W9-BDM-696

IMPORTANT:

HERE IS YOUR REGISTRATION CODE TO ACCESS
YOUR PREMIUM McGRAW-HILL ONLINE RESOURCES.

For key premium online resources you need THIS CODE to gain access. Once the code is entered, you will be able to use the Web resources for the length of your course.

If your course is using **WebCT** or **Blackboard**, you'll be able to use this code to access the McGraw-Hill content within your instructor's online course.

Access is provided if you have purchased a new book. If the registration code is missing from this book, the registration screen on our Website, and within your WebCT or Blackboard course, will tell you how to obtain your new code.

Registering for McGraw-Hill Online Resources

TO gain access to your McGraw-Hill web resources simply follow the steps below:

(1) USE YOUR WEB BROWSER TO GO TO: **www.mhhe.com/mediaethics5**

(2) CLICK ON **FIRST TIME USER**.

(3) ENTER THE REGISTRATION CODE* PRINTED ON THE TEAR-OFF BOOKMARK ON THE RIGHT.

(4) AFTER YOU HAVE ENTERED YOUR REGISTRATION CODE, CLICK **REGISTER**.

(5) FOLLOW THE INSTRUCTIONS TO SET-UP YOUR PERSONAL UserID AND PASSWORD.

(6) WRITE YOUR UserID AND PASSWORD DOWN FOR FUTURE REFERENCE.
KEEP IT IN A SAFE PLACE.

TO GAIN ACCESS to the McGraw-Hill content in your instructor's **WebCT** or **Blackboard** course simply log in to the course with the UserID and Password provided by your instructor. Enter the registration code exactly as it appears in the box to the right when prompted by the system. You will only need to use the code the first time you click on McGraw-Hill content.

Thank you, and welcome to your McGraw-Hill online Resources!

MCGRAW-HILL
ONLINE RESOURCES

REGISTRATION CODE

6GUB-V6FZ-T3KD-SQTO-K2VV

0-07-301893-7 T/A PATTERSON: MEDIA ETHICS: ISSUES & CASES, 5/E

Media Ethics:

ISSUES & CASES

FIFTH EDITION

Philip Patterson
Oklahoma Christian University

Lee Wilkins
University of Missouri-Columbia

Boston   Burr Ridge, IL   Dubuque, IA   Madison, WI   New York
San Francisco   St. Louis   Bangkok   Bogotá   Caracas   Kuala Lumpur
Lisbon   London   Madrid   Mexico City   Milan   Montreal   New Delhi
Santiago   Seoul   Singapore   Sydney   Taipei   Toronto

Higher Education

MEDIA ETHICS: ISSUES AND CASES
Published by McGraw-Hill, an imprint of The McGraw-Hill Companies, Inc. 1221 Avenue of the Americas, New York, NY, 10020. Copyright © 2005, 2002, by The McGraw-Hill Companies, Inc. All rights reserved. No part of this publication may be reproduced or distributed in any form or by any means, or stored in a database or retrieval system, without the prior written consent of The McGraw-Hill Companies, Inc., including, but not limited to, in any network or other electronic storage or transmission, or broadcast for distance learning.
Some ancillaries, including electronic and print components, may not be available to customers outside the United States.

This book is printed on acid-free paper.

1 2 3 4 5 6 7 8 9 0 DOC/DOC 0 9 8 7 6 5 4

ISBN: 0 07 288259 X

Editorial director: *Phillip A. Butcher*
Sponsoring editor: *Phillip A. Butcher*
Developmental editor: *Laura Lynch*
Senior marketing manager: *Leslie Oberhuber*
Executive producer: *Erin Marean*
Lead project manager: *Jean Hamilton*
Senior production supervisor: *Carol A. Bielski*
Associate designer: *Srjdan Savanovic*
Lead media project manager: *Marc Mattson*
Associate photo research coordinator: *Natalie C. Peschiera*
Permissions editor: *Marty Granahan*
Cover design: *Jenny El-Shamy*
Typeface: *10/12 Times Roman*
Compositor: *Carlisle Communications, Ltd.*
Printer: *R. R. Donnelley and Sons Inc.*

Library of Congress Cataloging-in-Publication Data
Patterson, Philip
   Media ethics: issues and cases / Philip Patterson, Lee Wilkins.—5th ed.
      p. cm.
   Includes bibliographical references and index.
   ISBN: 0-07-288259-X
   1. Mass media—Moral and ethical aspects. I. Title: Media ethics, issues and cases. II. Wilkins, Lee.
P94.M36 1997
174—dc21
www.mhhe.com   2004107528

To Amy, Andrew, Miranda, and Joshua
Four equally bright kids, unequally distributed between us

CONTENTS

CHAPTER III
ADVERTISING ETHICS: FROM LET THE BUYER BEWARE TO EMPOWERMENT   58

Cases

CHAPTER IV
LOYALTY: CHOOSING BETWEEN COMPETING ALLEGIANCES   84

Cases

CHAPTER V
PUBLIC RELATIONS: ADVOCATE OR ADVERSARY?   109

Cases

CHAPTER VI
PRIVACY: LOOKING FOR SOLITUDE IN THE GLOBAL VILLAGE   132

Cases

CHAPTER VII

THE MASS MEDIA IN A DEMOCRATIC SOCIETY:
KEEPING A PROMISE   157

Cases

CHAPTER VIII

MEDIA ECONOMICS: THE DEADLINE MEETS
THE BOTTOM LINE   188

Cases

CHAPTER XI
THE ETHICAL DIMENSIONS OF ART
AND ENTERTAINMENT   266

CHAPTER XII
BECOMING A MORAL ADULT   296

FOREWORD

CLIFFORD G. CHRISTIANS
RESEARCH PROFESSOR OF COMMUNICATION
University of Illinois–Urbana

The playful wit and sharp mind of Socrates attracted disciples from all across ancient Greece. They came to learn and debate in what could be translated "his
thinkery." By shifting the disputes among Athenians over earth, air, fire and water
to human virtue, Socrates gave Western philosophy and ethics a new intellectual
center (Cassier 1944).

But sometimes his relentless arguments would go nowhere. On one occasion,
he sparred with the philosopher Hippias about the difference between truth and
falsehood. Hippias was worn into submission, but retorted at the end, "I cannot
agree with you, Socrates." And then the master concluded: "Nor I with myself, Hippias. . . . I go astray, up and down, and never hold the same opinion." Socrates admitted to being so clever that he had befuddled himself. No wonder he was a favorite
target of the comic poets. I. F. Stone likens this wizardry to "whales of the intellect
flailing about in deep seas" (Stone 1988).

With his young friend Meno, Socrates argued whether virtue is teachable. Meno
was eager to learn more, after "holding forth often on the subject in front of large
audiences." But he complained, "You are exercising magic and witchcraft upon me
and positively laying me under your spell until I am just a mass of helplessness. . . .
You are exactly like the flat stingray that one meets in the sea. Whenever anyone
comes into contact with it, it numbs him, and that is the sort of thing you seem to be
doing to me now. My mind and my lips are literally numb."

Philosophy is not a semantic game, though sometimes its idiosyncrasies feed
that response into the popular mind. *Media Ethics: Issues and Cases* does not de-
bunk philosophy as the excess of sovereign reason. The authors of this book will not
encourage those who ridicule philosophy as cunning rhetoric. The issue at stake here
is actually a somewhat different problem—the Cartesian model of philosophizing.

The founder of modern philosophy, René Descartes, preferred to work in solitude. Paris was whirling in the early 17th century, but for 2 years even Descartes's
friends could not find him as he squirreled himself away studying mathematics. One
can even guess the motto above his desk: "Happy is he who lives in seclusion."
Imagine the conditions under which he wrote *Meditations II*. The Thirty Years' War
in Europe brought social chaos everywhere. The Spanish were ravaging the French
provinces and even threatening Paris, but Descartes was shut away in an apartment
in Holland. Tranquility for philosophical speculation mattered so much to him that
upon hearing Galileo had been condemned by the Church, he retracted parallel

arguments of his own on natural science. Pure philosophy as an abstract enterprise needed a cool atmosphere isolated from everyday events.

Descartes' magnificent formulations have always had their detractors, of course. David Hume did not think of philosophy in those terms, believing as he did that sentiment is the foundation of morality. For Søren Kierkegaard, an abstract system of ethics is only paper currency with nothing to back it up. Karl Marx insisted that we change the world and not merely explain it. But no one drew the modern philosophical map more decisively than Descartes, and his mode of rigid inquiry has generally defined the field's parameters.

This book adopts the historical perspective suggested by Stephen Toulmin:

> The philosophy whose legitimacy the critics challenge is always the seventeenth century tradition founded primarily upon René Descartes. . . . [The] arguments are directed to one particular style of philosophizing—a theory-centered style which poses philosophical problems, and frames solutions to them, in timeless and universal terms. From 1650, this particular style was taken as defining the very agenda of philosophy (1988, 338).

The 17-century philosophers set aside the particular, the timely, the local and the oral. And that development left untouched nearly half of the philosophical agenda. Indeed, it is those neglected topics—what I here call "practical philosophy"—that are showing fresh signs of life today, at the very time when the more familiar "theory-centered" half of the subject is languishing (Toulmin 1988, 338).

This book collaborates in demolishing the barrier of three centuries between pure and applied philosophy; it joins in reentering practical concerns as the legitimate domain of philosophy itself. For Toulmin, the primary focus of ethics has moved from the study to the bedside, to criminal courts, engineering labs, the newsroom, factories and ethnic street corners. Moral philosophers are not being asked to hand over their duties to technical experts in today's institutions, but rather to fashion their agendas within the conditions of contemporary struggle.

All humans have a theoretical capacity. Critical thinking, the reflective dimension, is our common property. And this book nurtures that reflection in communication classrooms and by extension into centers of media practice. If the mind is like a muscle, this volume provides a regimen of exercises for strengthening its powers of systematic reflection and moral discernment. It does not permit those aimless arguments that result in quandary ethics. Instead it operates in the finest traditions of practical philosophy, anchoring the debates in real-life conundrums but pushing the discussion toward substantive issues and integrating appropriate theory into the decision-making process. It seeks to empower students to do ethics themselves, under the old adage that teaching someone to fish lasts a lifetime, and providing fish only saves the day.

Media Ethics: Issues and Cases arrives on the scene at a strategic time in higher education. Since the late 19th century, ethical questions have been taken from the curriculum as a whole and from the philosophy department. Recovering practical philosophy has involved a revolution during the last decade in which courses in professional ethics have reappeared throughout the curriculum. This book advocates the pervasive method and carries the discussions even further, beyond freestanding courses into communication classrooms across the board.

In this sense, the book represents a constructive response to the current debates over the mission of higher education. Professional ethics has long been saddled with the dilemma that the university was given responsibility for professional training precisely at the point in its history that it turned away from values to scientific naturalism. Today one sees it as a vast horizontal plain given to technical excellence but barren in enabling students to articulate a philosophy of life. As James Carey concludes,

> Higher education has not been performing well of late and, like most American institutions, is suffering from a confusion of purpose, an excess of ambition that borders on hubris, and an appetite for money that is truly alarming (1989, 48).

The broadside critiques leveled in Thorstein Veblen's *The Higher Learning in America* (1918) and Upton Sinclair's *The Goose Step* (1922) are now too blatantly obvious to ignore. But *Media Ethics: Issues and Cases* does not merely demand a better general education or a recommitment to values; it strengthens the communications curriculum by equipping thoughtful students with a more enlightened moral awareness. Since Confucius we have understood that lighting a candle is better than cursing the darkness, or, in Mother Teresa's version, we feed the world one mouth at a time.

PREFACE

As you glance through this book, you will notice its features—text, illustrations, cases, photos—represent choices the authors have made. I think it's as important to point out what's missing as what's there, and why. I'll begin with what's been left out and conclude with what you'll find in the text.

First, you'll find no media bashing in this book. There's enough of that already, and besides, it's too easy to do. This book is not designed to indict the media; it's designed to train its future employees. If we dwell on ethical lapses from the past, it is only to learn from them what we can do to prevent similar occurrences in the future.

Second, you'll find no conclusions in this book—neither at the end of the book nor after each case. No one has yet written the conclusive chapter to the ethical dilemmas of the media, and I don't suspect that we will be the first.

What, then, is in the book?

First, you'll find a diverse, up-to-date, and classroom-tested compilation of cases in media ethics. Authors from more than 30 institutions and media outlets contributed real-life and hypothetical cases to this text to help students prepare for the ethical situations they will confront in whatever areas of the media they enter. The authors believe case studies are the premiere teaching vehicle for the study of ethics, and this book reflects what we think are the best available.

Second, binding these cases together and providing a philosophical basis from which to approach them constitutes the text. While it intentionally has been kept succinct, the text introduces students to the relevant ethical theory that will help eliminate "quandary ethics," which often results when cases are used as a teaching strategy.

Third, you'll find built-in discussion starters in the questions that follow each case. The questions at the end of the cases were written by the authors of each case, with the instructions that they were to be like concentric circles. The tightest circle—the micro issues—focuses only on the case at hand and the dilemmas it presents. The next circle—middle-range issues—focuses on the problem in its context, and sometimes manipulates the facts slightly to see if the decisions remain the same. The most abstract level—the macro issues—focuses on issues such as truth, equity, responsibility and loyalty. Properly used, the questions can guide discussion from the particular to the universal in any case in a single class period.

The book may be used either as the main text for a media ethics course or as a supplementary text for ethics modules in courses on newswriting, media and society, advertising and public relations, and photojournalism. The book works well for teachers who like to use the Socratic method in their classes, or as resource material for lecture classes.

Our approach in this text is best illustrated by an anecdote from a class. One student had the last hand up after a particularly heated case study. When I called on her, she asked, "Well, what's the answer?" I was surprised that she asked the question, and I was surprised that I didn't have a ready answer. I joked my way out of the question by asking if she wanted "The Answer" with a capital "a" or a lowercase one. If she asked today, I'd respond differently. I'd tell her that the answer exists within her, but that it won't emerge in any justifiable form without systematic study and frequent wrestling with the issues.

That's what this book is about. The chapters direct you in some systematic way through the philosophy that has explored these questions for centuries. The cases will make you wrestle with that knowledge in scenarios not unlike ones you might encounter while working. Together, they might not enable you to find "The Answer," but they might help you find *your* answer.

For the authors and contributors,

Philip Patterson

ACKNOWLEDGMENTS

The ethical dilemmas that challenge us require a "moral compass" to help us find our way down the winding paths of life. My compass was given to me by my parents at an early age, and it has worked for more than four decades. No one can ask for a better gift than that, and I thank them for their part in placing me where I am today.

No book of this type is a solo effort, and this book is certainly the result of hard work and encouragement by many people. To begin, each of the authors in the text has been a pleasure to work with. Lou Hodges, Cliff Christians, Ralph Barney, Jay Black, Deni Elliott, and others listened patiently to the idea in its many stages and offered advice along the way. Over the years I have been privileged to attend workshops on ethics sponsored by the Poynter Institute, the Freedom Forum, and the University of Nebraska. To Bob Steele, Ed Lambeth, Steve Kalish, and Robert Audi I owe a debt of gratitude for helping me continue to learn about ethics as I seek to teach my students. And Sue, we'll both miss you, and the field of journalism lost a giant in 2003.

A special thanks goes to the Ethics and Excellence in Journalism Foundation and to McGraw-Hill Higher Education for grants to cover costs incurred in this edition of the text. Finally, I thank my wife, Linda, and my children, Amy, Andrew and Joshua: I love you all.

p.d.p.

When ethics entrepreneur Michael Josephson opens his public speeches, he asks audience members to think of the most ethical people they know. Those people set ethical standards for others, by who they are and by what they inspire. It's fair for readers of this book to know who's on my list.

First, my mother, whose sense of human connection and compassion has been only incompletely copied by her daughter. Second, my father, who is the most principled human being I have ever met. Third, my stepmother, Carrie, who's managed to love the family she's married into—a feat worthy of far more than a Kantian sense of duty. My dissertation advisor and friend, Jim Davies, affirmed for me the ethical connection between people and politics. My former colleagues at the University of Colorado, Russ Shain, Steve Jones, Sue O'Brien, and Risa Palm, have proved that connection to be a very human one, as have my colleagues at the University of Missouri. They have also been willing to listen—*another ethical activity that too often goes unmentioned.* Barrie Hartman and the staff of the *Boulder Daily Camera* were wonderful reality checks.

I've received intellectual help as well. I've attended a number of conferences designed to teach me about ethics. The Hastings House, Gannett, the Poynter Institute, and the University of Nebraska have done their best to educate me in this field. The people connected with those efforts deserve special mention. Among them, Ed Lambeth, Ted Glasser, Deni Elliott, Cliff Christians, Lou Hodges, Martin Linsky, Roy Peter Clark, Don Fry, Sharon Murphy, Jay Black, Ralph Barney, Steve Kalish and Robert Audi have helped most profoundly. Many of them you will find mentioned in various contexts on the pages that follow. All of them have a special place in my intellectual psyche.

Two sets of acknowledgments remain.

For the past 25 years, my students at the state universities of Missouri and Colorado have taught me much more about ethics than I have taught them. They have suffered through portions of this manuscript with me. Their questions and their insights are evident on every page of this book.

Then there are Miranda and David—my daughter and my spouse. For the smiles, the hugs, the reading of first drafts, the talking, the listening, the suggestions, the lecture about using "skin" names, the films and all of the rest that being a family means. Love and thanks. I could not have done this without you.

l.c.w.

I

An Introduction to Ethical Decision Making

By the end of this chapter, you should be able to:

- **recognize the need for professional ethics in journalism.**
- **work through a model of ethical decision making.**
- **identify and use the five philosophical principles applicable to mass communication situations.**

MAKING ETHICAL DECISIONS

Scenario #1: You awaken the morning of September 12, 2001, and realize that the successful campaign you developed for Southwest Airlines with the tagline "You are free to move about the country" is no longer appropriate. In fact, if the ads continue to run in both print and broadcast media, consumers might consider Southwest both recklessly greedy and incurably insensitive to the events and pain of the past 24 hours. Yet, as an advertising practitioner you know that ads remind consumers of products they can purchase and the ability of your company to stay in business is now in serious doubt. Management wants to run a full-page ad in *USA Today* on the first day after planes are allowed to resume flying. Some of your superiors have expressed a desire to continue to trade on the equity built up in the well-known tagline—a risky strategy—while others want an entirely different campaign created in a near-impossible time frame. Your job is to decide what to do and, if necessary, to design an appropriate ad, respectful of the events that have occurred while at the same time urging flyers back to the air. What do you do?

Scenario #2: You are the chief information officer for a large metropolitan police force, trained in media and public relations. Your job ordinarily consists of acting as spokesperson for the department and also representing the department at a variety of community events. Your city is three weeks into a sniper spree that has left 10 innocent people dead. Now comes a break. Police have determined that the suspects are driving a blue Chevy Caprice with New Jersey plates. If this information is released to the public, citizens could potentially spot the car and assist police in the capture of the suspects. However, releasing the information might also enable the suspects to dump the car for another and continue their spree. How would you advise the chief? If the local media somehow obtain the information before a decision is made to release it, do you verify it or deny it?

Scenario #3: You are the producer for the nightly newscasts of the third-rated station in a Top-30 market. Poor ratings have caused the station to pay the lowest salaries in the market, meaning that most of the staff, like you, are relatively fresh out of college. Hoping to gain more market share, your station has formed an investigative team, and "I-Team" ads are airing throughout the day. Within weeks, they capture their first exclusive story. The I-Team has staked out the local airport—a medium-size facility with many domestic routes and four international flights daily. They have found several glaring security breaches, which they describe in detail, which could allow terrorists to gain access to passenger planes. Running the story will expose the loopholes and possibly cause responsible parties to close them. However, in the short term, the story could give important information to potential terrorists who might try to exploit other airports with your information. It is obvious that such a story would give a big boost to your new investigative thrust. What do you do?

The Dilemma of Dilemmas

The scenarios above are dilemmas—they present an ethical problem with no single "right" answer, even though the final decision is full of ethical ramifications. Resolving dilemmas is the business of ethics. It's not an easy process, but it is a process that can be anticipated and prepared for, and it is a process that has a wealth of theory to back up your final decision. In this chapter and throughout this book, you will be equipped with the tools to help solve dilemmas that arise in working for the mass media.

In the end, you will have tools, not answers. Answers must come from within you, but your answers should be informed by what others have written and experienced. Otherwise, you will always be forced to solve each ethical problem anew without the benefit of anyone else's insight or experience. Gaining these tools also will help you to prevent each dilemma from spiraling into "quandary ethics"—the feeling that no best choice is available and that everyone's choice is equally valid (see Deni Elliott's essay following this chapter).

Will codes of ethics help? Virtually all the media associations have one, but they have their limitations. For instance, the ethics code for the Society of Professional Journalists could be read to allow for revealing or withholding the information in the airport scenario above, two actions that are polar opposites. That doesn't make the code useless; it simply points out a shortfall in depending on codes.

While we don't dismiss codes—and all branches of mass media, public relations, and advertising and their trade associations have them and post them on their

Web sites—we believe you will find more help in the writings of philosophers, ancient and modern. We will turn to several of those writers in this chapter.

The goal of this book is to teach more than a set of rules. The goal is to give you the skills, analytical models, vocabulary and insights of others who have faced these choices, to make and justify ethical decisions.

Too many books insist that ethics can't be taught. It's situational, some claim. Since every message is unique, there is no real way to learn ethics other than by daily life. This analysis is partially correct. Most of us, outside of church or parental teachings, have learned ethics by the choices we've made or seen others make. Ethics, it is argued, is something you have, not something you do. But while it's true that reading about ethics is no guarantee you will perform your job ethically, thinking about ethics is a skill anyone can acquire.

While each facet of mass communication has its unique ethical issues, thinking about ethics is the same, whether you make your living writing advertising copy or obituaries. Each day at work, journalists make ethical choices, and some days those choices will have an influence far beyond a single broadcast or one newspaper's circulation area. Thinking about ethics won't make many of those choices easier, but, with practice, your ethical decision making can become more consistent. Ethics will then become not something you have, but something you do. A consistently ethical approach to your work as a reporter, photographer or copywriter in whatever field of mass communication you enter can improve that work as well.

Contemporary professional ethics revolves around these questions:

- What duties do I have, and to whom do I owe them?
- What values are reflected by the duties I've assumed?

Ethics takes us out of the world of "This is the way I do it" or "This is the way it's always been done" into the realm of "This is what I should do" or "This is the action that can be rationally justified." Ethics in this sense is "ought talk." The dual questions of duty and values can be answered a number of ways as long as they are consistent with each other. For example, if a journalist sees her primary duty as that of informing the public, she will place a high value on truth telling, tenacity in the pursuit of a story, etc. If a public relations practitioner sees his duty as promoting a cause, his choices would change accordingly.

It is important here to distinguish between *ethics,* which is a rational process founded on certain agreed-on principles, and *morals,* which are in the realm of religion. For example, the Ten Commandments are a moral system in the Judeo-Christian tradition, and Jewish scholars have expanded this study of the laws throughout the Bible's Old Testament into the Talmud, a 1,400-page religious volume. The Buddhist Eightfold Path provides a similar moral framework.

But moral systems are not synonymous with ethics. *Ethics begins when elements within a moral system conflict.* Ethics is less about the conflict between right and wrong than it is about the conflict between equally compelling (or equally unattractive) values and the choices that must be made between them.

Immanuel Kant, the most influential philosopher of the 18th century, described this famous ethical dilemma: What should you do when a man carrying a

---

A Word About Ethics

The concept of ethics comes from the Greeks, who divided the philosophical world into three parts. *Aesthetics* was the study of the beautiful and how a person could analyze beauty without relying only on subjective evaluations. *Epistemology* was the study of knowing, debates about what constitutes learning and what is knowable to the human mind. *Ethics* was the study of what is good, both for the individual and for society. Interestingly, the root of the word means "custom" or "habit," giving ethics an underlying root of behavior that is beneficial to the ongoing of society. The Greeks were concerned with the individual virtues of fortitude, justice, temperance and wisdom, as well as with societal virtues, such as freedom.

Two thousand years later, ethics has come to mean learning to make rational choices between what is good and bad, between what is morally justifiable action and what is not. Ethics also means distinguishing among choices, all of which may be morally justifiable, but some more so than others. Rationality is the key word here, for the Greeks believed, and modern philosophers affirm, that people should be able to explain their ethical decisions to others. That ability to explain ethical choices is an important one for journalists, who, in the course of reporting a single story, may have to make separate ethical decisions when dealing with sources, colleagues and, ultimately, the public. When an angry viewer telephones to ask why you broadcast the name of a rape victim, "It seemed like the right thing to do at the time" becomes a personally embarrassing and professionally unsatisfactory explanation.

---

gun arrives at your front door, asking the whereabouts of a second man (who is hiding in your closet) because he wants to kill him? Do you lie, or do you tell the truth? The Judeo-Christian moral system says that both killing and lying are wrong. Yet, you are being asked to make a choice between the two, and Kant's solution is a surprising and perplexing one.

When elements within a moral system conflict, ethical principles can help you make tough choices. We'll review several ethical principles briefly after describing how one philosopher, Sissela Bok, says working professionals can learn to make good ethical decisions.

BOK'S MODEL

Bok's ethical decision-making framework was introduced in her book, *Lying: Moral Choice in Public and Private Life.* Bok's model is based on two premises: that we must have empathy for the people involved in ethical decisions and that maintaining social trust is a fundamental goal. With this in mind, Bok says any ethical question should be analyzed in three steps.

First, consult your own conscience about the "rightness" of an action. *How do you feel about the action?*

Second, seek expert advice for alternatives to the act creating the ethical problem. Experts, by the way, can be those either living or dead—a producer or copywriter you trust or a philosopher you admire. *Is there another way to achieve the same goal that will not raise ethical issues?*

Third, if possible, conduct a public discussion with the parties involved in the dispute. These include those who are directly involved, that is, the reporter or the source, and those indirectly involved, that is, a reader or a source. If they cannot be gathered, conduct the conversation hypothetically. The goal of this conversation is to discover *How will others respond to the proposed act?*

Let's see how Bok's model works on the following sample scenario. In the section after the case, follow the three steps Bok recommends and decide if you would run the story.

How Much News Is Fit to Print?   In your community, one of the major charities is the United Way. The annual fund-raising drive will begin in less than two weeks. However, at a late-night meeting of the board of directors at which no reporter is present, the executive director resigns. Though the agency is not covered by the Open Meetings Act, you are able to learn most of what went on from a source on the board.

According to her, the executive director had taken pay from the agency by submitting a falsified time sheet while he was actually away at the funeral of a college roommate. The United Way board investigated the absence and asked for his resignation, citing the lying about the absence as the reason, though most agreed that they would have given him paid leave had he asked.

The United Way wants to issue a short statement, praising the work of the executive director while regretfully accepting his resignation. The executive director will also issue a short statement citing other opportunities as his reason for leaving. You are assigned the story by an editor who does not know about the additional information you have obtained but tells you to "see if there's any more to it [the resignation] than they're telling."

You call your source on the board and she asks you, as a friend, to withhold the damaging information because it will hinder the United Way's annual fund-raising effort that is just under way and jeopardize services to needy people in the community for years to come because faith in the United Way will be destroyed. You confront the executive director. He says, if you run the story you will ruin his chances of a future career.

What do you do?

THE ANALYSIS

Bok's first step requires you to *consult your conscience.* When you do, you realize you have a problem. Your journalistic responsibility is to tell the truth, and that means providing readers with all the facts you discover. You also have a larger responsibility not to harm your community, and printing the complete story about the

United Way director's actions might well cause at least some short-term harm. Clearly, your conscience is of two minds about the issue.

You move to the second step: *alternatives.* Do you simply run the resignation release, figuring that the person can do no further harm to the community and therefore should be left alone? Do you run the whole story but buttress it with board members' quotes that such an action couldn't happen again, figuring that you have restored public trust in the agency? Do you sit on the story until after the fund-raising drive and risk the loss of trust from readers if the story circulates around town as a rumor? Again, there do seem to be alternatives, but they are not without some cost.

In the third step of Bok's model, you will attempt to *hold a public ethical dialogue* with all of the parties involved. Most likely you won't ask the executive director, the story's source, average readers of the newspaper, a United Way donor, and your editor into the newsroom for a lengthy chat about the issues involved when you are on deadline. Instead you can conduct an imaginary discussion among the parties involved. Such a discussion might go like this:

EXECUTIVE DIRECTOR: "I think my resignation is sufficient penalty for any mistake I might have made, and your article will jeopardize my ability to find another job. It's really hurting my wife and kids, and they've done nothing wrong."

REPORTER: "But shouldn't you have thought about that *before* you decided to falsify the time sheet? This is a good story, and I think the public should know what the people who are handling their donations are like."

READER 1: "Wait a minute. I am the public, and I'm tired of all of this bad news your paper focuses on. This man has done nothing but good in the community, and I can't see where any money that belonged to the poor went into his pocket. Why can't we see some good news for a change?"

READER 2: "I disagree. I buy the paper precisely because it does this kind of reporting. It's stories like this that keep the government, the charities, and everyone else on their toes."

PUBLISHER: "You mean like a watchdog function."

READER 2: "Exactly. And if it bothers you, don't read it."

PUBLISHER: "I don't really like to hurt people with the power that we have, but if we don't print stories like this, and the community later finds out that we withheld the news, our credibility is ruined, and we're out of business." [To source] "Did you request that the information be off the record?"

SOURCE: "No. But I never thought you'd use it in your story."

REPORTER: "I'm a reporter. I report what I hear for a living. What did you think I would do with it? To use the same argument he used a minute ago, it's stories like these that allow me to support my family."

EXECUTIVE DIRECTOR: "So it's your career or mine, is that what you're saying? Look, no charges have been filed here, but if your story runs, I look like a criminal. Is that fair?"

PUBLISHER: "And if it doesn't run, we don't keep our promise to the community. Is that fair?"

NEEDY MOTHER: "Fair? You want to talk fair? Do you suffer if the donations go down? No, I do. This is just another story to you. It's the difference in me and my family getting by."

The conversation could continue, and other points of view could be voiced. Your imaginary conversations could be more or less elaborate than the one above, but out of this discussion it should be possible to rationally support an ethical choice.

There are two cautions in using Bok's model for ethical decision making. First, it is important to go through all three steps before making a final choice. Most of us make ethical choices prematurely, after we've consulted only our consciences, an error Bok says results in a lot of flabby moral thinking.

Second, while you will not be endowed with any clairvoyant powers to anticipate your ethical problems, the ethical dialogue outlined in the third step is best when conducted in advance of the event, not in the heat of writing a story. For instance, an advertising copywriter might conduct such a discussion about whether advertising copy can ethically withhold disclaimers about potential harm from a product. A reporter might conduct such a discussion well in advance of the time he is actually asked to withhold an embarrassing name or fact from a story. Since it is likely that such dilemmas will arise in your chosen profession (the illustration above is based on what happened to one of the authors the first day on the job), your answer will be more readily available and more logical if you hold such discussions either with trusted colleagues in a casual atmosphere or by yourself, well in advance of the problem.

Bok's model forces you to consider alternatives. It's in the pursuit of these alternatives that journalistic technique improves.

GUIDELINES FOR MAKING ETHICAL DECISIONS

Since the days of ancient Greece, philosophers have tried to draft a series of rules or guidelines governing how to make ethical choices. Obviously, in most ethical dilemmas such as the one above, you will need principles to help you determine what to do amid conflicting voices. While a number of principles work well, we will review five.

Aristotle's Golden Mean

Aristotle, teaching in the fourth century B.C., believed that happiness—which some scholars translate as "flourishing"—was the ultimate human good. By flourishing, Aristotle meant to exercise "practical reason" in the conduct of any particular activity through the setting of high standards.

Aristotle believed that practical reason was exercised by individuals. The *phrenemos,* or person of practical wisdom, was that human being who demonstrated ethical excellence through daily activity. For Aristotle, the highest virtue was citizenship, and the highest form of citizenship was exemplified by the statesman, a politician who exercised so much practical wisdom in his daily activity that he elevated craft to art. In contemporary terms, we might think of a *phrenemos* as a person who excels at one of a variety of activities—flautist Jean Pierre Rampal, poet Maya Angelou, filmmakers George Lucas and Steven Spielberg. They are people who flourish in their professional performance, extending our own vision of what is possible.

CALVIN AND HOBBES © Watterson. Reprinted with permission of UNIVERSAL
PRESS SYNDICATE. All rights reserved.

This notion of flourishing led Aristotle to assert that people and their acts, not particular sets of rules, are the moral basis of activity. His ethical system resulted in the creation of what is now called *virtue ethics*. Virtue ethics flows from both the nature of the act itself and the moral character of the person who acts. In the Aristotelian sense, the way to behave ethically is that (1) you must know (through the exercise of practical reason) what you are doing; (2) you must select the act for its own sake—in order to flourish; and (3) the act itself must spring from a firm and unchanging character.

It is not stretching Aristotle's framework to assert that one way to learn ethics is to select heroes and to try to model your individual acts and ultimately your professional character on what you believe they would do. An Aristotelian might well consult this hero as an expert when making an ethical choice. Asking what my hero would do in a particular situation is not necessarily a poor form of ethical analysis. The trick, however, is to select your heroes carefully and still think for yourself rather than merely copy behavior you have previously seen.

Aristotle's philosophy is often reduced to the somewhat simplistic *"golden mean:" Virtue lies at the mean between two extremes.* Courage, for example, is a mean between foolhardiness on one hand and cowardice on the other. But to determine that mean for yourself, you have to exercise practical wisdom, act according to high standards, and act in accordance with firm and continuing character traits. *In reality, therefore, the middle ground of a virtue is not a single point on a line that is the same for every individual.* It is instead a range of behaviors that varies individually, while avoiding the undesirable extremes, as shown in Figure 1.1.

Unacceptable behaviors	Acceptable behaviors	Unacceptable behaviors
Cowardice	Courage	Foolhardiness

FIGURE 1.1. Aristotle's golden mean

Continuing with the example of courage, this principle can be illustrated by considering two witnesses to a potential drowning. If one onlooker is a poor swimmer yet a fast runner, then it would be foolhardy for him to attempt to jump into the water and attempt a rescue, just as it would be cowardly for him to do nothing. For him, the courageous thing might be to run for help. If, on the other hand, the second onlooker is a good swimmer, it would not be foolhardy for her to attempt a rescue; in fact, it would be cowardly for her not to jump into the water. In each instance, both onlookers have done the courageous act, yet in radically different ways.

Seeking the golden mean implies that individual acts are not disconnected from one another, but rather that they form a whole that a person of good character should aspire to. In this age of questions about character, Aristotle's concept of virtue ethics has been rediscovered by a variety of professions.

Kant's Categorical Imperative

Immanuel Kant's *categorical imperative* asserts that an individual should act on the premise that the choices one makes for oneself could become universal law. Furthermore, he states that you should act so that you treat humanity always as an end and never as a means only. Kant called these two maxims "categorical" imperatives, meaning that their demands were not subject to situational factors. Many readers will recognize the similarity between Kant's categorical imperative and the Bible's golden rule: Do unto others as you would have others do unto you. The two are quite similar in their focus on duty.

Kant's ethical theory is based on the notion that it is the act itself, rather than the person who acts, in which moral force resides. This theory of ethics is unlike Aristotle's in that it moves the notion of what is ethical from the actor to the act itself. This does not mean that Kant did not believe in moral character, but rather that people could act morally from a sense of duty even though their character might incline them to act otherwise.

For Kant, an action was morally justified only if it was performed from duty, and in Kant's moral universe there were two sorts of duties. The strict duties were generally negative: not to murder, not to break promises, not to lie. The meritorious duties were more positive: to aid others, to develop one's talents, to show gratitude. Kant spent very little time defining these notions, but philosophers have generally asserted that the strict duties (i.e., not to harm) are somewhat more morally mandatory than the meritorious duties (e.g., to render aid).

To some, Kant's ethical reasoning indicates that as long as you perform the right act based on what the categorical imperative and duty demand, the consequences of that act are not important. We prefer a somewhat less austere reading of Kant. While Kant's view is that the moral worth of an action does not depend on its consequences, those consequences are not irrelevant. For example, a surgeon may show moral virtue in attempting to save a patient through an experimental procedure, but the decision about whether to undertake that procedure requires taking into account the probability of a cure. This framing of Kantian principles allows us to learn from our mistakes.

The test of a moral act, according to Kant, is its universality—whether it can be applied to everyone. For instance, Kant would insist that the ethical person drive at a speed and in a manner that would be appropriate for everyone else on the same highway. Under Kant's categorical imperative, journalists can claim few special privileges, such as the right to lie or the right to invade privacy in order to get a story. Kant's view, if taken seriously, reminds you of what you give up—truth, privacy and the like—when you make certain ethical decisions.

Utilitarianism

The original articulation of *utilitarianism* by Englishmen Jeremy Bentham and later John Stuart Mill in the nineteenth century introduced what was then a novel notion into ethics discussions: *The consequences of actions are important in deciding whether they are ethical.* In the utilitarian view, it may be considered ethical to harm one person for the benefit of the larger group. This approach, for example, is the ethical justification for investigative reporting, the results of which may harm individuals even as they are printed or broadcast in the hope of providing a greater societal good.

With its focus on the consequences of an action, utilitarianism completes a cycle begun with Aristotle (see Table 1.1). Aristotle, in developing the golden mean, focused on the *actor.* Kant, in his categorical imperative, focused on the *action,* while Mill, in his utilitarian philosophy, focused on the *outcome.*

Utilitarianism has been condensed to the ethical philosophy of the greatest good for the greatest number. While this pithy phrase is a very rough and ready characterization of utilitarian theory, it also has led to an overly mechanistic application of the principle: Just tally up the amount of good and subtract the amount of harm. If the remaining number is positive, the act is ethical. However, when properly applied, utilitarianism is not mechanical.

TABLE 1.1. The Shifting Focus of Ethics From Aristotle to Mill

Philosopher	Known for	Popularly Known as	Emphasized
Aristotle	Golden mean	Virtue lies between extremes.	The actor
Kant	Categorical imperative	Act so your choices could be universal law; treat humanity as an end, never as a means only.	The action
Mill	Utility principle	An act's rightness is determined by its contribution to a desirable end.	The outcome

In order to do justice to utilitarian theory, it must be understood within a historical context. Mill wrote following the changes of the Enlightenment. The principle of democracy was fresh and untried, and the thought that the average person should be able to speak his mind to those in power was novel. Utilitarianism as Mill conceived of it was a profoundly social ethic; Mill was among the first to acknowledge that the good of an entire society had a place in ethical reasoning.

Mill was what philosophers call a *valuational hedonist.* He argued that pleasure—and the absence of pain—was the only intrinsic moral end. Mill further asserted that an act was right in the proportion in which it contributed to the general happiness, wrong in the proportion in which it contributed to general unhappiness or pain. Utilitarianism can be subtle and complex. Mill acknowledged that the same act can make some happy but cause others pain. Mill insisted that both sets of consequences be valued simultaneously, a precarious activity but one that forces discussion of competing stakeholder claims.

Utilitarianism can be applied in both the specific and the general, what some philosophers have referred to as "act utilitarianism" as opposed to "rule utilitarianism."

For instance, one way of evaluating the ethical impact of investigative reporting is through the application of *act utilitarianism.* A producer might reason that an investigative report, while it would hurt the subject of the investigation, might further the general welfare. Crooks and cheats could be exposed, general societal problems aired. When the methods of obtaining information are ethical, investigative journalism can be justified because it contributes more to human happiness than it extracts in the pain it causes some individuals.

Rule utilitarianism, on the other hand, might be applied as follows. Take the assertion sometimes made that advertising itself is unethical. The rule utilitarian would note that in contemporary American culture advertising provides needed information about a variety of products and services. It is often entertaining, and it supports the media we enjoy. Of course, advertising sometimes can be in poor taste, it can be intrusive, and it can sometimes provide false or misleading information. When balancing the societal good against the societal harm, the rule utilitarian might well conclude that while the practice of advertising is ethical, certain forms of the activity—advertising products to children or advertising certain substances such as alcohol—should be regulated. Utilitarian theory does allow the sort of ethical reasoning that approves of particular activities while rejecting specific acts.

In utilitarian theory, no one's happiness is any more valuable than anyone else's—quantity and quality being equal. In democratic societies, this is a particularly important concept because it meshes well with certain social and political goals. In actual application, utilitarianism uniformly applied has a way of puncturing self-interest, although critics have argued that, when badly applied, it can actually promote selfishness.

Utilitarianism also suggests that moral questions are objective, empirical and even in some sense scientific. Utilitarianism promotes a universal ethical standard that each rational person can determine. However, utilitarianism is among the most criticized of philosophical principles because it is so difficult to accurately anticipate all the ramifications of a particular act. Different philosophers also have disputed how one calculates the good, rendering any utilitarian calculus fundamentally error prone.

While we recommend utilitarianism as a theory, we do caution you against exclusive reliance on it. Taken to extremes, the act of calculating the good can lead to ethical gridlock, with each group of stakeholders having seemingly equally strong claims with little way to choose among them. Sloppily done, utilitarianism may bias you toward short-term benefit. And a view to the short term, in an ethical sense, can often be shortsighted.

Pluralistic Theory of Value

Modern philosopher William David Ross (1930) bases his ethical theory on the belief that there is often more than one ethical value simultaneously "competing" for preeminence in our ethical decision making. In this, he differs from Kant or Mill, who proposed only one ultimate value. To Ross these competing ethical claims, which he calls duties, are equal, providing the circumstances of the particular moral choice are equal. Further, these duties gain their moral weight not from their consequences but from the highly personal nature of duty.

Ross proposed six types of duties:

1. Those duties that rest on previous acts of my own: duties of *fidelity,* based on my implicit or explicit promise, and duties of *reparation,* arising from a previous wrongful act.

2. Those duties of *gratitude* that rest on previous acts of others.

3. Those duties of *justice* that arise from the necessity to ensure the equitable and meritorious distribution of pleasure or happiness.

4. Those duties of *beneficence* that rest on the fact that there are others in the world whose lot we can better.

5. Those duties of *self-improvement* that rest on the fact that we can improve our own condition.

6. One negative duty: the duty of *not injuring others.*

We would recommend two additional duties that may be implied by Ross's list but are not specifically stated:

7. The duty to tell the truth, *veracity* (which may be implied by fidelity).

8. The duty to *nurture,* to help others achieve some measure of self-worth and achievement.

Ross's typology of duties works well for professionals who often must balance competing roles. It also brings to ethical reasoning some affirmative notions of the primacy of community and relationships as a way to balance the largely rights-based traditions of much Western philosophical theory.

Ross's concept of multiple duties allows the ethical decision maker to appreciate and consider important aspects of a situation without losing the value of following some rules. Like Kant, Ross divided his duties into two kinds. *Prima facie* duties are those duties that seem to be right because of the nature of the act itself. *Duty proper* are those duties that are paramount given specific circumstances. Arriving at your duty proper from among the prima facie duties requires that you consider what ethicists call the *morally relevant differences.*

Let's take an example using one of Ross's prima facie duties: keeping promises. In your job as a reporter, you have made an appointment with the mayor to discuss a year-end feature on your community. On your way to City Hall, you drive by a serious auto accident and see a young child wandering, dazed, along the road. If you stop to help you will certainly be late for your appointment and may have to cancel altogether. You have broken a promise.

But is that act ethical?

Ross would probably say yes because the specific aspects of the situation had a bearing on the fulfillment of a prima facie duty. You exercised discernment. You knew that your commitment to the mayor was a relatively minor sort of promise. Your news organization will not be hurt by postponing the interview, and your act allowed you to fulfill the prima facie duties of beneficence, avoiding harm, and nurturing. Had the interview been more important, or the wreck less severe, the morally relevant factors would have been different. Ross's pluralistic theory of values may be more difficult to apply than a system of absolute rules, but it reflects the way we make ethical choices.

Ross's concept of multiple duties "helps to explain why we feel uneasy about breaking a promise even when we are justified in doing so. Our uneasiness comes from the fact that we have broken a prima facie duty even as we fulfilled another. It helps explain why even the good consequences that might come from a failure to tell the truth or keep a promise do not always seem to us to justify the lie or breach of confidence" (Lebacqz 1985, 27).

Communitarianism

Classical ethical theory places its dominant intellectual emphasis on the individual and individual acts by emphasizing concepts such as character, choice, liberty and duty.

But contemporary politics points out the intellectual weakness in this approach. Consider the environment. On many environmental questions, it is possible for people to make appropriate individual decisions—today I drive my car—which taken together promote environmental degradation. My individual decision to drive my car doesn't matter very much; but when individual decisions are aggregated, the impact is profound. Furthermore, this environmental impact has consequences not for a single generation but for geologic time. Individual human beings cannot opt out of participation through daily living in the physical environment—unless they decide to live on the moon. While classical ethical theory acknowledges such problems, it provides little guidance for determining individual action or in understanding how individual actions fit within a larger whole.

Communitarianism, which has its roots in political theory, seeks to provide ethical guidance when confronting the sort of society-wide issues that mark current political and business activity.

Communitarianism spotlights society understood holistically and dynamically. Communitarianism returns to Aristotle's concept of the "polis"—or community—and invests it with moral weight. People begin their lives, at least in a biological sense, as members of a two-person community. Communitarian philosophy extends this biological beginning to a philosophical worldview. "In communitarianism, persons have certain inescapable claims on one another that cannot be renounced except at the cost of their humanity" (Christians et al. 1995, 14). In modern parlance, communitarians assert that when issues are political and social, community trumps individuals but does not trample them.

Communitarianism focuses on the outcome of individual ethical decisions, understood not as disconnected choices but analyzed as the impact of the sum of the choices on society. "Nurturing communitarian citizenship entails, at a minimum, a journalism committed to justice, covenant and empowerment. Authentic communities are marked by justice; in strong democracies, courageous talk is mobilized into action. . . . In normative communities, citizens are empowered for social transformation, not merely freed from external constraints" (Christians et al. 1995, 14).

Communitarianism asserts that social justice is the predominant moral value. While communitarians recognize the value of process, they are just as concerned with outcomes. They formally acknowledge one of history's more difficult lessons, that "good" process—for example, democratic elections or the writing of constitutions—can produce "bad" outcomes—for example, the 1933 takeover of Germany by a minority party headed by Hitler or the inclusion in the original U.S. Constitution of the three-fifths clause (African-Americans were equal to three-fifths of a single European Caucasian colonist for purposes of population count to determine the number of representatives each state would have in the U.S. Congress). Communitarians measure individual acts against the normative standard of their impact in creating a more just society.

Communitarian thinking allows ethical discussion to include values such as altruism and benevolence on an equal footing with more traditional questions such as truth telling and loyalty. Indeed, game theory (refined by John Nash and discussed in Case IX-A) has demonstrated that cooperation, one of the foundation stones of community, provides desirable results once thought to be possible only through competition (Axelrod 1984). Cooperation is particularly powerful when something called the "shadow of the future" looms sufficiently large. The "shadow of the future" means that people understand they will encounter the outcome of their decisions, in the form of their impact on others, in readily foreseeable time.

Communitarian philosophy suffers from a lack of a succinct summation of its general propositions. Amitai Etzioni, one of the movement's leaders, suggests that communitarianism emphasizes responsibilities "to the conditions and elements we all share, to the community." Political theorist Michael Sandel arranges communitarianism as both an extension of and a counterpoint to traditional political liberalism. Like traditional political liberalism—as expressed in this book by the philosophy of John Rawls and, to a lesser extent, the utilitarians—a communitarian community would be manifest in the aims and values of its individual participants. But it would differ from a traditional community in the sense that community members would include, as part of their understanding of self, their membership in the community. "For them, community describes not just what they have as fellow citizens but also what they are, not as a relationship they choose (as in a voluntary association) but an attachment they discover, not merely an attribute but as a constituent of their identity" (Sandel 1982, 150). Communitarian community resembles family more than it resembles town.

We believe that communitarianism is most helpful in discussing ethical issues that revolve around the journalistic role. Viewed this way, journalism cannot separate itself from the political and economic system of which it is a part.

Communitarian thinking makes it possible to ask whether current practice (for example, a traditional definition of news) provides a good mechanism for a community to discover itself, learn about itself, and ultimately transform itself into a more just and cohesive entity. Communitarian reasoning allows journalists to understand their institutional role and to evaluate their performance against shared societal values. For instance, the newsroom adage "if it bleeds it leads" might sell newspapers or attract viewers, but it might also give a false impression of community and its perils to the most vulnerable members. Communitarianism would not disallow the coverage of crime, but would demand context that would help viewers or readers decide if they need to take action.

Thinking as a communitarian mutes the competition among journalistic organizations while amplifying the collective effect that journalists and their organizations have on society and culture. Communitarian thinking can provide journalists with an effective justification for sometimes placing family before work, for including mobilizing information in a story about the local rape crisis center, or for inviting viewers and readers to help determine the sort of political stories in which they are most interested and then providing ample coverage of them.

Because communitarianism is a philosophy of ideals, it is difficult to find concrete journalistic examples of the theory in action. Many writers have linked communitarian philosophy with the civic journalism movement. Seminal examples of this type of civic journalism are the 1994 "Voices of Florida" project involving several leading newspapers in Florida and the 1996 "Your Voice, Your Vote" project by the *Charlotte Observer*. In the latter, the *Observer* polled the citizens of North Carolina twice about what issues concerned them in the upcoming elections and took these "everyday worries" to each statewide candidate for comment. Interestingly, one of the editors who headed the project, Chuck Clark (1997), would later write that most candidates, regardless of success in the election, enjoyed being engaged by the newspaper with the citizen's concerns while their political handlers "hated it" since it made it harder for them to "steer and manipulate the coverage." But like the philosophy of communitarianism, the practice of civic journalism has not yet been embraced by the mainstream of society.

THE "SCIENCE" OF ETHICS

Life in the 21st century has changed how most people think about issues, such as what constitutes a fact and what does or does not influence moral certainty. We will explore those changes, and the changes they have led to in the lives of mass-communication professionals, in more detail in the next chapter. But for now, it suffices to say that ethical theory, with its apparent uncertainties and contradictions, appears to have taken a back seat to science in much of modern life. Part of the reason people have become so concerned with ethics is that they seek "the answer" to ethical dilemmas in the same way they seek "the answer" in science. In such an endeavor, the vagaries of ethical choice as contrasted with scientific knowledge seem unsatisfactory.

We'd like to offer you a different conceptualization of "the facts" of both science and ethics. Science, and the seeming certainty of scientific knowledge, have undergone vast changes in the past hundred years. After all, before Einstein, most educated people believed that Sir Francis Bacon had accurately and eternally described the basic actions and laws of the physical universe. But Bacon was wrong. Scientific inquiry in the 20th century searchingly explored a variety of physical phenomena, almost always uncovering new relationships, new areas of knowledge, and most importantly, new and expanding areas of ignorance. What modern humanity regarded as the certainty of scientific truth has changed fundamentally in the last hundred years, and humanity has every reason to expect similar changes in this century. Science and certainty are not synonymous, despite our tendency to blur the two.

Contrast these fundamental changes in the scientific worldview with the developments of moral theory. Aristotle's writing, more than two thousand years old and with no fundamental changes, still has much to recommend it to the modern era, although, of course, there will continue to be new interpretations. The same can be said of utilitarianism and of the Kantian approach—both subject to more than a hundred years of critical review. Certainly, new moral thinking has emerged—for example, John Rawls's work on utilitarian theory (Chapter 6). But such work tends to build on rather than radically alter the moral theorizing that has gone before. This is not to assert that ethical philosophers do not have fundamental debates but rather to suggest that these debates have, in general, tended to deepen and enlarge previous insights rather than to "prove" them incorrect in some epistemological sense.

From this viewpoint, there is continuity in thinking about ethics that is lacking in the development of scientific thought. Further, thinking about ethics in a global way uncovers some striking areas of agreement. We are aware of no ethical system, for example, that argues that murder is an ethical behavior, or that lying, cheating and stealing are the sorts of activities that human beings ought to engage in on a regular basis. Applying the various ethical theories outlined in this chapter will deepen your understanding of these principles and the complexity of application, but they are unlikely to change your views about the ethical correctness of murder or lying.

When the average person contrasts ethics with science, it is ethics that tends to be viewed as changeable, unsystematic and idiosyncratic. Science has rigor, proof, and some relationship to an external reality. We would like to suggest that such characterizations arise from a short-term view of the history of science and ethics. In our view, ethics as a field has at least as much continuity of thought as developments in science. And while it cannot often be quantified, it has the rigor, the systematic quality, and the relationship to reality that moderns too often characterize as the exclusive domain of scientific thinking.

Suggested Readings

ARISTOTLE. *The Nicomachean ethics.*

BOK, SISSELA. 1978. *Lying: Moral choice in public and private life.* New York: Random House.

CHRISTIANS, CLIFFORD, JOHN FERRE, and MARK FACKLER. 1993. *Good news: Social ethics and the press.* New York: Oxford University Press.

GERT, BERNARD. 1988. *Morality: A new justification of the moral rules.* New York: Oxford University Press.

MILL, JOHN STUART. *On liberty.*

PETERS, JOHN D. 2000. *Speaking in the air: A history of the idea of communication.* Chicago: University of Chicago Press.

POJMAN, L. 1998. *Ethical theory: Classical and contemporary readings.* Belmont, CA: Wadsworth Publishing Co.

CHAPTER I ESSAY

Cases and Moral Systems

DENI ELLIOTT
University of South Florida—St. Petersburg

Case studies are wonderful vehicles for ethics discussions. Some of their great strengths include helping discussants

1. appreciate the complexity of newsroom decision making;

2. understand the context within which difficult decisions are made;

3. track the consequences of choosing one action over another; and

4. learn both how and when to reconcile and how and when to tolerate divergent points of view.

However, when case studies are misused, these great strengths become their fundamental weaknesses. Case studies are vehicles for an ethics discussion, not its ultimate destination. The purpose of an ethics discussion is to teach discussants how to "do ethics"—that is, to teach them processes by which they can practice and improve their own critical decision-making abilities. Each discussant should, through the use of the case-study vehicle, reach the end point: a reasoned response to the issue at hand.

When the discussion stops short of this point, it is often because the destination has been fogged in by one or more myths of media case discussions:

Myth 1: Every opinion is equally valid.

Not true. The best opinion (conclusion) is the one that is best supported by judicious analysis of fact and theory. In an ethics discussion, it is the one that best addresses the morally relevant factors of the case. An action has morally relevant factors if it is likely to cause some individual to suffer an evil that any rational person would wish to avoid (such as death, disability, pain, loss of freedom or pleasure), or if it is the kind of action that generally causes evil (such as deception, breaking promises, cheating, disobedience of law, or neglect of duty) (see Gert 1988).

Myth 2: Since we can't agree on an answer, there is no right answer.

It's tough to take into account all of the various points of view when working through a case. One way people avoid doing this is to refuse to choose among the different perspectives. But this retreat to fatalistic subjectivism is not necessary. It may be that there are a number of acceptable answers. But there will also be many wrong answers—many approaches that the group can agree would be unacceptable. When discussants begin to despair of ever reaching any agreement on a right answer or answers, it is time to reflect on all of the agreement that exists within the group concerning the actions that would be out of bounds.

Myth 3: It hardly matters if you come up with the "ethical thing to do," since people ultimately act out of their own self-interest anyway.

The point of ethical reflection is to find and deal with those situations when one should not simply do that which benefits oneself. Acting ethically means to refrain from causing unjustified harm, even when prudential concerns must be set aside.

Any institution supported by society, manufacturing firms or media corporations, as well as medical centers, provides some service that merits that support. No matter what the service, practitioners or companies that act only in the short-term interest, for instance to make money, will not last long. Free-market pragmatism, as well as ethics, dictates that it makes little sense to ignore the expectations of consumers and of the society at large.

The guidelines below can serve as a map for an ethics discussion. They are helpful to have when working through unfamiliar terrain toward individual end points. They can also help detour around the myths discussed earlier.

While discussing the case, check to see if these questions are being addressed:

1. What are the morally relevant factors of the case?
   (a) Will the proposed action cause an evil—such as death, disability, pain, loss of freedom or opportunity, or a loss of pleasure—that any rational person would wish to avoid?
   (b) Is the proposed action the sort of action—such as deception, breaking promises, cheating, disobedience of law, or disobedience of professional or role-defined duty—that generally causes evil?
2. If the proposed action is one described above, is a greater evil being prevented or punished?
3. If so, is the actor in a unique position to prevent or punish such an evil, or is that a more appropriate role for some other person or profession?
4. If the actor followed through on the action, would he be allowing himself to be an exception to a rule that he thinks everyone else should follow? If so, then the action is prudent, not moral. One way to test this out is for journalists to ask how they would react if a person in another profession did what they are thinking of doing. Would the journalists applaud the action, or would they write an exposé?
5. If, at this point, the proposed action still seems justified, consider if a rational, uninvolved person would appreciate the reason for causing harm. Are the journalists ready to state, explain and defend the proposed action in a public forum?

II

Information Ethics: A Profession Seeks the Truth

By the end of this chapter, you should be familiar with:

- **both the Enlightenment and pragmatic constructions of truth.**
- **the development and several criticisms of objective news reporting as a professional ideal.**
- **why truth in "getting" the news may be as important as truth in reporting it.**
- **how to develop a personal list of ethical news values.**

INTRODUCTION

Each of the traditional professions has laid claims to one of the central tenets of philosophy. Law, ideally, is equated with justice; medicine with the duty to render aid. Journalism, too, has a lofty ideal: the communication of truth.

But the ideal of truth is problematic. In routine interaction we consider truth a stable commodity: it doesn't change much for us on a day-to-day basis, nor does it vary greatly among members of a community. While we are willing to accept some cultural "lies"—for example, the existence of Santa Claus—we stand ready to condemn others—for example, income tax evasion or fraud. Most of the time, we seem to know what the boundaries are, at least when we deal with one another face-to-face.

However, the concept of truth has changed throughout human history. At one level or another, human beings since ancient times have acknowledged that truth may vary depending on individual points of view. Since Plato's analogy of life as shadows on the wall of a cave 3,000 years ago, people have grappled with the amorphous nature of truth.

Compounding the modern problem of the shifting nature of truth is the changing media audience. When a profession accepts the responsibility of printing and broadcasting the truth, facts that are apparent in face-to-face interaction become subject to different interpretations among geographically and culturally diverse viewers and readers. Ideas that were once readily accepted are open to debate. The whole concept of telling the truth becomes not merely a matter of possessing good moral character but something that requires learning how to recognize truth and how to convey it in the least distorted manner possible.

A CHANGING VIEW OF TRUTH

One pre-Socratic Greek tradition viewed truth—*alethea*—as encompassing all that humans remember, singled out through memory from everything that is destined for *Lethe,* the river of forgetfulness (Bok 1978). Linking truth and remembrance is essential in an oral culture, one that requires information be memorized and repeated so as not to be forgotten. Repeating the message, often in the form of songs or poetry, meant that the accumulated ideas and knowledge were kept alive or true for subsequent generations. Homer's *Iliad* and *Odyssey* or much of the Bible's Old Testament served this function.

This oral notion of truth, as noted in Table 2.1, was gradually discarded once words and ideas were written down. However, it has come to the fore again with the advent of television. Television allows viewers to hear the words of the president rather than wait for those words to be passed down orally or in writing. When we see something on television, we assume that it closely corresponds to reality—that it is in some sense true. The maxim "Seeing is believing" reminds us that truth has somehow become tangled up with pictures and presence. It is an oral concept of truth that has been a dormant form of knowledge for hundreds of years.

While the other ancient Greeks tied truth to human memory, Plato linked truth to human rationality and intellect. In *The Republic,* Plato equated truth with a world of pure form, a world to which human beings had only indirect access. In Plato's vision, there was an ideal notion of a chair—but that ideal chair did not exist in reality. What people thought of as a chair was as similar to the ideal chair as the shadows on the wall of the cave are to objects illuminated by the fire. Truth was knowable only to the human intellect—it could not be touched or verified.

TABLE 2.1.   A Philosophy of Truth Emerges

Source	Truth Equals
Ancient Greeks	What is memorable and is handed down
Plato	What abides in the world of perfect forms
Medieval	What the king, Church, or God says
Milton	What emerges from the "marketplace of ideas"
Enlightenment	What is verifiable, replicable, universal
Pragmatists	What is filtered through individual perception

Plato's metaphor has had a profound influence on Western thought. Not only did Plato link truth to rationality, as opposed to human experience, but his work implies that truth is something that can be captured only through the intellect. Platonic truth is implicit within a thing itself; truth defined the "perfect form." Plato's concept of truth separated the notion of something as true from the external world in which that thing existed.

Subsequent centuries and thinkers adhered to Plato's view. Medieval theologians believed truth was revealed only by God or by the Church. The intellectual legacy of the Reformation centered on whether it is possible for the average person to ascertain truth without benefit of a priest or a king. About two hundred years later, Milton suggested that competing notions of the truth should be allowed to coexist, with the ultimate truth eventually emerging (see Table 2.1).

Milton's assertions foreshadowed the philosophy of the Enlightenment, from which modern journalism borrows its notion of truth. The Enlightenment cast truth in secular terms and developed what is now called a "correspondence theory" of truth. The correspondence theory asserts that truth should correspond to some external set of facts or observations. The Enlightenment concept of truth was linked to what human beings could perceive with their senses harnessed through the intellect. Truth acquired substance. It was something that could be perceived, and ultimately perception of truth was something that could be replicated.

This Enlightenment notion of truth has remained with us and is essential to what contemporary scholars refer to as the scientific method. Truth has become increasingly tied to that which is written down, to that which can be empirically verified, to that which can be perceived by the human senses, and to that which does not vary among people or among cultures. It is a truth uniquely suited to the written word, for it links what is written with what is factual, accurate, and important in the most profound of senses. This Enlightenment view of truth undergirds the journalistic ideal of objectivity. Objectivity has its intellectual roots in the previous three hundred years. While objectivity has many definitions, it may be considered, most simply, a mechanism that allows journalists to divorce fact from opinion. Journalists view objectivity as refusing to allow individual bias to influence what they report or how they cover it. It is a journalism in which all facts and people are regarded as equal and equally worthy of coverage. Culture, an individual sense of mission, and individual and organizational feelings and views do not belong in objective news accounts. An Enlightenment view of truth allowed objectivity to be considered an attainable ideal.

However, philosophy was not the only reason, and some scholars have argued not even the most important reason, that objectivity became a professional standard in the early 1900s. The libertarian press of the Enlightenment was not really a mass press, and it garnered most of its financial support from political advertising and most of its readers through partisan political reporting. As the United States became urban in the late 1800s, publishers realized that to reach this large urban audience, they needed more support from a wider variety of advertisers. To convince potential advertisers that their advertising would be seen and possibly acted upon by a large audience, publishers had to make certain their publications would be read. Partisan publications could not ensure that, for strong views offended potential readers.

What publishers of the day needed was a product that built on an Enlightenment philosophical construction that guaranteed that facts would be facts, no matter who was doing the reading. Opinion would be relegated to specific pages. Both facts and opinion could be wrapped around advertising. Objective news reporting was born (Schudson 1978).

Objectivity came along at an advantageous time for yet another reason. The mass press of the early 1900s was deeply and corruptly involved in yellow journalism. Fabricated stories were common; newspaper wars were close to the real thing. Although many of the specific events of the era (for example, the apocryphal story that William Randolph Hearst began the Spanish-American War so he would have something to photograph) have been exaggerated, the excesses in pursuit of circulation tarnished the profession's image. Objectivity was a good way to clean up journalism's act with a set of standards where seemingly none had existed before. It fit the cultural expectations of the Enlightenment that truth was knowable and ascertainable. And it made sure that readers of news columns would remain unoffended long enough to glance at the ads.

The Enlightenment view of truth also was compatible with democracy and its emphasis on rational government. People who could reason together, who could arrive at some shared "truth" of how their political lives ought to function, could govern themselves. Information was essential to such a form of government, for it allowed citizens to scrutinize government. As long as truth was ascertainable by the rational being, government could function. Under this view, information—written, logical, linear—provided the social glue as well as the grease of such a society. Citizens and government need information in order to continue their rational function. Information, and the notion that it corresponded in some essential way with the truth, carried enormous promise.

Twentieth-century pragmatists—most notably Americans John Dewey, George Herbert Mead, Charles Sanders Pierce and William James—challenged the Enlightenment view of truth. They held that the perception of truth depended on how it was investigated and on who was doing the investigating. Further, they rejected the notion that there was only one proper method of investigation—that is, the scientific method. Borrowing from Einstein's insights, pragmatists argued that truth, like matter, was relative.

Specifically, the pragmatists proposed that knowledge and reality were not *fixed by,* but instead were the *result of,* an evolving stream of consciousness and learning. Reality itself varied based on psychological, social, historical, or cultural contexts. Additionally, reality was defined as that which was probable, not as something intrinsic (the Platonic view) or something determined by only one method of observation (the Enlightenment view).

Pragmatism found a comfortable home in the 20th-century United States. Under pragmatism truth lost much of its universality, but it was in remarkable agreement with the American value of democratic individualism. Soon pragmatism filtered through literature, science, and some professions, such as law.

Pragmatic notions of truth provided a philosophical basis to challenge objectivity. At roughly the same time that the journalistic community was embracing Enlightenment standards of objectivity, the culture itself was adopting more pragmatic notions of truth. That clash fueled criticism of objectivity on both a scholarly and a popular level. Several questions surfaced. If truth is subjective, can it be best obtained and reported by an impassive, objective and detached reporter? Does such a reporter exist? Is truth a construct that relies on the context of the source, the message and the receiver?

Postmodern philosophy (see *The Matrix* below) has taken these questions to their logical extension, suggesting that the concept of truth is devoid of meaning. Postmodernism asserts that context is literally everything, that meaning cannot exist apart from contextual understanding. This philosophical approach is antithetical to fact-based journalism, but designers and other visual journalists have employed it in everything from layout to typography.

The last 30 years have added yet another level of complexity to the problem: the information explosion. Not only do we as a culture now question the meaning of the terms *fact* and *truth,* but we literally cannot sort them all out. Facts and truth come to us quickly from all over the globe. Our ability to attend to these various messages, let alone construct rational meaning from them, is on the verge of being overwhelmed.

In short, the concept of objectivity, which was once equated with printing the truth, has been deeply undermined by both philosophical shift and technological innovation (Christians, Ferré, and Fackler 1992). Telling your readers and viewers the truth has become a complicated business.

> Telling the "truth" therefore is not solely a matter of moral character; it is also a matter of correct appreciation of real situations and of serious reflection upon them. . . . Telling the truth, therefore, is something which must be learnt. This will sound very shocking to anyone who thinks that it must all depend on moral character and that if this is blameless the rest is child's play. But the simple fact is that the ethics cannot be detached from reality, and consequently continual progress in learning to appreciate reality is a necessary ingredient in ethical action. (Bok 1978, 302–303)

It is to the issue of learning to appreciate reality that we will now turn. First, we will review some of the scholarly findings about news coverage and what the news does and does not reflect. Then we will ask you to apply these scholarly findings, as well as a question or two, to case studies that deal with the links between news and the truth.

The Matrix: **A Postmodern Examination of Truth**

"Do you ever have that feeling where you're not sure whether you are awake or still dreaming?"

  "Yeah, all the time. . . . It just sounds to me like you might need to unplug, man . . . get some R&R?"

  Thus begins Neo's journey down the rabbit hole (like Lewis Carroll's Alice) where reality literally turns inside out on itself. A computer wizard, and unknown genetic mutation, Neo—who is awak-ened to the possibilities courtesy of Morpheus—literally unplugs himself from the reality of a computer simulation where human beings serve as batteries for artificially intelligent machines that now run the world. The reality that most people know is nothing more than a computer code invented by the artificial intelligence and inserted electronically into billions of human neural systems from infancy onward.

Neo, as his name suggests, is the person who has the capacity to crack and overcome the code.

The Matrix set the standard in the latter part of the last century for smart films about the potential of the computers that increasingly power, and in some subtle ways govern, the information age. The film was also stylish; in fact, the long, black trench coats Keanu Reeves and Carrie-Anne Moss wore were eerily predictive of the attire worn by the Columbine High School shooters. The special effects and set design, based as they were on a comic book reality, gave form to one vision of hyper-reality, as did the film's otherworldly and sometimes violent content.

More importantly for our purposes, the film provides an accessible discussion of the postmodern approach to truth.

Postmodernism is a logical outgrowth of pragmatism. Instead of suggesting that truth varies with receiver, or sender, or context, postmodernism suggests that truth—if it exists at all—is unknowable. Those who believe they know the truth, like Neo at the beginning of the film, discover that their "reality" is merely false consciousness, founded on invalid assumptions that shift constantly in a chaotic environment.

Postmodernism rejects such concepts as the correspondence theory of truth, or even the Platonic ideal that truth is knowable only as an intellectual construct. In postmodernism, revealed truth, as medieval scholars understood it, does not exist, and the marketplace of ideas yields either false understandings or babble. In the film, dreams are real, reality shifts, and absolutely nothing is what it seems. Control, in the form of computer programs (malleable by both the programmers and the programmed), and death, in the form of biological waste, remain.

Almost all journalistic endeavors by their very nature reject this postmodern way of thinking. Some philosophers, for example Clifford Christians, reject postmodernism on the grounds that the essence of humanity itself provides an irrefutable challenge to the postmodern premise. Others have noted that postmodernism too easily falls into the trap of solipsism—or the notion that it is impossible to know anything outside of one's individual thoughts and perceptions. Solipsism, of course, negates any attempt at social ethics where values, principles and other people exist independently of individual thought and biological function.

While traditional theory may reject postmodernism, contemporary culture itself sometimes embraces what Morpheus calls "the desert of the real." Magazine designers employ postmodern sensibilities to create designs that play with the entire concept of text. Media critics argue that a media-generated reality, subject to no counterargument from other messages or critical examination by audiences, is not so different from the matrix that Neo encounters. And, digitizing and editing visual images and sounds through sophisticated computer programs is the stuff of elementary school play.

So, if postmodernism is an appropriate worldview, does that mean journalists and persuasion professionals should abandon their jobs or their ancient foundations in the face of overwhelming information overload? We think not.

Neo and Morpheus still have to act. They learn to think in new ways, but their actions remain centered on their belief in human independence and the "rightness" of thinking about and connecting with others. Even in this postmodern vision, ethical thinking still has a place. Neo's goal, after all, is to dismantle one matrix so humanity can make its own choices.

WHO'S DOING THE TALKING ANYWAY?

The pragmatic's critique of objectivity has called attention to the question of who writes the news. Journalists—who themselves are primarily male, Caucasian, well-educated, and middle to upper class—are often asked to cover issues and questions for which their life experiences have not prepared them. Stephen Hess (1981) noted that journalists, in terms of their socioeconomic status, look a great deal more like the people they cover than the people they are supposedly writing for. While the eastern elite press provides an extreme example of this tendency, other work on the national press corps has shown similar results (Weaver and Wilhoit 1993).

In the past 20 years, almost every professional journalistic organization has developed programs specifically to attract and retain women and minorities, many with limited success. Decades of programs to increase the minority presence in newsrooms has met with only incremental and sporadic success. This lack of access to the engines of information has not been lost on a variety of minority groups—from religious fundamentalists, who have in some cases established their own broadcasting networks, to racial minorities, who fail to find themselves either as owners or managers of media outlets or in front of the cameras and with front-page bylines. They argue that the result is news about middle-class Caucasians, for middle-class Caucasians, about a political-economic system that systematically excludes everyone but middle-class Caucasians.

How individual journalists and the corporations they work for should remedy the situation is unclear. But many editors and publishers as well as their corporate bosses worry that as the demographics change us from a culture that is predominantly Caucasian to one that is not, the mass media, particularly newspapers, will play an increasingly minor role unless journalists find a way to report news that is of interest to the new majority of their readers. Some are changing as a result. For instance, Gannett, the nation's largest newspaper chain, initiated the Gannett 2000 project in the early 1990s, a mechanistic attempt to ensure ethnic diversity and reader input in its news pages through formulas and heavy reliance on reader polls. The more recent civic journalism movement is another reflection of such efforts.

SEEING ISN'T BELIEVING

Another assumption embedded in the concept of objectivity centers on how the news is perceived. More than 80 years ago, journalist Walter Lippmann (1922) foreshadowed what modern psychology has now documented when he said, "For the most part, we do not first see, and then define, we define first and then see." He added that we tend to pick out what our culture has already defined for us, and then perceive it in the form stereotyped for us by our culture.

An example of this phenomenon is found in the study of a New York journalism professor, blind since birth, who could predict the race of football players being described in the play-by-play sports commentary by what was being said about them (Rainsville and McCormick 1977). Caucasian athletes were described as intellectually gifted while African-American athletes were described as physically gifted. In a culture that values brains over brawn, African-American football players were the subject of repeated stereotypical insults—all couched as praise in the play-by-play. And even though the professor's predictions and the study that validated them are now more than 30 years old, the tendency to go back to these stereotypes continues on sports broadcasts today.

Groups such as women, the elderly and the gay community have conducted studies with similar results. Their conclusion has been that while journalists maintain that they are objective, they (like their readers and viewers) bring something to the message that literally changes what they see and, hence, what they report (Lester 1996). What they bring, most often, is technology, and the technology of television has led scholars to question the role of objectivity in news reporting.

In a *Columbia Journalism Review* cover story in the summer of 2003 entitled "Rethinking Objectivity," author Brent Cunningham (2003) says that "our pursuit of objectivity can trip us up on the way to truth. Objectivity excuses lazy reporting. If you're on deadline and all you have is 'both sides of the story,' then that's often good enough." Cunningham cites numerous incidences of enterprising reporting spiked by editors who asked, "says who," when the facts went contrary to or beyond the conventional wisdom of the story based on the reporters' own work.

A slavish dedication to objectivity can keep reporters tethered to the government's version of the truth. Cunningham points to a study of 414 war stories on Iraq broadcast on ABC, CBS and NBC leading up to the 2003 conflict, where researcher Andrew Tyndall found that all but 34 originated from the White House, the Pentagon or the State Department. The result is that the "official truth" becomes the received truth, and only the bravest journalists dared depart from it, even when it was apparent to many that the administration had no comprehensive plan of how to rebuild a postwar Iraq.

E. J. Dionne (1996) claims that the press is in internal contradiction. It must be neutral, yet investigative. It must be disengaged, but have an impact. It must be fair-minded but have an edge. The conflicts make true objectivity in journalism virtually impossible to even define and even harder to practice.

DEFINING AND CONSTRUCTING THE NEWS

News reflects certain cultural values and professional norms. Those values and norms, often at odds with an Enlightenment concept of truth, lend themselves to a pragmatic version of the news, provided you remember who's doing the writing and story selection.

One professional norm that plays an important role in shaping the news is the journalistic imperative to tell a story to make a point. Often this leads to predictable narratives, many of them centering on crisis and politics (Nimmo and Combs 1985; Bennett 1988). Sociologist Herbert Gans (1979) studied how stories became news at *Newsweek* and CBS and found that almost all news stories reflected these six cultural values: ethnocentrism, altruistic democracy, responsible capitalism, individualism, an emphasis on the need for and maintenance of social order, and leadership. These dominant values helped to shape not only which stories were printed but also what they said. They are one basis for what communication scholars call "framing."

1993, Washington Post Writers Group. Reprinted with permission.

Gans called these values the "para-ideology" of the media, noting that "the news is not so much conservative or liberal as it is reformist." Researcher James Carey (quoted in Cunningham 2003) says that it is this para-ideology that is the source of charges of liberal bias against the media. "There is a bit of the reformer in anyone who enters journalism. And reformers are always going to make conservatives uncomfortable."

News stories about middle-class or upper-class people, those who tend to successfully adopt the culture's values, made the American news "budget," according to Gans, while stories about minorities, blue-collar Americans, and those sharply critical of governmental policy got lost on the cutting-room floor. While Gans focused on journalism about the United States, other scholars have noted the same phenomenon, called *domesticating the foreign,* in international coverage (Gurevitch et al. 1991). Journalists working for U.S. media outlets tell stories about international events in cultural terms Americans can readily understand but which also sacrifice accuracy and a non-American point of view. For example, routine coverage of elections in Britain or Israel is conveyed in horse-race metaphors even though both countries employ a parliamentary system where governing coalitions are common and who wins the horse race not nearly so important.

PACKAGING THE STORY: NEWS AS MANUFACTURED PRODUCT

The goal of telling a "good story" also raises other ethical questions, specifically those that focus on packaging to highlight drama and human interest. Ethical questions about packaging began with newspapers but have intensified with television. Television demands video, and television's video imperative has been found to dominate both story selection and placement (for example, Epstein 1974). If television arrives at a disaster before print journalists, it is television that frames the stories for the written word (Smith 1992). Photo availability sometimes contradicts the classic notion of objectivity that each story should stand on its own merits, but it certainly reflects the professional norms of particular media. *USA Today*'s graphic impact on the newspaper industry has not been applauded by everyone. Some see the paper as a further indication of the trivialization of news, with an emphasis on packaging. Political ads have helped journalists to frame news stories about the same issue (Jamieson 1992) to some extent because of compelling visuals in the ads.

Journalists also need something to package, which has led to a professional drive to find an "event" to report and to be there first. Few consumers realize it, but news is "manufactured" daily, just as surely as furniture, cars or the meal at your favorite fast-food restaurant—and often the process can be as messy as these other manufacturing enterprises. Journalists start the day with a blank computer screen or blank video tape with press time or broadcast time looming. And adding to the built-in tension is the challenge to be fair, complete, accurate and, above all, interesting. The daily challenge leads to ethical problems as the temptation of the shortcut, when available, always beckons.

The need to find an event has meant journalists have missed some important stories because they were not events but rather historic developments with both a past and a future. For example, major social developments such as the women's movement (Mills 1989), the civil rights movement, and the anti–Vietnam War movement were undercovered until their leaders created events such as sit-ins and demonstrations for the media to report. More recently, director Michael Moore said he began his wickedly funny 1989 film *Roger and Me* about the devastation of General Motors layoffs on his hometown of Flint, Michigan, because he "didn't see on the silver screen or the television screen what happened to people like us. It was a story then (in the mid-1980s) and it's a story now and that's part of the reason I did the movie" (Smith 1992).

This preoccupation with events affects coverage of several types of stories. Science is most frequently reported as a series of discoveries and "firsts" rather than as a process of discovery (Nelkin 1987). We are treated to stories about the next cancer or AIDS cure without the necessary context to interpret the latest research results. The twin dramas of "new hope" and "no hope" seem to drive most science reporting.

Stories are missed or misreported when they lack the easy "peg" editors look for. The socioeconomic, scientific and political causes of a disaster, such as the one that claimed thousands of lives in Bhopal, India, were seldom mentioned in news coverage that focused on the picture-friendly event (Wilkins 1987). Finally, phenomena not linked to specific events, such as the greenhouse effect or the growth of an American underclass, often go unreported or underreported until an appropriate news peg arrives to supply the needed event the coverage requires.

Elections become horse races with one candidate the "front-runner" and the "rest of the pack" struggling to narrow the gap with each new poll. But reporting an election as a contest fails to focus on the policy issues, which is what democratic elections are supposed to be about. The quintessential manifestation of this can be seen in the 2003 recall election of California's incumbent governor and the subsequent election of Arnold Schwarzenegger even though most Californians admitted not knowing any of his stances. And in a spectacular display of circular logic, many said they voted for the actor simply because they deemed him "electable."

The phenomenon of "pack journalism" has been chronicled in several films, dating back to the classic *The Front Page* and later recounted in Timothy Crouse's book *The Boys on the Bus* (1974) and Sabato's *Feeding Frenzy* (1992). All emphasize journalistic excesses and an unwillingness to engage in independent thought that would disturb enlightened and pragmatic philosophers alike.

And just like the candidates they cover, journalists seek to break out of the "pack" and the ticket to front-runner status (and the front page) is the "scoop," a story no other journalist has or one no one else is willing to run. The twin problems of pack journalism and the scoop mentality still dominate much reporting and editing. Because of this, important stories have been killed, while some poorly researched stories have been aired or published.

Journalists have also been cowed by the threat of litigation. The film *The Insider* presents a fictionalized but nonetheless fact-based account about the impact of litigation on reporting stories critical of big tobacco. Seymour Hersh's original reporting of the My Lai massacre during the Vietnam War, which eventually appeared in the *New York Times,* was held up because no other reporter had a similar story and a particular media outlet was afraid to stick its neck out.

On the other hand, the *New York Times* resorted to quoting the supermarket tabloid the *National Enquirer* in its coverage of the O. J. Simpson case largely in an effort to keep up with media competition. Equally significant, the *Enquirer* had the story right. And, the entire Washington press corps was confounded when Internet gadfly Matt Drudge, who styles himself a political reporter, published what became the first mention of the President Bill Clinton/Monica Lewinsky scandal. Drudge has said that he prints rumor as well as fact; traditional journalists, who want to separate the two, remain deeply troubled by the impact of the speed of the Internet on the need to check facts before more traditional publication.

Truth is more than just a collection of facts. Facts have a relationship to one another and to other facts, forming a larger whole. Yet analytic coverage of American institutions, of science and technology, of politics, and of social movements is rare. If the role of the mass media is not only to detail events and issues, but to do so in a way that relationships among them are clear, is merely retelling a story sufficient? Or do we need to do it better?

Stephen Hess (1981) has argued that journalists need to engage in reporting that looks more like social science than storytelling. Gans argues for news that is labeled as originating from a particular point of view. If readers and viewers are alerted to the worldview of those who have selected the news, just as they were during the era of the partisan press, they would be better able to place news in context. Other scholars argue for news that is analytical rather than anecdotal, proactive rather than reactive, and contextual rather than detached. And on a practical level, working reporters and editors insist that individual journalists need to do a better job of understanding their own biases and compensating for them.

These findings, from studies about how the media decide what is news to analyses of how individual audience members interpret the same news message, strike at the core of objectivity and its relationship to the complex truths of this century. Intellectually, we are living in a pragmatic era, but professionally we seem to be unable to develop a working alternative to the Enlightenment's view of truth.

DECEPTION: THE MEANS TO AN END

In a profession that values truth, is it ever ethical to lie? To editors? To readers? To sources, who may be liars themselves? Are there levels of lying? Is flattering some-

Stephan Pastis reprinted by permission of United Feature Syndicate, Inc.

one to get an interview as serious a transgression as doctoring a quote or photograph? Is withholding information the same thing as lying? And, what's the responsibility of news organizations that have published reports based on partial truth "fed" to them by other powerful institutions?

The war in Iraq provided abundant examples of varieties of deception. The front-page rescue of Pfc. Jessica Lynch from an Iraqi hospital was later documented as substantially different from the original (though never corrected) story put forth by the Pentagon. The case confronted journalists with the issue of how to correct erroneous reporting months after the initial accounts.

About the same time media outlets were trying to figure out how to find and report the truth from the difficult battlefields of Iraq, the *New York Times* faced a credibility crisis of its own. A 27-year-old reporter, Jayson Blair, fabricated all or part of more than forty stories he had written for the *Times.* After his May 1, 2003, resignation from the paper, the *Times* ran four full pages of corrections, including a front-page story, documenting every error discovered in Blair's reporting. The *Times'* correction, as well as subsequent reporting in other media outlets, made it clear that not only was Blair a person without a moral compass but that the newsroom organization at the *Times* had failed to correct the problem in earlier stages despite many opportunities to do so, an institutional failure of substantial proportions that toppled two *Times* editors as well.

Blair became a *Times* reporter after an internship with the newspaper. In a highly competitive reporting atmosphere, Blair rose through the ranks in part because of his interpersonal skills and hustle. The *Times* hired Blair based on his work at the paper and on the assumption that he had completed his college coursework. Had the editors investigated they would have learned that Blair never graduated from the University of Maryland. His editors found Blair's work fast but inaccurate. At one point, he was shifted to the sports desk, where he had similar problems, but he was returned to the regular newsroom to report on a series of sniper shootings in the Washington, D.C., area, in part because Blair's home was in northern Virginia, near where the shootings occurred.

Throughout his brief *Times* career, Blair systematically deceived his bosses on many levels. He filed stories from locations where he had never traveled. He added detailed description to stories by electronically accessing photographs taken at the scene and writing about what he saw in the pictures. He plagiarized accounts published in other news organizations, among them the *Washington Post*. He doctored his expense accounts, and failed to document many expenses that he should have incurred had he been doing his job honestly.

Some of the errors were small—blue flowers in front of a house instead of pink; others were substantial—quotes from people he had never interviewed. Sometimes, Blair's sources complained to the *Times* about the inaccuracy of his coverage. Most telling are the ones who said they did not call because they assumed "that's the way things are done." The paper did publish some corrections. But it wasn't until a single editor served notice to his superiors that Blair did not "belong" at the paper that the organization decided it needed to look into a pattern of behavior that now stretched over more than 18 months of work.

In a subsequent analysis of the case, many at the *Times* and other places suggested that one reason Blair's actions had been unchecked for so long was because of his race. Blair was African-American, and he had been hired as part of the *Times'* diversity program. His mentors at the paper, Executive Editor Howell Raines and Managing Editor Gerald Boyd, who also is African-American, were among Blair's strongest supporters. Raines, who had been raised in the South, was particularly sensitive about racial issues. Boyd had personally mentored the young writer. While the *Times* denied that race was the reason that Blair had been promoted, Blair himself did not.

Errors in Journalism: Inevitability and Arrogance

Confounding truth and deception in journalism is the problem of errors. Inadvertent mistakes in stories are common. One freelance fact checker (Hart 2003) wrote in *Columbia Journalism Review* that she had not experienced an error-free story in three years of fact checking for *CJR,* one of journalism's leading watchdog publications. Her calls to fellow fact-checkers at other publications led her to believe that articles with errors are the rule, not the exception.

However, mistakes are different from fabrication (discussed more fully in Chapter 10) and do not indicate a lack of dedication to the truth. Some, if not most, mistakes are matters of interpretation, but others are outright errors of fact. In her article, "Delusions of Accuracy," Ariel Hart says that hearing journalists proudly claim to have had no errors or fewer errors than the *Times* found in Blair's writing is "scary, not the least because it encourages delusions of accuracy."

One problem seems to be audience members so disconnected from the media that they don't bother to correct our mistakes or, worse, assume as readers of the *Times* evidently did, that fabrication is *de rigueur* for journalists. "Journalists surely make mistakes often, but I think we don't—or can't—admit it to ourselves because the idea of a mistake is so stigmatized. . . . So mistakes need to be destigmatized or re-stigmatized and dealt with accordingly. They should be treated like language errors," Hart argues.

In interviews after his resignation, in which he was unrepentant for his actions, Blair said he believed that his race had had a great deal to do with why he had been hired and how he had been treated at the *Times*. "Anyone who tells you that my race didn't play a role in my career at the *New York Times* is lying to you," Blair told the *New York Observer*. "Both racial preferences and racism played a role. And I would argue that they didn't balance each other out. Racism had much more of an impact."

Other journalists reporting on the debacle noted that Blair's editors at the paper had been fearful of confronting the highest levels of management about the quality of Blair's work because they did not want to be perceived as racists. Other reporters had some indication about Blair's behavior but remained silent because he appeared to be close to the paper's top managers and because they did not want to be perceived as racists themselves. As Blair himself saw it, he had become the beneficiary of racial discrimination—in his favor. Many news organizations with diversity programs used the Blair case to examine how they were mentoring and overseeing young reporters of all races. The profession almost unanimously rejected any suggestion that diversity programs in and of themselves were somehow contributory to Blair's acts.

However, Blair wasn't the only bad news for the *Times* during these weeks. Pulitzer Prize–winning reporter Rick Bragg also resigned from the paper after it became public that he, too, had published stories based largely on the reporting of stringers who did not receive a byline in the *Times*. Furthermore, some of his stories filed with non–New York datelines had been written on airplanes and in hotel rooms where Bragg was functioning more as a rewrite editor rather than doing actual on-the-scene reporting. Bragg said his practices were known at the *Times* and common in the industry. Others vehemently disagreed. At the conclusion of this tumultuous six-week period, both Raines and Boyd resigned. In addition, the *Times* appointed an external review committee to examine the cases, and the organization's response to them, for the paper.

So, how do journalists feel about deception as an ethical problem? A recent survey of members of Investigative Reporters and Editors, perhaps journalism's most prestigious professional organization, provides some insight into the profession's thinking (Lee 2002). Journalists think about deception on a continuum. At one end, there is almost universal rejection of lying to readers, viewers and listeners. IRE members regard such lies as among the worst ethical professional breaches. At the other end, more than half of the IRE members surveyed said they approved of flattering a source to get an interview, even though that flattery could be considered deceptive and certainly was insincere. Lies of omission—such as withholding information from readers and viewers and also editors and bosses—were considered less of a problem then fabricating facts in a story or fabricating entire stories, which was almost universally condemned. IRE members were more willing to withhold information in instances when national security issues were involved. The journalists also said some lies were justified; they approved of lying if it would save the life or prevent injury to a source.

The journalists surveyed also noted that there were outside influences on these judgments. Broadcast journalists were more accepting of hidden cameras and altering video than were print journalists. And, those who worked in competitive markets were more willing to accept deception than were those who saw themselves in less competitive environments. Finally, the more experienced a journalist was, the less likely he or she was to accept any form of deception.

This recent history is only the latest chapter in journalist's challenging relationship with "the truth." (For a review of some of those historic cases, for example Nellie Bly, Janet Cooke and the Mirage Bar scam, see the Web site for this book.) While the Blair case illustrates that there are bad actors in any system, how organizations deal with those actors raises important questions. More important is the apparently fine-grained reasoning about ethics and the impact of professional circumstance on ethical thinking that the survey of Investigative Reporters and Editors reveals. In all these instances, what journalists worry about is the impact such reporting methods have on the believability of news accounts and on journalists' ability to cover subsequent stories.

Ethical theory suggests that many cases revolve around two issues: Is it ethical to lie to liars? Is withholding information the same thing as lying? If not, under what circumstances might it be appropriate? If it is, are there ethically based justifications for such an act?

Sissela Bok has written eloquently on lying to liars. She argues that such an act raises two questions. Will the lie serve a larger social good, and does the act of lying mean that we as professionals are willing to be lied to in return? Bok suggests that most of the time, when we lie we want "free rider" status—gaining the benefits of lying without incurring the risks of being lied to. In other words, some journalists may believe it's acceptable to lie to a crook to get a story, but they professionally resent being lied to by any source, regardless of motive.

Many philosophers have asserted that lying is a way to get and maintain power. Those in positions of power often believe they have the right to lie because they have a greater than ordinary understanding of what is at stake. Lying in a crisis (for instance, to prevent panic) and lying to enemies (for instance, to protect national security) are two examples. In both circumstances journalists can be, either actively or without their knowledge, involved in the deception. Do journalists have a right to counter this lying with lies of their own, told under the guise of the public's need to know?

Then there is the omission versus commission issue—a line professional journalists do appear willing to draw in some circumstances. Reporting via the Internet has given new urgency to the issue of lying by omission. In most instances failing to identify yourself as a reporter when collecting information electronically from news groups, chat rooms, or other modes of public discussion the Internet makes possible is considered problematic. Journalists, when pressed, note that the U.S. Supreme Court has ruled Internet transmissions are public. The ethical issue emerges when most of those involved in the discussion are not aware of the legal standards and expect, instead, the more ethically based relations of face-to-face interactions.

Ethical thought leaves journalists with difficult choices. Bok asserts that a genuinely white lie may be excusable on some grounds, but that all forms of lying must stand up to questions of fairness and mutuality. Even lying to liars can have its downside.

> In the end, the participants in deception they take to be mutually understood may end up with coarsened judgment and diminished credibility. But if, finally, the liar to whom one wishes to lie is also in a position to do one harm, then the balance may shift; not because he is a liar, but because of the threat he poses. (Bok 1978, 140)

Since so many of the lies journalists are told emanate from powerful sources, the issue of telling some form of lie to report a socially beneficial story remains a troubling and important one. Another ethical issue centers on exactly how much truth journalists ought to tell. Completeness and accuracy are sometimes used synonymously with truthfulness and objectivity, but important ethical distinctions can be made among the concepts. If truth itself is relative, then how should a journalist balance getting the story against providing his or her readers with the essential information needed to evaluate it? Again, the issue becomes one of the means to a specific end, both now and in the long run.

ETHICAL NEWS VALUES

Most mass media courses present a list of qualities that, collectively, define news. Most such lists include proximity, timeliness, conflict, consequence, prominence, rarity, change, concreteness, action and personality. Additional elements may include notions of mystery, drama, adventure, celebration, self-improvement and even ethics. While these lists are helpful to beginning journalists, they probably will not help you decide how to recount the news ethically.

We suggest you expand your journalistic definitions of news to include a list of ethical news values. These values are intended to reflect the philosophic tensions inherent in a profession with a commitment to truth.

If news values were constructed from ethical reasoning, we believe the following elements would be emphasized by both journalists and the organizations for which they work.

Accuracy—using the correct facts and the right words and putting things in context. Journalists need to be as independent as they can when framing stories. They need to be aware of their own biases, including those they "inherit" as social class, gender and ethnicity, as well as learned professional norms. Their news organizations need to trust journalists when they report independently rather than expect them to act as part of a pack.

Tenacity—knowing when a story is important enough to require additional effort, both personal and institutional. Tenacity drives journalists to provide all the depth they can regardless of the individual assignment. It has institutional implications, too, for the individual cannot function well in an environment where resources are too scarce or the corporate bottom line too dominant.

Dignity—leaving the subject of a story as much self-respect as possible. Dignity values each person regardless of the particular story or the particular role the individual plays. Dignity allows the individual journalist to recognize that news gathering is a cooperative enterprise where each plays a role, including editors, videographers, designers, and advertising sales staff.

Reciprocity—treating others as you wish to be treated. Too often, the journalistic enterprise is defined as "writing for the lowest common denominator." Reciprocity eschews the notion of journalism as a sort of benevolent paternalism—"We'll tell you what we think is good for you"—and recognizes that journalists and their viewers and readers are partners both in discovering what is important and in gleaning meaning from it.

Sufficiency—allocating adequate resources to important issues. On the individual level, sufficiency can mean thoroughness, for example, checking both people and documents for every scrap of fact before beginning to write. On an organizational level, it means allocating adequate resources to the newsgathering process.

Equity—seeking justice for all involved in controversial issues and treating all sources and subjects equally. Like the ethical news value of accuracy, equity assumes a complicated world with a variety of points of view. Equity demands that all points of view be considered, but that not all be framed as equally compelling. Equity expands the journalistic norms of "telling both sides of the story" to "telling all sides of the story."

Community—valuing social cohesion. On the organization level, a sense of community means that media outlets and the corporations that own them need to consider themselves as citizens rather than mere "profit centers." On the individual level, it means evaluating stories with an eye first to social good.

Diversity—covering all segments of the audience fairly and adequately. There appears to be almost overwhelming evidence that news organizations do not "look like" the society they cover. While management can remedy part of this problem through changing hiring patterns, individual journalists can learn to "think diversity" regardless of their individual heritages.

Like all lists, ours should not be considered inclusive or without some measure of internal contradiction. We believe those contradictions, however, provide an important continuum within which informed ethical choice can be made.

Suggested Readings

BENNETT, LANCE. 1988. *News: The politics of illusion.* Longman: New York.

BOK, SISSELA. 1983. *Lying: Moral choice in public and private life.* New York: Random House.

GANS, HERBERT. 1979. *Deciding what's news: A study of CBS Evening News, NBC Nightly News, Newsweek and Time.* New York: Vintage.

JAMIESON, KATHLEEN HALL. 1992. *Dirty politics.* New York: Oxford University Press.

LESTER, PAUL M. 2003. *Images that injure.* Westport, CT: Greenwood Press.

LIPPMANN, WALTER. 1922. *Public opinion.* New York: Free Press.

PLATO. *The republic.*

SABATO, LARRY. 1992. *Feeding frenzy: How attack journalism has transformed American politics.* New York: Free Press.

Cases on the Web

"News as Persuasion: The *New York Times* vs. Wen Ho Lee" by Lee Wilkins

"Columbine: News and community—A balancing act" by Lee Wilkins

"The doctor has AIDS" by Deni Elliott

"Taste in photojournalism: A question of ethics or aesthetics" by Lou Hodges

"Reporters and confidential sources" by Steve Weinberg

"Rodent wars and cultural battles: Reporting hantavirus" by JoAnn M. Valenti

"Too many bodies, too much blood: A case study of the 'family-sensitive newscast'" by Bill Babcock

"Nine days in Union: The Susan Smith case" by Sonya Forte Duhé

CHAPTER II ESSAY

Informing the Public Must Come First
CHRISTOPHER HANSON
University of Maryland

Journalists who will stop at nothing to get a story—from paparazzi photographers pursuing Princess Diana, to TV crews shoving mikes into the faces of traumatized children—have given the news business a reputation for recklessness and cruelty. This might explain why many beginning journalism students believe avoiding harm should be the reporter's primary duty. Their strong inclination is to kill the story of the "family values" mayor downloading porn or the congresswoman drunk before noon in order to spare spouse, children and extended family the pain of disclosure.

Some would kill as "sensationalistic" any photograph that someone in the audience might find disturbing, from images of the World Trade Towers aflame to hospital scenes of Iraqi war victims to Enron executives in handcuffs.

Well intended though it may be, this approach cannot lead to sound journalism because its top priority is being kind and gentle, not informing the public. If minimizing harm were the universal threshold test for airing a story, we would have lots of blank pages and dead air, because stories of tragedy and wrongdoing tend to upset people.

Hence the responsible journalist leans strongly toward publication. Her imperative is not to kill that disturbing story or photo but to present it in a way that minimizes pain without holding back what the public needs to know.

This imperative to inform—and zeal in doing so—is essential if our system is to be open and democratic in practice and not just in principle. The most crucial role of journalists is to wrest "power from groups bent on retaining or accumulating it [and] redistribute power to the public by disseminating information." (Jay Black, Bob Steele, Ralph Barney, *Doing Ethics in Journalism,* 3rd ed., 20.) Consider these examples:

- In 1997, Sergeant Major Gene McKinney, the Army's most powerful non-commissioned officer, was appointed to a panel aimed at ferreting out sexual harassment in the military. Infuriated, former McKinney aide Brenda Hoster told the *New York Times* he had sexually harassed her, driving her to quit the service. The *Times'* front-page story led to McKinney's resignation from the panel, his court-martial and conviction for obstruction of justice. Using information as her lever, an obscure ex-soldier forced the mighty United States Army to act.
- Rep. Wes Cooley, R.-Ore., made much of his Korean War combat record. But the *Oregonian's* revelation that the record was fabricated depleted his power to play the hero. It empowered voters, including many who had backed him, to make a more informed choice—thumbs down.
- When *Consumer Reports* rates a new model car a lemon or the *New York Times* pans a play, they shift power from producer to consumer.

There are cases, to be sure, when a news organization must withhold information. In the 2003 Iraq war, for instance, reporters refrained from disclosing advance knowledge of when and where U.S. military units would strike because a perishable scoop was not worth risking American lives.

Yet journalists who hold back information should always do so with uneasiness. The practice can be habit forming, especially for beat reporters who face the temptation to go soft on key sources. In 1972, Washington's seasoned political and White House correspondents had no stomach to investigate the Watergate break-in. It took two zealous but lowly metro reporters with no stake in coddling sources to crack the case and implicate Nixon's top lieutenants.

Information is power. Journalists perform a bold, even radical public service each time they break up an information monopoly that had allowed some politician, businessman or corrupt clergyman to operate unchecked.

Unfortunately, journalists do not perform the service enough. The powers that be spare no effort to rope journalists, break their zeal and filter their reports—with offers of access, exclusive stories and high status, with threats, complaints to the boss and hyped estimates of the damage a story would do.

It works. As Black, Steele and Barney put it, "All too often, journalists 'wimp out.' "

Such choices have consequences. The less energy journalists throw into spreading information, the less power citizens have to choose the best leader, influence government policy, avoid shoddy or unsafe products, make the most of their money and otherwise control their own lives.

Zeal to inform the public is the paramount journalistic virtue. Sadly, it is in too short supply.

CHAPTER II CASES

CASE II-A
Visualizing September 11th
SARA GETTYS
University of Missouri

The morning of September 11, 2001, AP photographer Richard Drew was cover-ing a fashion show in downtown Manhattan. When two planes slammed into the World Trade Towers, AP called Drew and sent him to the story (Cheney 2001). As people jumped, he photographed several of the jumpers, tracking one man in a white coat and dark pants in several frames. Drew remembers, "I've been at the AP for 32 years. I've covered my share of disasters and earthquakes and fires. . . . [So when], all of a sudden, people started falling out of the tower, I started photo-graphing it" (Abransky 2002).

Papers across the country, including the *New York Times,* picked the photo to run as part of the coverage. The *Times* ran the photo above the fold on Page 7 of the A section in full color, the art for the lead story jump from Page A1. The photo ran alone surrounded by text that included a chronological accounting of the day's events.

That same morning, Milagros Hernandez received a frantic phone call from her brother Norberto Hernandez, who worked as a pastry chef at Window on the World, a restaurant on the 107th floor of Number One World Trade Center. After speaking briefly with him, Milagros turned on her television set to watch cover-age of the tragedy. She knew her brother worked above the burning floors, and she remembers her brother saying that if he ever were to be trapped, he would jump rather than burn to death.

Television coverage included pictures of people jumping, and one man in particular—wearing a white coat—caught her eye. But the fleeting image pro-vided no clues as to the jumper's identity. When she opened the *New York Times* the next day, the victim's white jacket and dark complexion sent a shock of recog-nition through her. "Oh my God! That's my brother!" she remembers thinking.

Throughout the day on September 11th, *Times* editors, along with their col-leagues at other news organizations, worked to cover the attack. At the *Times,* staffers in the advertising and strategic planning departments worked the dictation desk, tak-ing reports from reporters and eyewitness accounts (Tugend 2001). In an event where every aspect of coverage was graphic, violent, and horrifying, the decisions about what to show to tell the totality of the story became the decisions that relied heavily on the standards of those working the desks. Stories from the September 12 edition of the paper included photos of firefighters grieving for lost comrades, pictures and first-person accounts of the towers falling, and pictures of wounded victims waiting for help. There were no ads in the A section of the paper that day, with the exception of a full-page Verizon ad on the back cover.

When the photo ran, the *Times* started receiving calls from outraged readers who felt that this photo in particular was sensationalistic and exploited a man at the mo-ment just before his death (Mitchell 2001). Papers nationwide that ran the photo

AP Photo/Richard Drew.

received similar calls. In Allentown, Pennsylvania, more than 60 people called the local paper to complain. The *Arizona Daily Star* posted the photo on its Web site but took it off in response to complaints.

In the midst of the tragedy and public outrage, Peter Cheney, a reporter for the *Toronto Globe and Mail,* was covering the attacks and cleanup and rescue attempts when he saw a missing person's poster of Norberto Hernandez and thought he might be the man in the photo. He contacted Milagros and decided to tell the story of the family who believed that the man pictured was their relative. In doing so, he addressed both the life of the victim the family believed was pictured and the grieving process of the survivors. He also included the family's response to the photo—from Milagros's belief that the man pictured was undeniably her brother, to Norborto's daughter, who didn't believe that the man in the photo was her father.

While the identity of the man in the photo remained uncertain, Cheney explored that possibility and allowed the family to express its grief and to celebrate the life of a loved one whose last moments may have been shared with millions of readers.

Micro Issues

1. Should AP photographer Drew have continued to "follow" the jumper once he realized what was happening?
2. Does it matter that it is difficult, some say impossible, to clearly identify the man in the photo?
3. Was it appropriate to place the photo on an inside page? Should it have run on Page A1? Should other publications in distant places have run the photo?
4. Was the story reporter Chaney wrote an invasion of privacy at this time of grief?
5. While Nerborto Hernandez was included in a list of profiles that the *Times* ran on the victims, Hernandez's profile was only two paragraphs long and failed to mention the possibility that he was the man pictured on September 12th. Is this appropriate?

Midrange Issues

1. Does the placing of the photo on an inside page somehow mitigate what many concluded was an invasion of privacy?
2. How should the *Times'* editors have considered the fact that "the jumper" was alive when the photograph was taken?
3. Are the justifications for television running the video of the jumper somehow ethically distinct from those the *Times* adhered to? Should they be?
4. If the *Times* and other media outlets had failed to provide visual information about this element of the story, would those organizations have failed to recognize and report on the decisions these people made?
5. Compare this photo with the Pulitzer Prize–winning photo by Stanley Foreman in Case IV-D of the girl falling to her death from a faulty fire escape in Boston. What are the differences? What are the similarities? Do you make the same decision for both photos? Justify your answer.

Macro Issues

1. Should the *Times* have altered the photo—or published a different one—where the individual jumper was less recognizable? Why or why not?
2. What values do you believe the *Times'* editors weighed as they arrived at their decision?
3. Because September 11th was a horrific event, did coverage—in order to be accurate—have to picture some of the horror of that day? Would you apply the same reasoning to coverage of international events—say, conflict in the Middle East?
4. By publishing the photo, to whom or what is the *Times* being loyal?
5. Do the *Times* and other media outlets that published and broadcast such photos share any responsibility for the public emotion connected with the events of 9/11?

CASE II-B
The Spouse Is Squeezed: A South Carolina TV Reporter's Attempt to Conceal Her Source
SONYA FORTE DUHÉ
University of South Carolina

It seems like a typical news day.

A man telephones WIS-TV Senior Reporter Heather Hoopes, claiming to possess a "bombshell videotape" that she must see.

The source tells the Columbia, South Carolina, NBC affiliate reporter the tape is available to her only if she comes to his house to get it. He says he won't mail it or drop it off at the station. If she wants it, she *has* to come and get it.

Concerned for her safety, Hoopes asks her husband, Jim Matthews—who for more than twenty years has worked with the Department of Justice's Drug Enforcement Administration and now heads the local Columbia office—to drive her to the caller's home. He agrees.

Matthews has no idea that the videotape contains a privileged conversation between a murder defendant and his lawyer, secretly videotaped by a local sheriff's deputy. Hoopes isn't exactly sure what she is getting either.

After reviewing the tape, she broadcasts a story about the videotaping of the privileged conversation. To Hoopes and colleagues, the tape is a clear violation of the prisoner's rights. Hoopes's move to have Matthews drive her to retrieve the videotape from this confidential source leads to numerous court battles and thousands of dollars in legal costs for her, her husband and her employer.

CONTEXT

In 1995, Lexington County sheriff's detectives arrested B. J. Quattlebaum and charged him with the murder of William Swartz. Quattlebaum was taken to the Lexington County Jail, where he called his attorney.

The men used a small room to talk. Unknown to them, a deputy sheriff was secretly and illegally videotaping their meeting.

At a later time, the same confidential source, who was subsequently identified as Columbia attorney Jack Duncan, called Hoopes at WIS to alert her to this alleged wrongdoing. Hoopes, her news director, and her editors decided to use a portion of the videotape to expose the illegal action. However, in an attempt to protect the arrested man's rights, the news team didn't use the audio portion of the tape.

The FBI attempted to obtain the name of Hoopes's confidential source but could not meet Justice Department protocol because of First Amendment questions. When the FBI's efforts to subpoena WIS ran into roadblocks, it attempted to make Matthews reveal the person's identity.

In a May 10, 1999, story in the *Washington Post,* Hoopes was quoted as saying, "I consider it a backdoor tactic. I don't understand why the Justice Department is doing this. It's very stressful for me and my husband. I carry an extra burden because I put him in the situation."

Prosecutors subpoenaed Matthews, and a federal grand jury demanded that the DEA agent testify about the case.

Matthews's lawyer, along with the WIS legal team, filed motions with U.S. District Court asking that Matthews not be forced to testify. Lawyers argued that forcing him to be a witness would violate his First Amendment rights. These motions were dismissed. Written pleas to Attorney General Janet Reno, FBI Director Louis Freeh, and Justice Department official Beneva Weintraub also did not recuse Matthews from a court appearance.

The Radio Television News Director Association is the world's largest professional organization devoted exclusively to electronic journalism. The organization represents local and network news executives in broadcasting, cable, and other electronic media in more than thirty countries. In those letters, RTNDA President Barbara Cochran called on the Justice Department to end FBI attempts to force Matthews to testify.

"On behalf of the 3,400 members of the RTNDA, I am writing to express our grave concern about FBI attempts to force the husband of a South Carolina television station reporter to reveal to a grand jury what he knows about his wife's confidential source," wrote Cochran.

"Efforts to force Mr. Matthews to betray the confidence of his spouse not only raise compelling questions about marital privilege, but they represent a blatant attempt to circumvent the reporter's privilege recognized by the Constitution, the state, and the Justice Department," she continued.

"It is well recognized that news-gathering activities are protected under the First Amendment of the United States Constitution. This protection extends to information given in confidence to a reporter, including the source of that information. The South Carolina legislature has also expressed a strong public policy of protecting news-gathering activities, enacting a shield law whose aim is to protect the free flow of information to the public. Moreover, Department of Justice regulations expressly recognize that: Because freedom of the press can be no broader than the freedom of reporters to investigate and report the news, the prosecutorial power of the government should not be used in such a way that it impairs a reporter's responsibility to cover as broadly as possible controversial public issues."

Cochran continued, "RTNDA is certainly aware of no case where a reporter's spouse has been ordered to disclose a confidential source. If prosecutors are allowed to obtain confidential news information from a third party where efforts to obtain the same information from the reporter have failed, then the protections afforded by the First Amendment and state press shield statutes would be meaningless." Hoopes said, "I would have thought they [authorities] would have applauded the efforts of my source and WIS to bring this to light. Instead it seems like we're the criminals."

Quattlebaum was later convicted of first-degree murder and sentenced to death. In January 2000, the South Carolina Supreme Court overturned Quattlebaum's conviction, due in part to the videotape incident.

A federal judge ordered the deputy who videotaped the conversation to pay a $250 fine for civil rights violations. As for Hoopes's confidential source, he was sentenced to and spent several months in jail for lying to a federal grand jury and was disbarred.

Micro Issues

1. Should the reporter have taken the videotape? Why?
2. Should the reporter have asked someone to accompany her to pick up the videotape? If so, who?
3. Was it okay for the reporter to air the videotape?
4. Should the reporter have aired the audio from the videotape?

Midrange Issues

1. Does the reporter have the right to air videotape of an illegal act? When would it be inappropriate?
2. Was it the journalist's responsibility to expose this illegal taping of a privileged conversation?
3. Did the journalist breach her source's confidentiality by allowing her husband to accompany her to pick up the videotape?

Macro Issues

1. Should reporters be allowed to keep sources confidential if a criminal act has occurred?
2. What responsibilities do reporters have to law enforcement officials? Why?
3. Should spouses of reporters have the same First Amendment rights that reporters possess?
4. What role should nonjournalists play in the newsgathering process?

CASE II-C
When Is Objective Reporting Irresponsible Reporting?
THEODORE L. GLASSER
Stanford University

Amanda Laurens, a reporter for a local daily newspaper, covers the city mayor's office, where yesterday she attended a 4:00 P.M. press conference. The mayor, Ben Adams, read a statement accusing Evan Michaels, a city council member, of being a "paid liar" for the pesticide industry. "Councilman Michaels," the mayor said at the press conference, "has intentionally distorted the facts about the effects of certain pesticides on birds indigenous to the local area." Mr. Michaels, the mayor continued, "is on the payroll of a local pesticide manufacturer," and his views on the effects of pesticides on bird life "are necessarily tainted."

The press conference ended at about 5:15 P.M., less than an hour before her 6:00 P.M. deadline. Laurens quickly contacted Councilman Michaels for a quote in response to the mayor's statement. Michaels, however, refused to comment, except to say that Mayor Adams's accusations were "utter nonsense" and "politically motivated." Laurens filed her story, which included both the mayor's accusation and the councilman's denial. Laurens's editor thought the story was fair and balanced and ran it the following morning on the front page.

The mayor was pleased with the coverage he received. He thought Laurens had acted professionally and responsibly by reporting his accusation along with Michaels's denial. Anything else, the mayor thought, would have violated the principles of objective journalism. The mayor had always believed that one of the most important responsibilities of the press was to provide an impartial forum for public controversies, and the exchange between him and the councilman was certainly a bona fide public controversy. Deciding who's right and who's wrong is not the responsibility of journalists, the mayor believed, but a responsibility best left to readers.

Councilman Michaels, in contrast, was outraged. He wrote a scathing letter to the editor, chiding the newspaper for mindless, irresponsible journalism. "The story may have been fair, balanced, and accurate," he wrote, "but it was not truthful." He had never lied about the effects of pesticides on bird life, and he had "never been on the payroll of any pesticide manufacturer," he wrote. "A responsible reporter would do more than report the facts truthfully; she would also report the truth about the facts." In this case, Michaels said, the reporter should have held off on the story until she had time to independently investigate the mayor's accusation; and if the accusation had proved to be of no merit, as Michaels insisted, then there shouldn't have been a story. Or if there had to be a story, Michaels added, "it should be a story about the *mayor* lying."

By way of background: The effects of pesticides on bird life had been a local issue for nearly a year. Part of the community backs Mayor Adams's position on the harmful effects of certain pesticides and supports local legislation that would limit or ban their use. Others in the community support Councilman Michaels's position that the evidence on the effects of pesticides on bird life is at best ambiguous and that more scientific study is needed before anyone proposes legislation. They argue that pesticides are useful, particularly to local farmers who need to protect crops, and because the available evidence about their deleterious effects is inconclusive, they believe that the city council should not seek to further restrict or prohibit their use. The exchange between Mayor Adams and Councilman Michaels is the latest in a series of verbal bouts on the subject of pesticides and the city's role in their regulation.

Micro Issues

1. Did Laurens do the right thing by submitting her story without the benefit of an independent investigation into the mayor's accusations about Councilman Michaels?
2. Is the mayor correct in arguing that Laurens acted responsibly by providing fair and balanced coverage of both sides of a public controversy without trying to judge whose side is right and whose side is wrong?
3. Is the councilman correct in arguing that Laurens acted irresponsibly by concerning herself only with reporting the facts truthfully and ignoring the "truth about the facts"?

Midrange Issues

1. Is it sufficient when covering public controversies to simply report the facts accurately and fairly? Does it matter that fair and accurate reporting of facts might not do justice to the truth about the facts?
2. Does the practice of objective reporting distance reporters from the substance of their stories in ways contrary to the ideals of responsible journalism?
3. If reporters serve as the eyes and ears of their readers, how can they be expected to report more than what they've heard or seen?

Macro Issues

1. What distinguishes fact from truth? For which should journalists accept responsibility?
2. If journalists know that a fact is not true, do they have an obligation to share that knowledge with their readers? And if they do share that knowledge, how can they claim to be objective in their reporting?
3. Justify or reject the role of objectivity in an era where more media outlets are available than ever before.

CASE II-D
Monitoring *The Monitor*: Taste, Politics and an Explosive Photo
GINA BRAMUCCI
University of Missouri

The Monitor newspaper, launched in 1992, is the only independent paper in the small nation of Uganda in East Africa. The paper has an average daily circulation of 25,000, although it is estimated that at least 10 people read each paper in Uganda. Charles Onyango-Obbo, one of the paper's founding editors, is a high-profile critic of the government of President Yoweri Museveni. He has been imprisoned for what *The Monitor* has published, writes a weekly column for another paper, and is well known to the foreign media.

On April 28, 1999, an unnamed source brought a photo to *The Monitor*'s offices in Kampala, the Ugandan capital. The photo pictured a young woman, nude and pinned down by seven men. The men, wearing the uniforms of the Ugandan army, were shaving the woman's genital area with scissors. The photo is not printed in this book.

Deputy Editor David Ouma Balikowa received the photo, and shortly afterwards Ugandan security agents arrived to ensure that it would not be published. *The Monitor* editors wanted to talk with the security agents, but according to Ouma it was evident that if they shared the photo with the agents it would be confiscated. For the paper's editors, the attempt to suppress the photo was added incentive for publication. Gulu police confirmed that a case such as the one in the photo had been reported to them.

In his May 17, 1999, column on the incident Onyango-Obbo wrote: "The word was out that the paper had the picture. The paper's credibility as the country's only serious independent media voice was on the line. Here we were about to participate in what might seem like a cover up or take a risky plunge and get hurt."

The photo ran on May 11, 1999, on *The Monitor*'s back page with no accompanying story. The caption read:

> This picture was brought to *The Monitor* by someone who claimed to have taken it in Gulu barracks early this year without being noticed. Recent days have seen what locals say is renewed tension by state operatives to disrupt the calm that was returning to the region.

The northern barracks must be placed in context in order to grasp the significance of *The Monitor*'s claim. Since 1986, when Museveni first took power in Uganda, a small rebel insurgency in the north has plagued his presidency. The Lord's Resistance Army, or LRA, trumpets a pseudo-religious cause based on the premise of overthrowing Museveni and creating a utopian society that will be ruled by the Judeo-Christian Ten Commandments. To this end, the LRA targets its own people, the Acholi tribe, abducting children for soldiers, ambushing vehicles, and killing and maiming haphazardly.

The LRA is not the only threat to civilians in northern Uganda, however. The U.S. State Department and nongovernmental organizations such as Human Rights Watch and Amnesty International have regularly found government troops guilty of severe human rights abuses, and have documented a pattern of looting, rape, torture and extrajudicial killings. The Gulu barracks, where *The Monitor* claimed the photo was taken, are the northern operational headquarters for these troops, the Ugandan People's Defense Force, or UPDF. It is in this context—a history of documented abuse—that *The Monitor*'s editors made the decision to publish the photo.

The publication of the photo caused immediate reaction from the media and civilians in Uganda. Reactions ranged from outrage to wholehearted support for *The Monitor.* Perhaps surprisingly, some of Uganda's women's rights groups criticized the paper's editors for their decision, as did Miria Matembe, the national minister of ethics and integrity. Matembe, who has been known for her advocacy on the part of women, felt that women and children would be disturbed by the graphic photo.

Arguments like Matembe's were countered forcefully by those in the media who felt that the photo's publication promoted basic equalities and liberties for women, the least advantaged party in Uganda's patriarchal society.

On the evening of May 12, with public discourse growing louder, Onyango-Obbo received a letter from the Criminal Investigation Department, or CID, of Uganda's police force. According to Onyango-Obbo, the editors spent six hours at CID before being taken to court. The state charged the men with sedition and publishing false news that could create "fear and alarm." The journalists pleaded not guilty of the charges and were released on bail of $63 each.

The UPDF released its own statement on May 12, denying that the photograph had been taken in Uganda and saying that "activities like rape as depicted in the picture cannot take place in any military barracks or for that matter in the UPDF operational zones." The army claimed that the fatigues worn by the soldiers pictured were not those used by the UPDF, and that the woman pictured has a West African hairstyle.

After a delay, the trial of *The Monitor* editors opened on Nov. 9, 1999, with Magistrate Pamela Mafabi hearing the case. In their testimony, UPDF officers repeated their claim that the uniforms of the soldiers pictured were not used in the Gulu barracks. But when presented with photos of well-known UPDF officers in uniforms similar to those pictured, one officer admitted that he wasn't familiar with all of the uniforms used. Although it's unclear when, at some point in 1999 northern UPDF officials also testified that women are regularly punished at army facilities by having their heads shaved with blunt razors.

After his first day in the courtroom, the defense lawyer for *The Monitor* editors, James Nangwala, was shot by unidentified gunmen in front of his home. He was hit in the shoulder, and Mafabi adjourned the trial until January 2000.

The trial of 24-year-old Kandida Lakony, who came forward prior to the original trial and claimed to be the woman pictured in the photo, caused a further delay in *The Monitor* case. Lakony told officials the man shaving her was a former boyfriend and a soldier in the Gulu barracks. After a few days of protection in the state house of President Museveni, she was brought before a Ugandan court and accused of lying and giving misleading information to the police. The public was largely sympathetic to Lakony and her testimony was highly publicized, but the court found her guilty and she was sentenced to 12 months in prison. Lakony died shortly after her release.

Nearly two years after the photo's appearance in *The Monitor*, on March 6, 2001, Onyango-Obbo, Oguttu and Ouma were acquitted of the charges of sedition and publication of false statements. Another magistrate, Joshua Maruk, ruled that the state had failed to prove its case. "Looking at the caption of the photo, all that is indicated was a claim, the interpretation being that the publication was not vouching for the truth of the photo," Maruk wrote.

Micro Issues

1. Considering the circumstances, how should the paper have verified the photo's accuracy?
2. If it was impossible to verify the photo's accuracy, should the paper have published it?
3. Would your reasoning be different had the incident occurred in the United States?

Midrange Issues

1. Use utilitarian reasoning, and then the veil of ignorance, to analyze this case. How does the particular philosophical theory help you think through the issues?
2. How should journalists weigh their personal safety and well-being against their role as professionals?
3. Is this photo as described too offensive to be published in the United States? Is a different standard appropriate in different cultures?

Macro Issues

1. What is the role of the media in developing nations? How might that role influence ethical decision making?
2. This case asks you to think about whether there is such a thing as universal ethical principles. Is there a universal standard you believe should be applied in this case?

CASE II-E
A Hometown Hero Takes a Spill
M. W. MULCAHY
Former editor, Cape Cod Times

Todd Eldredge was a major contender in the 1996 Olympic Games figure skating competition. As he went into his final routine, he had a good chance of taking home the gold medal. Many in his hometown community of Chatham, Massachusetts, and throughout Cape Cod, had been following his progress for years.

Then came the fall that dashed his hopes at the gold and pushed him back to fourth place.

In designing the front page of the next day's Sunday *Cape Cod Times,* night production editor Ron Sikora said the decision was a simple one. It was the biggest story of the day for the community, and an Associated Press photograph of the fall told the story best. The photo was played big across the top of the page. While none of the key editors were in the newsroom that Saturday night, all later agreed that they supported Sikora's call. The paper ran the photo of Eldredge sprawled on the ice.

By Monday morning the phone calls, e-mails, and letters were all pouring in from irate readers who wanted to know how the editors could be so insensitive as to show one of Cape Cod's local sons in his very moment of defeat. Why couldn't the paper show more support for Eldredge by picking a more upbeat photo?

The consensus at the paper was supportive of Sikora's decision, saying this photo best conveyed what happened and the agony on Eldredge's face showed that in that split second he realized that the fall meant defeat. In the newsroom, it came down to the issue of telling the truth. Based on callers' responses, it appeared the community felt the issue was more one of failing to support a local hero in his darkest hour.

As the paper's news editor, I fielded many of these calls. While some simply wanted to complain about our insensitivity or to suggest we had made the photo smaller or played it in the sports section, one caller started off the conversation with the question "What were you thinking?" When I told her the editors felt a responsibility to tell the truth and that photo did the best job of conveying what really happened to Eldredge's Olympic dream, the caller still disagreed with the decision but felt some consolation in understanding the reasoning behind it.

Shortly after that call, the editors at the *Times* held a meeting to discuss how to best address the public outcry. There was general agreement that we must run as many of the letters as we could fit on the editorial page, but editor Cliff Schechtman dismissed the idea of an editorial, explaining our position by stating it would come off as being too defensive. The letters would run. The readers would have their say and that would be that.

But the caller's question, "What were you thinking?" kept pestering me after the meeting. Don't we have a responsibility to our community to explain our decisions? Aren't they entitled to understand the logic and philosophy used to defend the use and play of the photograph? By staying silent, I felt we were essentially saying, "It's our newspaper, and we do what we want, and we don't have to explain ourselves to anyone."

AP/WIDE WORLD PHOTOS. *Used with permission.*

I wrote up a short explanation of the thought process that went behind the decision and gave copies to Schechtman and managing editor Alicia Blaisdell-Bannon. Schechtman made some changes but agreed to run it as a note from the editor to explain what we were thinking. Although a few calls and e-mails still trickled in the next day, it appeared that the note to our readers served the community by helping them to understand the reasoning behind our actions.

While the editors at the *Cape Cod Times* stood behind Sikora's decision, there was an interesting epilogue weeks later when Eldredge was in another skating competition. When it looked as though he was going to win a gold medal in that competition, the editors agreed they would reserve a spot on page one for the story—and a photo reflecting his victory—in the event that he took home the gold. Unfortunately, he came in third and the story and photo were pushed back to the sports section.

Micro Issues

1. Should the newspaper have featured the fall as its main photo of Eldredge?
2. If a photo of Eldredge skating in the competition had been used, what different "truth" would have been told?

Midrange Issues

1. Could the fall have been better covered in an inside photo?
2. When is it appropriate in news coverage to show a person in tragedy? In triumph?
3. What type of official response did the public outcry warrant?
4. Even though Eldredge's fall happened at a public event, his feelings were private, but they were made public by the circumstances and magnified by the photo. Balance the competing values of his privacy and the interest of his fans in what had happened to him.

Macro Issues

1. When a local newspaper reports on the athletic efforts of one of its own favorites, are the standards of reporting different? What if the local celebrity is a politician?
2. Critique the decision by Schechtman to not write an editorial on the basis that it might look too defensive.

CASE II-F
SARS: The Bug That Would Not Go Away
SEOW TING LEE
Illinois State University

On Feb. 21, 2003, 64-year-old Liu Jianlun arrived in Hong Kong from Guangzhou, China, to attend his nephew's wedding reception. The retired professor, nursing a fever and a dry cough, checked into the Metropole, a three-star hotel popular with tourists. That evening, he had a raging fever. In his ninth-floor room, he struggled to dress in anticipation of a joyous reunion-of-sorts with his sister and brother-in-law. While waiting for an elevator, he sneezed and coughed, unaware that he was expelling a highly infectious virus. On March 4, he was dead, but not before passing the bug to seven hotel guests who would later carry the virus to Canada, Singapore, and Vietnam. Like Liu, they all stayed on or visited the ninth floor of the hotel and used the same elevator lobby.

The seven hotel guests infected hundreds of people outside mainland China, and unleashed international spotlight on a mystery killer illness—later named SARS, or Severe Acute Respiratory Syndrome by the World Health Organization. From Guangdong, the virus traveled in humans to 30 countries and areas of the world, sparking off public health crises in Hong Kong, Taiwan, Vietnam, Singapore and Canada. As of July 7, 2003, 8,439 people have been afflicted by SARS, and 812 people have died. Mainland China accounted for 5,327 cases and 348 deaths.

The Chinese professor's role in the story was typical of the pattern of SARS transmission: an imported hospitalized case infected health care workers and other patients, who in turn infected their close contacts and moved the disease to the community at large. Liu was a military physician in the Guangzhou Army's General Hospital in the southern China province of Guangdong, believed now to be the epicenter of the outbreak. He attended scores of patients of a pneumonia-like disease.

The first recorded case appeared in the Guangdong city of Foshan on Nov. 16, 2002, when a businessman checked into a hospital with a mysterious strain of pneumonia. Two weeks later, in the industrial city of Heyuan 120 miles away, doctors and nurses at the Heyuan Municipal Hospital began to fall ill and die. The official prognosis of Chinese physicians at that time was "chlamydia pneumonia."

Initially, Chinese media coverage of the virus hovered between silence and denial. When the mystery pneumonia first emerged in Guangdong, local officials ignored the problem, hoping that it would go away. Fearing criticism from Beijing and negative publicity from abroad, Guangdong officials moved to suppress media reports about the disease. The media blackout, however, only served to fan rumors and fear among the populace. Through cellphones, text messages about "a fatal flu in Guangdong" circulated. Another rumor said that bioterrorists had struck Guangzhou's World Trade Center and 100 people had died. Guangdong shops began to experience a run on antiviral medicines and white vinegar, believed by the Chinese to contain disinfecting properties.

On Jan. 3, 2003, the *Heyuan News* published a brief story denying the existence of an "epidemic virus," urging local residents not to panic. According to the paper, "No epidemic disease is being spread in Heyuan. Symptoms like cough and fever appear due to the relatively colder weather." It was the first media reference, and the last for more than a month, to the disease. The Chinese media, although aware of the number of rising cases, was ordered by authorities not to report on the outbreak. A reporter at a Shenzen newspaper recounted how the ban came even as his editor was handing out Chinese herbal medicine to reporters to fight the disease.

In response to the intensifying rumors and panic, Guangdong provincial health officials hurriedly convened a press conference on Feb. 11, 2003. The director general of the provincial board of health admitted that there was a virulent strain of pneumonia sweeping the province. Health officials announced that 305 people were afflicted but only five had died. But two days later, Guangdong saw a renewed panic buying of salt and rice as rumors resurfaced.

On Feb. 9, 2003, Swiss pharmaceutical giant Roche held a news conference and handed out press kits touting the effectiveness of its antiviral medicine, Tamiflu. Sales exploded. Guangdong authorities issued a warning to the company, which denied allegations of profiteering. It said sales of Tamiflu had been strong even before the news conference. On Feb. 18, the *Southern Metropolis Daily* reported that Roche was being investigated for stirring up public fears to boost profits. Little else was reported on SARS in Chinese newspapers until early April 2003.

As SARS spread from southern Guangdong to Beijing and other provinces, the Chinese government resorted to centuries-old strategies of bureaucratic secrecy and xenophobia. Topmost on the minds of Chinese leaders was foreign investment and tourism revenue. In the euphoria of the country's ability to draw billions of dollars of foreign investment and its successful bid for the 2008 Summer Olympics, its leaders were also keen to maintain its freshly minted international reputation.

China, they further reasoned, is a big country and an epidemic or two is inevitable. There is no reason to cause panic among the populace of 1.3 billion people. A widening gap between the rich and the poor was weakening the social fabric, as economic reforms bred a huge underclass of have-nots. Tens of millions of Chinese are unemployed despite the country's dazzling progress from embarking on the capitalist road in 1978. Mindful of the country's history of mass revolts toppling dynasties and regimes, Chinese officials were cautious.

Even after the Chinese media broke the silence on SARS, the official line was that "the disease was already brought under effective control" and "Beijing remained as normal and safe as ever." The World Health Organization (WHO), prompted by the Toronto outbreak, issued its first global alert about SARS on March 12. The alert was unreported in China. On March 16, China handed its first data to the WHO, but refused to let the WHO team enter Guangdong for weeks even as scientists successfully linked SARS to the outbreak in the Chinese province. The state-owned *Guangming Daily* reported on April 3 that China's health minister Zhang Wenkang rejected the theory that SARS originated in Guangdong.

As the epidemic raged on in Hong Kong, Chinese officials did not budge. Even as SARS could no longer be contained in Guangdong, officials ordered state-run television CCTV to air stories of smiling, camera-toting tourists at the Great Wall. As doctors and nurses in Beijing hospitals whispered of hundreds of SARS cases in epidemic wards, the official stand was that all cases outside Guangdong were "imported" from abroad. The country's Ministry of Central Publicity issued three instructions: don't talk to the media about SARS, don't talk to the public about the disease, and don't talk to WHO officials.

The Chinese government, however, could not control the flow of information from health care workers. Doctors and nurses, angry at government-orchestrated cover-ups, turned whistle-blowers and supplied more accurate figures of SARS casualties to the foreign media. On April 3, 2003, Jiang Yanyong, 72, a former director of the People's Liberation Army Hospital No. 301, was watching a live telecast of a press conference by China's health minister, Zhang Wenkang. The minister announced that Beijing had only 12 cases of SARS and three deaths. "You are safe here whether you wear the gauze mask or not," the upbeat minister was shown telling a foreign photojournalist wearing a gauze mask at the conference. Furious, Jiang held a press conference to denounce the government for lying about the numbers of SARS casualties in Beijing. Jiang's charges were not reported in the local newspapers and television but were posted on the Internet, generating a furor in Beijing.

Next, Jiang wrote an e-mail to the state-run CCTV-4 and Phoenix TV, providing them with the number of cases he had verified from several military hospitals. He wrote: "I simply couldn't believe what I was seeing. . . . All the doctors and nurses who saw yesterday's news were furious." The two media organizations did not respond to his e-mail, which found its way into the hands of the foreign media and made news worldwide.

The first foreign journalists to contact Jiang were from *The Wall Street Journal* and *Time.* Susan Jakes, a correspondent with *Time,* interviewed Jiang on April 8, and the interview was published on the *Time* Web site that evening. The next day, Jakes' article, "Beijing's SARS Attack," was translated into Chinese and was accessed heavily by Chinese Internet surfers. Jiang continued to speak to various international media outlets, and the WHO, reacting to these news reports, quickly demanded access to Beijing's military hospitals. On April 16, the WHO confirmed Jiang's data on Beijing SARS cases.

Mounting international scrutiny and pressure forced the Chinese government to rethink its strategy as the virus spread quickly outside mainland China. On April 9, 2003, Chinese premier Wen Jiabao conceded that the SARS situation "is grave," in an about-turn from his earlier reassuring statements that China was safe. The figures of infections and deaths continued to be underreported, however. The turning point came in a press conference on April 22, 2003, when, overnight, the Ministry of Health confirmed 346 cases and 18 deaths in Beijing. Health minister Zhang Wenkang and former Beijing Mayor Meng Xuenong were sacked from their posts.

The media blackout fanned rumors and speculation about the SARS situation on the Internet and through cellphone text-messaging—two channels of information over which the Chinese government has little control. The impact of SARS in the United States may be smaller—75 cases and no deaths, but it helped reinforce anti-Asian prejudices and stereotypes. The reaction of the University of California at Berkeley—banning from its summer programs all students from mainland China, Hong Kong, Taiwan and Singapore—illustrates how powerful the fear of a disease can be. There were alarming cases of prejudice against Chinese-Americans, as well as other Asians in different parts of the world. The financial fallout is also considerable. According to the Asian Development Bank, SARS will cost Asian economies US$28 billion, and is expected to wipe half a percentage point off growth for 2003 in Asia, with serious ramifications for a global economy.

Clearly, China's handling of the SARS outbreak has not impressed anyone. Andy Ho, a columnist in the *Straits Times,* Singapore, echoed a common sentiment around the world faulting the Chinese government for its suppression of news, offers of incomplete statistics and stalling of WHO visits. "Had the Guangdong authorities alerted the world to the outbreak there from November last year, Singapore would not have chalked up 32 deaths from SARS."

Micro Issues

1. How would American journalists cover the SARS story, if, say, the outbreak had originated in Missouri or New York?
2. Under these circumstances, how does a Chinese journalist function?
3. To whom were Chinese officials loyal? To whom should Chinese journalists have been loyal? Other journalists?
4. If you were the public relations person for Roche, how would you have handled the press conference?

Midrange Issues

1. What are the potential problems in dealing with whistle-blowers like Dr. Jiang Yanyong?
2. In a press conference, China's health minister Zhang Wenkang rejected the theory that SARS originated in Guangdong. He was quoted as saying, "The assertion that the location where SARS cases were discovered early is the place where it originated is not correct. The United States reported AIDS first, but we can't say AIDS originated in the United States." Given your reading of the situation, what did Zhang mean by this?
3. What is the role of the Internet and new information technologies such as text-messaging in emerging democracies? How does journalism "use" these technologies effectively?

Macro Issues

1. How does watchdog journalism contribute to social stability in times of crisis? Are there things journalists should not do at such times?
2. In war, truth is the first casualty, observed historian Phillip Knightley, who provided a compelling account of war reporting in his book, *The First Casualty.* What is the role of media in war or national crises? Consider September 11 and the war in Iraq.
3. Which philosophical theory best supports China's approach to the SARS outbreak? The decision of Roche?

III

Advertising Ethics: From Let the Buyer Beware to Empowerment

By the end of this chapter, you should be familiar with:

- **why both advertising and news can be evaluated as symbol formation.**
- **the balance and cognitive dissonance persuasion theories and their role in advertising.**
- **the issues surrounding the interaction between ads and vulnerable audiences.**
- **the TARES test for evaluating the ethics of individual ads.**

INTRODUCTION

Since the days of ancient Greece, a major function of communication has been to persuade. Greek citizens used the art of rhetoric to their advantage in the Greek city-states where democracy was practiced through an elaborate court system. Eventually, the courts of Athens became crowded with those who sought to use their persuasive powers for gain. Today's airwaves and printing presses are likewise filled with messages designed to increase the influence and wealth of their sponsors.

But ancient Athens has morphed into a 21st-century democracy that runs on the engines of capitalism, fueled in large part by advertising. While the ancient Greeks overtly attempted to persuade, contemporary advertising employs elements that act on the human psyche in more subtle ways. Indeed, communication theory has evolved in an attempt to discover how it is that some messages persuade and others do not. And, although the ancient Greeks accepted all speech as persuasion, contemporary understandings have separated advertising from news.

We think the Greeks had the right idea some 3,000 years ago. We suggest that both advertising and news be understood as elements of the same activity: symbol formation (Wilkins and Christians 2001). Both news and advertising are rooted in culture. Both make some assumptions about the relationship between mediated messages and the individuals who receive them. Most important, if news and advertising really are different parts of the same process, then the same ethical tools—and standards—can be applied.

The similarities between advertising and news are particularly important when the lines between the activities blur (as they do in advertorials) or when advertising about newsworthy issues, such as who should be elected president, becomes an important way people learn about those questions. A set of ethical standards shared between both activities will give contemporary practitioners a better chance at "doing the right thing" in an increasingly competitive media environment.

But before we talk theory, let's talk some economic fact.

YOU PAY WHEN YOU WASH, NOT WHEN YOU WATCH

Anyone in the management end of a media business understands this truth: the role of programming on television (either news or entertainment) and the role of copy (news, features or editorials) in newspapers is to deliver an audience to advertisers.

The United States is the only country in the world that has chosen to fund its media system almost exclusively through private dollars. The public broadcasting system receives a tiny fraction of 1 percent of the U.S. budget; requirements for the publication of legal advertising may keep weekly newspapers alive, but those revenues are insignificant to such media behemoths as the *New York Times.* While Americans may find advertising intrusive, seriously misleading, and environmentally unfriendly (think of the trees we could save if McDonald's didn't have to package every burger and fry with its own logo), it funds the world's most robust media system. As George Gerbner (1987) says, "You pay when you wash, not when you watch."

Contrary to what news journalists believe, most people regard advertising as another form of information. Experiments have shown that people prefer newspapers with advertising to newspapers that lack ads. Auction Web sites, one of the most popular kinds of Internet activity, provide further evidence that an audience with a purpose will seek out advertising to help make an informed choice.

These facts of media life do not blunt some of the deepest criticisms of advertising. The nature of the advertising message itself—short, highly visual and intentionally vague—supports criticism about advertising's reliance on stereotypes, its glorification of consumerism at the expense of community, and its apparent willingness to indulge in any excess to "make a buck." Indeed, some of the most compelling evidence that advertising works has arisen from studies of the impact of tobacco advertising on children under 18. The United States—and the rest of the world—have the cancer rates to prove it.

As a nation, the United States has chosen to regulate some of advertising's most egregious excesses, but we have also chosen to continue this method of paying for news and information. If advertising practitioners are ever to be ranked above the bottom of the occupational trustworthiness scale, then ethical thinking needs to become every bit as much a part of the advertising process as market research and strategic communication plans.

THINKING ABOUT THE AUDIENCE:
FROM PERSUASION THEORY
TO PHILOSOPHICAL ANTHROPOLOGY

Psychologists first began to try to understand persuasion by working with a stimulus–response model. This early behaviorist approach led many to believe that the media could act as a "hypodermic needle" or a "magic bullet," sending a stimulus/message to an unresisting audience. These researchers, called "powerful effects theorists," found examples to support their theory in the public panic after Orson Welles's *War of the Worlds* broadcast on October 30, 1938, and in the success of propaganda during both world wars.

But, the stimulus–response model proved a poor predictor of much human behavior. By the 1940s, most researchers were concluding that media effects were limited or nonexistent. However, by studying only behavior change (i.e., changing my vote), the researchers overlooked the true power of the media in the cognitive (knowledge) and affective (emotional) realms.

Later, communication theorists focused on cognitive psychology. Rather than analyzing persuasion as a simple behavioral reaction to a sufficient stimulus, these

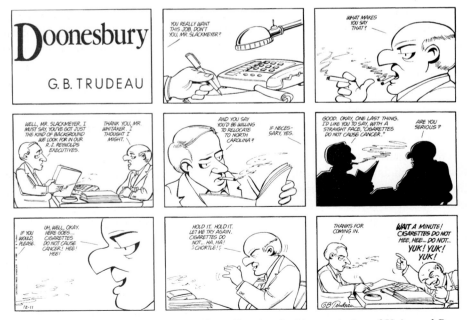

Doonesbury Copyright 1988 G. B. Trudeau. Reprinted with permission of Universal Press Syndicate. All rights reserved.

scholars theorized that how people think helped to explain persuasion. According to these theories, people strain toward cognitive balance. Simply put, we are most comfortable when all of our beliefs, actions, attitudes and relationships are in harmony, a state theorists called "symmetry."

Such theories have become known as "balance theories," since they stress the tendency of people to strive for cognitive balance in their lives. A person achieves balance only when his or her attitudes, information and actions are in harmony. Leon Festinger (1957) coined the term *cognitive dissonance* to describe the state where a message and an action give conflicting and uncomfortable signals. The desire to eliminate that dissonance is a strong one, strong enough to influence purchasing behavior and voting habits or opinions—at least some of the time.

Advertisers use this theory. A frequent scenario in advertising copy is to knock a consumer off balance early and to promise restoration of that balance through the purchase of a product. For instance, the headline of an ad might suggest that your dandruff is making you a social outcast, and the subsequent copy promises you social approval if you use the correct shampoo. A television ad might suggest that the wrong choice of tires means you don't care about your family's safety, while the correct choice of tires restores peace of mind by providing needed protection.

This social science–based approach to understanding advertising helped in creating ads and, to a more limited extent, explained their effectiveness. However, the social science approach makes some assumptions about the nature of people that advertising itself calls into question. For example, advertising scholars have tried to outline how people cognitively "process" or think about ads. Yet the same studies indicate that people are often irrational, emotional, and not necessarily well informed about the various claims made in ads.

Despite the equivocal findings of social science–based research, the ultimate practical justification for advertising was summed up in the ancient Roman phrase *caveat emptor,* "Let the buyer beware." In other words, the creators of the ads were willing to assume little responsibility for the impact of their work, and academic studies gave them partial cover: if you can't prove that something's been effective, then it's unreasonable to suggest you take some responsibility for it.

Philosophical anthropologists assert that human rationality exists on equal footing with human beings who explain themselves through daily experience, language and symbols. Culture and experience balance rationality (Wilkins and Christians 2001). If philosophical anthropology is correct, then ethical analysis of advertising founded in "Let the buyer beware" is morally untenable. Instead, the ethical goal of advertising should be the empowerment of multiple stakeholders. If the concept of human being as creator of culture and dynamic user of symbols becomes an ethical foundation for thinking about the audience, then advertising practitioners could be expected to operate within the following framework:

- Clients and the public need information that gives them "a good reason to adopt a course of action" (Koehn 1998, 106). The reason needs to be nonarbitrary and capable of helping people support one action instead of others.
- Rather than offering only expert opinion, advertising should foster ongoing discussion so that people can explore when options are sound and when practical knowledge (common sense) is superior.

- Advertising, just like news, can help foster reflective community, including the community of consumers.
- Advertising needs to take seriously the role of culture in our lives. That means that advertising must authentically reflect the diverse voices that comprise our culture.
- Advertising will speak to the role of organizations in our lives. Questions of history and background can be conveyed in ads, but that must be done accurately and in context.

Given these general guidelines, let's explore a specific framework that puts ads to an ethical test.

THINKING ABOUT THE MESSAGE: THE TARES TEST

The TARES test (Baker and Martinson 2001) suggests the creators of every ad should ask themselves a series of questions. If the answers are "yes," the ad passes the test. If the answers to some or all of the questions are "no," then the creator must justify—in the sense that Bok discusses—the ad content decisions. While the TARES test will not solve all ethical problems in creating ads, it does give creative people, marketing directors and strategic communication planners a tool.

The first element of the test—**T**—stands for **truthfulness.** Are the ad claims, both verbal and visual, truthful? If the message communicates only part of the truth (and many ads do this), are the omissions deceptive? Conversely, an ad would pass the test if it meets a genuine human need to provide truthful information, even if some facts are omitted.

The Cheerios television ads that emphasize eating Cheerios as part of a heart-healthy lifestyle could easily pass the first element of the TARES test. People do have to eat, and the ads provide needed information. The ads also omit some information—for example, the other components of a heart-healthy lifestyle or the fact that other breakfast cereals also meet these requirements. But the omitted information does not lead the mature consumer to make false assumptions and bad choices.

Step two in the TARES test—**A** for **authenticity**—is closely linked to step one. Authenticity suggests that it's important not only to do the right thing, but also "to do it with the right attitude" (Pojman 1999, 158). We link this notion to the concept of sincerity. First, is there a sincere need for this product within the range of products and services available? Second, are the reasons given the consumer purchasing

---

The TARES Test of Ethical Advertising

1. Are the ad claims *T*ruthful?
2. Is the claim an *A*uthentic one?
3. Does the ad treat the receiver with *R*espect?
4. Is there *E*quity between the sender and the receiver?
5. Is the ad *S*ocially responsible?

the product presented in such a way that they also would motivate the person who developed and wrote the ad?

Let's take a set of ads about products designed to help elderly or infirm people live more independently. Although some of these products—for example, devices that turn on lights in response to a hand clap—may seem little more than high-tech toys, anyone with a grandparent in a wheelchair, a sibling crippled by an illness like rheumatoid arthritis, of even a young person suffering from the imposed immobility of a broken leg can readily understand the need for such devices. But in making this point, if the ads stereotype elderly people as frail, helpless, weak or easily panicked, they do not authentically reflect the reality of life beyond age 65. Indeed, such stereotypical and fear-filled appeals omit a substantial number of consumers who might benefit from the product. The ad lacks authenticity. Thus, the TARES test would suggest rethinking the specific appeal in the ad to one that scares and stereotypes less and informs more. For creative people, such a switch is readily accomplished. Just as important, a fresher approach might well sell more.

The **R** in the TARES test stands for **respect,** in this case, respect for the person who will receive the persuasive message. However, as a shorthand way of thinking through this element of the test, it might be appropriate for advertising practitioners to ask themselves, "Am I willing to take full, open, public and personal responsibility for the content of this ad?" As Aristotle might add, a *phrenemos* respects himself as well as others. Mutuality is an ethical virtue. It's to this notion of mutuality that the TARES test now turns.

The **E** in the TARES test stands for **equity.** We conceptualize mutuality as follows: is the recipient of the message on the same, level playing field as the ad's creator? Or, to correctly interpret the ad, must that person be abnormally well informed, unusually bright or quick-witted, and completely without prejudice? Advertising copy that takes advantage of these common human frailties would not pass the equity portion of the TARES test. Phrased another way, the ad would fare well behind John Rawls's veil of ignorance (see Chapter 6).

Think about this corporate image ad for Mobil Oil—the one with the pristine scenery, glorious sunset and an oil tanker. The ad claims that Mobil has the best interest of the environment at heart by building tankers with double hulls. While Mobil's claim—that it builds double-hulled tankers—is literally true, correctly interpreting the ad requires a rapid and thorough recall of recent legislative history. Mobil, and all other oil companies, were required by Congress to build double-hulled tankers after the single-hulled tanker, the *Exxon Valdez,* ran aground and spilled an enormous amount of oil in Alaska, an environmental disaster of the first magnitude. (For more on this episode, see the Exxon case on the Web site for this book.) For the image ad to work, it counts on the average person not knowing—or not being able to connect—legislative requirements with corporate behavior. In fact, the ad assumes an unequal relationship between the knowledge of the person who created the ad and the consumer. It flunks the concept of equity.

Finally, the **S** in the TARES test. Is the ad **socially responsible?** This is perhaps the most difficult element of the test for the simple reason that advertising practitioners have duties to many groups, among them their clients, the agencies for which they work, consumers, people who see the advertising but do not buy a particular product, and society at large. Because this text emphasizes social ethics, we suggest interpreting this portion of the TARES test in the following fashion:

- If everyone who is financially able to purchase this product or service did so and used it, would society as a whole be improved, keeping in mind that recreation and self-improvement are worthy societal goals?
- If there are some groups in society who would benefit from using this product as advertised, are there others that could be significantly harmed by it? Are there ways to protect them?
- Does this ad increase or decrease the trust the average person has for persuasive messages?
- Does this ad take the notion of corporate responsibility, both to make money and to improve human life and welfare, seriously and truthfully?

Using this concept of social responsibility should enable you to think ethically about television's decisions to air condom advertising. MTV, the network targeted at teenagers, chose to air such ads in 2000. More traditional network television outlets did not. Which decision do you believe is more ethically justified? Why? Has the notion of social responsibility any place in your analysis?

The TARES test is a demanding one. But asking these questions, particularly during the process of creating an ad, can also be a spur to better, more creative execution and be rewarded in the capitalistic marketplace. The TARES test may help advertising practitioners warn their corporate clients about the kind of advertising that could do them, as well as society at large, great long-term harm.

ADVERTISING'S SPECIAL PROBLEMS: VULNERABLE AUDIENCES

Advertising in a mass medium reaches large, heterogeneous audiences. Sometimes, advertising intended for one group is seen by another. Sometimes the results are humorous, and maybe even a little embarrassing, as when ads for contraception make their way into prime-time programming.

However, in the case of the tobacco and the motion picture industries, this "confusion" of intended audience with actual recipients appears quite deliberate. Congressional hearings into Hollywood's advertising practices in 2000 produced internal documents that proved that the motion picture industry targets children between the ages of 12 and 17 with ads for movies carrying the advisory "No one under 17 admitted without parent or guardian." The tobacco industry agreed to withdraw its cartoon spokesperson "Joe Camel" from magazines and billboards after internal documents revealed the industry targeted underage smokers. In other cases—for example, the beer industry—advertising intended for adults is often seen by those who cannot legally drink but do remember the catchy commercials and the presentation of drinking as something connected with fun and good times. Even young children know about the Budweiser lizards, and most adult alcoholics report having had their first drink when they were underage.

These examples revolve around the same ethical question: are there certain types of audiences who deserve special protection from advertising messages? In keeping with thousands of years of ethical thinking, U.S. law has answered this question in the affirmative, particularly in the case of children. Thus, there are a number of legal restrictions on advertising targeted at children, in everything from Saturday-morning television programming to the sorts of messages and characters that advertisers may employ. The reason is that children, unlike adults, are not assumed to be autonomous moral actors. They reason about advertising imperfectly, and in an attempt to protect them American society has accepted some regulation of commercial speech.

However, the issue gets murkier when the target audience is formed of adults— for example, ethnic consumers. Exactly when advertisers began to actively court ethnic consumers is uncertain. Brooks (1992) quotes a 1940 *Business Week* article that reported an organization was established in Los Angeles to help guide advertisers who wished to garner the patronage of African-American consumers. The businesses were cautioned against using words such as "boss," "boy," and "darkey" in their advertisements. Instead, the advertisers were urged to refer to African-American consumers as "Negroes" who want the same things as other shoppers.

The real attempt to court ethnic audiences began when those audiences acquired buying power. Hispanics are now the largest minority in the United States. The buying power of African-American consumers now tops more than $300 billion. The Asian-American market has also increased substantially. Yet, a relative handful of advertisements reflect this emerging demographic reality, and commercials designed to appeal to this market segment sometimes employ troubling stereotypes or encounter other difficulties. For example, R. J. Reynolds Tobacco Company spent millions developing a cigarette aimed at African-Americans and putting billboards in African-American neighborhoods to announce it, only to pull the product when consumer outrage over the impact of tobacco on the health of the target market became public.

Other tendencies in advertising combine, in troubling ways, cultural understandings and product sales. Magazines pointed at teenage girls seldom reflect the reality of teenage bodies. Scholarly studies have shown that women, when exposed to advertising images, find their own bodies less acceptable. The same goes for facial features. Scholars have noted that the ideal image of beauty, even in magazines targeted at African-Americans, is a Caucasian one of small noses, thin lips, and lighter skin tones. African-American women simply don't see themselves in these advertisements. Scholars in the cultural studies tradition argue that the impact of these repeated images is cumulative—the culture itself comes to accept without question what is, in reality, nothing more than a gender or a racial stereotype.

Few scholars have suggested that adults who are members of minority communities need special protection from advertising. What they have noted is that ads that abuse the trust between consumer and product have both short-term and long-term consequences. In the short term, products may not sell or may find themselves the target of regulation. In the long term, the load of cynicism and societal distrust increases. People sense they are being used, even if they can't explain precisely how. The buyer may learn to beware of advertising itself rather than to use advertising to help make better-informed decisions.

Suggested Readings

BAKER, S. and MARTINSON, D. 2001. "The TARES test: Five principles of ethical persuasion." *Journal of Mass Media Ethics* Vol. 16, Nos. 2 & 3.

FESTINGER, L. 1957. *A theory of cognitive dissonance.* Stanford, CA: Stanford University Press.

KOEHN, D. 1998. *Rethinking feminist ethics.* New York: Routledge.

LEISS, WILLIAM, STEPHEN KLINE, and SUT JHALLY. 1986. *Social communication in advertising: Person, products and images of well being.* New York: Methuen Publications.

O'TOOLE, JOHN. 1985. *The trouble with advertising.* New York: Times Books.

PATTERSON, THOMAS E., and ROBERT D. MCCLURE. 1972. *The unseeing eye.* New York: G. P. Putnam's Sons.

SCHUDSON, MICHAEL. 1984. *Advertising: The uneasy persuasion.* New York: Basic Books.

CASES ON THE WEB

"A case of need" by Deni Elliott

"Exxon's whipping cream on a pile of manure" by JoAnn M. Valenti

"A sobering dilemma" by Beverly Horvit

CHAPTER III CASES

CASE III-A
Daisy Girl Redux: Using Fear as a Political Weapon
ANDREA MILLER
Louisiana State University

In the twenty-first century, an old fear, one that many felt came tumbling down with the Berlin Wall, has been rekindled. The fear of nuclear war appears as real now as it was when people built concrete bunkers back in the 1960s. In 2003, the saying "everything old becomes new again" was manifested in the controversial "Daisy Girl" anti–nuclear war ad.

Broadcast a single time on television in 1964, the "Daisy Girl" political advertisement showed a little blonde girl picking the petals off a daisy. As the petals are plucked one by one, a voice counts down to a nuclear bomb blast. The ad was originally created by legendary adman Tony Schwartz for Lyndon Johnson's presidential campaign against conservative Barry Goldwater. The implied message was that a vote for Goldwater was a vote for nuclear war. The Republican Party claimed the ad slandered Goldwater. In the fearful Cold War climate, the advertisement aired once before viewer protests forced it to be pulled.

In January 2003, a group with another agenda attempted to replant the seeds of fear. The grass-roots organization MoveOn.org had a new version of the "Daisy Nuke" ad created to protest the United States' seemingly inevitable path to war with Iraq. The reincarnation's message was less subtle this time. As the young girl picked the petals, the voiceover said: "War with Iraq. Maybe it will end quickly. Maybe not. Maybe it will spread. Maybe extremists will take over countries with nuclear weapons."

Images of wounded soldiers and burning oils wells appeared on the screen. The nuclear explosion and mushroom cloud appeared with the final message: "Let the inspections work."

The group spent $400,000 for the ad to air on local stations in 13 major cities, including New York, Chicago, and Miami.

The organization behind the ad's revival, MoveOn.org, was formed in the 1990s to oppose the impeachment of former President Bill Clinton. Prior to the airing of "Daisy 2," the group had also spent more than $300,000 on newspaper ads urging President Bush to avoid war with Iraq. Eli Pariser, MoveOn.org's international campaign director, told the Associated Press that the goal of "Daisy 2" was to encourage a national discussion. But critics argued that, just as the original did 40 years ago, the ad stirred more fear than debate.

Two network-affiliated television stations decided not to run the ads.: KNBC-TV in Los Angeles and WRC-TV in Washington, D.C. Both are owned by NBC. NBC's owner, General Electric, released the following statement concerning the ad's "non-acceptance": "We prefer to handle controversial issues in our news and public affairs programming, where we can be fair and balanced." Responses from the individual stations mirrored the parent company's statement.

Four decades after the first Daisy Girl ad, "Daisy 2" was less controversial than historically and psychologically significant. The ad was reincarnated hoping to capitalize on its familiarity and the emotion the ad evokes: fear. In the post 9/11 world, Americans have an unprecedented level of fear for safety—physical and economic. Because a person's fears can shape their perception of the facts (Jamieson 1993), the ad could cause people to believe in the reality of the worst-case scenario it represents. The link that was created was tenuous, but not improbable, especially after millions watched the impossible crash of a passenger jet into the World Trade Center.

The ad's history garnered more attention than the ad itself. Because of the ad's historical significance, the news media covered the release of the ad extensively. The ad was scheduled to air for only five days and in just over a dozen large television markets. However, MoveOn.org released the ad to the media prior to its broadcast. Most Americans saw the ad in the television coverage of the ad or read about its contents in the newspapers. As with the original "Daisy Girl" ad, MoveOn.org got its money's worth in free publicity.

Micro Issues

1. Was the decision by the two NBC affiliates not to air the "Daisy" ad an appropriate one?
2. Should other stations have joined in the decision? Defend your answer.
3. What were some possible positive and negative consequences of the ad?

Midrange Issues

1. How was the agenda behind the ad different between the 1964 and 2003 versions? Does that make a difference in the appropriateness of the ad?
2. Fear of nuclear war? Fear of no future for your children/grandchildren? Fear of another Vietnam-like conflict? This ad evoked a strong negative emotion that is usually associated with the primal instinct to flight. Is that what MoveOn.org hoped to accomplish?
3. Did the media play an additional role in the controversy by covering the story of the ad itself? Does the story have news value from an ethical standpoint?

Macro Issues

1. Advertisers play on the emotions of viewers all the time to sell products. How is the use of fear different? Is the use of fear to sell an idea different than using fear to sell a product?
2. Images and ideas that question patriotism also evoke a visceral response. What role does or should war play in patriotism? Does duty ethics come into play in the issues of war, patriotism, and safety?
3. Conflict is a necessary part of ethical decision making. What ethical theory could MoveOn.org have used to justify their decision to reincarnate this ad? What ethical theory could television stations have used to justify their decision not to air the ad?

CASE III-B
Superman's Super Bowl Miracle
RENITA COLEMAN
Louisiana State University

In 1995 actor Christopher Reeve, best known as Superman, was paralyzed from the neck down in a horseback-riding accident. Five years later, he "walked" across a stage to receive an award. This was no miracle of modern medicine; rather it was a miracle of computer animation. And, the occasion was an advertisement rather than a real awards ceremony or fund-raising effort for spinal cord research.

Reaction to the commercial for Nuveen Investments was swift. The phones started ringing at the National Spinal Cord Injury Association. Paralyzed people fooled by the image wanted to know where Reeve went to get cured. People with spinal cord injuries and physicians saw the commercial as either heartwarming or contemptible. Reeve was portrayed as either a saint or snake-oil salesman, peddling false hopes or raising hope and money for research.

More than 131 million viewers saw the 60-second spot, which aired twice during the Super Bowl. It featured an auditorium full of people gathered to present an award for research that cured spinal cord injury. No specific date is given, and narration in the beginning puts the gathering sometime after 2006. The New York skyline has a few new, futuristic skyscrapers, and there are two outdoor shots of a subway train and a newsstand with a TV screen hanging overhead. But, once the screen moves inside the auditorium, there are no clues that this is a "flash-forward." Reeve looks barely older than he does today.

An announcer in a tuxedo talks about the advances science has made against AIDS and cancer and tells the audience that someone special is to present the awards for some amazing breakthroughs in spinal cord injuries. The camera focuses on the lower body of a man getting up from a chair and walking stiffly to the stage; it is a beaming Christopher Reeve. The special effects are achieved with a computerized image of Reeve's head grafted onto another man's body. He walks haltingly to the stage with the help of canes and walkers. A voice-over says, "In the future, so many amazing things will happen in the world. What amazing things can you make happen?" The screen fades to black and three taglines read, "Invest well." "Leave your mark." "Nuveen Investments."

Was this commercial misleading or creative?

Many disabled people and their advocates were aghast. It cruelly offered false hope and unreasonable expectations to people who should be adapting to life with disabilities, they said. It was not just psychologically harmful, but practically harmful too, especially to young people, said one doctor with a spinal cord injury of his own. People could end up spending untold hours each day preparing their bodies for the time when the cure comes instead of preparing themselves for the realities of their new world. Others felt the commercial left the impression that people with spinal cord injuries were consumed by a quest for a miracle cure. Reeve's own wife was against the commercial. "I didn't like it because I worried that the commercial would result in disabled people being carried away by this fantasy of dramatic recovery," Dana Reeve told the *New York Daily News*. Some accused Reeve of parading his own fantasies in public to convert others. The *New York Times'* advertising column called it "crass and more than a little creepy."

However, not everyone connected with spinal cord injury was upset. It offered much needed hope, some said, and it helped focus attention on the need for research. Reeve himself defended it, saying breakthroughs are imminent and getting people interested and investing in research is paramount. In fact, since his injury Reeve has worked tirelessly for a cure, raising millions, setting up a research center, and persuading Congress to add $10 million for research. There is a genuine reason for optimism, Reeve said, citing scientific information he was given before it was published in academic journals.

Some doctors agree that a cure is in the foreseeable future; others caution any cure is more likely to benefit the newly injured, not people like Reeve.

In a released statement, Reeve called the commercial a "vision" and likened it to John F. Kennedy's setting a goal to land astronauts on the moon. "I was pleased to be involved in this spot because the message is that all of us must give back to society and leave our mark in some unique way."

The firestorm obscured one question: what was this commercial selling? Nuveen Investments is a 101-year-old Chicago-based company that has been shifting from municipal bond underwriting to money management for brokers and financial advisers. The company had a net income in 1999 of $97.3 million. Some speculated that Reeve's endorsement would boost the company's name recognition and credibility.

The connection between a cure for paralysis and investing money is unclear in the $4 million ad. Nuveen spokesman Chris Allen said the point of the ad was "to inspire a dialogue on money, to have a new dialogue and get away from buying bigger boats and bigger cars and think about the impact that money can have on the future."

Many viewers didn't know what the commercial was advertising then and still don't today. Less in doubt was the immediate effect of free publicity. The commercial was rebroadcast as news by hundreds of television stations, and it dominated radio and television talk shows and newspaper columns for weeks.

Additionally, there is the issue of how visual images can fool even media-savvy viewers. The commercial was filmed to look like news coverage. There was no explicit statement that this was a futuristic vision, no visual cues that this was a flash-forward. The visual image of Reeve walking was laced with emotional appeal. Reeve himself told *Adweek* that seeing a paralyzed person walking is "very emotional and almost overwhelming. So, it created a visceral response." Finally, there was the claim by some that the ad helped to raise money for spinal cord research.

Micro Issues

1. Ethicists suggest that the claims made in an advertisement should be open to rational discussion. What are the claims in this ad? Could a consumer rationally respond to them based on information in the ad?
2. Should this ad have included visual cues about its hypothetical nature?

3. Since the goal of advertising is to sell something, how would you evaluate this ad's effectiveness?
4. Is this ad like or unlike ads in which now-dead film stars are inserted through use of digital animation to sell products such as Diet Coke or Coors beer? Why or why not?

Midrange Issues

1. Should news journalists have run stories about this commercial? Why or why not? What should those stories have said?
2. Research indicates that visual information and emotional responses tend to circumvent the brain's logic centers. For what sort of products might such ads be appropriate? Are there products or causes for which such an approach is inappropriate?
3. Do you believe this ad passes the TARES test? Justify your decision.

Macro Issues

1. Do the ends justify the means in this ad? Does the possible good of increased awareness and funding for spinal cord injury justify what many said was a deception?

CASE III-C
Breaking Through the Clutter: Ads That Make You Think Twice
FRITZ CROPP IV
University of Missouri

Controversial advertising campaigns were nothing new for Benetton when it unveiled its spring–summer 2000 worldwide communication campaign. In January 2000, "We, on Death Row," a statement against the death penalty featuring U.S. death row convicts, brought Benetton an unprecedented level of criticism, complete with an apology from its president and the loss of a potentially lucrative contract with a mainstream American retailer.

Benetton, the Italian clothing company, had a 15-year record of concerning itself with social issues, including peace, war, AIDS awareness, and multiculturalism. Previous imagery featured a dying AIDS patient surrounded by his anguished family, a picture of a black horse and a white horse copulating, an unwashed newborn baby with an uncut umbilical cord, a buttock branded with an HIV-positive stamp, a priest and a nun kissing, the blood-soaked uniform of a dead Bosnian sniper, a white baby nursing at a black breast, and the like.

Such ads invite controversy. The Vatican criticized the ad featuring a nun and priest kissing, and a French court ruled that the company had exploited human suffering in a campaign depicting dying AIDS patients and ordered it to pay damages to French citizens infected with the HIV virus. Yet Benetton seemed to invite the controversy, proclaiming its approach "looks reality in the face" (hyperlink: http://www.benneton.com) by tackling social issues. Company President Luciano Benetton said 10 years ago that "our campaigns are an attempt to get away from traditional advertising in the belief that it has no power and no value any more." Adds Oliviero Toscani, Benetton's photographer and creative director, "My brief is not to concern myself with commercial images to sell more T-shirts but rather to create an image for the company that touches people in all of the countries in which Benetton is present" (Mondow 2000, 61).

While one cannot directly or singularly credit the advertising, Toscani's work has coincided with Benetton's worldwide growth. While critics decry the seeming vacuum between the provocative campaigns and the relatively mainstream Benetton stores and products, the company enjoyed a steady increase in worldwide sales and net profits through the 1990s. Benetton now sells clothes, accessories, and sporting goods in more than 7,000 stores in 120 countries, with 70 percent of its sales originating in Europe (Conley 2000).

"We, on Death Row" began when Toscani began working with freelance journalist Ken Shulman to photograph and interview 26 U.S. prisoners on death row. The work culminated in a 96-page supplement in the January 11, 2000, edition of *Talk* magazine, followed by a series of individual pictures of the prisoners in selected U.S. magazines and on billboards in major U.S. cities.

"The campaign is about the death penalty," proclaims the Benetton press release on the company's Web site. "Leaving aside any social, political, judicial or moral consideration, this project aims at showing the public the realities of capital punishment, so that no one around the world will consider the death penalty neither as a distant problem nor as news that occasionally appear [sic] on TV."

The *Talk* magazine supplement included pictures and comments from the prisoners, along with quotes from Pope John Paul II and the Dalai Lama. Questions were decidedly soft. Shulman asked inmates about their families, prison food, what they dream, and what they miss, with no mention of the victims, no discussion of current feelings of remorse.

Given space limitations, the advertisements, which Benetton claims were decided upon after the pictures and interviews had been taken and completed, were limited to a picture of an inmate, a description of his crime, the method by which he would be killed, the words "Sentenced to Death," and the "United Colors of Benetton" logo. Seven inmates agreed to allow their photographs to be used for this campaign. Even less context is provided in this format. There was no warning for the victims' families that the pictures were about to appear.

When they did, criticism came from many angles.

Sears, Roebuck and Company canceled a franchising contract it had recently signed with Benetton. The contract was forged to help Sears with its declining clothing sales and help Benetton reestablish itself in the United States, which accounts for just 5 percent of the company's business. Further, Sears pulled from its shelves all brands owned by the global parent company.

California House leader Scott Baugh drafted a resolution urging all California residents to boycott Benetton until the campaign disappeared. The bill passed 59 to 8. Pennsylvania Attorney General Lynne Abraham called for a nationwide boycott. Activists from Parents of Murdered Children staged a protest outside Benetton's U.S. office in New York City. The company also was targeted in Texas by Justice for All, the New York group Center for the Community Interest, and the International Union of Police Associations. Missouri Attorney General Jay Nixon filed a circuit court suit, saying that representatives from Benetton tricked their way into Missouri's jails by pretending to be journalists. "Selling sweaters on the back of death row inmates is sick and wrong," he said.

Advertising critics were equally appalled. Bob Garfield, a columnist at *Advertising Age,* wrote, "There is no brand—not a single one—that has the right to increase its sales on the backs, on the misery, on the fates of condemned men and women, much less their slaughtered victims" (Steuver 2000, C01).

In April 2000, Benetton announced that Toscani, who once said there is no such thing as going too far (Hughes 2000), was leaving after 18 years. The company did not address whether the "We, on Death Row" campaign was a factor.

In the end, it is difficult to assess the cost or benefits to Benetton of "We, on Death Row." The $1.8 million in royalties to have been generated by the Sears deal represents a fraction of the company's $2 billion in annual sales. Similarly, the $15 million the company said it spent on global distribution, combined with the undisclosed production costs, may be balanced by the resulting publicity, which continues to build upon Benetton's edgy image among its young target as a socially conscious company. "A substantial number of consumers seem to sense genuine integrity and principle behind Benetton's actions," notes Patrick Allossery of the *Financial Post* (2000, C3).

Micro Issues

1. The twenty-six prisoners interviewed by Toscani and Shulman were convicted of 37 murders. Should Benetton have considered the victims' families before running its campaign? Should the company have given them advance warning that the images would appear?
2. Responding to 144 consumer complaints, the British Advertising Standards Authority accepted Benetton's explanation that the campaign was intended to encourage debate and remind people that even death row prisoners have human rights. Thus, it ruled that its duty was to uphold an advertiser's freedom of speech. When a clothing company exploits shocking issues in its advertising, is it an abuse of that freedom?
3. Was it okay for Benetton to expand its campaign to print advertisements and billboards without seeking the same type of permission it was granted prior to interviewing the prisoners for the *Talk* magazine insert?

Midrange Issues

1. It's been said that there's no such thing as bad publicity. Does the end of free publicity justify the means?
2. Does this type of campaign illuminate the issues—or potentially trivialize them?
3. If the point of "We, on Death Row" was to raise awareness of issues surrounding the death penalty, is a one-sided approach appropriate? Should Benetton have sought opinions from people in favor of the death penalty?

Macro Issues

1. Should the definition of advertising be altered to include efforts such as "We, on Death Row," or should such campaigns be considered differently by review boards and by the media outlets that sell time and space?
2. Should standards be developed to prevent advertisers from insensitive or potentially irresponsible actions, or does paying for space or time supersede the need for balance, fairness or objectivity?
3. Benetton claims to "tear down the wall of indifference, contributing to raising the awareness of universal problems among the world's citizens." However, there are cultural chasms to be addressed. In this case, the company's belief that the death penalty is inherently wrong is consistent with European opinion on the issue, but inconsistent with what many Americans believe. Should advertisers—or companies paying for space to espouse their own commentary—be sensitive to cultural differences? If so, what guidance should be provided for them?
4. Jim Faulds, an advertising executive in Edinburgh, says ads that go beyond the boundaries of good taste also push back those boundaries. People become numbed to the shock tactics, and the only recourse is to shock further. Asks *Scotsman* reporter Michael Kerrigan (2000, 22), "As we recall the outrage that greeted those late 1990s campaigns we do indeed seem to be harking back to an age of innocence, long gone by. Have we, too, been implicated in Benetton's little habit?"

CASE III-D
The Plagiarism Factory
JOHN P. FERRÉ
University of Louisville

Terry had not long been advertising manager for the *Louisville Cardinal* when she received camera-ready copy of an advertisement for ready-made research papers. "RESEARCH PAPERS," it announced, "16,278 to choose from—all subjects. Custom research also available—all levels. COD or Visa/MasterCard." The ad urged students to send two dollars or to call a toll-free hotline for a catalog. With the camera-ready advertisement, the company enclosed a check for a year's space in the weekly university newspaper.

Because the *Cardinal* is an independent student paper, Terry was not compelled or prohibited by university administrators from running questionable advertisements. Furthermore, the newspaper had run the advertisement weekly for years. Tradition was on the side of publishing the ad, yet Terry felt uneasy about it. She voiced her uneasiness at the next staff meeting, and the staff agreed to reject the ad. Terry mailed the following letter:

> I am sorry to inform you that we cannot run your advertisement for research assistance. The staff of the *Louisville Cardinal* reserves the right to refuse any advertisement it feels could be harmful or insulting to the students of this university. Therefore, out of respect for the integrity of the student body and for the protection of the ethical policies of the University of Louisville, I am returning your check for $111.36. I apologize for any budgeting inconveniences this may have caused you.

Although Terry lost a commission and the newspaper lost some revenue, the staff of the *Cardinal* felt confident that they had made the right decision. The mail-order research paper firm contacted the newspaper a couple of years later to no avail.

At least one of the newspaper's advisers was highly critical of the staff's decision. "Newspapers should print ads, not reject them," he argued, "especially since the *Cardinal* is the only newspaper on campus. It should not act as a censor. Its advertising columns should be open to anyone who is willing to pay for the space, whatever the product or service. Editorial judgments should be made only in regard to news and feature stories."

Despite the adviser's fear that the student newspaper was beginning a campaign of advertising censorship, the *Cardinal* has refused space to no other national advertiser. It prints advertisements for alcoholic beverages, for instance, even though alcoholism and drunk driving are arguably more dangerous for students than academic dishonesty. Apparently, the *Cardinal*'s primary moral criterion for the acceptance of advertisements is honesty. All ads that neither deceive nor encourage others to deceive are acceptable in the pages of the *Cardinal*.

Micro Issues

1. If the research paper company queries the newspaper once again, should the newspaper reconsider its decision, or should it stand firm?
2. Is the financial health of the paper an ethically relevant factor? If the paper's budget was in the red, could an argument be made that it is better for the student body to have a newspaper with offensive ads than it is to let the paper die?
3. At some time in the future, the paper receives an ad for *Cliffs Notes*. The staff knows that some students are tempted to rely on plot summaries rather than read whole novels that are assigned in various courses in the humanities. Furthermore, the campus bookstore stocks a wide variety of *Cliffs Notes*. What should the newspaper do? If your answer differs from your decision on the research-paper ad, distinguish between the two products.

Midrange Issues

1. What types of advertisements should student newspapers reject? Community newspapers?
2. Should papers decide advertising policy in advance, or should they make these decisions on a case-by-case basis? What would such a policy look like?
3. Suppose your campus newspaper receives an advertisement from a local nightclub for a "Drink or Drown" promotion—all the beer you can drink for one price. Do you accept the ad? Suppose the campus radio station has refused air time to the advertiser. Is the newspaper under any obligation to reject it in light of the radio station's decision?
4. Has the proliferation of term paper sites on the Internet made this case study moot? Since such papers are now readily available for downloading, should this change the stance of the newspaper? If so, how?

Macro Issues

1. Are a newspaper's advertising columns a common carrier—selling space without discrimination—or should they operate with the same editorial freedom that applies to news and feature stories?
2. Is a newspaper morally responsible for everything it prints, whether or not the content originated at the newspaper?
3. Is it right to impose one's standards on information others receive? Is the newspaper doing so in this case?

CASE III-E
If You Let Nike Play . . .
RENITA COLEMAN
Louisiana State University

It takes you by surprise. A television commercial without a product. Just a half dozen or so preteen girls of various ethnic backgrounds in a working-class playground. With the rhythm and cadence of a song, they voice the refrain "If you let me play; if you let me play sports." The verse goes like this:

> I will like myself more.
> I will have more self-confidence.
> I will be 60 percent less likely to get breast cancer.
> I will suffer less depression.
> I will be more likely to leave a man who beats me.
> I will be less likely to get pregnant before I want to.
> I will learn what it means to be strong.

At the end of 30 seconds, the screen goes black and the familiar Nike logo appears with the slogan "Just Do It."

Unusual, certainly. Only a few advertisements have departed so radically from standard practice. Is this commercial socially responsible or ethically questionable? Is its audience children or their parents? This 30-second commercial is startlingly effective precisely because of its ambiguity. It grabs your attention with its rapid-fire visuals; it makes you sit up and pay attention with its hard-hitting issues; and it makes you curious to know what this unusual ad is all about. The net effect is that this subtle pitch of a sportswear company becomes all the more memorable.

The Nike "If you let me play" ad makes unique use of the time-honored advertising technique of cognitive dissonance. It knocks the viewer off balance with the incongruous image of preteen girls discussing such adult subjects as spouse abuse, breast cancer, and depression. It is emotionally and cognitively unsettling to hear children discussing such things because we assume youth equals innocence. We would rather not have to face the fact that many children today are intimately acquainted with such topics. Perhaps a mother or other family member has battled depression or even lost a fight with breast cancer. More unsettling yet, perhaps children have seen daddy hitting mommy.

Even absent firsthand knowledge, children today are subjected to such situations via the news and entertainment media. Who really thinks children have been shielded from the facts of O. J. Simpson's battering of his ex-wife Nicole? From Columbine High School? And the trend is for family secrets to be less concealed than they once were. Children today are not the innocents of the past or the innocents we would still like to believe they are. This Nike ad is an in-your-face testimonial to that. And true to the formula of ads that use cognitive dissonance as a tool, Nike proposes a solution to restore the viewer to balance: let me play, and inferentially, let me do so in Nike apparel.

"Our goal wasn't to be alarmist, just direct," said Andrea Bonner, who helped create the "If you let me play" commercial. "We just wanted to be real." She acknowledges that this issue-oriented commercial is "a different kind of animal for Nike." In fact, she says, it "borders on being a pro bono message."

Nike has been questioned on ethical grounds in the past. In 1994, a commercial featuring basketball's bad boy, Dennis Rodman, was criticized for reinforcing an ends-justifies-the-means mentality when Santa Claus grants Rodman his Christmas wish of expensive new shoes despite his unsportsmanlike conduct. African-Americans criticized the company for using Rodman as a role model when other, more positive African-American role models were available. Nike has similarly been criticized for advertising its shoes on billboards located in poor, inner-city neighborhoods where parents can ill-afford $100 shoes.

The company was even accused of helping to cause thefts and violence in ghettos where the apparent reason for the assault was the victim's expensive sports shoes. The children in the "If you let me play" ad appear to be from working-class families. While it is rather ambiguous, the appearance of the playground and the children's clothes provide visual cues to suggest this. Perhaps Nike tried to avoid being accused of marketing expensive products to socioeconomic groups that either cannot afford them or would do without necessities in order to purchase them.

The subject of target markets also brings up the issue of advertising to children. The poor and elderly as well as the young have often been singled out as audiences deserving special sensitivity and responsibility from advertisers. Because they are potentially more vulnerable, less experienced and adept at sorting out product claims, and more subject to peer pressure and advertising's influence, children's advertising must assume a greater sensitivity than advertising to the general population, an audience considered to be active and autonomous.

Research by Carol Gilligan and others has shown that adolescence is a particularly formative time for a girl's self-esteem. Adolescence is a time for issues of attachment for girls, and identity formation takes place within relationships. There is special vulnerability for girls in finding a way of caring for themselves while maintaining connections to others. The topics in this commercial are all of a connective nature—pregnancy involves a male and a child; domestic violence involves a relationship with a male, at least; strength, self-confidence, depression, and even breast cancer, with its strong ties to feminist issues, are all issues of self-caring and identity formation.

Another controversy centers on the source of the statistics in the ad. In "If you let me play," Nike claims it got its statistical information from the Women's Sports Foundation (WSF), a nonprofit organization that collects studies regarding athletics and women and girls. However, a representative of the WSF said the foundation would never knowingly provide its research to Nike because it is sponsored by Reebok, Nike's chief competitor. The advertising agency that created the commercial also claims that the information was obtained from WSF.

Micro Issues

1. Is Nike guilty of using "scare tactics" to sell its clothing line?
2. Nike claims the message borders on being a pro bono message, in other words a free public service ad for a worthy cause. Critique that claim.

Midrange Issues

1. Would the same commercial have been any less arresting had it featured adult women? Would it be less effective?
2. Nike never produced a similar ad for boys, although there are documented health and social benefits for males who play sports. Why do you think there was not an "If you let me play" ad made featuring young boys?

Macro Issues

1. The Women's Sports Foundation gets its research data from a variety of academic and not-for-profit sources. Given its goals of promoting fitness through sports for women, why would it consider the statistics in the Nike ad to be proprietary information? Shouldn't the foundation be pleased at the larger audience generated by the Nike ad?
2. Obviously many girls who do not play sports do not suffer any of the maladies mentioned in the ad later in life either. Is Nike guilty of portraying women as more vulnerable than they are in order to sell clothing?

CASE III-F
Channel One: Commercialism in Schools
ROZALYN OSBORN
University of Missouri

Channel One is a 12-minute newscast designed for teenagers—middle school through high school—broadcast via satellite into classrooms across the United States. It is viewed in more than 350,000 classrooms, in 12,000 schools, and by about 8 million students every day—about 40 percent of the nation's total students in this age group (Fox 1996; Bormly 1996; Bormly 1999; Hoynes 1998; Kennedy 2000; Walsh 2000). It was first developed by Chris Whittle of Whittle Communications in 1989 in Knoxville, Tennessee. The program was purchased in 1994 by K-III Communications, now known as Primedia Inc., the owner of the *Weekly Reader, New York* magazine, and *Soap Opera Digest.*

The *Channel One* offer is difficult for schools to resist, especially schools in poor districts or with little funding. The corporation provides schools with communication technology equipment, including a satellite dish, networked cable wiring, a VCR, and a 19-inch television for every classroom. The equipment, valued in the 1990s at about $50,000, is provided, installed, and maintained at no cost to the school. In return, schools agree to air *Channel One* to a large majority of their students every day.

What lies at the center of the debate over *Channel One* and programs like it is advertising. As part of the twelve-minute program, students view 2 minutes of advertising. In one school year, that means students who view *Channel One* see about 700 commercials, the equivalent of about one day of class time (Dudley 1998, Fox 1997). In its first year of operation, *Channel One* sold $51 million of commercials, more than ESPN or CNN sold at similar times (Robertson 1999). The ads, with a cost of about $185,000 per 30 seconds, are the largest contributor to *Channel One's* annual $100 million in profit (Dudley 1998).

William Hoynes, a Vassar College sociology professor, says *Channel One* is a "promotional vehicle for itself and for youth culture and style. This approach . . . promotes a friendly environment for advertising" (Walsh 2000, 15).

Channel One supporters maintain the technology and information the outlet provides are invaluable, particularly in poorer schools. They contend that brief exposure to advertising is worth the gain in technology and materials. Most teachers and students approve of *Channel One* (Bormly 1999) and say they believe the acquisition of the technology in the schools is without risk and that the programming seems to combat chronic lack of knowledge of current events among teenagers. Though many are concerned with the impact of the commercials, most think the benefits outweighed those negative aspects. Teachers particularly said the programming promoted current events knowledge and that it presented hard-to-discuss subjects important to teens' lives.

Critics focus on the outlet's commercial aspect, maintaining that schools should be a protected environment. By accepting the commercialization that comes with *Channel One,* opponents argue that schools are targeting a captive audience (Fox 1997; Kennedy 2000; Robertson 1999). As consumer activist Ralph Nader said in hearings held before the U.S. Senate in 2000, *Channel One* harms "children, schools, taxpayers, and democracy by forcing students to view the ads." *Channel One* opponents maintain that money made from the selling of commercials is tantamount to selling out students and their minds to advertisers and corporations (Bell 1999; Fege & Hagelshaw 2000; Hoynes 1998; Robertson 1999; Walsh 2000).

Opponents also claim the programming does not result in a significantly better understanding of current affairs (Hoynes 1998). Moreover, *Channel One* promotes materialistic attitudes, say critics. According to Commercial Alert, a Washington, D.C., watchdog group, "*Channel One* doesn't belong in schools because it conveys materialism and harmful messages to children, corrupts the integrity of the schools, and degrades the moral authority of schools and teachers" (Kennedy 2000, 21). Based on academic studies of students exposed to the programming, scholars note, "Students who watch *Channel One* news evaluate advertised products more highly and express substantially more consumption-oriented, materialistic attitudes than do students who do not watch *Channel One*" (Hoynes, 1998, 340).

In 1999 Commercial Alert sent letters to all *Channel One*'s major advertisers, asking them to discontinue advertising on the program. Only one company, Nabisco, replied, saying, "We do not believe evidence supports the charge that two minutes of daily advertising is putting our children's future at risk" (Walsh 2000, 16).

Micro Issues

1. How is *Channel One* different from the student newspaper or yearbook that sells advertising? From the PTA fund-raiser?
2. Are there certain sorts of ads that should be censored from *Channel One*?
3. A news service called ZapMe! installs and maintains computer labs for schools, providing they agree that schools log 4 hours per day per computer and allow ZapMe to place ads of marketers on its Internet connections. It also tracks student demographic information. The company asks your local school district for permission to sign a contract. Do you write an exposé of the practice or an editorial praising it?

Midrange Issues

1. Are there certain areas of U.S. life that should be protected from commercialization? Why?
2. How would you respond to the argument that *Channel One* helps students learn, particularly about difficult issues?

Macro Issues

1. How do you respond to Nader's comments that commercialism in the schools is a threat to democracy?
2. What other sorts of commercialism appear in public schools? How is *Channel One* like or unlike those forms of commercialism?
3. How might John Rawls analyze the impact of *Channel One,* particularly in less affluent school districts?
4. Should other nations adopt this method of supporting public education? Why?

CASE III-G
Fried Chicken as Health Food? The FTC Cries Foul
PHILIP PATTERSON
Oklahoma Christian University

Say "fried chicken" to the typical consumer and many images come to mind. The image of fried chicken as health food is not near the top of the list, or even on the list. But according to commercials aired in the fall of 2003 by KFC (the former Kentucky Fried Chicken), their signature product, Original Recipe fried chicken, can be a part of a balanced diet, and may even help you lose weight.

First came consumer skepticism and the late-night comedians' jokes. Then came action by the Federal Trade Commission (FTC), which sent a civil subpoena asking the franchise chain to justify the health claims made in two television ads that debuted in November of 2003. The action was another attempt by government to manage weight-loss products and weight-loss claims, all while the growing obesity problem in the United States threatens to overwhelm the nation's health care system.

The two ads in question were developed for KFC by the advertising agency Foote, Cone and Belding. In a press release announcing the campaign, a KFC executive was quoted as saying that "consumers should no longer feel guilty about eating fried chicken" (Matthews and Steinberg, 2003 B-1).

In one television ad a man notices a slimmer appearance in one of his friends. "Is that you, man? You look fantastic," he says. When asked what he had done, the friend announces (through a mouthful of food) "Eatin' chicken." An off-camera announcer claims that one Original Recipe chicken breast has 11 grams of carbohydrate and 40 grams of protein and implies that fried chicken fits neatly in low-carbohydrate, high-protein diets that have been popular in the United States in the past decade.

In the second ad, a woman arrives home where her husband is watching television. "Remember when we talked about eating better? Well, it starts today," she says as she sets down a KFC bucket. The off-screen announcer claims that two Original Recipe chicken breasts have fewer fat grams than a Burger King Whopper sandwich (the difference later revealed in small print to be only five grams). The spot goes on to say that you could "go skinless for just three grams of fat per piece," even though decades of KFC advertising has touted the formula of spices in its chicken breading.

Both commercials contained a small disclaimer on the bottom of the screen urging viewers to eat the chicken as part of a balanced diet and exercise. Other disclaimers were also necessary, including one that admits that the bucket of chicken shown in the ad typically contains pieces other than breasts and that KFC chicken is not a low-sodium product—something obvious to anyone who has ever tasted the product.

Consumer reaction ranged from skepticism to outrage. The Center for Science in the Public Interest sent a letter to the FTC calling the ads "outrageous" and urged government action. Their complaint included the charge that basing the numbers on single-piece servings simply was not realistic for many consumers.

In previous cases, the FTC has used the "net impression" test to determine if the totality of the ad—words, pictures and disclaimers—is misleading to the consumer. While the FTC allows "puffery" in advertising (such as ads claiming that KFC tastes "best" even in the absence of empirical evidence), ads may not be misleading.

Early indications were that the FTC would focus on the disclaimers and whether they could be easily read. At least one partner in a New York law firm specializing in advertising law told *The Wall Street Journal* that because the health claims are intentionally vague, it might be difficult to prove that they were misleading.

Micro Issues

1. Given the fact that these ads fly in the face of all conventional dieting wisdom, is it plausible that the average American would be convinced by these ads to begin eating KFC's Original Recipe fried chicken to lose weight? Should the government have to prove that in order to make KFC stop the ads?
2. By comparing one poor dietary choice—fried chicken—favorably to a poorer dietary choice—a Burger King Whopper—which parts of the TARES test, if any, are being violated?
3. Is the standard for an "ethical ad" simply one that doesn't mislead or should there be a higher standard? If so, what would that standard be?

Midrange Issues

1. These ads featured models as regular people—two friends, a couple—who are discussing chicken in a living room setting. If the ads had featured actors as doctors, pharmacists, or some other trusted health care authority, possibly wearing lab coats, would that have crossed any legal or ethical line?
2. Does the inclusion of small printed disclaimers about the spoken and visual claims absolve the company from charges of misleading consumers?
3. Does the fact that few consumers eat only one piece of chicken at a sitting and virtually none peel the skin off before eating prevent KFC from ethically basing its health claims on those serving choices?
4. Many advertising critics argue that it's the total number of messages—rather than individual messages—that matter. Should ethical thinking on this issue consider the totality of the messages rather than individual ads?

Macro Issues

1. The ads featured normal-sized models. Given the percentage of Americans who are overweight, and especially the percentage of fast-food patrons who are overweight, should at least one of the four actors have been overweight? Would that have detracted from the message KFC was trying to send? What does this casting decision say about our nation's thinking on body image?
2. Advertising deals in "strategic ambiguity." By being less than specific about health claims or individual results, is KFC being cautious or being purposely ambiguous to stay out of court, or both?
3. Fast food has its place in American culture. In a time-starved culture, franchises such as KFC sell a product that is equal parts convenience and nutrition. It can be argued that in these ads, KFC simply wants people to feel good about choices they are already inclined to make. Should the FTC be using the finite resources of government to police these kinds of ads, especially when products such as dietary supplements have the potential to do real harm? Or should the FTC try to tackle both with equal vigor, even if one drains resources from the other? Justify your answer.

IV

Loyalty: Choosing Between Competing Allegiances

By the end of this chapter, you should:

- **understand why the articulation of loyalties is important in professional ethics.**
- **know Royce's definition of loyalty and at least one of the major problems with that conceptualization.**
- **understand how journalists' role in society provides them with an additional set of loyalties to consider.**
- **be familiar with and able to use the Potter Box as a justification model for ethical decision making.**

LOYALTY AS PART OF THE SOCIAL CONTRACT

Decisions involving loyalty occur routinely for media professionals. When journalists make a decision to air or not to air a story, they have decided to whom they will be loyal. When recording executives cancel the contract of a controversial artist to avoid a boycott, they have chosen a loyalty. Most ethical decisions come down to the question "To whom (or what) will I be loyal?"

The original discussion of loyalty in Western culture was written by Plato in *The Trial and Death of Socrates* (see Russell 1967). In Plato's *Phaedo,* Socrates bases his defense against the charges brought against him on his unwavering adherence, or loyalty, to divinely inspired truth. When asked by his accusers if he will stop teaching philosophy, Socrates responds:

> Men of Athens, I honor and love you: but I shall obey God rather than you, and while I have life and strength I shall never cease from the practice and teaching of philosophy, exhorting any one whom I meet. . . . For know that this is the command of God; and I believe that no greater good has ever happened in the State than my service to God.

While the word "loyalty" is not present in English translations of the *Phaedo,* the overall tone of the work is a tribute to loyalty, in this case a willingness to die for a cause. This willingness to make one of the ultimate sacrifices has troubled those who wrote about loyalty in subsequent centuries.

Social contract theorist Thomas Hobbes was the first major Western philosopher to assert that God did not have to be the focus of loyalty and that people could have competing loyalties. In his historic work on the theory of the state, *The Leviathan,* Hobbes asserted loyalty is a social act, that it is the core of the agreement that allows people to form the social contract that is the basis of political society. However, Hobbes, unlike Socrates, admitted loyalty has its limits. Loyalty to the ruler stops when continued loyalty would result in a subject's death. One has a higher loyalty to self-preservation in this instance than to the ruler. The turmoil surrounding U.S. involvement in the Vietnam War is a classic example of this type of conflict of loyalties.

Hobbes made two central alterations in the Socratic notion of loyalty. First, he emphasized its social nature. Second, he acknowledged that people could have more than one loyalty and might, at certain times, be forced to choose among them. These two elements, in addition to the original insights of Socrates and Plato, provide the basis of contemporary philosophical discussion of the concept.

THE CONTRIBUTIONS OF JOSIAH ROYCE

American theologian Josiah Royce, who taught at Harvard in the early 1900s, believed that loyalty could become the single guiding ethical principle. In *The Philosophy of Loyalty* (1908), Royce wrote, "My theory is that the whole moral law is implicitly bound up in one precept: 'Be loyal.'" Royce defined loyalty as a social act: "The willing and practical and thoroughgoing devotion of a person to a cause." Royce would be critical, therefore, of the stereotypical journalist found in Ben Hecht's *The Front Page*—a cynic of everything and everyone, a professional who gets a story at all costs and whose only loyalty is to himself. In Royce's view, loyalty is an act of choice. A loyal person, Royce asserted, does not have "Hamlet's option"—or the leisure not to decide. For in the act of not deciding, that person has essentially cast his loyalty.

Loyalty also promotes self-realization. Royce spent much of his academic career fascinated with what were then the new insights of Freudian psychology, and he viewed loyalty in a psychological and developmental light. As a person continued to exercise loyalty, Royce believed, he or she would develop habits of character that would result in systematic ethical action. Like other aspects of moral development, loyalty can be learned and honed, Royce believed.

Loyalty as a single ethical guide has problems. *First,* loyalty, incompletely conceived, can be bias or prejudice cloaked in misleading language. *Second,* few people maintain merely a single loyalty, and if loyalty is to become a guiding ethical principle, we need to develop a way to help distinguish among competing loyalties. *Third,* with the advent of a mass society, the entire concept of face-to-face loyalty has lost much of its power to compel ethical action. *Finally,* one of the most troubling questions arising from the concept of loyalty is whether an ethical person can be loyal to an unethical cause, for example racism or gender discrimination.

However, Royce suggested a way to determine whether a specific cause was worthy of loyalty. A worthy cause should harmonize with the loyalties of others within the community, which can be defined in a number of ways. For instance, the loyalty of the journalist should be in harmony with the loyalty of the reader. The loyalty of the advertising agency should not conflict with the loyalty of either its client or the consumer. Surely, loyalty to the concept of free and unfettered political discussion—the basis of modern democracy and journalism—would meet Royce's test of loyalty.

A true understanding of loyalty allows people to reject unethical causes, Royce believed. The true problem was not a poor choice of loyalties but failure to adhere to chosen loyalties: "The ills of mankind are largely the consequence of disloyalty rather than wrong-headed loyalty" (Royce 1908). The cause that is capable of sustaining loyalty, Royce noted, has a "super-individual" quality, one that is apparent when people become part of a community. A spirit of democratic cooperation is needed for Royce's view of loyalty to result in ethical action. For instance, advertising agencies are demonstrating an ethical loyalty when they view their role as providing needed information for intelligent consumer choice, but more often they opt for loyalty to the bottom line.

Royce's thought has been criticized on a number of grounds. First, some philosophers assert that Royce's concept of loyalty is simplistic and that the adoption of loyalty as a moral principle may lead to allegiance to troubling causes. For instance, the advertising copywriter who scripts distorted television spots about an opponent in the belief that she must get her candidate elected is demonstrating a troubling allegiance to a politician over the democratic process. Similarly, a reporter who must get the story first, regardless of its completeness or accuracy, would be demonstrating a misplaced loyalty to the professional ideal of the scoop.

Second, others have noted that Royce provides no way to balance among conflicting loyalties other than his assertion that loyalty to a particular cause should evoke a similar response in others. Who the others are, in this case, becomes an important question. The executive producer who relegates all but the most important foreign news to the end of the broadcast because Americans aren't interested in hearing about activities in other nations may have an excessively narrow definition of whom the viewers are concerned about.

Third, it is unclear how Royce's ethical thinking would balance majority notions against minority views. Royce's notion of loyalty could inspire adherence to the status quo or strict majority rule. For instance, advertisements that stereotype groups of people despite evidence to the contrary help perpetuate incorrect images. The ads work because they appeal to the majority, but by stereotyping they have crowded out more accurate impressions.

Yet despite these criticisms, Royce's thought has much to recommend it. First, Royce speaks to the development of ethical habits, something most modern ethical theorists believe is necessary for continuing ethical behavior. Second, Royce reminds us that the basis of loyalty is social, and loyalty requires we put others on an equal footing with ourselves. In this sense, his view of ethics is not a purely rational one, but one that is founded in a concept of relationships. When you acknowledge loyalties, you are also acknowledging that things could have been otherwise. Most important is the overriding message of Royce's work: *when making ethical choices, it is important to consider what your loyalties are and how you arrived at those loyalties.* We believe this is particularly pertinent when people are acting in a professional role in a society that has given the profession both rights and responsibilities.

JOURNALISM AS A PROFESSION

Loyalty is not a fixed point but a range within a continuum. In *Loyalty: An Essay on the Morality of Relationships,* George Fletcher identifies two types of loyalty. The first is minimal loyalty: "Do not betray me." The second is maximum loyalty: "Be one with me." Between these two poles is a range of possibilities for allegiance and for corresponding media behavior. The location on the continuum for *Spy* magazine will differ from that of *The Nation* magazine.

One of the problems modern news media face is that a large percentage of the U.S. public subscribes to the notion that if the media are not maximally loyal—that is, one with government, the military and so forth—then they are traitorous. The media have been called disloyal by more than one politician on the election trail, often for no greater sin than fulfilling the watchdog role. Fulfilling this role puts the journalist, and their media outlets by extension, on trial in the court of public opinion. For instance, in the summer of 2003, as journalists called for the Bush administration to provide proof that Iraqi dictator Saddam Hussein had possessed weapons of mass destruction, polls showed that Americans were willing to give the president the benefit of the doubt in the absence of the weapons, even though their supposed existence was one of the primary reasons Americans went to war with Iraq.

Loyalty can be linked to one's role. A role is a capacity in which we act toward others. It provides others with information about how we will act in a structured situation. Some roles are occupationally defined—account executive, screenwriter, editor. Others are not: mother, spouse, daughter. We all play multiple roles, and they help us sort out situations and know what to expect from others.

When the role you assume is a professional one, you add ethical responsibilities. Philosophers claim that "to belong to a profession is traditionally to be held to certain standards of conduct that go beyond the norm for others" (Lebacqz 1985, 32), and journalism qualifies as one of those professions with a higher expected norm of conduct.

However, not all journalists agree in practice. Hodges (1986) makes the distinction in this manner: When asked what she does for a living, one journalist says, "I am a journalist" while another says "I work for the *Gazette.*" Hodges claims the first speaker is a journalist who recognizes her responsibility as a professional while the latter merely acknowledges her loyalty to a paycheck. The first would be expected to be loyal to societal expectations of a journalist, the second may or may not.

Journalists and their employers have debated whether journalism should be considered a profession. For some, the concept of professionalism itself is not inherently positive. Advocates of professionalism assert that professionalism among journalists will provide them with greater autonomy, prestige and financial rewards. Critics see the process of professionalization as one that distances readers and viewers from the institutions that journalists often represent.

Despite these debates, we intuitively sense that journalists have two central responsibilities that are distinct because of the role journalists play in modern society. First, they have a greater responsibility to tell the truth than members of most professions. Second, journalists also seem to carry a somewhat greater obligation to foster political activity than the average person.

Philosophers note that while specific ethical dilemmas are transitory, roles endure. Role expectations carry over from one situation to another. Most of the time, loyalty to the profession means loyalty to the *ideals* of the profession. To Aristotle, loyalty to a profession also would mean being loyal to and maintaining high professional standards. The Aristotelian notion of virtue means being the best television producer or advertising executive you can be in the belief that you are being loyal to the profession and its abstract ideals.

CONFLICTING LOYALTIES

As the foregoing discussion indicates, we are no longer talking about merely a single loyalty. We live in an age of layers of loyalties, creating added problems and complications.

Sorting through competing personal and professional loyalties can be difficult, particularly when loyalties in one role appear to conflict with the loyalties of another. However, those concerned with professional roles and the loyalties they generate have done some thinking about this issue. We have adapted one such framework from William F. May, who outlined these layers of loyalties for college professors. We suggest a similar approach for those who work in the media.

1. Loyalties arising from shared humanity:

   - demonstrate respect for each person as an individual.
   - communicate honestly and truthfully with all persons.
   - build a fair and compassionate social and cultural environment that promotes the common good.

2. Loyalties arising from professional practice:

   - fulfill the informational and entertainment mission of the media.
   - understand your audience's needs.
   - strive to enhance professional development of self and others.
   - avoid the abuse of power and position.
   - conduct professional activities in ways that uphold or surpass the ideals of virtue and competence.

3. Loyalties arising from employment:

   - keep agreements and promises, operate within the framework of the law and extend due process to all persons.
   - do not squander your organization's resources or your public trust.

- promote compassionate and humane professional relationships.
- foster policies that build a community of ethnic, gender and socioeconomic diversity.
- promote the right of all to be heard.

4. Loyalties arising from the media's role in public life:

- serve as examples of open institutions where truth is required.
- foster open discussion and debate.
- interpret your professional actions to readers and viewers.
- serve as a voice for the voiceless.
- serve as a mirror of society.

The problem of conflicting loyalties is evident in the media employment reality of today. Most media practitioners work for a corporation. They owe at least some loyalty to their corporate employers. However, such loyalty is tenuous because it seldom involves a face-to-face relationship. Modern corporations often demand employee loyalty but are much less willing to tell employees their corporate loyalties or responsibilities. These mutually understood promises are essential to corporate loyalty, where the fear is that one's allegiance to the organization will advance the interest of the organization without reciprocal loyalty to the employee.

In the final analysis, most ethical decisions are not about loyalties to corporations or abstract concepts such as freedom of the press. They are about how you treat the subject of your interview or the consumer of your advertising. An element that is essential in such ethical decisions is the notion of *reciprocity.* Simply articulated, reciprocity requires that loyalty should not work against the interest of either party.

Copyright © Ed Stein. Reprinted with permission of Rocky Mountain News.

Even in an era of sometimes shifting loyalties, there are some loyalties that should only be most reluctantly abandoned. We recommend you give further consideration to two of them: loyalty to humanity and loyalty to truth. *Virtually no situation in media ethics calls for inhumane treatment or withholding the truth.* Maybe you can think of other loyalties you would rarely, if ever, break. Even if you can't devise a list of every conceivable conflict of loyalties, knowing where your ultimate loyalties lie isn't a bad place to start.

THE POTTER BOX

In Chapter I, you learned an ethical decision-making model developed by Sissela Bok, one that could help you make an ethical choice. In this chapter, you will learn a second decision-making model, one that incorporates articulation of loyalties into the reasoning process. The model was developed by Harvard theologian Ralph Potter and is called the Potter Box. Its initial use requires that you go through four steps to arrive at an ethical judgment. The case below will help familiarize you with the model.

> You are the assistant city editor for a newspaper of about thirty thousand circulation in a western city of about eighty thousand. Your police reporter regularly reports on sexual assaults in the community.
>
> While the newspaper has a policy of not revealing the names of rape victims, it does routinely report where such assaults occurred, the circumstances surrounding the attack and a description of the assailant, if police can provide it.
>
> Tonight the police reporter is preparing to write a story about a rape that occurred in the early-morning hours yesterday on the roof of the downtown bus station.
>
> Police report that the young woman who was raped went willingly to the roof of the bus station with her attacker. Although she is 25, she lives in a group home for the educable mentally handicapped in the city. She is one of seven women living in the facility.
>
> She could not describe her assailant, and police have no suspects.
>
> Your reporter asks you for advice about how much detail, and what detail, he should include in the story.

The Potter Box has four steps (see Figure 4.1) that should be taken in order. They are (1) understanding the facts, (2) outlining the values inherent in the decision, (3) applying relevant philosophical principles and (4) articulating a loyalty. You proceed through the four steps in a counterclockwise fashion, beginning with the factual situation. We will examine each step individually.

Facts	**Loyalties**
Values	**Principles**

FIGURE 4.1. The four steps of the Potter Box

Step One: Understanding the facts of the case. In the scenario, the facts are straightforward. You, the newspaper editor, have the information. Your ethical choice rests with how much of it you are going to print.

Step Two: Outlining values. "Values" is a much abused word in modern English. People can value everything from their loved ones to making fashion statements. In ethics, however, values takes on a more precise meaning. In this sense, when you value something—an idea or a principle—it means you are willing to give up other things for it. If, as a journalist, you value truth above all things, then you must sometimes be willing to give up privacy in favor of it. In the foregoing case, such a value system would mean that you would print every detail, because you value truth, and would risk invading the privacy of a person who is in some important ways unable to defend herself. If, as a journalist, you value both truth and privacy, then you may be willing to give up some truth, the printing of every detail, to attempt to preserve the victim's privacy.

Values often compete, and an important element of using the Potter Box is to be honest about what you really do value. Both truth and privacy are lofty ideals. Less lofty, most of us value keeping our jobs. Journalists often value getting the story first. A forthright articulation of all the values wrapped up in any particular ethical situation will help you see more clearly the choices that you face and the potential compromises you may or may not have to make.

Step Three: Application of philosophical principles. Once you have decided what you value, you need to apply the philosophical principles outlined in the first chapter. For example, in the previous scenario, a utilitarian might argue that the greatest good is served by printing a story that alerts the community to the fact that some creep who rapes women who cannot defend themselves mentally or physically is still out there. Ross would argue that a journalist has duties both to the readers and to the victim, and they must be weighed before making a decision.

Aristotle's golden mean would counsel a middle ground that balances printing every detail against printing no story at all. Kant would suggest that the maxim of protecting someone who cannot protect herself is a maxim that could be universalized, making a decision to omit some information justifiable.

In this case, application of several ethical principles leads to the same general conclusion: the newspaper should print some story, but not one that inadvertently reveals the victim's identity or that makes her out to be hopelessly naïve in her trust of strangers.

However, you should be alert that while application of different ethical principles in this scenario leads to the same conclusion, other ethical dilemmas may not produce such a happy result. This is precisely why use of the Potter Box demands the application of more than one ethical principle, for if ultimate judgments may vary, you need to be able to explain why.

Step Four: Articulation of loyalties. Potter viewed loyalty as a social commitment, and use of the Potter Box will reflect that sort of ethic. In the fourth step, you need to articulate your loyalties—and to decide whether any of them conflict. In the foregoing case, you may have a loyalty to telling the truth, to alerting the community to a potential danger, to protecting individual privacy, or to doing your job well. Again, in this case, your loyalties are not in severe conflict with one another unless you adopt an absolutist view of the truth the community needs to know. It is possible to counsel your reporter to write a story that tells the truth but omits some facts (for example, the woman's residence in a group home and her mental retardation), alerts the community to a danger (there's a creep out there who police haven't caught), protects the victim's privacy (you won't print her name or where she lives), and allows you to take pride in the job you've done (you've told the truth and not harmed anyone).

However, use of the Potter Box often highlights a conflict between loyalties. In these instances, we refer you to Royce's conception of loyalty itself. What you choose to be loyal to should be capable of inspiring a similar loyalty in others who are both like and unlike you. Journalists are often accused of being "out of touch" with their viewers or readers, and it is at precisely this point of idiosyncratic loyalties that the profession is most highly criticized. Nowhere was that more evident than in the Persian Gulf War, when the majority of the press chafed at military restrictions out of a loyalty to freedom of the press, yet the majority of the public didn't care about the sanctions—demonstrating a loyalty to patriotism instead. However, you should be warned that loyalties are not subject to popular opinion, and that you might often hold unpopular loyalties in your particular professional role in society.

Our experience with the Potter Box has been that the vast majority of ethical decisions will allow you to sustain a variety of loyalties. Those decisions that are truly most troubling are ones in which loyalty to one particular cause or principle becomes so dominant in your reasoning process that you are forced to abandon a variety of other loyalties that once seemed quite essential to you.

While you may initially find the stepwise process of the Potter Box somewhat cumbersome, as you learn to use it you will become fluent in its application. You may also discover that you can go through the Potter Box on different levels of abstraction.

The following case study, "The Pimp, the Prostitute, and the Preacher," illustrates how you might use the Potter Box when making an ethical decision.

The Pimp, the Prostitute, and the Preacher

You are the court reporter for a daily newspaper in a city of about 150,000 in the Pacific Northwest. About a year ago, the local police force began to crack down on prostitutes working the downtown mall. However, the stated goal of the department's activities was to limit prostitution by arresting pimps—men who make money from prostitutes—rather than by arresting either the prostitutes or their customers. The first of those arrests has now come to trial, and your paper has assigned you to cover the story on a daily basis.

In his opening statement, the local assistant district attorney tells the jury that in order to convict a person of pimping under state law, the state must prove first that money was exchanged for sexual favors, and second that the money was then given to a third party, the pimp, in return for protection, continued work, etc. During the first two days of the trial, he calls as witnesses four young women, ages 14 to 16, who admit they have worked as prostitutes in the city but are a great deal less clear on the disposal of their earnings. Your story after the first day of the trial encapsulates the police activities, the prosecutor's goals in the case and the public testimony of two of the young women without disclosing their names.

Near the end of the second day in the trial, the prosecuting attorney begins to call as witnesses men who say they paid one or more of the four young women to have sex with them. Among those who testify is a middle-aged man who in an almost inaudible response to a question lists his occupation as a minister at one of the more conservative Protestant churches in the city. He admits to having paid one of the young women for sex, and that day's portion of the trial ends soon after his testimony is complete.

About 45 minutes later you are back in the office to write the story of that day's testimony when the newsroom secretary asks you if you have a few minutes to speak with "Reverend Jones." The name itself doesn't register, but you look up and realize you are facing the minister who testified earlier in the day. In the open newsroom he begs you, often in tears and at one point on his knees, not to print his name in your story. He even holds out a copy of the story you wrote, which appeared on page one of this morning's paper, outlining why the names of the prostitutes had not been used. He asserts that, should a story with his name appear, his marriage will crumble, his children will no longer respect him and he will lose his job.

After a few minutes and a whispered conversation with the newsroom secretary, the paper's managing editor realizes what is happening and calls you, the minister and the news editor into his office for a conference. What do you say?

Using the Potter Box, determine how you would report this story. Your decision will reflect a set of loyalties as well as the values and principles you have chosen. Others may choose differently. A justification model such as Potter's or Bok's (introduced in Chapter I) does not eliminate differences. What it will do, ideally, is ensure that your choices are grounded in sound ethical reasoning.

When you are finished, the final casting of loyalties will inevitably create another fact for the first quadrant of the box. For instance, in this case, if the decision is to run the name, anything that might subsequently happen to the minister as a result—firing, divorce, even possible suicide—is now an additional "fact" for the first quadrant of the Potter Box. If you decide not to run the minister's name and his parishioners discover his indiscretion anyway, the loss of credibility the newspaper suffers from those who find out the name was withheld is also a "fact" to be entered into the first quadrant of the Potter Box. Considering these additional "facts" (even though they are at present hypothetical), you may want to go through the process again to see if your decision will remain the same.

Now that you've made a concrete decision about revealing the name of the minister based on the facts, we'd like to introduce you to additional facts. After you read them, go through the Potter Box again while focusing less on the minister and more on larger issues that affect how the story is written and how it is run in the newspaper. This time, think about the notions of stereotyping, how members of minority communities are portrayed in news reports and the idea of what exactly we mean by the journalistic watchwords "objectivity" and "truth."

As the trial continues, it becomes increasingly clear to you that there are other factors at work. In your largely Caucasian community, the only people arrested for pimping have been African-American. All the young women who work as prostitutes are Caucasian, as are the customers who testify. As far as prostitution goes, your Pacific Northwest version is relatively mild. There are no reports of drug use among the prostitutes and their customers, and none of the prostitutes has complained of physical violence. Further, the prosecuting attorney cannot make any of the young women admit under oath that they ever gave the pimps any money. The jury verdict in this case is not guilty.

Do the new facts change your loyalties articulated in the first application of the model to the facts?

We recommend that you try using both the Bok and Potter justification models at various times in your ethical decision making. Becoming a competent practitioner of both methods will provide you with greater flexibility and explanatory power. We also recommend, regardless of the approach you use, that an unvarnished and critical discussion of loyalty becomes part of your ethical dialogue. We believe it will enable you to anticipate situations as well as react to them.

Suggested Readings

FLETCHER, GEORGE P. 1993. *Loyalty: An essay on the morality of relationships.* New York: Oxford University Press.

FUSS, PETER. 1965. *The moral philosophy of Josiah Royce.* Cambridge, MA: Harvard University Press.

HANSON, KAREN. 1986. "The demands of loyalty." Idealistic Studies, 16, pp. 195–204.

HOBBES, THOMAS. 1958. *Leviathan.* New York: Bobbs-Merrill.

OLDENQUIST, ANDREW. 1982. *"Loyalties". Journal of Philosophy,* 79, pp. 173–93.

POWELL, THOMAS F. 1967. *Josiah Royce.* New York: Washington Square Press, Inc.

Cases on the Web

"She chose before losing the choice" by Tom Lyons
"Standing behind a reporter: The CBS/*News Journal* Controversy" by John Sweeney
"The anchor as activist" by Fred Bales
"The wonderful world of junkets" by Ralph Barney

CHAPTER IV CASES

CASE IV-A
"Where Everybody Knows Your Name: Reporting and Relationships in a Small Market"
GINNY WHITEHOUSE
Whitworth College

Everybody is a source when you're covering an agricultural town with a population under 12,000.

But Sunnyside Police Sergeant Phil Schenck had not been a source for Jessica Luce when he asked her out for a date during a Halloween party in 1999. Luce had worked as a general assignment reporter at the *Yakima Herald-Republic* for almost a year. Sunnyside, Washington, was one of four communities she covered in this first job out of college. The two spent time together infrequently over the next two months.

"I was interested in him, we had fun, but if I had been asked what was going on I would have said we were friends," Luce said.

Nonetheless, a co-worker was incredulous. Luce remembers him saying, "You can't go out on a date with a source. It's one of the biggest taboos in journalism!"

The *Herald-Republic*'s four-page code of ethics advises staff to avoid conflicts of interest and to disclose those that are unavoidable. Prohibition of gifts and free travel is clearly explained. However, no specifics are given describing personal relationships that might cause conflicts of interest.

Luce decided to keep her relationship with Schenck, however it might be defined, quiet. Even with all the police stories she had written, she had never needed Schenck as a source and never thought the occasion would arise.

Schenck's boss, however, was another matter. Sunnyside Police Chief Wallace Anderson had been accused of shooting a great blue heron outside the police station, storing explosives at the station house and of having a threatening temper. Following a lengthy and expensive investigation, Anderson resigned in November.

By New Year's Day, Luce and Schenck decided they were definitely dating. "I kept my relationship under wraps save for a few confidants at work. I felt the relationship would be perceived as something wrong," Luce said. "But I didn't see it interfering with my job. Phil and I didn't talk about work as much as normal couples might. We knew it wasn't fair to either one of us."

In mid-February, Schenck was named acting captain, giving him the number two position in the Sunnyside police department and making him the official media spokesman. Luce realized she needed to be pulled off the Sunnyside police beat immediately. Her editors agreed.

"It was hard to talk with them about my private relationship, and I was forced to define things about the relationship that I hadn't even done for myself," Luce said.

Craig Troianello, her city editor, sat her down for a long conversation. "Jessica made it easy because she was straightforward. We didn't ask intimate questions— that's irrelevant in this case," Troianello said. "By taking the proactive ethical stand that she did, it was easy for us to deal with this."

Luce said Troianello emphasized that his concern did not mean he was questioning her integrity. However, he had to make sure he hadn't overlooked something that could be perceived as a conflict by readers.

"This was a lesson on perception versus reality," Luce said. Luce's reporting did not affect Schenck's promotion, nor had Schenck ever implied that a story should or should not have been covered. Nonetheless, Schenck benefited from the chief's departure.

Troianello said he was never worried that Luce's reporting was compromised, but he wanted to make sure the newspaper was above suspicion. "Issues involving the police department were in the forefront of the news," Troianello said. "People could read anything into it—that she was protecting the chief, that she was trying to bring the chief down. Those kinds of spins drove my concern."

On the other hand, Schenck questions whether a strict conflict-of-interest standard is realistic in a small town. "Everybody is a potential source—even the clerk at the grocery store. We eat food. If her husband or boyfriend is a farmer, you could say she is promoting eating. This is an ideal that might be somewhat impractical," Schenck said. "If you can't be a real person, how can you report on real people?"

Luce says if she had to do it all over again she would not have kept the relationship a secret as long as she did. Nonetheless, it would still be hard to talk to a supervisor about dating. Troianello said he understands the complexities of a journalist's personal life but would rather Luce had brought the relationship to the newspaper's attention by New Year's Day when the two began dating.

However, he understands the dynamic of the situation. "She's in a small town where the number of people with four-year degrees and professionals is small," Troianello said. "It seems like there will be some mixing at some point. Relationships could occur as naturally as it does in the newsroom. I married a copy editor."

Once their relationship went public (they were later engaged), Luce was surprised at how supportive the community and city officials were, including the new police chief (someone other than Schenck). "What we as journalists see as an ethical problem and conflict of interest isn't necessarily going to be seen as an ethical problem by the public."

However, Luce never heard comments one way or another from the former chief or his supporters. On several occasions, city officials have questioned whether Schenck leaked information to Luce or *Herald-Republic* reporters. Schenck simply explained that he had not. "I deal with stuff every day that Jessica would love to get her hands on," Schenck said. "But we just don't talk about it."

Luce now covers education in the city of Yakima.

Micro Issues

1. Did Luce have a responsibility to tell her editors about her relationship with Schenck? If so, when should Luce have informed them?
2. What responsibility did the *Yakima Herald-Republic* editors have to explain expectations on conflicts of interest? Is spelling out those expectations necessary or appropriate in a code of ethics?
3. How would the ethical questions have changed if Schenck worked in another capacity for the city, such as being a teacher?
4. How would the ethical questions have changed if Luce and Schenck had remained only friends?

Midrange Issues

1. What aspects of their lives should journalists be able to keep private?
2. Is public perception of an ethical problem truly relevant?
3. Journalists spend most of their time with two groups: their sources and their co-workers. Considering those limitations, is dating possible or advisable?
4. Recently, NBC *Dateline* correspondent Maria Shriver took a leave of absence as her husband, Arnold Schwarzenegger, ran a successful race for governor of California. As she returns to her duties, what limitations, if any, should be imposed on her reporting? Justify your decision.

Macro Issues

1. Can journalists cover communities effectively if they are expected to remain remote and removed?
2. How specific should codes of ethics be on conflicts of interest?

CASE IV-B
A Question of Role: Is a Documentary Filmmaker a Friend, a Journalist, or an Entertainer?
NANCY MITCHELL
University of Nebraska—Lincoln

In 1998 independent filmmaker David Sutherland wrote, produced, directed and edited a story about a young Nebraska farm couple, Juanita and Darrel Buschkoetter, and their three daughters. It is a riveting story of the family facing the dual hardships of trying to keep the family farm and the family intact. Taken from more than two hundred hours of film shot in rural Nebraska over a period of three years, Sutherland painted a portrait of the impact of the economic struggles of family life.

Sutherland interviewed forty families before he decided on featuring the Buschkoetters. During his initial stay with the couple, Sutherland said he showed the couple examples of his work so they knew what they were getting into. During the making of the film, neither Sutherland nor his crew ever became friends with the family. However, he said he did develop a friendship after the project wrapped up.

The series won much critical acclaim. The documentary was nominated for four Television Critics Association awards, including Program of the Year. The project also was included in many critics' list for Best of TV for 1998, including the *Chicago Tribune, TV Guide* and the *Boston Globe.* (David Sutherland Web site)

Steve Johnson, critic for the *Chicago Tribune,* said: "One of the extraordinary television events of the decade. 'The Farmer's Wife' is a breathtaking piece of work, a harrowing intimate love story set against an unforgiving physical and cultural landscape . . . [it] is bigger than just a farm story, offering lessons for a culture that acts as if poverty only occurs in inner cities, that piles up debt and ducks out by declaring bankruptcy, or that hits a rough patch in a marriage and scurries off to see a divorce lawyer."

Another rave came from David Bianculli, *New York Daily News,* who said: "It's a heavy viewing load, but certainly nothing compared to the trials and troubles, on the farm and in the home, thrown at Juanita and Darrel Buschkoetter. And watching 'The Farmer's Wife' is time very well spent: This is an honest, haunting, unflinching instructive and intimate study of a family that seems doomed to fail, but refuses to give up easily. 'The Farmer's Wife' has a coherent and compelling story worthy of a classic novel. (Four stars)."

Ron Miller of *The Oregonian,* wrote, "not until this week's 'The Farmer's Wife' has any filmmaker probed so deeply into the heart of an American family with such gut wrenching results. Sutherland's film ultimately gets at a truth about human relationships that surely will resonate through every household that tunes into 'The Farmer's Wife.' "

And tune in they did. The film attracted 18 million PBS viewers when it first aired in September 1998, according to Sutherland's Web site, making it one of the most watched series in PBS history. The six and one-half hour documentary aired in three segments. The first segment introduced viewers to the Buschkoetters, who tell the story (without the intrusion of a narrator) of the troubles they face both in their marriage and the risk of losing the farm after years of drought.

The second segment chronicles family life and the relentless challenge to make ends meet. At this point, the family is in danger of losing its farm. The loan officer, Hoy Bailey of the USDA, tells the Buschkoetters that they need to ask all the creditors for an extension. In one compelling scene Juanita drives at night to the office of one of the creditors, where she asks for a two-year extension. The creditor, Rich Kucera, listens to her and eventually agrees. The next scene finds Darrel in the kitchen of their home and Juanita arrives home to tell Darrel that Kucera has agreed, even if reluctantly, to extend their agreement. Darrel comments that he can't believe that Kucera was nice:

DARREL: "He wasn't even nasty?"
JUANITA: "No."
DARREL: "Richard, not nasty? That's a first. . . . I couldn't even imagine that guy being nice."

In the ensuing scene, Darrel calls Hoy Bailey. The loan officer tells Darrel that all of the extensions have been granted except for one for $100, and without that, they'll lose the farm in a buyout.

DARREL: "You mean $100 would cause a buyout?"
HOY: "Yep."
DARREL: "Don't you think that's a little bit ridiculous? I mean, if it had to be, I could go out and sweep a street and make $100 and eliminate a buyout."

In the next scene, the couple is working with Hoy and is apparently not in danger of losing the farm anymore. The second segment ends without the viewer knowing how the Buschkoetters resolved the financial questions.

The last episode depicts the resolution of their problems. Darrel harvests a bumper crop but suffers the stress of working his farm and another to make enough money to feed the family. After Darrel lashes out at his wife, Juanita takes their girls to her sister and leaves him. Juanita and the girls return after a week or so. Darrel seeks counseling, and the couple seems to be working things out. The Buschkoetters save their farm and their relationship through their hard work and commitment.

Sutherland describes himself as "a portraitist, not an investigative reporter. I'm not driven by the spectacular, the sensational, but I am interested in all the nuances of personality in making the portrait."

Sutherland said he crafted the film in such a way as to let family interactions and the family's interactions with outsiders tell the story. A narrator was never involved. Sutherland described the approach as "third person, close up, not first person, not omniscient." Sutherland said he had no agenda for the film but was concerned about the agendas those he interviewed might bring to the project. Sutherland said he is as concerned about those being filmed trying to use him to promote their agenda as he is with filmmakers' potential to use the subjects for their selfish gain.

Just how far would Sutherland go to observe a journalistic convention of not interfering with the subjects because that might change the story? "If someone's life were in the balance, I'd have come up with the money [to save the farm]." Sutherland saw himself in Juanita and Darrel; he said their dream of saving the family farm was parallel with his own dreams of creating a documentary that was not just a story about a farm family, but an intimate portrait with a social issue as a backdrop. To Sutherland, it was important to "talk to them [the subjects] from your heart, being an outsider and not taking advantage of them."

In the final episode, when Juanita left Darrel, Sutherland chose not to follow her even though Juanita gave him permission. Sutherland trusted the story could be told in another way at another time, and he eventually captured a summary of the event after the family was reunited.

Response to the series and the publicity led to opportunities for the Buschkoetters. They testified before Congress on the plight of the family farm; they traveled on publicity tours and gained experience from speaking engagements. Sutherland believes that the Buschkoetters' girls gained more self-esteem. Sutherland said he, too, was changed. He said the project "made me fall in love with America again. It was about people who tried their best. What more could you ask for?"

Micro Issues

1. If you were the producer, would you have lent the Buschkoetters the $100 if doing so meant they wouldn't lose the farm? What does it do to the story if you lend the money? What does it do to the story if you don't lend the money? What does it do to the family?
2. Would you answer the question differently if you were a news journalist working on an in-depth piece on the same subject?
3. Did Sutherland make the right decision about filming the marital breakup? How would you explain his decision to an editor, using concepts of professional excellence and the philosophy surrounding the issue of privacy?

Midrange Issues

1. When asked if he thought the personal rewards of creating a documentary might be construed as using people for personal gain, Sutherland responded: "I'm as uptight about them [subjects of his documentaries] using me." Evaluate this statement. Is this same tension prevalent in news journalism?
2. Sutherland describes himself as a portraitist, not an investigative reporter (e-mail, September 7, 2003). Do you think this gives him freedom to make different choices than he would had he claimed to be an investigative reporter?
3. Does having a camera present change the story? Do you think filming the meeting when Juanita asks the creditor for the extension on the loan changed the creditor's behavior? Does that matter?
4. When, if ever, can a journalist or documentarian become friends with those he has written about? What do you think a philosopher such as Kant or Ross would say about your response?

Macro Issues

1. Is it possible to produce a documentary from an objective point of view? What should be a guiding principle in creating this type of work?
2. Does a documentary need to conform to different ethical understandings then other entertainment forms—for example, reality television or a prime-time magazine show? Why?

CASE IV-C
Conflicted Interests, Contested Terrain: The *New York Times* Code of Ethics
BONNIE BRENNEN
Temple University

In January 2003 the *New York Times* broke a lengthy tradition and published its new ethics code on the Web. The *Times* decision was an important one, for ethics codes are one manifestation of what scholars such as Raymond Williams refer to as a "contradictory and conflict-ridden social history" of a specific culture (Williams 1981, 176). Using this approach, ethics codes can be an important marker of specific social practices created under particular social, economic and political conditions at distinct times in history.

For example, members of the American Newspaper Guild in 1933 crafted one of the first ethics codes developed by journalists rather than managers. That code suggested the "high calling" of journalism had been tarnished because news workers had been pressured by their employers to serve special interests rather than the public good. Conflict of interest was centered on the relationship between reporters and sources, and the code made a particular point that business pressures were putting undue stress on newsrooms, specifically the suppression of sensitive news and the "suppression of legitimate news concerning 'privileged' persons or groups, including advertisers, commercial powers and friends of newspapermen." The code recommended that to combat business pressures the news should be edited "exclusively in newsrooms."

Ethics codes in general are controversial among professionals and scholars. Some maintain that ethics codes are nothing more than generalized aspirations—too vague to be of any use when specific decisions must be made. Others insist codes can be helpful to beginning journalists, photographers and public relations practitioners; they provide some guidance in the form of rules that can be internalized as professional expertise and experience deepen. And still others agree with Williams; codes are a manifestation of the ideology of an era. They are more about power and politics than they are about ethics.

The new *Times* code linked its creation to the public perception of the "professional reputations of its staff member(s)." The code was directed to "all members of the news and editorial departments whose work directly affects the content of the paper."

The code focused primarily on issues of conflict of interest. In fact, the code did not mention accuracy and fairness and devoted only a single sentence to issues of privacy.

However, when addressing the issue of conflict of interest, the code was both specific and detailed. The *Times* code considered the impact that spousal relationships might have on news coverage. The *Times'* willingness to consider spousal relationships was an acknowledgment of the changing role of women in the workforce and the ethical issues that this social change raises. It also addressed whether journalists working abroad should abide by the ethics and mores of the countries in which they are stationed, most of which do not provide the equivalent of First Amendment protections.

The code required staff members to disclose yearly speaking fees in excess of $5,000, and prohibited staff members from accepting gifts, tickets, discounts or other "inducements" from organizations the *Times* covered. Staff members could not invest in companies they covered, and payment for favorable or altered coverage was specifically forbidden. However, staff members were allowed to do certain sorts of unpaid work—for example, public relations for a child's school fund-raising event. But, *Times* staffers were forbidden from giving money to candidates or causes, marching in support of public movements, or appearing on radio and television shows to voice views that went beyond those of the paper. When family members, such as spouses, participated in such activities, *Times* staffers were required to disclose those activities to management and recuse themselves from certain sorts of coverage.

The *Times* code was also protective of the newspaper's place in the marketplace. Staffers were prohibited from disclosing confidential information about the operations, plans or policies of the newspaper to other journalists. Such questions were to be referred to management. If readers asked such questions, *Times* staffers were encouraged to respond "openly and honestly." *Times* staff members also were prohibited from doing freelance work for any media outlet that competed with the *Times*. "Staff members may not appear on broadcasts that compete directly with the *Times'* own offerings on television or the Internet. . . . As the paper moves further into these new fields, its direct competitors and clients or potential clients will undoubtedly grow in number."

Like the earlier American Newspaper Guild code, the new *Times* code reflects the ongoing tension between economic realities and a social responsibility philosophical framework of traditional American journalistic issues. It may also be useful to consider Williams's notion that codes ironically suggest that a more complete understanding of the relationship between journalism practices and societies exists apart from the actual codes. The *New York Times'* attempt to codify specific relationships may actually work to obscure them.

Micro Issues

1. Should managers and owners be subject to a code of ethics, particularly for publications as influential as the *Times*?
2. Why is the notion of perception—as opposed to action—important in considering the issue of conflict of interest?
3. Should the *Times* code have addressed a variety of common journalistic issues—such as accuracy, fairness and privacy?
4. Evaluate the code of the American Newspaper Guild on these issues.

Midrange Issues

1. Disclosure is often suggested as a remedy for conflict of interest. Evaluate this remedy.
2. Should conflict of interest rules be different at a small newspaper or television station as opposed to the *Times*?

3. Does the *Times* code infringe on staffers' First Amendment rights? Do journalists give up some of their rights as citizens in order to do the work of journalism?

4. Are there instances when recusing oneself from an assignment is unsatisfactory? What should journalists do if such a case arises?

5. Should a conflict of interest extend as far as prohibitions against a journalist being an officer in the parent-teacher association (i.e., PTA or PTO) of his or her child's school? An officer in your local homeowners association? Does the potential for those organizations to get involved in the news pages (i.e., teacher problems, zoning protests) influence your decision?

Macro Issues

1. What are the specific historical developments in the field of journalism that may have promoted the development of this particular version of the *New York Times* code?

2. Research indicates that codes that are developed by the newsroom have a much better chance of influencing behavior than codes that are superimposed by management. If the *Times* had used this approach, would it have "discovered" the actions of reporters such as Jayson Blair (details of the Blair case may be found in Chapter II)? Should the development of codes include the potential for discovering wrongdoing?

3. Does the *Times* code place the organization's financial health in an equal footing with the public trust? Is that appropriate?

CASE IV-D
One Person's Tragedy, Another Person's Prize
PHILIP PATTERSON
Oklahoma Christian University

July 22, 1975, was a busy day for *Boston Herald* photographer Stanley Forman. Early in the day he climbed towers and rode elevators all over Boston to get pictures of the city's skyline for a Sunday magazine feature. During that time, he remained on call for other daily assignments.

After returning his film to the newspaper, he was hoping to leave for the day when a call came about a fire in one of the city's older sections of Victorian row houses. The dispatcher mentioned that some people might be trapped in the burning structure. Forman followed the fire engine to the scene and heard on his scanner an SOS ordering a ladder truck to the scene. When he arrived, he followed a hunch and ran down the alley to the back of the row of houses.

There he saw firefighter Bob O'Neil and two people, a 2-year-old girl and her 19-year-old godmother, on the fifth-floor fire escape. The fireman was calling for help from a fire truck below. The truck raised its aerial ladder to the trio. Forman climbed aboard the bed of the truck to get a better angle on what he anticipated would be a routine rescue.

Meanwhile the WBZ radio traffic helicopter had landed on the next roof, and the pilot was offering to take the child. Though he is visible in most of the photos, he never got a chance to help.

As Fireman O'Neil reached for the ladder of the fire truck below, there was a loud noise—either the sound of a scream or the shriek of metal bending. The fire escape gave way, sending the two victims falling and leaving O'Neil clinging for his life to the ladder. Forman saw it all through his 135 mm lens and took four photos as the two were falling, before turning away to avoid seeing them hit the ground. The woman, Diana Bryant, broke the fall of the girl, Tiare Jones, who survived. Bryant sustained multiple head and body injuries and died hours later.

O'Neil was shaken by the experience. "Just two more seconds. I would have had them," he said repeatedly. Though Forman took a few more pictures, he was shaking too much to hold the camera still.

Returning to the newspaper, he waited anxiously to see if he had the photos that he thought he had. When it was obvious he did, he stayed to help with some of the prints and went home, exhausted. At 8:00 P.M. he learned that Bryant had died. He wondered if the newspaper would still run the photos.

He saw the first morning edition of the paper shortly after 2:00 A.M. and was surprised to see that the key photo in the sequence (the one reprinted here) was printed on Page 1 and measured $11^{1}/_{12}$ inches by $16^{1}/_{12}$ inches—virtually the entire tabloid page. A full sequence of the four photos ran on Page 3.

By 4:00 A.M., Forman had made a set of prints for the Associated Press, which gave the pictures worldwide distribution that same day. Tearsheets on the photos came from 128 U.S. papers and several foreign countries.

Stanley J. Forman, Pulitzer Prize 1977. Used with permission.

Within 24 hours, action was taken in Boston to improve the inspection and maintenance of all existing fire escapes in the city. Fire-safety groups around the country used the photos to promote similar efforts in other cities.

Numerous awards came as well. The Pulitzer Prize committee gave Forman its 1976 news photo prize. The National Press Photographers Association named the photo Picture of the Year. Several other groups, including the Society of Professional Journalists, honored the photo as well. Forman went on to win the Pulitzer Prize again the following year, making him the only photographer to win consecutive Pulitzer Prizes for news photography. His awards earned him a Nieman Fellowship at Harvard and lecture engagements around the world.

Micro Issues

1. What are the rights of victims of a tragedy such as this one? Should they have protection from being photographed? Being interviewed?
2. Forman's instincts and resourcefulness enabled him to capture photos that no other photographer got. Is the exclusive nature of the photos a factor in whether to run them?
3. Forman said that when he heard Bryant had died, he assumed that the photos would not run. Should the death of one of the girls have affected the treatment of the photos?
4. Did the newspaper sensationalize the photo shown in this case by its size or placement?
5. Do the rights of the other people pictured—O'Neil and the helicopter pilot—enter into the decision of whether to use the photos?

Midrange Issues

1. Is the repair of aging fire escapes a morally justifiable reason for running the photos?
2. Many newspapers outside of Boston ran the photos as well. When the local news peg (the fire) is absent, what is the ethical reasoning for running the photos?

Macro Issues

1. Photos such as Forman's are often singled out for awards within the industry. In fact, more than half of all photos that have won the two major prizes in photojournalism have involved tragedy. Should one person's calamity be a photojournalist's good fortune?
2. Are prizes too important to the profession of journalism? Are they ethical in a field such as journalism?

CASE IV-E
Keeping Secrets: A Public Relations Dilemma
JAY BLACK
University of South Florida

Nancy B. is a public affairs officer in Jonesville for the city's largest employer, the National Steel Corporation (NSC). In her middle-management position she has access to her firm's immediate and long-range plans. She has attended a meeting of top management and the company's board of directors at which it was decided that economic conditions have made it absolutely necessary to close down permanently NSC's Jonesville plant. Factors include a glut of inexpensive, imported steel, which is diminishing the market for NSC's products, plus the government's insistence that the Jonesville plant's 40-year-old blast furnaces and scrubbers are environmental hazards that will cost $10 million to remedy.

Jonesville is in a sensitive economic position. It is a town of 20,000, located 80 miles south of the state's capital and economic center. There are few job possibilities for Jonesville's unemployed, who would probably have to sell their houses and move. Until a generation ago, the region was primarily agricultural, with only a moderate amount of manufacturing. After World War II, the NSC plant's growth changed the economic balance. The sons of farmers became ironworkers or developed skills in fields allied to the steel mill, and the numerous family farms were consolidated into several larger farms, with far fewer employment possibilities. Today, 3,000 people work at the NSC plant. The plant has paid decent wages, and most of its workers own their own homes in or around Jonesville.

Nancy B. is a single parent of two high school children. She owns her own home and has been saving money to send her children to a moderately expensive out-of-state college. She has a sister, Elizabeth, who is the mother of three children and works part-time as a real estate salesperson. Elizabeth is very excited about having five "hot" prospects for house sales in town; the deals should go through in about three weeks. Elizabeth's husband, Frank, has been employed by NSC for 15 years and now has a good-paying job as a shift foreman. Elizabeth and Frank have been very close to Nancy, especially since 10 years ago when Nancy's husband died in an industrial accident at the NSC plant.

At the board meeting where the decision was reached to close down the plant, arguments were made that a great deal of harm would come to the company—its reputation, its inability to fill a final set of orders for one last major contract and the response of the stock market—if word about the impending closure got out. All persons attending the meeting were asked to promise not to say anything to anyone about the closure, or to act in any way that would set off either rumors or a panic.

Nancy B. was among those who were told by top management that NSC would make every effort to secure equivalent employment for them at another division of the corporation. In her case, her immediate supervisor reminded her of how well the firm had treated her upon her husband's death a decade earlier: she had gone from secretary to executive secretary to public relations assistant to public relations officer in quick succession.

Micro Issues

1. Should Nancy protect herself by searching for a job and putting her home on the market?
2. Should she help Frank and Elizabeth by giving them the information?
3. Are her duties or responsibilities in this matter changed in any way by the fact that she is a single parent?

Midrange Issues

1. If Nancy acts out of loyalty to family and tells Elizabeth the news, can Elizabeth then claim the same loyalty to her clients who might need to sell their homes quickly? Do you see any difference in the situations?
2. What should Nancy do if she gets a call from the press attempting to confirm a rumor that the company is closing the plant and leaving?
3. Nancy will be offered a chance at another job and probably will get her relocation costs paid. Frank and Elizabeth, however, will not. Nancy has information that they need, but she badly needs to keep her job. Is she protecting her own comfort at their expense?

Macro Issues

1. The request to remain quiet about the move was unilateral: Nancy listened to the request but did not make a promise to abide by it. Does this silence free her to do as she pleases, or is it implied that she understood the request and agreed to abide by it? Can a duty be assumed by failure to object to it?
2. Is it ever justifiable to lie to the media? If so, under what circumstances?
3. If you were in Nancy B.'s position, can you think of arguments that would persuade management to be more forthright with employees? How would the concept of proactive public relations help or hurt in this regard?

V

Public Relations: Advocate or Adversary?

By the end of this chapter, you should be familiar with:

- **why the relationship between the media and public relations is both symbiotic and strained.**
- **how the concept of advocacy can provide an ethical justification for public relations.**
- **how public relations practitioners help news journalists function.**

JOURNALISM AND PUBLIC RELATIONS: THE QUINTESSENTIAL STRUGGLE

Public relations began as a profession in the late 19th century when newsmakers sought to find a way to get past journalism's gatekeepers to get their stories told. From simple press releases to elaborate publicity stunts (such as the "torches of freedom" march for women smokers envisioned by Edward L. Bernays in the early years of the 20th century) PR practitioners offered a way to unlock the gate and get stories into the newspapers for their clients. At the same time they offered "free" news to publishers. Consequently, any controversy surrounding public relations as a profession must be viewed in light of the alternative. If the more than 200,000 public relations professionals in the United States did not exist, many stories would go unreported.

Despite the occasional animosity between journalists and public relations practitioners, the relationship is truly symbiotic—they simply could not live without each other. No news organization is large enough to gather all the day's news without several public relations sources. Business pages are full of press releases on earnings, new product lines and personnel changes, all supplied by writers not paid by the media. Travel, entertainment and food sections of newspapers would be virtually nonexistent if not for press releases. On the other hand, the media provide the all-important audience for an institution that wants the publicity.

With this common need, why are the two professions sometimes at odds? Editors point their fingers at public relations practitioners who perceive their jobs in terms of the quantity (much) and the quality (favorable) of exposure they can get for their clients or causes. These practitioners, in turn, point to editors and reporters who come to each story with an agenda (a polite word for bias) that influences the outcome of the final story, usually in a manner unfavorable to the public relations professional's client. Much of the problem stems from how each of the two professions defines news. To the public relations professional, the lack of breaking news is newsworthy. Plants that operate safely and are not laying off any employees, nonprofit organizations that operate within budget and provide needed services, companies that pay a dividend for the 50th consecutive quarter are all signs that things are operating smoothly and make for a story that the public should hear.

However, to the journalist, news is a change in the status quo: a plant that pollutes, employees who embezzle, firms that go bankrupt—all are worthwhile news stories. Caught in the middle, the news consumer probably prefers a choice of both stories. However, shrinking "newsholes" (the amount of space available for news copy) and static amounts of airtime won't allow both, and the editorial bias is toward disruption more often than efficiency.

As the journalistic gap has grown between the two professions, public relations professionals have found it necessary to resort to staging events to get their good news on air or in newspapers. Such events—ribbon cuttings, press conferences, open houses, and the like—are a phenomenon Daniel Boorstin (1962) called the "pseudo-event." The timing, the staging and the location of a pseudo-event are set with the cameras in mind. Media owners, sensing a cost-efficient story with good visuals that fosters community goodwill, have historically been willing to attend (Epstein 1974).

An Associated Press story from Minneapolis illustrates the quintessential pseudo-event. The story announced that former University of Oklahoma law professor Anita Hill, who in 1991 publicly charged then Supreme Court Justice-elect Clarence Thomas with sexual harassment, would *not* be coming to Minneapolis. Advance publicity about her visit had generated so many donations for an endowed professorship in her name that Hill did not need to appear in person, said the promoters. In short, the publicity about the pseudo-event had made the real event unnecessary.

Pseudo-events can breed more pseudo-events. In April of 2003, Martha Burke, head of the National Council of Women's Organizations, made national news with a pseudo-event—a protest at The Masters golf tournament in Augusta over the all-male membership policies of the host course, Augusta National. The made-for-television event was largely deemed a failure due to the small turnout and refusal of Augusta National to change its policy. A few months later, Burke issued a press release saying she would *not* be returning to Augusta to protest in 2004, leaving editors in the curious position of having to decide whether it was newsworthy to announce that a pseudo-event *would not* happen.

Boorstin claims that as much as one-fourth of all news fits the pseudo-event scenario—events that would not have occurred or would have occurred differently if not for the presence of a camera, including such examples as bill and treaty signings, official send-offs, most press conferences, photo opportunities, and most demonstrations, sit-ins and strikes. Reporters and photographers don't always share their publisher's enthusiasm for these events for two reasons. First, they feel used. Second, reporters prefer stories that they research themselves to stories handed to them.

Public relations professionals often attempt to trade on the credibility of the news to advance their cause. A news story carries more clout with readers or viewers than does an advertisement. Although readers and viewers may not know the terminology, they have a sense that a media gatekeeper is at work screening stories of dubious reliability. When the public relations professional successfully places a story in the media, it has the credibility of having passed through the gate, a benefit of the doubt paid advertising does not receive.

Add to that the serendipity that the story is free and an ad is not, and the motivation is great for the public relations professional to attempt to influence the editorial content. This is done either by hyping an unimportant story or by putting the company's "spin" on a legitimate story, making sure that only the company line gets heard. With the stakes high—promotions, for instance, hang in the balance for those who continually get favorable coverage for their institutions—the chance for abuse is high as well.

Public relations professionals place a strain on news desks with their constant flow of news releases to the print and electronic media. As many as 90 percent of all press releases received are dumped by editors after a quick glance. Yet the flow of news releases continues virtually unchecked, since many organizations measure the effectiveness of a PR office by output, not publication. This system creates resentment on the part of the public relations professional whose articles never seem to be printed, and resentment from the editor who must sift through the mass of releases against the possibility of overlooking a usable one.

SELLING CANDIDATES, INDUSTRY AND WAR: A PROFESSION IS BORN

Public relations as a profession is a modern development based on a rationale as old as the ancient proverb affirming that "a good name is more desirable than great riches." And good names, just like useful symbols, are essential in politics.

Samuel John Adams recognized the value of using events or symbols to arouse emotion during the American Revolution. He used slogans like "Taxation without representation is tyranny," and he staged the Boston Tea Party. In the 1820s, Andrew Jackson's presidential campaign attempted to reach the common folk, using techniques that foreshadowed many public relations practices. Amos Kendall, a member of the famous "Kitchen Cabinet," was Jackson's pollster, counselor, ghostwriter and publicist. Though Kendall did not hold the title, he also served as the first presidential press secretary and congressional liaison. Matthew St. Clarke, though a political enemy of Kendall's (they clashed over the National Bank headed by St. Clarke), nonetheless learned from his adversary and used similar techniques to create the myths surrounding the historical figure Davey Crockett. Later, Edward Stanton, Abraham Lincoln's secretary of war, would initiate press techniques during the Civil War still in use today.

After decades of use in the political arena, attempts to influence public opinion moved to the private sector. This new wave of public relations was originally called "press agentry." One of its earliest and best practitioners was P. T. Barnum, who also exemplified the early attitude of press agents in his statement "There's a sucker born every minute." The public, under this notion, was both ignorant and monolithic in nature, easily seduced by a clever pitch.

The building of great business empires in the 19th century—sometimes referred to as "industrial trusts" run by robber barons—often angered the public and the press. Workers were beginning to organize themselves into unions and management, and the trusts were criticized by many. Journalists who reported on their often un-savory practices were called "muckrakers," a term coined by President Theodore Roosevelt. Their stories helped to spur public opinion to support trust-busting leg-islation, the Sherman Antitrust Act being the best known.

Beleaguered business leaders also turned to public relations to counteract what they viewed as negative news and, more importantly, impending government regu-lation. In 1889, George Westinghouse established the first corporate public relations department to wage a fierce struggle in the media with Thomas A. Edison over the relative merits of AC and DC electric current. Westinghouse won, and today we use alternating current in our homes. Other businesses followed Westinghouse's lead.

Ivy Lee, considered one of the founders of modern public relations, became pub-licity adviser to a group of U.S. coal mine operators beset by labor problems early in the 20th century. As a Pennsylvania Railroad employee, Lee pioneered the practice of giving the press full information about railroad accidents, bringing about new think-ing in public relations as a source of complete rather than one-sided information. Lee's efforts foreshadowed one of the dominant contemporary theories of public relations, the notion that public relations practitioners, their corporate employers and the pub-lic need to have an equal—or symmetrical—relationship (Grunig and Hunt 1984).

World War I forced the government into the public relations business. In 1917 Woodrow Wilson authorized the creation of the Committee on Public Information, headed by George Creel. The committee conducted a national campaign to mobilize public support for the war, to encourage enlistment in the armed forces and to pro-mote the sale of Liberty Bonds. World War II again brought the federal government into the public relations business. The Office of War Information (OWI) was founded in 1942 to once again act as a catalyst to recruit U.S. soldiers and factory workers and to find funding for the war. After the war the OWI became the United States Information Agency, a powerful tool for U.S. propaganda. One of the agency's responsibilities was and is the Voice of America radio broadcasts, sending news and features about the United States to the rest of the world.

By the 1990s, the government had turned high-tech, producing "news releases" on video and distributing them via satellites to television stations. For instance, when television news showed "smart bombs" hitting their targets during the first Persian Gulf War, the footage was produced by the military and the public relations firm of Hill and Knowlton (Safer 1992). Much of the video coverage of this first war against Iraq came courtesy of these military video news releases, commonly referred to as VNRs.

Following an exposé of the practice in *TV Guide,* the public relations industry created a "Code of Good VNR Practice for Video News Releases." Operating within the guidelines of the code would give the VNR packager a "seal of approval" to be affixed to the video. One of the main tenets of the code was that VNRs would have to be clearly identified by source. By the time of the 2003 war in Iraq, the Pentagon had retreated from its earlier position and allowed "embedded" journalists to follow troops into action.

Another manifestation that PR adapts to technology is seen in what Chris Mooney (2000) has dubbed "e-spin," canned attacks and counterattacks by political candidates delivered daily to the e-mail accounts of political reporters covering elections. Born in the closely contested Bush-Gore election in 2000, the phenomenon, like press releases and VNRs, adds one more tool to the PR arsenal of tools attempting to influence political coverage.

The founding of the Public Relations Society of America (PRSA) in 1948 was a major step in the professionalization of the field. Today, its ethics code is the professional standard. By the end of the 20th century, more than 2,000 PR firms operated in the United States, with many more around the world. The scope of public relations today is hard if not impossible to define, with no uniformly accepted simple definition of the craft or art of public relations. What is known is that thousands today work in a profession designed to "spin" or otherwise manipulate the news in favor of their clients. At the individual level, the goal of the profession is information acquisition, opinion change and often behavioral change. At the system level, public relations provides the media and the public with necessary assistance in the information and news-gathering process.

ADVOCACY IN AN ADVERSARIAL SOCIETY

Hegel argued that thesis and antithesis should produce synthesis—a coming together of ideas. And if democracy has a central philosophy it could be that society benefits when people of different thoughts arrive at collective judgments about public issues through public debate. It is perhaps illuminating to note that the partisan press was the predominant medium when the Constitution was written. And in the midst of this cacophony of one-sided and often virulent broadsides, the states ratified what we now call the First Amendment, which states that "Congress shall make no law respecting . . . freedom of speech." According to the Founders, speech need not be neutral or two-sided to be protected.

As the United States grew and diversified into a country of labor and management, urban and rural, rich and poor, and people of all races, inevitable conflicts grew. Because it was a land where every individual enjoys a right to "life, liberty, and the pursuit of happiness," and where the courts settled important disputes by the rule of law, many individuals and institutions decided they could function more effectively if they paid someone to "advocate" for their point of view.

The justice system has long recognized the need for each side to have an advocate to navigate the adversarial system of the courts. Landsman (1984) says the system requires a "zealous advocate." According to adversary theory, "when each actor performs only a single function the dispute before the court will be resolved in the fairest and most efficient way" (pp. 45–46). In the system, each advocate must find and present the most persuasive evidence and downplay that evidence that might be harmful to the client.

The original practitioners of public relations—Edward L. Bernays and Ivy Lee—both claimed to act as "lawyers in the court of public opinion." Their role, as they saw it and as most in the profession understand it today, was to win the battle for public opinion through targeted media messages. Often these messages presented a one-sided or highly selective point of view, but in a country where multiple opinions found a voice, such messages were viewed as ethical.

Does the claim to be similar to a lawyer in a court of law make the public relations professional an advocate for a client's truth or an adversary to media professionals who must find the truth about a client? Does a public relations professional, whose output might end up in the media and therefore influence public opinion, have any more right to be selective in that truth telling than journalists? Does the fact that the rules of the marketplace, or the legislature, differ from those of a courtroom mean that advocacy may be a good, but incomplete, guide to ethical behavior?

Those who support the advocacy model argue that any misleading information put out by public relations professionals will be somehow "self-corrected" by the gatekeepers of the media or by the self-righting "marketplace of ideas." Those who reject the advocacy model do so on two grounds: first, they assert that advocacy too easily morphs into distortion and lies; second, that the long-term health of many enterprises, from business to government programs, is ill-served by "spin" and better served by honest, timely communication—even at the expense of short-term losses.

This concept of telling the truth in times of crisis, or becoming an advocate for the long-term health of a particular client, has become one of the foremost professional principles for public relations practitioners engaged in crisis communication. The history of the field would suggest that businesses and agencies whose actions demonstrate that public health and safety are more important than short-term profits—in sum, telling the truth even when it hurts—are quite likely to profit substantially in the long term. That was the lesson that public relations practitioners learned a generation ago from Johnson & Johnson's handling of the "Tylenol scare," when seven people in the Chicago area died as a result of taking Tylenol capsules laced with cyanide. Johnson & Johnson voluntarily pulled the product off the shelves, reimbursed consumers who had purchased it but could no longer use it, and cooperated completely and openly with both government investigators and the media.

Less than two years after the incident, the result was that Tylenol's market share had increased and the corporation itself was trusted by the public. Contrast this set of actions with those of Firestone/Bridgestone's stonewalling over the recall of faulty tires on sport utility vehicles—and the long-term impact of those actions on corporate health. Public relations practitioners who advocate telling the truth in times of crisis can serve both their clients and the public without fear of compromising professional or personal ethics.

Deaver (1990) provides a useful tool (see Figure 5.1) in which he identifies four layers in a continuum of truth and the intent of those who practice it. At the top are those intending to inform, followed by those intending to persuade, followed by those who often intend to entertain, and finally by those who intend to deceive. It is

Message	**Intent**
TRUTH/truth	to inform accurately and fully
facts and information	with no apparent bias
journalistic news	
PR copy	an intent to persuade by using
editorials/columns	selective information; the truth
advertising copy	but not the whole truth
propaganda	
parables and allegories	nontruths told with no intent to
fiction	deceive
honest error	
deceit	intent to deceive, even if for a
"white lies"	purpose claimed to be justifiable
BLATANT LIES	

FIGURE 5.1. The continuum of truth

interesting to note that Deaver distinguishes between "TRUTH," which is absolute and usually derived from an ultimate source of authority, and "truth," which is the documentable facts and information we deal with every day.

Deaver's configuration puts public relations and advertising safely within the realm of what society deems acceptable behavior. Their purposes are distinct from those of their journalistic peers, but well above the level of deceit.

Hodges (1986) says that the notion of professional responsibility can be summed up in a single question: For what am I prepared to respond ably? In other words, what have my education and my experience equipped me to do and to assume responsibility for? Ask a public relations practitioner "To what are you ably equipped to respond?" and he or she might answer "To respond to a crisis for a client" or "To generate favorable media attention for a client." However, there are greater responsibilities.

Hodges further states that responsibilities come from three sources. First there are those that are *assigned,* such as employee to employer. Second there are those that are *contracted,* where each party agrees to assume responsibilities and fulfill them. Third there are the *self-imposed* responsibilities, where the individual moral actor takes on responsibilities for reasons indigenous to each individual. It is our contention that public relations, practiced ethically, will not only fulfill the assigned or contracted responsibilities with the employer or the paying client but also take on the greater calling of self-imposed responsibilities. These self-imposed responsibilities could include such constructs as duty to the truth and fidelity to the public's good. The more self-imposed responsibilities the PR professional assumes, the more ethical the profession will become as practitioners see their personal good as being synonymous with the public's good.

CONCLUSION

While the proliferation of news releases is a source of mild irritation between the professions of journalism and public relations, it is a minor nuisance compared to the differences in how the two sides approach "hard" news stories. Unfortunately, some public relations practitioners see their jobs not only as telling the good news about their company but also as keeping the bad news from being told. This stand-off results in the perpetuation of a vicious cycle. Business executives perceive that the press is out to "get" them, so they refuse to speak, while the press perceives that a corporation has something to hide by its silence.

Public relations began as a profession when certain newsmakers wanted more media coverage. Today because of what business perceives as a negative bias, many public relations professionals are used as dissemblers of legitimate stories. Some businesses have found it expedient to refuse to cooperate with the media, and some have extended the policy to all employees. For instance, one major retailer does not even allow its managers to grant interviews about the expected best-selling toys for the upcoming Christmas season. Though this policy seems a bit extreme in a Christmas feature story, it is based on the assumption that most of the time the media will want information that will harm a business.

The average news consumer rarely observes this constant struggle for control over the content of the news, yet he or she is affected by it. How should we evaluate a profession with the goal of persuading in a manner that does not look like traditional persuasion or the goal of preventing the dissemination of information that might harm the illusion that has been created?

Practitioners in the field justify their profession with the following arguments: First, the stories they attempt to tell are the unreported or the underreported stories of products that work, employees who are honest, and corporations that are good community citizens. Second, the rules are set by the other players in the game—the media. Finally, if the media would ever agree that good news *is* news, the animosity and duplicity might diminish.

Suggested Readings

BOORSTIN, DANIEL. 1962. *The image.* New York: Atheneum.
CUTLIP, SCOTT. 1994. *The unseen power: Public relations—a history.* Hillsdale, NJ: Lawrence Erlbaum Assoc.
HODGES, LOUIS. 1986. "Defining press responsibility: A functional approach." In D. Elliott (ed.), *Responsible journalism.* (pp. 13–31). Newbury Park, CA: Sage Publications, Inc.
VONNEGUT, KURT. 1952. *Player piano.* New York: Dell Publishing Co.

Cases on the Web

"Handling the media in times of crisis: Lessons from the Oklahoma City bombing" by Jon Hansen
"Public relations role in the Alar scare" by Philip Patterson
"A case of need" by Deni Elliott

CHAPTER V CASES

CASE V-A
Quit, Blow the Whistle, or Go with the Flow?
ROBERT D. WAKEFIELD
Wakefield Communications

Anyone who spends sufficient years in public relations will face a crisis of conscience. Practitioners are trained for the tenuous task of balancing institutional advocacy with the "public interest" (Newsom, Turk and Kruckeberg 1996). Yet this role can lead to personal conflict, as it did in my case.

The setting was an urban school district with about 40 schools and more than 35,000 students. Its superintendent had a national reputation for innovative community outreach, and he was a media favorite. I worked with him for five years before he accepted a statewide position. His replacement was a quiet man with conservative views who, along with the administrative team he brought with him, believed that educators were trained to run the schools and could do so best with minimal interference.

Like most inner-city school districts, the system was losing students as people moved to the suburbs. In the previous decade, a student population that once filled four high schools could now fill only three.

The seven-member school board had approached—and then abandoned—the question of closing one of the schools because the proposal aroused such strong feelings among students, faculty and parents. However, the new administration, trying to balance those responses against the financial drain of supporting an additional high school on taxpayer dollars, decided to broach the question again.

Promised a tumultuous situation, the new administrators aggravated the problem by how they handled it. Rather than sharing the issue with the community or with school faculties to seek a mutually agreeable solution, they tried to resolve the entire problem behind closed doors.

I first learned about the closed-door approach at a "study meeting" with the school board. The new superintendent held these informal meetings during his earliest days in the district; they tended to be so boring and ambiguous that journalists seldom attended.

Before the meeting in question, the superintendent asked me whether any media would be present. I told him one reporter might come late. As the meeting began, I was surprised to hear him tell the board and the few staff members, "If any reporter shows up, I will change the subject—but today we're going to talk about closing a high school." He then outlined the results of meetings he had already held on the issue, discussed a proposal from a local community college to buy the building so it would not be abandoned and sought the support of the four high school principals.

Thus began my ethical conundrum. I agreed that the enrollment problem was serious and that closing a school was probably the best alternative, but I opposed the administration's method of resolving the issue. As public relations officer, I believed that public institutions must be open and that involving those affected by the closure in the actual decision-making process would eventually generate long-term support for whatever decision was made. I was appalled at the attempts to exclude the public; but I said nothing.

Closed doors can quickly swing ajar, and it took less than one day for news of the decision to leak. The school targeted for closure was one of the oldest in the state. It had recently received a U.S. Department of Education award as an exemplary inner-city school, but its community was the least affluent and arguably the least politically powerful.

The day after the "study session," and with a regular board meeting scheduled for the same evening, reporters called to verify what they were hearing. (Chief executives often forget that supervisors of individual units within the system have their own allegiances. In this case, one of the high school principals left the "study meeting" and informed his teaching staff that they would be receiving transfer students "from that inner-city school." The rumors began.)

After the phone calls, I asked the superintendent what he planned to say at the board meeting and was told, "We will discuss space utilization needs." I told him about the calls and that our jobs would be threatened if we were not truthful with the community. To his credit, he responded quickly and openly. The evening meeting unfolded as expected. The room was jammed with district patrons and with the media. The expected lines were drawn. Underlying the fervor was a common theme: closing a traditional high school was awful enough, but the secretive way in which the administration had reached its conclusions was unforgivable.

The next several weeks were an intense period of work for a young public relations officer. I did media interviews, talk shows, and forums to explain the situation. I also met with dozens of teachers, parents and citizens, both to hear their comments and to take their suggestions. I had to be careful that my words represented the district instead of myself. I had worked with some local reporters for several years and felt comfortable giving them background so they could seek additional materials without revealing me as the original source. It was a personal risk, but the reporters never betrayed my trust.

Two additional incidents epitomized my ethical struggles. The first occurred after the initial board meeting, when a top administrator said the community misunderstood why decisions were made behind closed doors. I lobbied for openness. The administrator admonished me to remember who paid my salary, a rebuke that confirmed the new administration did not share my own values.

The second incident occurred when I was asked to meet with a man who had been chosen to speak on behalf of the community. I had taken only a few steps into his office when he said to me, "You don't agree with your administration, do you?" My response was silence while he explained his position.

For some reason, it was this encounter that forced my crisis of conscience: Do I quit, blow the whistle, or keep quiet? I had a wife and child to support; the employment picture at the time was not robust. Right or wrong, I surmised that the various relationships I had developed could appease many angry feelings. I also believed in the importance of education. So, I decided to stay through the crisis, then seek new employment.

About one month into the crisis, the board retained a consultant who, like me, believed in open communication. Two weeks later, four board members came to my office and requested a meeting. Because this constituted a majority of the board, such an assembly violated the law requiring the meeting be made public. I violated the law and invited them to stay. They said they were worn down by the constant tension and asked what I, as a public relations practitioner, thought they should do.

To me, the answer was straightforward. Relying on basic public relations formulas and common sense, I suggested that they could diffuse the tension by reverting to what should have been done in the first place: announce that selected representatives from throughout the city would form a committee to help review the situation and come to a decision that would then be discussed by the board.

To my surprise, the board members took this advice to the administration, and much of what I recommended was done. A few months later, the school was closed in a tearful farewell. And, five weeks after the school closed, I accepted a job with a local public relations firm.

Micro Issues

1. What sort of press releases or other talking points should Wakefield have prepared once the rumors began?
2. Should Wakefield have gone off the record with reporters he trusted?
3. Are there some sorts of decisions governmental bodies make that really should be kept from the media and hence the public? Is this one of them?
4. How should Wakefield have responded to the racial subtext of some of the protests about the closing of the school?

Midrange Issues

1. Should Wakefield have "blown the whistle" on the board members who requested an illegal meeting?
2. Was it appropriate for Wakefield to advise the board to take an approach different from that suggested by the superintendent?
3. How much does Wakefield's previous experience with a different superintendent influence his understanding of how the district works? How did this "workplace" socialization influence his ethical thinking?

Macro Issues

1. To whom should Wakefield be loyal?
2. Should he ever have told members of the community of his own personal views?
3. How does Wakefield's job compare with that of a press secretary for a political figure?
4. Is it ever appropriate to keep journalists in the dark about how political decisions are made?

CASE V-B
Getting the Story, Getting Arrested: Photojournalism and Activism
LEE WILKINS
University of Missouri

British photojournalist Steve Morgan had worked as a freelancer for more than 20 years. Among his repeat clients was Greenpeace, an environmental organization that some characterize as radical, in part for tactics designed to stop various sorts of activities the group feels will degrade the environment. Supporters note that Greenpeace uses peaceful means to promote environmental change. However, the organization and its members have not shied away from direct confrontation, for example, attempting to physically prevent the killing of whales, when the environmental group and its members believe such action warranted. All would agree that Greenpeace has a point of view.

On July 14, 2001, Morgan, along with Spanish videographer Jorge Torres, accompanied a group of 15 Greenpeace members as they protested a missile test off the coast of California, near Vandenberg Air Force Base. The protest involved boarding boats and sailing into the test path, an action that potentially could have stopped such a test. There had been previous protests at Vandenberg, but of the 50 people arrested as part of them, all had been charged with misdemeanors, which usually lead to a fine and probation.

Morgan's assignment from Greenpeace was to take pictures of the protest and to make certain those photos were circulated internationally by news services such as Reuters and AFP (Agence France-Presse). Greenpeace often employed the news media in this way to publicize its views. Morgan took a boat to the site of the protest, shot his photos and returned to shore. There he was arrested by the FBI, which charged him with trespassing, disobeying the orders of a federal officer and conspiracy—a felony.

Morgan's press credentials were examined and discarded by the FBI, Morgan said. He spent six days in the county jail, and was then allowed to fly home to Great Britain upon posting $20,000 bond, over protests of the prosecutor. About six months later Morgan returned to California with his wife and two children, where he was given probation by a U.S. court. The charges the journalists faced, and their sentences, were the same as those given to the protestors.

"It was never my intention to go to the U.S. to break any laws," Morgan said. "I was attempting to document a protest, rather as I would if I were working for AP, Reuters, *The Guardian* or the *Independent,* and, as far as it's possible to be, I was there to be objective. As far as I was concerned, I was doing my job."

At the time of his sentencing, Morgan told the British newspaper *The Guardian* (which is considered the most left-of-center of the elite British print media), "As a photojournalist, my interpretation of events is shaped by my personal views and not by the persons or organizations who commission the assignments." A few months earlier, soon after his arrest, Morgan said, that he would agree to work for Greenpeace again. "I would have no qualms about working for Greenpeace again—it would be determined by the kind of assignment offered. Greenpeace is an organization that in general I believe has done a lot of good. I may not agree with everything that they do, but agree in general as do most people that we all want to live on a clean and peaceful planet. But if I was asked to cover a demo involving the U.S., inflatables and the military, I think the answer would be pretty clearly: 'no, thanks.'"

Greenpeace saw the arrest as politically motivated and capable of setting precedent for other photojournalists. "There is no question that there's some political motivation behind these charges," said Aaron Dyer, the group's lead attorney. "It doesn't appear to be related to September 11, because it predates the attacks, but it does appear to be based on the desire of the Air Force to make a statement about these protests; and the government, the U.S. attorney general's office, seems to be assisting their efforts, It's inappropriate and it's unprecedented in U.S. jurisprudence."

Micro Issues

1. Should Morgan and the other journalist have been in the same boat as the protestors?
2. Does getting close enough to get a good picture—a professional necessity—lend some notion of support to the group?
3. Does the fact that Greenpeace hired Morgan constitute a real or potential conflict of interest for Morgan?
4. Should Morgan tell international news agencies that he is being paid by Greenpeace when he offers his work for sale?

Midrange Issues

1. How are freelance journalists like or unlike their salaried counterparts in terms of loyalty to their employers?
2. If you were a public relations professional, would you suggest that your organization hire its own photographer to cover events and provide the local media with the images? Does the kind of event matter?
3. Is Greenpeace's action in hiring a photographer ethically distinctive from political candidates who provide "photo ops"?

Macro Issues

1. In Europe, and in much of the rest of the world, news organizations are expected to have a point of view. How might that expectation change how editors would evaluate the newsworthiness of Morgan's pictures?
2. Was Morgan, a British citizen, ethically justified in relying on the U.S. First Amendment in his work? Should American journalists working in other nations rely on U.S. understandings of ethics and law, or should they adopt the local standards?

CASE V-C
Selling Brand America
PATRICK LEE PLAISANCE
Colorado State University

Less than a month after the terrorist attacks of Sept. 11, 2001, Charlotte Beers was given what many described as the toughest public relations challenge ever: Selling the idea of a benevolent, moral America to a hostile and embittered Arab world.

In a high-profile advertising career, Beers built a reputation on Madison Avenue as a shrewd and tireless generator of Big Ideas That Worked. The "Queen of Branding," *Business Week* once crowned her. She capped her career by heading Ogilvy & Mather and later J. Walter Thompson, two of the world's advertising behemoths. She quickly was recruited by Bush administration officials eager to launch a public relations front in the war on terror. Her work generated a wave of commentary and triggered fits of soul-searching among many media practitioners. Was her work misguided propaganda or admirable outreach?

Countering misperceptions with assertive dialogue, Beers argued, is critical—especially in the Middle East. "We have all been made aware of the polls which report our eroding goodwill with the rest of the world," Beers said during a December 2002 speech at the National Press Club. "But it's considerably more intense and more deliberately manipulated by extremist factions in the Middle East. It serves their purpose, you understand, to paint us as decadent and faithless; a place and a people who are inimical to the tenets of Islam. These distortions happen every day in their press, in their magazines and from their pulpits. Our share of the mainstream voices is at an all-time low in terms of being heard. Our silence, I believe, is dangerous."

Beers received credit for helping to jump-start the long-dormant "public diplomacy" arm of the State Department, persuading the foreign-service corps that devising strategies to get the U.S. message out should be a critical part of foreign-policy decisions. One of her first moves as Undersecretary of State for Public Diplomacy and Public Affairs was to produce a glossy brochure that detailed, with grisly photos, the human carnage of Sept. 11. The brochure, called "The Network of Terrorism," was distributed in Middle East countries as a newspaper supplement. And at her behest, the State Department Web site aimed at foreigners added a feature on "Muslim life in America," illustrated with pictures of mosques and smiling Muslim families.

The centerpiece of her campaign became a series of short video presentations of Muslims describing their lives in the United States. The video campaign was called "Shared Values." In one of four video segments that government officials in Indonesia, Kuwait and Morocco allowed to air in late 2002, a Muslim family in Toledo, Ohio, is shown at a school softball game extolling American virtues. "I didn't see any prejudice anywhere in my neighborhood after Sept. 11," says Rawia Ismail, a Lebanese-born mother, who also is a schoolteacher. The other videos tell the stories of a prominent Arab doctor, the Algerian-born director of the National Institutes of Health, a Libyan-born baker, and a medic with the New York Fire Department.

Also in 2002, Beers launched a new campaign, reminiscent of the Cold War cultural exchanges of the 1960s, in which 15 American writers such as Richard Ford and Michael Chabon were recruited to write essays answering the question, "In what sense do you see yourself as an American writer?"

For Beers and other officials involved with the information campaign, the mission was clear: to get the word out that America was a badly misunderstood place and that many Muslims live here happily and safely and interact with people of other faiths. "The whole idea of building a brand is to create a relationship between the product and its user," Beers said in an interview during her first month on the job. "We're going to have to communicate the intangible assets of the United States— things like our belief system and our values."

The State Department spent about $15 million on the "Shared Values" videos, which were produced by the advertising company McCann-Erickson using State Department research. The videos were targeted to run in Muslim countries through Ramadan, the traditional period of fasting and reflecting that lasts from early November to early December.

The campaign also featured junkets to show America to Arab journalists, government-published books such as *Iraq: From Fear to Freedom,* and a new radio station, Radio Sawa, that broadcasts in the Arab world, playing pop music in Arabic and English and providing top-of-the-hour news from an American point of view.

Renowned "brand consultant" Wally Olins, who has worked with Spain and several central European countries in image-building projects, said marketing strategy, directly and indirectly, has always been part of national diplomacy. "Historically, nations have always used powerful and consistent ways of branding themselves—the issue is whether it is done consciously. For example, nations emerged as powerful entities during the late 18th-century French Revolution and later on with the German idea of *die Volk.* People think of this as sociocultural political history—not branding. But that's what it was." Rance Crain, editor of *Advertising Age,* praised Beers. "Charlotte Beers knows how to crystallize that message and drum it home to her target audience," Crain said. "That's what advertising can do."

Beers dismissed charges that launching an advertising campaign to "sell America" was misguided. "Just because I'm from Madison Avenue doesn't mean I think I'm selling," she told the National Press Club. "There is not an assumption that we have a ready buyer out there. So please believe me when I say that these mini-documentaries are presented as offering to create a dialogue, which is a really different starting point than a pitch."

When he appointed Beers, Secretary of State Colin Powell was unapologetic. "We are selling a product," Powell said. "We need someone who can rebrand American policy, rebrand diplomacy."

But from the outset, questions and doubters proliferated. Could the same strategies that Beers used to sell Craftsman power tools, Hoover vacuums and Uncle Ben's rice also sell Uncle Sam? How was a slick veneer of marketing going to change hostile attitudes without any changes in the largely pro-Israeli policies, at which the hostility is directed? Was a $30 million propaganda campaign the best way to address anti-American sentiment? Crafting an effective message was one thing; getting it out to Arab populations was another. The vast majority of the media outlets in Muslim countries are state controlled, and many eventually refused to broadcast Beers's campaign packages. Saudi Arabia and Egypt, among other countries, refused to air the "Shared Values" video packages; Egyptian broadcast officials said they don't accept "propaganda from a foreign country."

It also didn't help Beers's efforts when, just before launching the Muslim ad campaign, news of plans for a Pentagon "disinformation" office leaked. In February 2002, the Defense Department announced plans for an Office of Strategic Influence, which would plant false or misleading stories in foreign media outlets and would hire people to organize pro-American rallies. Defense Secretary Donald Rumsfeld quickly called a halt to the office once it was publicized.

Combating deeply entrenched hostility to U.S. policy with feel-good ads is a dubious endeavor, critics said. "The problem is that America isn't a product and Brand America isn't necessarily a good analogy for what public diplomacy is all about," said Martin Kaplan of the Annenberg School of Communication at the University of Southern California. "For one thing, public diplomacy is a two-way street. It's not, 'We sell, you buy.' It's rather, 'We have to listen to each other. We have to demonstrate some mutual respect.' Unfortunately, in our country, we are notorious for not being interested in other nations."

No amount of public diplomacy spin will "make a dent in the public opinion in the Arab world, that largely opposes American policies toward Israel and Palestine," Kim Andrew Elliott, a broadcast veteran and an analyst in the Office of Research at the U.S. International Broadcasting Bureau, wrote in a *New York Times* opinion column. Rather than propaganda, Elliott said the United States should promote independent broadcasting.

In the middle of Beers's speech to the National Press Club, protesters interrupted her by chanting, "You're selling war but we're not buying!" Such U.S. protesters, however, weren't the only ones not buying Beers's message. The ad campaign was regularly mocked and derided in the Arab media. Mohamad Wahbi, a prominent Egyptian journalist, said Beers's strategy was simplistic. "They're not going to sell America to the Arab world the way you would sell any commodity," he said.

Christopher Simpson, a communications professor at American University and author of *Science of Coercion: Communication Research and Psychological Warfare, 1945–1960,* said Beers's campaign was based on two fundamental misconceptions. The first was that selling a product simply is not the same as promoting a belief. "Advertising and propaganda is well known to have an impact on short-term decisions—are they going to buy Tide detergent or Cheer, vote Gore or Bush," Simpson said. "It's also well known to have very little impact on more fundamental beliefs." The second problem is that Beers operated on the belief that anti-American sentiment is based on a misunderstanding of America—that to know America is to love it. "The central illusion here is that the U.S. is somehow not getting its message across," Simpson said. "The large majority of people in the Middle East understand pretty well what the United States is actually saying and doing, and no amount of propaganda is really going to change that."

Others agreed that a major flaw in the strategy was that Beers and her team insisted that the problem of anti-American sentiment was really a "communication" problem.

"The ads were extremely poor," said Youssef Ibrahim, a senior fellow at the Council on Foreign Relations. "It was like this was the 1930s and the government was running commercials showing happy blacks in America. It is the policy itself we have to explain."

But Beers defended the "Shared Values" campaign and suggested it was the kind of strategy that the United States needed to do more of. The advertising-oriented strategies didn't seem to take. In late 2002, the White House took over the job of selling Brand America from Beers's State Department office. Beers's "Shared Values" television campaign was abandoned in January 2003 after it met with stiff resistance from some crucial allied nations.

Beers resigned in March 2003 at age 67, after 17 months in office.

Micro Issues

1. Research by the British Council has shown that while people may love the American way of life represented by the films of Hollywood, they hate American foreign policy and diplomacy, which many perceive as self-serving, arrogant and insensitive to other cultures. How might you argue that Beers's campaign was a positive effort to address this dichotomy?
2. What other kinds of media messages might Beers have constructed to counter anti-American sentiment among Muslim populations?

Midrange Issues

1. Some have said the Muslim-friendly video ads that Beers produced suffered from an inherent contradiction: They were slickly produced TV ads designed to convince Arab audiences that America was not all slick TV. How might PR practitioners view the relationship between their message and the methods through which it is presented or delivered?
2. Can advertising campaigns such as the "Shared Values" videos be considered a "dialogue," as Beers suggested?
3. Foreign protests against America are largely "pseudo-events" staged for the media. Does that fact carry any "moral relevance" in whether the Pentagon could organize pro-American rallies? Defend your answer.

Macro Issues

1. What would be some key features of a public-diplomacy campaign that treated audiences as means rather than as ends?
2. Nancy Snow, a professor at the University of California-Fullerton and author of *Propaganda Incorporated: Selling America's Culture to the World,* argues that propaganda is not necessarily evil, but *how* groups or governments engage in propaganda can raise serious ethical questions. When can propaganda serve as an effective and ethical tool?

CASE V-D
Endowment or Escarpment: The Case of the Faculty Chair
GINNY WHITEHOUSE
Whitworth College

The *Washington Post* called Ken Lay's portrait hanging in the University of Missouri's College of Arts and Science something "larger-than-life." The *Columbia Missourian,* hometown paper to the university, says the painter believed Lay had the "air of a stubborn man."

The painting was commissioned to show the Enron chief executive officer in his element: standing in his office above the Houston skyline, leading one of the world's largest and most successful corporations. The Lay Family Foundation made generous donations to several institutions from a portfolio of $52.2 million before federal investigators swept in at Enron and the company stock, which made up 90 percent of the Foundation holdings, plummeted.

Major Lay Family Foundation gifts ranged from Rice University to the Houston Holocaust Museum to Bethel Baptist Church in Columbia, Missouri, Lay's father's last pulpit before he was laid to rest in the church's cemetery. The Foundation was not able to honor all its 2002 pledges, Linda Lay announced in a media release, and no new pledges of support would be made until current obligations are fulfilled.

However, the University of Missouri's Kenneth L. Lay Chair of Economics was already well established. Lay donated $1.2 million to create the endowed chair. Endowments help universities draw top faculty; however this particular post has never been filled. While universities sometimes spend years seeking the right faculty to hold such top positions, there is no small irony that this chair remains vacant as of this writing.

Federal investigators charge that Lay made nearly $247 million by selling his stock options while encouraging employees to keep their own life savings in Enron stock. Many of those employees soon found themselves out of work and without retirement funds.

Lay certainly is not the first controversial figure to provide major funding to a university. Contentious steamship and railroad magnate Cornelius Vanderbilt was the richest man in America when he died, and the major philanthropic act of his life was when he gave $1 million to the Nashville, Tenn., university that soon took his name. Duke University (founded on tobacco money) acknowledges that former President Richard Nixon, one if its most controversial alumni, contributed heavily to the Duke School of Law's scholarship funds.

As scrutiny into sources of public funding escalates, Harvard University has accepted funds from a string of controversial donors: Socrates Kokkalis, a billionaire who gave $5 million to the Kennedy School of Government and later was investigated in his native Greece on allegations of fraud, embezzlement, and Cold War spying; A. Alfred Taubman, the former chairman of Sotheby's who gave $15 million and was jailed for price-fixing; and Abdullah bin Laden, who denounced his half-brother Osama, earned a Harvard doctorate in 2000 and gave the university $2 million. Other bin Laden family members have contributed to Harvard as well.

The ethical questions here center on substantive credibility versus the appearance of credibility. The wealthy bin Laden name has been tarnished by a terrorist, but the donors themselves have no known links to terrorism. Is their money somehow tainted anyway?

Are these public figures from Ken Lay to Socrates Kokkalis trying to buy goodwill? Certainly. Do they support the mission of the institutions they fund? They say they do. Unquestionably the kinds of schools they fund reflect their own interests.

However, Peter Jackson, CEO and president of Foundation Northwest, says maintaining positions such as the Missouri's Ken Lay Chair of Economics "just doesn't ring true." He suggests that in accepting and keeping gifts, fund-raisers should consider whether the contribution furthers the academic mission of the university.

Jackson said: "What Mr. Lay represents in his business life runs counter to the university's fundamental ideals and associating his name with the institution is demeaning the ideals of the institution. . . .The agony is that you've got the money. Do you take his name off the chair?"

At what point does the goodwill purchased by a donor tarnish the image of the institution so badly that the money gained in one area means contributions lost in another? That's hard to tell. If a donor appears credible on the day a check is written and is arrested a month later, should the university give the money back? Most fund-raisers will say no. Their faculty and students may say otherwise. What if the donor's check comes after the controversy? What is the price of the university's good name and integrity?

These questions are important to graduates pursuing careers in fund-raising, a growing public relations field as government funding priorities shift and nonprofit institutions seek out communications professionals to maintain their financial footing.

The *Chronicle of Philanthropy* notes that most fund-raisers stay with a given institution for around two years. Jackson says the fund-raiser then may have only limited loyalty to the institution but nonetheless a clear responsibility to bring in a certain level of funds. "How far will they go and what are they willing to do to meet that goal?" he added.

Dickinson College President William G. Durden says these kinds of questions are not new. In fact, they stretch to the earliest days of the nation. In a letter to the *New York Times,* Durden quoted Dr. Benjamin Rush, who signed the Declaration of Independence and helped found Dickinson. Rush told a friend helping raise college funds: "Go on with your collections. Get money—get it honestly if you can. But get money for our College."

Micro Issues

1. Your favorite professor has just received an endowed chair from a corporation that laid off one of your parents. You know a great deal about this corporation's employment practices and consider them unethical. Do you continue to take this professor's classes? What, if anything, do you say to your professor?
2. You receive a major scholarship from this same corporation described above. You and your family have limited funds for your education. Accepting the scholarship means that your loan debt will be significantly reduced. What do you do?

3. You just landed your first job after graduation in the Institutional Advancement (fund-raising) office of your alma mater. You and your colleagues have a hefty financial quota to fill, not only to keep your university afloat but also to justify your own paychecks. What do you say to your colleagues when this same corporation described above approaches your office about making a sizable gift?

Midrange Issues

1. Fund-raisers and other nonprofit public relations professionals frequently develop personal relationships with their major donors, particularly with more aged contributors. The donor generally knows that a request for funds is forthcoming as this relationship is built. What might be an ethical way to build a personal relationship with a donor?
2. What might be unethical?

Macro Issues

1. Is enlightened self-interest, the assumption that corporations should contribute to the community in ways that will further the corporations' goals, an ethical policy? If so, explain why. If not, identify ethical alternatives.
2. Many U.S. universities divested stock in South African companies during the Apartheid era, protesting against and attempting to end a racist and oppressive regime. What standards should universities hold in accepting money as well as investing stock in corporations based in the United States and around the world?
3. Look at the questions raised in the text on the previous page and supply answers to them.

CASE V-E
The Gym Shoe Phenomenon: Social Values vs. Marketability
GAIL BAKER
University of Florida

Sprinkled between the abandoned burned-out buildings and the glass-covered vacant lots of Chicago's South Side are bigger-than-life billboards featuring famous athletes wearing expensive Nike gym shoes. Basketball superstar Michael Jordan claims he can jump higher while wearing the shoes; former football great Bo Jackson boasts he can run faster in Nike athletic shoes. Controversial movie director Spike Lee says people of different backgrounds would get along better wearing good athletic shoes.

The company is excited about the "Air Jordan" and "Bo Knows" athletic shoe campaigns it developed for the African-American market. And to ensure that the campaigns are sensitive to African-American consumers, Nike hired legendary Georgetown University basketball coach John Thompson as a $200,000-a-year consultant.

In addition, Nike is careful to select only athletes with "squeaky clean" reputations. Neither Jordan nor Jackson has ever been involved in drugs. Both are family men who are active in their communities. The company believes these two men can clearly be considered role models for the African-American youths who see, hear and read the advertisements. It is thought that these celebrities add credibility to the product and enhance the image of the expensive shoes, which cost between $50 and $125 a pair.

Back in the Chicago ghetto, a 16-year-old black youth is shot and killed on his way to school. Police surmise that he is murdered for his $125 gym shoes, the only clothing missing from his bloody body when the authorities arrive. Unfortunately, this is not the first case of assault or murder provoked by a pair of expensive shoes. Because they have become so fashionable and because they are so expensive, inner-city children are robbing and killing each other to look more like the athletic celebrities they wish to emulate.

Some gangs name themselves after the shoes and shave the name into their haircuts. Parents sometimes sacrifice necessities to purchase the shoes for their children.

The popularity of the shoes and the violence that is sometimes associated with them is noticed by leaders in the African-American community. Nike is criticized in the media for selecting black athletes as spokespersons.

Eric Perkins of the Educational Testing Service calls the use of black athletes "exploitative, because advertisers are playing into the subliminal fascination with black superiority in the white collective psyche." Others criticize Nike for what they believe to be a lack of minority hiring and black community support. Nike is also accused of promoting athletics over academics. Only one in 10,000 high school athletes ever becomes a professional, and only 20 percent of all black college athletes ever finish college.

Jesse Jackson and other religious and civil rights leaders call for a national boycott of Nike to protest the company's business practices. Reverend Jackson is particularly critical of the African-Americans who endorse athletic shoes, saying, "They are exploiting an ethos of mindless materialism."

Operation PUSH (People United to Save Humanity), a civil rights organization founded by Reverend Jackson, joins the boycott effort. PUSH officials complain that sales of Nike shoes to blacks total $200 million annually, while the company has no high-ranking black executives and does not do business with black-owned advertising agencies. The company responds by saying that sales to nonwhites account for only 14 percent of its sales. Nike also states that 7.5 percent of its 4,200 U.S. employees are black.

Fourteen weeks into the boycott, the Rev. Tyrone Crider, executive director of Operation PUSH, says the boycott would continue "until Nike decides to put money in black-owned banks, advertise with black-owned media, do business with black-owned businesses, and put a black on its board of directors."

On the other side of the issue, Nike spokespersons say it is just good marketing to use Bo Jackson and Michael Jordan in their advertisements. "He [Jackson] is a person kids can look up to. He's crazy about his kids and his wife and family. He's somebody who has applied himself and came from a really humble background," says Melinda Gable, public relations executive for Nike.

Jordan, Lee and Thompson meet with Jackson in an effort to stop the boycott. The meeting is unsuccessful and the boycott continues.

Nike announces during the boycott that it will hire a minority vice president and name a minority to its board of directors by 1992. The company also hires a minority advertising agency, Muse Codero and Chen, out of Los Angeles, to handle a portion of its account.

Nike shoe sales, unaffected by the boycott, increase 58 percent over the same period the previous year. After several months and a number of news articles and television stories, the Nike boycott fades from the national headlines and Nike continues its use of black athletes in its advertising campaigns. Inner-city crime continues, but few news reports link the violence to clothing or shoes.

Following the boycott, the company develops a "Bo Knows School" campaign featuring Jackson and distributes thousands of book jackets to inner-city schools. On it Jackson appears in a graduation cap and gown, a band uniform, a scientist's white lab coat, and a Greek philosopher's toga. The book jacket reads, "Bo knows all this stuff because he stayed in school."

Although the company now receives applause for its interest in education, critics still question the tie-in with African-American athletes.

Micro Issues

1. Is Nike advertising responsible for the inner-city violence that occurred after its campaign?
2. Did Nike's decision to hire an ethnic advertising agency relieve the company of its social responsibility or was it just a public relations ploy?

Midrange Issues

1. Is Nike guilty of stereotyping African-Americans by using athletes in their ads?
2. If Nike didn't use athletes to promote athletic shoes, whom should it select?
3. Should athletes be used as role models in advertising aimed at black youths, since such a small percentage of African-Americans ever play professional sports?
4. Do product manufacturers need to be sensitive to the social and economic conditions of their potential clients, or should they be able to market any product that sells, as long as it's legal?

Macro Issues

1. Should advertisers respond to pressure placed upon them by community activists?
2. Can advertising be held accountable for social problems that stem from poverty and lack of opportunity?

VI

Privacy: Looking for Solitude in the Global Village

By the end of this chapter, you should be able to:

- **appreciate the difference between the right to privacy and a need for privacy.**
- **distinguish between the law and ethics of privacy.**
- **understand the concepts of discretion, right to know, need to know, want to know, and circles of intimacy.**
- **understand and apply Rawls's veil of ignorance as a tool for ethical decision making.**

WHY PRIVACY IN THE NEW MILLENNIUM?

If there was one area in media ethics that was stretched almost beyond recognition in the latter part of the 20th century, it was privacy. And the assault involved no less a person than the President of the United States. What the world got to see was a public discussion of sex—and what constitutes sex—played out before the U.S. Congress, the national television audience, and newspaper readers across the country. Americans learned that an intern, noticed by former President Bill Clinton when she brought him pizza late one night, had become his partner in oral sex for many months, the proof being a semen-stained dress she retained from the affair.

Congress learned of the affair because a "friend" of Monica Lewinsky's had taped her telephone conversations, which included hours of distraught discussion about her relationship with the president. We watched thunderstruck as Hillary Clinton, now a U.S. senator, denied knowing of the affair, a claim she would continue to make in her best-selling autobiography in 2003. We also watched her public stoicism when her husband admitted that he had lied to her as well as the rest of the American people.

We watched the impeachment proceedings, and read newspaper accounts of independent counsel Kenneth Starr's sexually explicit report. Many U.S. newspapers printed the report verbatim. Just in case they did not, the U.S. House of Representatives made it available on the Internet without benefit of editing or warning about subject matter and content. Shortly after that Larry Flynt, *Penthouse* magazine publisher, promised a $1 million reward for accurate information about Republican congressional figures who engaged in behavior similar to that of President Clinton, but without the benefit of an independent counsel inquiry. The fallout reached to the highest levels of leadership in Congress as leaders dropped out of public positions because of private indiscretions.

The Clinton-Lewinsky affair came to symbolize the media's apparent inability to make distinctions between news and what one scholar has characterized as "mediated voyeurism," described as "the consumption of revealing images of and information about others' apparently real and unguarded lives, often yet not always for purposes of entertainment but frequently at the expense of privacy and discourse, through the means of the mass media and the Internet" (Calvert 2000, 23). Calvert lists such diverse activities as hidden camera reports, the paparazzi phenomenon, and video surveillance in businesses as well as private homes, and suggests that such technology-based media content has forever changed journalism. "Our notions of news and human interest stories have shifted over time. Today, voyeurism passes as news" (Calvert 2000, 29).

The nation's capital is not the only place an overheated press can pursue a story, trampling on the rights of victims and families in the process. One only needs to remember the feeding frenzy of the press pursuing the stories of the murder of young JonBenet Ramsey, the murder of Laci Petersen and her unborn baby, or the disappearance of Washington intern Chandra Levy to see firsthand what happens when getting the story trumps the privacy interests of the individuals involved. Voyeurism becomes news.

Yet some stories that might be considered voyeuristic can have an important purpose. In early 2000, NBC *Today Show* host Katie Couric, whose husband had died about two years earlier from colon cancer, had her own colonoscopy broadcast on national television. Several months before that, talk-show host Oprah Winfrey videotaped women having mammograms—although visual images of the women's breasts never aired due to carefully selected camera angles. The goal in both cases was a worthy one: protecting the public health by demonstrating that routine medical screening exams don't hurt and can save a life. In these instances, Couric and the women in Winfrey's report gave up some element of privacy that most Americans continue to cherish.

Not everyone is so open. After the 2000 presidential election, NBC's well-regarded political correspondent Tim Russert noted in an interview with Vice President-elect Richard Cheney that for months he had asked for specific information regarding the health of Cheney's heart only to be stonewalled with generalities. It was only after Cheney had a mild heart attack that the public got an accurate and detailed response to Russert's questions and learned that Russert had asked them in the first place.

Domestic politics are not the only place where the lines between what is private and what is public seem to have disappeared. Reality television treats us to *Survivor* and *Temptation Island,* the Internet brings us images of women giving birth and teens losing their virginity. We watch in horror as the victims of Kosovo emerge, only to flip the channel to *Real World* and *Road Rules*. The travails of O. J. Simpson (accused of murder) or Kobe Bryant (accused of rape) or Martha Stewart (accused of lying to the government) become a sort of reality television for the all-news set. Through it all we remain confused about whether we are responding as normally curious human beings, citizens who need information, or journalists doing important work in a democratic society.

THE NEED FOR PRIVACY

Much has been written on the "right to privacy," a right made problematic by the fact that the term never appears in the U.S. Constitution. Relatively little, however, has been written about the "need for privacy." Philosopher Louis W. Hodges has attempted to focus attention on the need for privacy. He says that "without some degree of privacy, civilized life would be impossible" (Hodges 1983). Both a personal and societal need for privacy exists, Hodges claims.

First, we personally need privacy to develop a sense of self. Constance T. Fischer (1980) states that people need privacy to "try out" new poses, future selves, and so on, without fear of ridicule by outsiders. If we are to become the person we wish to be, a certain degree of privacy is needed to develop that person apart from observation. Religious cults that seek cognitive control over their members do so in part by depriving the members of any real degree of privacy, restricting both growth and reflection.

Second, society needs privacy as a shield against the power of the state. As the state gains more information about its citizens, it is increasingly easy to influence, manipulate or control each one.

Precisely because the state is seen as the agency of the citizens' own authority, its independent power is feared, and limitations on the power of the state, such as the Bill of Rights, were established in order to protect private life (Neville 1980). Throughout history, totalitarian regimes have used extensive government surveillance—the near absence of privacy—as a major component of any attempt to create a uniformly subservient citizenry, a subject that dominates Orwell's *1984*.

Therefore, while much of the debate focuses on the *right* to privacy, an equally compelling argument must be made for the *need* for privacy. Privacy is not to be viewed as a luxury or as an option or even a gift of a benevolent government. It is a necessary component of a democracy upon which many of its values, such as freedom, individual dignity and autonomy, rest.

Perhaps no issue in contemporary journalistic ethics has been as troubling as invasions of privacy. That trouble exists for at least two specific reasons. First, community and national standards are changing. What was once strictly private, for instance the mention of breast surgery in the newspaper or on television, is not only common but also credited with saving lives. Second, privacy is both a legal concept in the domain of the courts and an ethical concept debated by philosophers. Confusion over which analysis is appropriate confounds our thinking.

The result is that journalists have been caught between what the law allows and what their consciences will permit. This confusion has led to ethical bungling on a scale that has probably undermined the entire profession's credibility and fed two stereotypical notions: one, that journalists will do anything to get a story, and two, that audiences will willingly consume anything the journalist delivers. These images not only are at odds with reality, but also make getting and understanding legitimate stories even more difficult.

LEGAL AND ETHICAL DEFINITIONS

The legal notion of privacy began in 1890 with a *Harvard Law Review* article, written by lawyers Samuel Warren and Louis D. Brandeis (who eventually became a U.S. Supreme Court justice), calling for a constitutional right to privacy. Today privacy is guarded legally in four distinct ways:

1. Intrusion upon a person's seclusion or solitude, or into private affairs, such as invading one's home or personal papers to get a story.

2. Public disclosure of embarrassing private facts, such as revealing someone's notorious past when it has no bearing on that person's present status.

3. Publicity that places a person in a false light, such as enhancing a subject's biography to sell additional books.

4. Misappropriation of a person's name or likeness for personal advantage, such as using Michael Jackson's likeness to sell Pepsi without his permission.

While this four-part list is straightforward, the court's interpretation of it is not, placing privacy among the least satisfactory areas of constitutional law. Not only are decisions themselves contradictory, but also some of the concepts themselves are open to question or change. What once might have been an embarrassing, private fact—for example, that an unmarried woman is pregnant—is now commonplace knowledge and, quite often cause for celebration. In recent years, one's sexual orientation has increasingly moved toward this same level of commonplace knowledge. But at the same time, information once available for the asking, such as a student's telephone number or the address of an individual based on driver's license registration, is now closed by a maze of privacy legislation enacted in the 1970s and 1980s.

To further cloud the issue, the claim to privacy is different for different categories of people. Public figures, for example, are subject to a different standard than are others, as are "limited" public figures and even "accidental" public figures thrown into the spotlight by chance. Just exactly who the courts will consider a public figure fluctuates. When the media invade privacy, the legal remedies occur after the fact. A huge monetary award can make a plaintiff rich, but it cannot return that sense of control the initial invasion takes away. For this reason alone, the law provides an unsatisfactory solution. Ethical thinking prior to broadcast or publication is preferable to a court battle.

The ethical basis for privacy is much older than the legal one and appears throughout literature. The bulk of this work asserts that privacy is something we all possess by being human. Modern philosophical interpretations make the assumption that privacy is considered a need, a way of protecting oneself against the actions of other people and institutions. Privacy carries with it the connotation of control and limited access. The individual should be allowed to control who may have certain sorts of information and, sometimes, the context within which that information is presented.

Part of what is confusing about the concept of privacy is that, as a concept, it cannot stand apart from community. Responsibility for keeping things private is shared: individuals have to learn when to withhold information, the community has to learn when to avert its eyes completely or to narrow its gaze. Legal scholar Jeffrey Rosen notes that this attention to the role of the community in avoiding the unwanted gaze stems from Talmudic law. "Jewish law, for example, has developed a remarkable body of doctrine around the concept of *hezzek re'iyyah,* which means 'the injury caused by seeing' or 'the injury caused by being seen.' This doctrine expands the right of privacy to protect individuals not only from physical intrusions into the home but also from surveillance by a neighbor who is outside the home, peering through a window in a common courtyard. Jewish law protect neighbors not only from unwanted observation, but also from the possibility of being observed" (Rosen 2000, 18–19). Part of the problem with a "shoot first, edit later" philosophy for photographers and videographers at the scene of a tragedy is that the "injury caused by being seen" has already been exacerbated by the camera.

Medieval law, too, recognized the possibility of injury due to the unwanted gaze, a deep foreshadowing of telephoto lenses or hidden cameras and microphones that have become an almost reflexive part of some forms of investigative/entertainment journalism. Like the philosophical approach developed by the Greeks, in both these instances privacy is linked to our ability to "become" human and retain some element of dignity while doing it. "Only citizens who respect one another's privacy are themselves dignified with divine respect" (Rosen 2000, 19).

THE CONTINUING CONFLICTS

Most would agree with Grcic (1986) that while privacy is a prima facie right, it sometimes can be negated by other, more compelling rights. In simpler times, the right to invade privacy belonged almost exclusively to the government. The government can demand, for example, that an individual relinquish control of a substantial amount of private information to complete federal and state income tax forms. Further, failure to provide such information makes one legally liable. For the survival of the entire political community, the government demands that its citizens provide it with certain information that is otherwise private. However, specific rules govern such disclosure. The government cannot legally give your tax return information to other interested parties. Such a check on government power theoretically allows the maintenance of some level of individual privacy.

However, the government is not the only institution today that can demand and receive private information. Banks, credit companies, doctors and attorneys, all can request (and usually receive) a variety of highly private information, the bulk of it willingly disclosed. Inevitably, such disclosure is one-directional. While you are required to provide your physician with your medical history to ensure proper treatment, your physician might be surprised if you inquired about his or her success rate with a particular surgical procedure, and she certainly is not required to give it to you. Doctors in Massachusetts were uncomfortable and protested when the state passed a law requiring such information be made available to patients.

Computers and databases have become tools for gathering and repositories for storing private information. Huge industries have cropped up selling a single commodity: private information. When you buy a house or apply for a job, you will watch as the information industry disgorges huge amounts of legal and financial information about you with about a 40 percent chance of some error, according to industry figures. The tensions over what should or should not remain private are not resolved; they are merely accounted for and debated in today's complex society.

However, Warren and Brandeis had the press, not the government or financial institutions, in mind when they wrote their precedent-inspiring article. The pair developed their novel legal argument after a breakfast in celebration of Mr. Warren's wedding was covered by the press, an article that would be a benign social mention today if it made the press at all. Offended by this "outrage," Warren and Brandeis could not have anticipated trash television, "kiss-and-tell" books, computerized databases, or the myriad other ways the mass media disseminate private information about people who are more or less willing to disclose it. The issue is not more complex today than it was during the country's formative years, but the ways privacy is violated are substantially different, and perhaps more threatening.

DISTINGUISHING BETWEEN SECRECY AND PRIVACY

People tend to think of private information as something they would like to keep secret, but such thinking confounds these two related but separable concepts.

Secrecy can be defined as blocking information intentionally to prevent others from learning, possessing, using or revealing it (Bok 1983). Secrecy ensures that information is kept from *any* public view. Privacy, however, is concerned with determining who will obtain access to the information. Privacy does not imply that information will never reach public view, but rather that an individual has control over what information becomes public and to whom.

Secrecy often carries a negative connotation. However, we agree with Bok in asserting that secrecy itself is neither morally good nor bad. Privacy and secrecy can overlap but are not identical. "Privacy need not hide; and secrecy hides far more than what is private. A private garden need not be a secret garden, a private life is rarely a secret life" (Bok 1983, 11). Privacy can and should be balanced against other considerations; secrets are something an individual decides to keep.

In *Dietemann v. Time,* jurist Alan F. Westin viewed privacy as the ability to control one's own "circles of intimacy." In the case, two reporters lied to Dietemann to

PUBLIC   PUBLIC

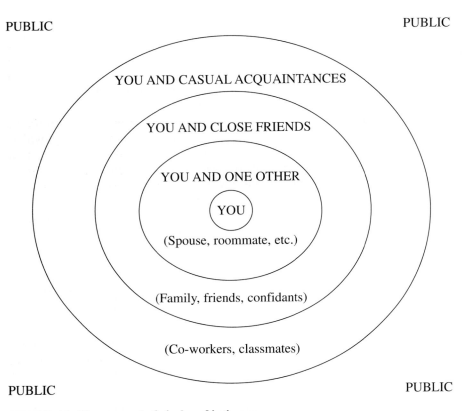

PUBLIC   PUBLIC

FIGURE 6.1. The concept of circles of intimacy

enter his home and later expose him as a medical quack practicing medicine without a license, at home. While the courts saw some social utility in exposing such behavior, Dietemann, they ruled, had a reasonable expectation of privacy in his own home.

Philosopher Louis W. Hodges has used the concept of circles of intimacy to develop a working concept of privacy for journalists and other professionals. If you conceive of privacy as a series of concentric circles, as Figure 6.1 illustrates, in the innermost circle you are alone with your secrets, fantasies, hopes, reconstructed memories, and the rest of the unique psychological "furniture" we bring to our lives.

The second circle you probably occupy with one other person, perhaps a sibling, a spouse, a parent, roommate, or loved one—a person who might change at various times in your development. In that circle, you share private information. In order for that relationship to work well, it needs to be reciprocal, and it should be based primarily on trust.

The third circle contains others to whom you are very close—probably family or friends, perhaps a lawyer or clergy member. Here, the basis of relationships is still one of trust, but some communications can be primarily one way—and you do not expect to have complete control over them. As the ripples in the pond of intimacy continue to spread, what you reveal about yourself becomes progressively more public and less intimate, and you progressively lose more control over information about you.

Using this model of expanding circles, privacy can be considered individual control over who has access to your various circles of intimacy. Invasion of privacy occurs when your control over your own circles of intimacy is wrestled from you by people or institutions. Rape victims who unwillingly see their names in print or their pictures broadcast frequently speak of the loss of control they felt during the experience as being similar to the loss of control during the rape itself.

Journalists, both as individuals and as representatives of powerful institutions, can and sometimes do invade circles of intimacy. Awareness of the concept will allow you to consider the rights of others as well as balance the needs of society in critical ways, particularly when the issue is newsworthy. Under at least some circumstances, invasion can be justified, but under other circumstances invading privacy constitutes usurping an individual's control and stripping him or her of individuality and human dignity. Part of the ethical growth of a journalist is to know when the rule applies and when the exceptions should occur.

DISCRETION: WHETHER TO REVEAL PRIVATE INFORMATION

With the distinction between privacy and secrecy in mind, the next problem confronting the ethical journalist is "discretion"—a word not usually associated with journalism. Bok (1983, 41) defines discretion as "the intuitive ability to discern what is and is not intrusive and injurious."

We all decide at times to reveal private information, and doing so wisely is a mark of moral growth. Discretion demands moral reasoning where the interests of more than one party are balanced. Once a source decides to reveal private information, a reporter's discretion remains the sole gatekeeper between that information and a public that might need the information or might merely want the information. The journalist is forced to rely on moral reasoning to decide if he is feeding the voyeur or the citizen in each of us.

What is a journalist to do with information resulting from another's indiscretion? Kantian theory would suggest that the journalist treat even the indiscreet source as the journalist herself would wish to be treated, making publication of the indiscretion less likely. Yet many journalists claim that, in practice, everything is "on-the-record" unless otherwise specified. In situations like these, a return to Ross's list of prima facie duties could be helpful. What is my duty to an often vulnerable and sometimes unwitting source? To a curious readership or viewership? To a media owner who wants (and pays for) my story? Which duties emerge as foremost to the journalist who should make such decisions more consistently?

Perhaps no new medium is more "on-the-record" than the Internet. We speak of information as "being posted" without examining the assumptions or the motives of those doing the posting. The courts are unclear on whether posting on the Internet constitutes actual publication.

However, considering media behavior, it appears that not everyone is willing to wait for ethical thinking to take hold. In the last few years of the 20th century, the courts, the U.S. Congress, and state legislatures, particularly in California, are imposing a form of discretion—at least on journalists. California law now provides that a person may be held liable for a "constructive invasion of privacy" even if no physical trespass occurs. This statute was aimed primarily at paparazzi who stalk Hollywood celebrities, but according to some it would have impact on journalists as well. Paul Tash, executive editor of the *St. Petersburg Times* and chair of the Freedom of Information Committee of the American Society of Newspaper Editors, told Congress when it was considering similar legislation that it "would protect villains, frauds and scoundrels against diligent photojournalists who would bring them and their activities to light," (quoted in Calvert 2000).

WHEN THE RIGHT TO KNOW IS NOT ENOUGH

Just as the distinction between secrecy and privacy is easily confused, there is also a misconception on the part of both journalists and the public among the concepts of "right to know," "need to know," and "want to know." However, the three concepts are distinct and not interchangeable.

Right to know is a legal term often associated with open-meeting statutes and based on the philosophy that government runs more honestly in the open. Right to know is a way to counterbalance government power. In recent years both federal and state governments have passed right-to-know laws. These laws are a legal, not ethical, construct. Journalists have a legal right to the same information that other members of the public may obtain—for example, the transportation of hazardous materials through their communities.

Ethical problems can emerge from right-to-know information. Is it ethical to print everything a journalist has a legal right to know? For instance, police reports routinely carry the names of suspects, victims, and witnesses to a variety of crimes. Does the journalist publish such information, even though it has been legally obtained? If a reporter has information that might harm national security if printed, should it be withheld? Clearly, even right to know carries with it ethical considerations.

Need to know originates in the realm of philosophy. Media ethicists such as Deni Elliott (1986) have argued that one of the functions of the mass media is to provide information to citizens that will allow them to go about their daily lives in society, regardless of political outlook. Citizens may have a legal right to much of this information, but perhaps not all of it. In this view, providing information the public needs to know includes within it the concept of journalistic tenacity and responsibility.

Too often, when journalists assert that the public has the "right to know" a fact, what they mean is that citizens "need" such information to get along in their daily lives. For example, the average citizen cannot examine bank records. That duty is left to auditors and the government. But with the recent turmoil in the financial sector, journalists could reasonably argue that at least some information about the health of financial institutions and the character of those who run them is needed by

Public Outing, Public Outcry

The firestorm around columnist Robert Novak in 2003 and 2004 demonstrates the hazards of reporting sensitive information, even when the law is on the side of the reporter. Novak's problems began when he "outed" a covert CIA operative in his column. The context was a column about how former ambassador Joseph Wilson had been chosen to go to Niger by the Bush administration in late 2002 to investigate whether Saddam Hussein attempted to purchase yellow-cake uranium for a nuclear weapons program in Iraq. Wilson concluded the information was erroneous, and reported that to the administration. Despite Wilson's report, President Bush used the erroneous information in his 2003 State of the Union address as part of his justification for going to war with Iraq.

When journalists began to inquire about the lack of evidence in Niger, the administration recanted, but not before Wilson wrote an op-ed piece for the *New York Times* that summarized his findings. Shortly after that, an unnamed administration official leaked to Novak that Wilson's wife was a covert operative for the CIA. Novak published her name and her status as a spy in his column, in the context of a story on why Wilson was picked for the Niger job— his wife suggested him to the administration. Not only was printing the name a possible felony, but the public "outing" could have endangered the lives of the operative and her contacts. However, Novak, as the recipient of the leak, was covered by a "shield law" that protected him from being forced to divulge his source. Novak became the focus of professional debate, some of it supportive and some critical.

What made the incident more troubling was that Novak was one of six journalists who received the same information by a leaker intent on hurting Wilson, yet he was the only one who published it. Novak's defense was that the name was "out there," and he simply published what was commonly known, not knowing it was classified. It was important in the context of the story, he said, since Wilson's wife had suggested her husband for the Niger assignment and accompanied him on it. The incident, is still under investigation as this book goes to press.

the public to make informed economic decisions. Need to know often requires a tenacious journalist, as the law is not a tool to access information for such stories.

Need to know is the most ethically compelling argument of the three. Need to know demands that an ethical case be constructed for making known information that others wish to keep private. Need to know also demands that journalists present the information in a manner that will make its importance evident to a sometimes lazy citizenry.

When an argument is framed in terms of right to know, it reduces the journalist to ethical legalism: I will do precisely what the law allows. When an argument is framed in terms of need to know, however, it means that counterbalancing forces have been weighed and that bringing the information to light is still the most ethical act. Asserting your right to know may be the best way to get the facts regarding a crime, but only by weighing the public's need to know will you be satisfied with the decisions you make in airing the story.

Finally, there is the issue of want to know, which speaks to the curiosity in all of us. Want to know is the least ethically compelling rationale for acquiring information and disseminating it. We all want to know a lot of things—what our neighbors do in the evening hours, how much money other people earn, and who in Hollywood is sleeping with whom. While we may want that information, however, we don't really need it and most certainly have no right to it. It serves the function of gossip, providing us with small talk or a smile.

By nature of their occupation, journalists often become repositories for much "want to know" information. A number of media outlets have been founded on the public's desire to know about celebrities, criminals, and even common folk. More than half a century ago, *Police Gazette* titillated its readers with information they wanted to know that no other media outlet provided.

Today, providing "want to know" information is an entire industry. Yesterday's *Police Gazette* is today's *America's Most Wanted,* or any other number of reality-based television shows, some of them focusing on the work of police but all designed to garner ratings and hence profits. Reality television, and its Internet permutations, provide evidence that U.S. culture itself is shifting the concept of privacy more toward want to know. That shift raises an important professional issue: when "want to know" becomes enmeshed in the profit motive, is the long-term result a loss of public understanding of the distinctions between journalism and entertainment that will make it more difficult for journalists to do their important work in the coming decades?

JOHN RAWLS AND THE VEIL OF IGNORANCE

Preserving human dignity in times of crisis is a difficult task. Political philosopher John Rawls, considered this century's most articulate proponent of the social contract theory of government, has provided a helpful exercise to help make decisions about particularly thorny privacy issues (Rawls 1971).

Rawls's theory of "distributive justice" is designed to take the best from utilitarian theory while avoiding some of its more fundamental problems. It begins with the premise that justice should be equated with fairness. In order to achieve "justice as fairness," Rawls suggests an exercise he calls the "veil of ignorance." In the exercise, before any member of a community can make an ethical decision affecting others, he or she must consider the options behind a veil of ignorance.

Behind the veil, everyone starts out in an "original position" as equals who do not know whether they will be powerful or powerless when they emerge into the community from behind the veil. Rawls suggests that rational people would be willing to make and to follow those decisions when individual distinctions such as gender or socioeconomic status are laid aside.

For example, if the issue is whether to photograph or interview survivors at the scene of an airline crash, one could gather many people with diverse views behind the veil. Among them could be a reporter, a photographer, a survivor, a victim's family, an average reader or viewer, the management or owner of the media outlet, the owner of the airline, paramedics at the scene, the flying public, and others. Behind the veil, in the original position, none of the participants would know what their status would be when they emerged. Their arguments would then be free of bias that comes from points of view. The participants would argue the pros and cons of the public's need to know and the victim's right to privacy without knowing whether they would emerge as a reporter, a reader, or a victim.

Rawls's veil of ignorance provides journalists with an important tool to use when they begin an ethical dialogue with the stakeholders in your decision much like the one Bok recommends (see Chapter I). Behind the veil of ignorance it is possible to walk in the shoes of the stakeholders, to air various views, and then to make a reasoned choice.

When people begin their deliberations behind such a veil, Rawls suggests that two values emerge: we will act so that *individual liberty is maximized; however, weaker parties will be protected.* We will look at each concept separately.

First, Rawls suggests the liberty of all will be valued equally. Behind the veil, freedom of the press (a liberty journalists cherish) becomes equal to freedom from unwarranted intrusion into private life (a liberty readers cherish). How one retains both becomes a debate to be argued from all points of view without the bias of status since each participant is in the original position, ignorant of personal position or status.

Second, under the framework the weaker party is usually protected. Few participants would make an ethical decision that might not be in the interest of the weaker party unless the evidence was overwhelming that it would better the lot of the entire group. Behind the veil participants would be forced to weigh the actual and potential harm that journalists, as powerful people representing powerful institutions, could inflict on people who are less powerful.

It is important to note that consensus is not required, and maybe even not expected, behind the veil. The veil of ignorance is designed to facilitate ethical discussions, not stymie them from lack of unanimity. Using the veil of ignorance, the ethical decision maker arrives at what Rawls calls "reflective equilibrium." In the state of reflective equilibrium some inequalities are allowed. However, they will be the inequalities that contribute in some significant way to the betterment of most individuals in the social situation. For instance, the consensus of the group behind the veil might be to run a photo of a victim of tragedy if it might prevent a similar tragedy from occurring.

Reflective equilibrium summons what Rawls calls our "considered moral judgment." Decisions would be based on the principles we would be most unwilling to give up because we believe doing so would result in a grave wrongdoing for all. Balancing the liberties of various stakeholders, while protecting the weaker party, allows for a thorough exploration of all of the issues involved, which utilitarianism sometimes fails to address.

Using the concepts of right to know, need to know, discretion, and circles of intimacy, along with Rawls's concept of distributive justice, will provide you with the ethical tools to begin the work of balancing conflicting claims of privacy. These tools will enable you to better justify your choices, to make decisions systematically and to understand what went wrong when mistakes occur.

Selected Readings

ALDERMAN, ELLEN, and CAROLINE KENNEDY. 1995. *The right to privacy.* New York: Alfred A. Knopf, Inc.

BOK, SISSELA. 1983. *Secrets: On the ethics of concealment and revelation.* New York: Vintage.

GRCIC, JOSEPH M. 1986. "The right to privacy: Behavior as property." *Journal of Values Inquiry* 20, 137–44.

HIXSON, RICHARD F. 1987. *Privacy in a public society.* New York: Oxford University Press.

HODGES, LOUIS W. 1983. "The journalist and privacy." *Social Responsibility: Journalism, Law, Medicine* 9, 5–19.

ORWELL, GEORGE. 1949. *1984.* San Diego: Harcourt, Brace, Jovanovich.

RAWLS, JOHN. 1971. *A theory of justice.* Cambridge, MA: Harvard University Press.

ROSEN, JEFFREY. 2000. *The unwanted gaze: The destruction of privacy in America.* New York: Random House.

SCHOEMAN, FERDINAND D., ed. 1984. *Philosophical dimensions of privacy: An anthology.* New York: Cambridge University Press.

Cases on the Web

"Naming names: Privacy and the public's right to know" by John B. Webster

"Public grief and the right to be left alone" by Philip Patterson

"A reporter's question: Propriety and punishment" by Stanley Cunningham

"Computers and the news: A complicated challenge" by Karon Reinboth Speckman

"Honor to die for: *Newsweek* and the Admiral Boorda case" by Philip Patterson

"Culture, law and privacy: Should ethics change in a cultural context" by Lee Wilkins

---

CHAPTER VI CASES

CASE VI-A
Naming Names: A Basketball Star and His Accuser Make the News
PHILIP PATTERSON
Oklahoma Christian University

On June 30, 2003, Los Angeles Lakers star Kobe Bryant had intercourse with an employee of the Lodge and Spa at Cordilera, where he was staying in the remote town of Edwards, Colorado. The sexual encounter occurred after the 19-year-old concierge at the four-star resort, whom he had met earlier in the afternoon, went to Bryant's room at his request. That much is agreed on by the two parties, but not much else.

According to Bryant, the sex was consensual. According to the employee, it was not.

Fans of Bryant, a perennial NBA all-star and the winner of three league championships with the Lakers, hoped that the enormously popular star would not be charged. However, after a week of investigation by Colorado authorities, Bryant was arrested and charged in Eagle County court with one act of Class 3 Sexual Assault, which is the equivalent of rape under Colorado law. As this book went to press, he had appeared in court and entered a plea of not guilty to the charge.

Most news organizations have policies against naming assault victims, and almost all major media outlets honored those policies in this case. However, the accuser's name was made available almost instantly on Internet sites created by fans of Bryant, complete with photos from her high school yearbook, her e-mail address and even her cell phone number.

Sports talk show host Tom Leykis, whose radio show originates in Bryant's adopted hometown of Los Angeles, began using the name of Bryant's accuser in the first week. His show is heard on 60 stations across the country. Leykis told Reuters news service "We're told that rape is violence, not sex, and if that's true there's no reason she should feel shame or embarrassment." He added that he felt it would be unfair to name Bryant and not his accuser and said he believed Bryant to be the "real victim" in the case.

Even the media outlets that would not name the victim participated in researching her life. It was soon known that she had a troubled past, including an episode when she overdosed on medication and was taken by ambulance to the hospital for treatment. It was also widely reported that she had tried out unsuccessfully for the *American Idol* television series, with the unstated context that she sought celebrity.

The *Online Mirror* at the University of Northern Colorado, where she spent her freshman year, reported in July that it had "exclusive" interviews with students who knew the accuser. All spoke anonymously, a safeguard for the accuser, according to the *Mirror*. The acquaintances told the *Mirror* that she had "issues with her boyfriend" and that they "fought throughout the school year." They added that "male guests frequently visited her overnight" and that she "bragged about her sexual encounters." The article also recounted the overdose story that was already making the rounds in mainstream media.

Bryant appeared at a news conference in Los Angeles after the initial story broke, with his wife, Vanessa, by his side, and confessed to adultery but adamantly denied that the sexual encounter was anything but consensual.

Discussion about naming the accuser filled the airwaves and Internet in the days after the original accusation and Bryant's initial court visit in August. On the Poynter Institute's Web site, Bob Steele wrote, "I believe we have a professional obligation to assess, the best we can, the vulnerability of individuals as we write stories about the most painful and difficult elements of their lives. As journalists, we generally write a story and move on. Those we write about will be forever connected to that story. We have a duty to show great care and concern."

Geneva Overholser was the editor of the *Des Moines Register* when that newspaper won a Pulitzer Prize in 1991 for a series written by Jane Schorer that documented one woman's path through the criminal justice system after her rape. With her own consent, the victim was named in the story. Overholser argued that the practice of withholding the accuser's name reinforces the stigmatization that society puts on the rape victim. On the Poynter Web site she wrote: "The responsible course for responsible media today is this: Treat the woman who charges rape as we would any other adult victim of crime. Name her, and deal with her respectfully. And leave the trial to the courtroom."

Micro Issues

1. Is this a fairness issue? Are Leykis and others who claim to be fair to both the accused and the accuser by running both names missing the point? How would you support or refute the "fairness" argument?
2. Geneva Overholser made the argument for running the name of the accuser without ever using her name. Her name is not used in this case study. Can her name be used in the context of robust debate? Should it be used?
3. Do any of your answers change if the charges are dropped for "lack of evidence"?

Midrange Issues

1. In her essay, Overholser points out: "As a practical matter . . . newspapers are not—as they once were—the gatekeepers of such information. . . . Details about the Kobe Bryant accuser are being bandied about by shock jocks and on the Net netherworld." Does the fact that the name is "out there" justify airing it on the local news or running it in the community newspaper?
2. In the online article, the student newspaper said that the accuser had plans to return to Greeley (home of the university) in the fall. Should this change the way the newspaper covers the case as it goes to trial? Are the standards different because it is a student newspaper? Are they different if she is living in the community? If so, in what way?
3. What is the difference in refusing to name the accuser, presumably to protect her privacy, but at the same time bringing up issues from her past that might violate that privacy?
4. When Overholser said to "leave the trial to the courtroom," is she referring to this type of coverage? What information about her past included in this case is relevant to print? Ethical to print?

Macro Issues

1. Read Bob Steele's comments again. He speaks of a "duty" we have to show care and concern. List all the parties to whom you may have a duty in this story and try to resolve how you can keep your duty to each of them with the decision you have made about running the name.
2. Is rape just like any other crime or should it be treated differently by the media? By the courts?

CASE VI-B
A Person of Interest
CARA DeMICHELE
University of Missouri

Scarcely a week after America was attacked on September 11, 2001, terrorism took a different twist—letters tainted with deadly anthrax. The first such letters were postmarked from Trenton, New Jersey, on September 19, 2001, and sent to the *New York Post* and NBC Nightly News anchor Tom Brokaw. A New Jersey letter carrier began to show symptoms of an unusual illness on September 27, but it wouldn't be identified as anthrax exposure until after the death of Bob Stevens, a photo editor at American Media, Inc., in Boca Raton, Florida: Stevens died of inhalation anthrax. By the end of November, five people would die from the disease, and 17 more would be infected, while nearly 30,000 others would be given antibiotics. Congress shut down for two days after contaminated letters were mailed to Senators Tom Daschle and Patrick Leahy.

Multiple agencies tried to trace the infection, and by October 2001 it became clear that the anthrax had originated in the United States, from a strain grown at Iowa State University in Ames. Tests also showed not only that some of the anthrax was very refined but also that some had been "weaponized," making it more likely to be inhaled. There were at least 200 people in the United States who were thought to have the expertise to be capable of such a crime, but only 30 to 40 of them had access to the Ames anthrax strain.

Careful not to label anyone a "suspect" prematurely, the FBI spent months repeatedly interviewing and investigating 20 to 30 "persons of interest" who had worked or did work for federal laboratories on contract. Media outlets worldwide followed the investigation. Part of that reporting process demanded that journalists keep an eye on discussion boards and statements coming from the Federation of American Scientists (FAS) on the Web. Dr. Barbara Hatch Rosenberg, a molecular biologist at the University of New York at Purchase and chairwoman of a biological weapons panel at FAS, is familiar with the work of scientists in the close-knit biological weapons community and had been acting as advisor to the FBI.

On Feb. 19, 2002, Rosenberg made a statement at Princeton University claiming that the FBI had identified and twice questioned the man responsible for the anthrax attacks but was "dragging its feet" because the man was a former government scientist. In her comments, which also had been the subject of discussion at the FAS Web site for months, Rosenberg stated that many scientists in the field knew of the suspect who may have formerly worked at the U.S. Army Medical Research Institute of Infectious Diseases at Fort Derick, Maryland, and was currently working as a contractor in the Washington, D.C., area. Her comments were first reported in the *Trenton Times* newspaper, and then were slowly picked up by other U.S. media outlets.

The news coverage died down in the ensuing month until early June, when news organizations were tipped that the FBI would be searching the Maryland apartment and Florida storage locker of a bioweapons expert on June 25, 2001. Dr. Steven J. Hatfill is a former Fort Derick scientist who was first interviewed by the FBI in December 2001. Like some of the other 20 to 30 scientists who were deemed "persons of interest," Hatfill consented to the searches. At that time, the agency had searched the homes and offices of 25 other scientists with little to no media coverage. Just like the other searches, the FBI found nothing in the Hatfill searches but chose to keep him a "person of interest." And, unlike the other searches, the Hatfill investigation received extensive and ongoing media coverage.

It is likely that some news organizations had been aware that Hatfill was a possible target since December 2001 because his name and gossip about him had appeared on the FAS Web site. According to the articles and transcripts that covered the Hatfill case, there was plenty about his past that made him a likely suspect. ABC News, among others, reported that the FBI was interested in Hatfill partly because in the late 1970s Hatfill attended medical school in Zimbabwe near a Greendale elementary school. "Greendale School" appeared as the phony return address on one of the tainted letters sent to the Senate. In the early 1990s, Hatfill worked as a researcher for the National Institutes of Health. During this time he was widely quoted in newspaper articles as a bioterrorism expert and often gave lectures on the dangers of biowarfare.

After leaving the NIH, Hatfill had worked in the virology division of the Army's biodefense laboratory at Fort Derick from 1997 to September 1999. A Fort Derick spokesman told the Association Press that the virology division studies how to protect military personnel from biological weapons. The spokesman stated that while Hatfill probably had access to labs that contained the Ames anthrax strain, it wasn't part of his primary duties. In 1999, however, Hatfill commissioned a report that describes placing 2.5 grams of a simulated form of anthrax into a business envelope, which has only fueled speculation.

On March 4, 2002, Hatfill was fired from his job at Science Applications International Corporation, a Pentagon and CIA contractor that helps the government with biological defenses. Hatfill told the *Baltimore Sun* that he had been fired because journalists were constantly pursuing him. Most recently, Hatfill lost his research job at Louisiana State University as a result of the investigation.

On Aug. 1, 2002, the FBI performed a second search of Hatfill's apartment and again found nothing. By the time of Hatfill's Aug. 11 press conference to again deny any involvement with the anthrax attacks, the FBI had searched his home twice, his car, his storage facility in Florida, and his girlfriend's apartment with no success. Despite not being able to place Hatfill in New Jersey when the letters were sent, the FBI decided not to change Hatfill's "person of interest" status. Two years later, out of 20 to 30 "persons of interest" still being investigated by the FBI, Hatfill's name is the only one to have been released publicly. He has never been formally charged with any crime or officially named a "suspect."

Micro Issues

1. When, if ever, did Hatfill become news? When, if ever, did the case cease to be newsworthy?
2. When the original allegations surfaced, what sort of questions, if any, should journalists have asked Dr. Rosenberg, who made the original allegations?
3. When should Hatfill have been contacted to respond to the suspicions? How should his responses have been reported?
4. Would a legal action on Hatfill's behalf be a better remedy than an ethical one? Why or why not?

Midrange Issues

1. Journalists covering this beat almost certainly knew about Hatfill but did not report what was being said about him until Dr. Rosenberg's comments were made in public. Evaluate this news judgment.
2. Should journalists attempt to obtain the names of other "persons of interest"? Should they publish those names?
3. Are journalists responsible for Hatfill losing his job?
4. Do you think the news media were used by the FBI to try to pressure Hatfill? If you do, how should the journalists have responded?

Macro Issues

1. When, if ever, does the FBI's failure to solve the anthrax case become news?
2. How do you think the fact that journalists themselves were the targets of some of the anthrax letters figures into the media accounts of the investigation?
3. Using both utilitarian theory and Kant's categorical imperative, develop a newsroom policy that provides guidelines for covering "persons of interest."

AP/WIDE WORLD PHOTOS. Used with permission.

CASE VI-C
Competition, Deadlines, and the Mistreatment of Richard Jewell
GREG LISBY
Georgia State University

On July 27, 1996, around 12:45 A.M., Richard Jewell, a security guard employed to protect AT&T's interests and property in Atlanta's Centennial Olympic Park during the Summer Olympic Games, showed an agent with the Georgia Bureau of Investigation an unattended green knapsack lying beneath a bench outside a sound and light tower that was being used for a performance at the AT&T Global Olympic Village stage. Federal agents called to the scene determined that the knapsack contained a bomb, and Jewell and other law enforcement officers quietly began evacuating the area.

At 12:58 A.M., a bomb threat was called in to law enforcement officials from a pay phone three blocks from the scene. The tower and most of the immediate area surrounding the bomb had been cleared by the time it exploded at approximately 1:20 A.M., killing one visitor, leading to a fatal heart attack for a foreign journalist on the scene, and injuring 111 others.

For the next two days, the 33-year-old Jewell was hailed as a "hero." He was interviewed by several major newspapers and television networks, including NBC's *Today* show, about his role in spotting the knapsack, alerting authorities, evacuating the area, and helping the injured.

On Tuesday, July 30, however, FBI agents interviewed Jewell about the bombing while telling him he was participating in a training film on how to investigate suspicious packages. When agents asked Jewell to "pretend" to waive his right to an attorney, he called his lawyer and ended the meeting.

That same day, the *Atlanta Journal-Constitution* learned of police suspicions and revamped the front page of its special afternoon Olympics "Extra" supplement to spotlight Richard Jewell as "the focus of the federal investigation." Although the story was not attributed to any source, the paper has since said that three of its employees independently confirmed the investigation. The newspaper was distributed around 4:30 that afternoon, and a CNN anchor read the story verbatim on the air shortly afterward.

That night each of the three major networks' newscasts picked up the story, and the next day virtually every one of the country's major newspapers gave the story front-page billing. An exception was the *New York Times,* which ran a piece inside its "B" section, focusing more on the media than on Richard Jewell.

Many news organizations later cited not wanting to "appear foolish" by not running a story or the suspect's name when so many other organizations were. Many were also careful to point out that Jewell had not been charged, or even officially named as a suspect. Investigators had been discovered staking out Jewell's apartment, and by late afternoon the media, led by CNN and local Atlanta television stations, joined them. By midday Wednesday, an estimated 200 national and international journalists were on the scene as federal investigators, including agents from the FBI and the Bureau of Alcohol, Tobacco and Firearms, searched the apartment Jewell shared with his mother, and took away boxes of belongings and Jewell's pickup truck. In one of the few statements he made to the media at the time, Jewell "categorically" denied being the Centennial Olympic Park bomber in response to a reporter's question, an exchange that was also shown on CNN and NBC.

NBC also reported on July 31 that agents that day had searched the shed near a cabin Jewell had rented in northeast Georgia before he had moved to Atlanta in May. ABC and CBS, however, reported that the FBI's suspicions of Jewell might be diminishing, with ABC citing the lack of evidence—of fingerprints at the phone from which the 911 call originated, of a voice match, and of the short time span between the 911 call and the explosion.

On Thursday, August 1, the front page of the *Atlanta Constitution* detailed the search in an article that included the name and location of Richard Jewell's apartment complex. The apartment number, its address, and a map detailing its location were included in an inside story.

According to the *Constitution,* Jewell became a suspect after the president of Piedmont College, a small campus in north Georgia, contacted authorities after seeing Jewell interviewed on television. He said that Jewell, who had once worked as a security guard for the college, had been "overzealous" in the pursuit of his duties there, harassing students and asking to work undercover.

Prior to his job at the college, Jewell had been a deputy for the Habersham County Sheriff's Department until he wrecked his patrol car, was demoted to jailer, and subsequently resigned. His 1990 arrest for impersonating a police officer in DeKalb County in metropolitan Atlanta was also widely reported. Media organizations stated that the FBI was looking at whether Jewell fit the "profile" of a loner who might have planted the bomb in order to draw attention to his heroism; indeed, some said he had sought out interviews after the bombing. (It was later revealed that an AT&T spokesperson, not Jewell, had solicited interviews on his behalf.)

On Friday, August 2, two of the bombing victims filed suit against Richard Jewell. They alleged that he failed to clear the area around the bomb before it exploded.

On August 3, the FBI returned to Jewell's apartment with a subpoena for hair samples and fingerprints. Jewell and his lawyer, G. Watson Bryant Jr., refused to allow more voice samples or a polygraph test. About two weeks later, Jewell passed a lie detector test administered by an expert his legal team hired because they "didn't trust" the FBI to conduct the exam. In an article detailing the results, the *Atlanta Journal-Constitution* quoted several people extolling the expert's integrity, but the next day reported that the expert had also "cleared" two other men subsequently convicted as felons.

Richard Jewell left his apartment for the first time in five days on Sunday, August 4, when Bryant spirited him past law enforcement officers and the media still keeping vigil in the parking lot. He met with criminal lawyer Jack Martin, who with Bryant on Monday tried without success to unseal the affidavits filed by the FBI to obtain its search warrants.

During the next week the *Journal-Constitution* reported on Bryant's assertion that a piece of bomb shrapnel recovered by the FBI from the apartment was a "souvenir" given to Jewell by other guards at the park, and on Martin's demonstration, by walking the route involved with a reporter, that Jewell didn't have the time to make the 911 call.

The role and behavior of the media during the investigation were examined on ABC's *Viewpoint* on August 22. Discussing "The Bizarre Case of Richard Jewell" were Martin and Bryant, along with representatives from CNN, ABC, CBS, NBC, and NBC's Atlanta affiliate. The FBI, the Georgia Bureau of Investigation, and the *Journal-Constitution* declined to attend.

Four days later, at a news conference called by Jewell's lawyers, Richard Jewell's mother made an emotional appeal to President Bill Clinton, asking him to direct the Justice Department and the FBI to state whether or not they intended to charge her son. She also asked the media to leave them alone, stating that their life was a "nightmare." The White House did not comment, but a few days later Attorney General Janet Reno declined to exonerate Jewell, saying that she understood the Jewells' feelings but that the investigation had to be pursued. The *Journal-Constitution* commented that the exchange was part of a public relations campaign mounted by Jewell's lawyers—by then four in number—to get the FBI and the Justice Department to clear and apologize to their client.

A federal magistrate ruled on September 14 that the lawyers would be permitted to see portions of the FBI affidavits submitted to justify the search warrants. On September 22, Richard Jewell gave his first public interview since coming under investigation, appearing on CBS's *60 Minutes*. The discussion with correspondent Mike Wallace focused on whom he would sue if he were not charged.

By the end of September, the FBI agreed to "less obtrusive" surveillance of the Jewell apartment, and on Saturday, October 5, returned most of the property it had seized from the apartment and the north Georgia sites, including Mrs. Jewell's collection of Tupperware. The following day, in lieu of taking an FBI polygraph, Jewell submitted to a six-hour interview in what the *New York Times* called a deal approved by the Justice Department in which Jewell would receive within six weeks of the interview a letter clearing him if no damaging information was revealed during the questioning. Attorney Lin Wood later told the *Journal-Constitution* there was no guarantee of such a letter.

In a court hearing on October 8, U.S. District Judge J. Owen Forrester rebuked the media for "the worst example of media coverage I've ever seen since watching *La Dolce Vita*" (Federico Fellini's 1960 film depicting journalists as vultures). Forrester cited published reports of material in the sealed affidavits for search warrants as evidence of a probable leak by law enforcement officials, and was assured by U.S. Attorney Kent Alexander that a Justice Department and FBI investigation into the leaks was under way.

Fourteen guns were returned to Richard Jewell that day. Two days later, the *Journal-Constitution* published a "letter to the editor" from Alexander that defended the FBI's conduct in the investigation.

On Saturday, October 12, the *Journal-Constitution* reported "little progress" in the bombing investigation "as the FBI turns its attention away from Richard Jewell." The next day, it reprinted an *American Journalism Review* article critical of the media coverage the Jewell story had received.

Less than two weeks later, on October 24, Judge Forrester ordered public disclosure of the affidavits in response to a motion filed by the *Journal-Constitution* and the Atlanta ABC affiliate, WSB-TV, saying he believed Jewell was no longer the focus of the investigation.

Although the affidavits had already been released to Jewell's legal team, and the disclosure of such documents during a criminal investigation was unusual, Forrester called the situation "unique."

On Saturday, October 26, Alexander issued a letter to Richard Jewell's lawyers notifying them that Jewell was no longer considered by the Justice Department to be a target of the investigation. The letter expressed regret that "the Jewells have . . .

endured highly unusual and intense publicity that was neither designed nor desired by the FBI." The absolution received front-page treatment in the *Journal-Constitution* and the *New York Times* the next day.

Richard Jewell held a news conference on Monday, October 28, which was carried live by CNN and all three network affiliates in Atlanta. Introduced by his lawyer as the "114th victim" of the Olympic bombing, Jewell characterized press coverage of him as "all lies," said he had never asked for media attention before that day, and declared the day the start of "the other part of my nightmare—trying to restore my reputation and good name."

Micro Issues

1. In the days following Jewell's press conference, media organizations defended the manner in which they had reported the story, saying they were following "common procedures." Identify the "common procedures" of reporting a news story such as the one described here. Discuss the ethics of each procedure.
2. Richard Jewell's attorneys indicated that he was planning to sue several news organizations, including the *Journal-Constitution,* NBC News, and NBC anchorman Tom Brokaw. However, many people don't sue to win; instead they win by suing. What are the ethical issues involved in Richard Jewell's attempt to restore his reputation by threatening a lawsuit for libel, when—as a public figure—he would have an extremely difficult time establishing the necessary legal standard of fault required to collect monetary damages?

Midrange Issues

1. The results of an ABC News poll conducted at the time of Jewell's exoneration revealed that 69 percent of Americans thought Jewell had been unfairly treated by the media; 82 percent said it was not acceptable for the media to identify a suspect before he or she was charged. Under what circumstances, if any, is it ethically permissible for the media to identify a suspect before he or she is charged with a criminal offense?
2. Justify your answer to the previous question using ethical reasoning and principles.
3. In late 1996, NBC agreed to pay Jewell more than $500,000 to avert a lawsuit over comments made by Tom Brokaw. In your opinion will the threat of lawsuits "chill" the media from reporting on suspects in the future?

Macro Issues

1. Deadline pressure, the competition for news and "pack journalism"—the individual assignments of a number of reporters to follow a single person or issue for weeks or months at a time "like a pack of hounds sicked on a fox" (Crouse 1974, 7)—all contributed to the media's coverage of Richard Jewell's heroics at the Olympics. How might deadline pressure have been handled differently yet within an ethical framework? How might the journalists have competed for news differently in this situation?
2. How is the journalistic standard of objectivity twisted by "pack journalism"?
3. How did the concept of authority as an accepted source of information affect the media's attitude toward Richard Jewell? Under what circumstances, if any, is it ethically permissible for the media to allow themselves to be used as either an investigative or surveillance arm of the police? Do they have any different ethical obligations than do ordinary citizens witnessing a similar situation?

CASE VI-D
Arthur Ashe and the Right to Privacy
CAROL OUKROP
Kansas State University

"Tennis great Arthur Ashe has AIDS," began the dispatch fed by *USA Today* to its overseas edition and the Gannett News Service on April 8, 1992.

Ashe, a disciplined athlete who overcame racial barriers, was 48. He was the first African-American to win the U.S. Open and Wimbledon tennis championships. He was reluctant to go public with his disease, but was given little choice.

On April 7 he had been contacted by *USA Today* reporter Doug Smith about a rumor telephoned in to the newspaper that Ashe had AIDS. After speaking with Smith, Ashe talked with *USA Today*'s executive editor for sports, Gene Policinski. Policinski asked Ashe if he was HIV-positive, and the response was "could be." Ashe asked Policinski to delay the story for 36 hours. Policinski would not promise Ashe the delay. Ashe called a press conference for April 8.

The call from *USA Today,* Ashe said at the press conference, put him in the unenviable position of having to lie if he wanted to protect his family's privacy.

"I am sorry that I have been forced to make this revelation at this time. After all, I am not running for some office of public trust, nor do I have stockholders to account to. It is only that I fall in the dubious umbrella of, quote, public figure, end of quote."

Later Ashe wrote in the *Washington Post* that going public with a disease such as AIDS was "akin to telling the world in 1900 that you had leprosy."

© 1992 Gary Markstein. Used by permission.

Ashe was married and was the father of a 5-year-old daughter, Camera, thought to have been protected from knowledge of his disease prior to the call from *USA Today*. Ashe had known since 1988 that he had AIDS, apparently contracted from a blood transfusion required during heart surgery in 1983. Blood was not routinely checked for the virus before 1985.

It is clear in articles appearing since Ashe's press conference that a number of journalists knew about Ashe's disease but chose to protect "Arthur Ashe's Secret" (Frank Deford, *Newsweek,* April 20, 1992).

"Keeping my AIDS status private," Ashe wrote in the *Washington Post,* "enabled me to control my life."

Was *USA Today* right or wrong? An editorial in *The Christian Century* (April 22, 1992) called this a "tale of media irresponsibility and corporate greed," an example of "entertainment posing as information."

In the editorial in *The Christian Century,* Peter Prichard, editor of *USA Today,* claims that "when the press has kept secrets . . . that conspiracy of silence has not served the public. . . . Journalists serve the public by reporting news, not hiding it. By sharing his story, Arthur Ashe and his family are free of a great weight. In the days ahead, they will help us better understand AIDS and how to defeat it."

Public-figure privacy decisions are often difficult, this one perhaps particularly so. Ashe had, over the years, earned much respect. In addition to his accomplishments in tennis, he had participated in human rights struggles in the United States and was a leading critic of apartheid in South Africa. He was the author of a lauded history of African-American athletes in the United States.

Arthur Ashe died from AIDS-related complications in February 1993.

Micro Issues

1. Should Policinski have promised Ashe the requested 36 hours during which to prepare a statement?
2. Were Deford, Roy Johnson, and others who knew about Ashe's disease months before the press conference right to keep Ashe's secret?

Midrange Issues

1. What if Ashe's ailment were an inoperable lung cancer or Lou Gehrig's disease? Would the media decision have been justifiable then?
2. If Ashe had contracted AIDS through a homosexual encounter, should that have been part of the story? Would it change the decision-making process? Justify your decision.

Macro Issues

1. Does the Ashe case really differ significantly from, say, the rape of a celebrity? Both are public figures, but according to the policy of many news media, the rape victim would be afforded anonymity. Is that fair?
2. What is the public's stake in knowing Ashe had AIDS? Does that stake override his right to privacy?

VII

The Mass Media in a Democratic Society: Keeping a Promise

By the end of this chapter, you should be familiar with:

- how a society's media are shaped by the form of its government.
- many of the criticisms leveled at the way the U.S. media cover government and elections.
- the special problems of reporting on terrorism and hate.
- why the media should be concerned with social justice for the powerful and the powerless alike.

INTRODUCTION

Americans view the written word as essential to political society. The First Amendment to the U.S. Constitution states:

> Congress shall make no law respecting an establishment of religion, or prohibiting the free exercise thereof; or abridging the freedom of speech, or of the press; or the right of the people peaceably to assemble, and to petition the government for a redress of grievances.

Scholars such as John C. Merrill (1974) assert that the First Amendment should be interpreted purely as a restriction on government. This view emphasizes the role of freedom of expression and downplays assertions of journalistic responsibility.

Some journalists concur. *Washington Post* Managing Editor Leonard Downie, speaking to a meeting of journalism educators, said he expects his reporters to act "as if they live on an island." "I know that makes me unpopular," he said, "but my interpretation of the First Amendment is that it means strictly that government should not interfere with the press." Downie has consistently claimed he neither votes nor belongs to a political party, saying that he prefers to remain totally objective in the political process.

We prefer a different view. Madison, Hamilton, and Jay, in the *Federalist Papers,* asserted that communication among the citizens serves an important political purpose.

The founders expected citizens to be informed and then to participate in politics. They expected that political debate, including what was printed in the press of the day, would be partisan and biased rather than objective, but they also believed that from this cacophony of information the rational being would be able to discern the truth.

As the authors made clear by circulating those documents as a series of newspaper articles, one way to enhance political learning was publication in the media of the time. Citizens had an obligation to read such information; the press had an obligation to provide it.

Tucked within all of this, we believe, is a promise that the mass media, both in 1791 and more than two hundred years later, will provide citizens with what they need to know to get along in political society. Scholars have labeled this analysis of the media's role in a democratic society the "social responsibility theory" of the press. However, assuming such a responsibility is becoming progressively more difficult. Some of the difficulties emanate from the structure of the contemporary American political system and, hence, are appropriately the subject for political reform. Others reflect the ethical choices contemporary journalists are making. After providing some historic context, it is to those issues we will turn.

A DEMOCRACY WITHOUT MASS COMMUNICATION

In ancient Greece, the highest form of human existence was the *polis*—literally "community." But the polis was special, for as Aristotle noted, it was "an association of free men." The polis governed itself; the ruled were the rulers.

In the ancient myth, the art of politics was a gift from the gods, who provided men with *adios,* a sense of concern for the good opinion of others, and *dike,* a sense of justice, or that which makes civic peace possible through the adjudication of disputes. In the ancient myth, these gifts were bestowed on everyone, not just on some ruling economic or social elite. All men were able to exercise the art of politics through rhetoric and argument in the assembly, a form of direct democracy that survived for only a few years in Athens. Certain Native-American tribes exercised a similar form of democratic decision making, but in Europe, ancient Greece was the first—and last—place it was seriously attempted.

Socratic teaching took issue with the myth. Not everyone, according to Plato and Socrates, was capable of knowing *adios* and *dike.* Democracy was the refuge of the herd; it took a philosopher-king to rule. Indeed, in his book *The Trial of Socrates,* I. F. Stone maintains that the Athenians condemned Socrates to death not because he insisted on teaching philosophy but because the philosophy he taught was profoundly antidemocratic.

The Greeks, of course, had no media system; their political interaction was face-to-face, at least among the men who ruled. But their democracy, founded as it was on conceptions of knowing and rhetoric, never assumed an uninformed or lackadaisical citizenry. The Greeks didn't need newspapers or television to govern themselves, but they did demand political and cultural literacy. Without knowing it, their highly developed vision of democratic theory, one which viewed political information as a citizen's fundamental right (not the commodity that contemporary news organizations consider it), anticipated the core of modern problems in 21st-century democracies.

MODERN MEDIATED PROBLEMS: LEARNING ABOUT LEADERS

Athens was small enough that "pure" democracy was possible. By the late 1700s when the framers were crafting the U.S. Constitution—on which almost all other modern democracies have been modeled—the architects of government knew it was not possible for each citizen to be involved in every political decision. They established a representative democracy in which certain members would be elected by their fellows to speak for them—to represent their views—in the legislature. (In ancient Athens, leaders were named by drawing lots.) This concept of representative government drew heavily from the ancient Greek tradition of *adios,* a concern for the good opinion of others.

In the 21st century, the issue has been reframed: Can people become acquainted well enough with any candidate to acquire an opinion? Except for a small group of government and corporate insiders, the mass media have become the primary mode of receiving political discourse. In addition to providing voters with facts, something that is generally assumed to be the role of news, the media also provide citizens with a framework to understand those facts, the realm of culture and myth that is the role not only of news but also of entertainment and advertising.

Candidates have been quick to learn that the public uses a variety of media sources to get to know their candidates. One study by the Pew Charitable Trusts in 2004 found that more than 50 percent of Americans under the age of 50 get their news about politics "regularly" or "sometimes" from late-night comedians. However, Pew research showed those respondents who "regularly" turned to late-night comedians for information were among the least likely to know basic facts about the candidates.

Comedy Central consistently gets its highest ratings and industry awards for its late-night news show with anchor/comedian Jon Stewart. Dennis Miller and Bill Maher have taken political commentary mixed with often biting humor to the premium television channels. And most major candidates for the 2000 and 2004 presidencies visited Leno and Letterman for a chat during the campaign.

The trend to reach the masses through popular culture channels reached new heights when actor Arnold Schwarzenegger announced on the *Tonight Show with*

Jay Leno that he was running for governor of California in the summer of 2003 while a full pressroom of mainstream political reporters waited for the announcement backstage. With the declining readership in newspapers and the graying of the audience for the nightly news shows of NBC, ABC and CBS, the trend of using entertainment media to convey political messages will continue. Researchers Bruce Williams and Michael Delli Carpini (2002) writing about this phenomenon in the *Chronicle of Higher Education,* noted that "it becomes as important to know Dennis Miller's sources and slants as Dan Rather's" in this new electoral world.

Study of media coverage of political campaigns has uncovered some disturbing trends. Journalists function as a pack; there is seldom any really distinctive political reporting during elections (Crouse 1974; Sabato 1992). However, campaign assignments remain sought after by members of the national press corps for reasons of personal prestige. The person who covers the winning candidate for the network will almost assuredly become the White House correspondent for the next four years, a guarantee of celebrity status, increased income and, many would argue, real political power. Because of the financial ramifications, journalists covering a national election have almost as much at stake as the candidates they cover.

Further, journalists treat front-runners differently than they do the remainder of the candidate pack (Robinson and Sheehan 1984). Front-runners are the subject of closer scrutiny, but those examinations are seldom about issues, even though it is issue-oriented reporting that tends to provoke political interest and public participation (Patterson 1980). Instead, electoral reporting focuses on character and personality, key components of political leadership, but certainly not the only ones.

Candidates and their paid consultants seem to have intuitively understood what academic research has shown. They've developed strategies that will allow them either to capitalize on front-runner status and image or to compensate for a lack of it. Free media—synonymous with a positive story on the 5:00 P.M. news—has become the watchword of most state and national political campaigns. The candidates have created the "photo opportunity" and the "Rose Garden strategy." Both seem designed to thwart anything but the most carefully scripted candidate contact with the voting public.

The 2003 Schwarzenegger campaign perfected this strategy in a shortened campaign season brought about by the California gubernatorial recall initiative. In the brief weeks leading to the election, Schwarzenegger rarely gave speeches of substance. Instead, he resorted to the prop of a broom, vowing to "sweep" the sitting governor out of the office in a gesture reminiscent of the film *O Brother Where Art Thou.*

At the same time candidates try to script their every move, the media have the right, and some would say even the responsibility, to get "behind the curtain" (Molotch and Lester 1974) to the real candidate. What happens then often makes news in ways the candidates could not have foreseen, as the following illustrations show.

In 1972, going into the New Hampshire primary, Senator Edwin Muskie of Maine was considered the Democratic front-runner. Just days before the primary, Muskie, reacting to media criticism of his wife, broke down in tears according to reports in the *Washington Post.* The crying was disputed by some on the scene, including Muskie, but the damage was done. Muskie was finished as a political contender.

During the 1980 primary season, CBS correspondent Roger Mudd concluded an interview with Democratic challenger Edward Kennedy with this question: "Mr.

Senator, why do you want to be president?" The rambling answer that resulted clearly revealed that Kennedy had no scripted answer for why he was challenging incumbent Jimmy Carter of his own party and led many of his critics to continue to claim he was running only on the family name. Only a larger story—the taking of the American embassy in Iran and the capturing of American hostages—kept the gaffe from getting more airtime. Kennedy did not win the nomination.

In the 2000 presidential race, future President George W. Bush refused to provide details of what he characterized as "youthful mistakes" to the press corps, many of whom were asking questions about previous cocaine use. Several months later, a novice television reporter at a Fox affiliate in Maine broke the story that Bush had been arrested for drunk driving when he was 40. Neither revelation had an impact on the result of the presidential contest.

Journalists face a number of questions in cases such as these. Just because the information is available and even accurate does not automatically mean that it is relevant. While political character is definitely a bona fide issue in an election of national importance, where is the threshold for what counts as a mark of character or the lack thereof? Voters must winnow the field of candidates in some way. The question is whether this sort of journalism is adequate for making that political decision.

These changes in the electoral process take place in a culture where the word "politician" has become synonymous with "crook" and "liar." Instead of being perceived as the honorable calling it was in ancient Greece, politics for many Americans is viewed as an unsavory activity. Such images come to us not only through the news but also through entertainment. Frank Capra's film *Mr. Smith Goes to Washington* paints the exceptional politician as common man and hero, against a backdrop of crooked politics as usual. A similar vision is manifest in the 1993 film *Dave.* Our current views are equally skewed. Whether it's *The Candidate, Bulworth,* or *Primary Colors,* the entertainment media portray politicians at best as absent or weak, at worst as downright sleazy.

MODERN MEDIATED PROBLEMS: GETTING ELECTED

Political scientists agree that the mass-mediated election has redefined electoral politics. It's also changed our understanding of mass communication, blurring the distinctions between advertising and news from the voters' point of view. As many researchers have noted, all politics—and hence all political communication—is symbolic.

Let's begin with some research findings. Voters sometimes learn more about candidates' stands on issues from advertising than they do from news (Patterson 1980). Factual accuracy, therefore, must be the starting point for ethical political advertising. As philosopher Hannah Arendt has noted, "Freedom of information is a farce unless factual information is guaranteed and the facts themselves are not in dispute" (Arendt 1970). Other scholarly studies have found that news stories about elections emphasize strategy and tactics rather than stands on issues (Sheehan and Robinson 1984).

The media system is interactive—voters who want to become informed about the candidate's policy choices get the information from ads, some of them labeled "negative" or "attack" ads, in part because policy information is missing from news stories. Negative political ads are literally as old as the republic. One early patriot, Yale President Reverend Timothy Dwight, claimed that if Thomas Jefferson were

Copyright © Ed Stein. Reprinted with permission of Rocky Mountain News.

elected, the Bible would be burned, the French national anthem sung in Christian churches, and women dishonored in the most biblical of senses. The majority of voters obviously didn't believe him.

Contemporary voters are providing scholars with evidence that they, too, can discern among the various types of political ads. Comparative ads, ones that contrast candidate positions on specific issues, are viewed as information rich, and voters view them as an appropriate part of political discourse. Attack ads, ones that are personal and negative, that contain no "positive" or "issue-oriented" information, are disliked and distrusted. Voters appear to be able to distinguish between negative, comparative, and positive or biographical ads (Jamieson 2000). Furthermore, recent analysis indicates that the majority of political ads fall into the positive or contrast categories (Benoit 2000), providing ample evidence that it is possible to create ethical political advertising on the local, state and national levels.

Journalists are deciding that covering the advertising a campaign produces can result in legitimate news stories focused on policy issues. These news stories, often called "ad watches," appear in both broadcast and print and have the goal of putting the claims in political ads to the tests of truthfulness and context. While the scholarly findings are not conclusive, anecdotal evidence from states as diverse as Colorado, California, and North Carolina suggests that aggressive news journalism focusing on attack ads and negative campaigning can have an impact on the voters' knowledge of particular candidates and their evaluation of those candidates. In addition, we would suggest that it is the responsibility of journalists to evaluate political advertising as legitimate news and to hold candidates publicly accountable for the advertising sponsored by a campaign or, in the grayer areas, advertising paid for by political action groups in favor of a particular candidate that same candidate refuses to disavow.

For example, an important, but largely unreported, news story of the 2000 election was the hundreds of political radio ads paid for by the National Rifle Association and its assorted state political action committees in favor of specific candidates, but which included the tagline "the [insert name of candidate here] campaign is not responsible for this ad." Journalists should be willing to ask who is responsible for the public statements of political action committees.

Everyone seems to agree on a single starting point: political advertising is unique (Kaid 1992). Ideally, the same ethical principles that apply to advertising (see the TARES test outlined in Chapter 3) should be applied to political advertising as well. Further, many philosophers link facts with rationality, particularly in the area of political debate. The use of emotional arguments designed to stir listeners or viewers "to set aside reason" has been characterized as a "violation of democratic ethics" (Haiman 1958, 388). There may, however, be times when valid issues have strong emotional content, such as the ongoing debate over abortion. At those times, the melding of emotion with issue content in such cases is not prima facie unethical.

Students of history will realize that many totalitarian regimes have used emotional appeals to either gain or retain power. However, such ads usually lack any public revelation of evidence to support the claims. Making the evidence behind political assertions public—what Kant called the "transcendental principle of publicness"—has historically been the role of the news media. We believe such reporting stands on firm ethical ground. The lack of this sort of journalism was foreseen by Lippmann: "In the absence of debate, restricted utterance leads to the degradation of opinion. By a kind of Gresham's law the more rational is overcome by the less rational, and the opinions that will prevail will be those which are held most ardently by those with the most passionate will" (Lippmann 1982, 196).

If political advertising is indeed a special case, then journalists and their audiences should demand higher standards, more regulations or both. While some of the solutions to the current problems have First Amendment ramifications, they are worthy of discussion. They include the following:

- Allot limited amounts of free time to qualified candidates for major office to level the playing field for candidates without destroying the bottom line at already strapped broadcast outlets.
- Strengthen state regulations against corrupt campaign practices and find ways to enforce those regulations.
- Establish a federal campaign commission to hear complaints about ethical abuses in campaign communication, particularly in advertising.
- Encourage journalists to stop covering the "horse race" aspect of campaigns and focus on problem and policy solutions.
- Hold candidates accountable for their ads, not only in verbal terms but in visual and audio terms as well.
- Teach journalists to read and report on the visual imagery of a campaign, and to ask candidates questions about it.
- Allow attack ads only if they include the image of the candidate directing the attack.
- Reject unfair or inaccurate ads created by political action committees.
- Conduct ad watches as part of media coverage of a campaign, analyzing the ads for omissions, inconsistencies and inaccuracies.

It takes money to buy ads, and in contemporary democratic societies that means the candidate with the most money often has the loudest voice. Many of those in public life, such as former New Jersey Senator Bill Bradley or Arizona Senator John McCain, argue the influence of money in the political system is pervasive and corrosive. How to deal with the money that finances political advertising is an important policy question, one with significant ethical overtones, but there seem to be no good candidates for conducting an investigation. Politicians are too entrenched in the existing system to be objective, and the media that could presumably investigate political money and its negative influence are compromised by the act of receiving so much of the cash. The problem cannot be "solved" in this brief chapter, but it is worth considering whether a highly profitable media system such as the one in the United States might not be able to find a way to "give back" access to political candidates who cannot raise enormous sums to purchase newspaper space and broadcast airtime.

MODERN MEDIATED PROBLEMS: COVERING POLITICAL CHARACTER

Conceptualizations of character have changed significantly since the founding of the republic, when character was defined in Aristotelian terms—an observable collection of habits, virtues and vices. Freudian psychology has altered that definition to include motivation, the subconscious and relationships that help to form all of us as people. What journalists cover is "political character": the intersection of personality and public performance within a cultural and historical context. Character is dynamic; it represents a synergistic interaction of a person within an environment (Davies 1963).

Journalists who explore character often do so for an ethical reason, despite apparent invasions of privacy. Privacy in Western culture is regarded as a right that can be negated by other more compelling rights (Grcic 1986, 141). Political figures are powerful people. Ethicist Sissela Bok (1978) has noted that when an unequal power relationship is involved, it is possible to justify what would otherwise be considered an unethical act. To paraphrase Bok, at the core of any serious investigation of the private character of public people is the notion that if the person one wishes to investigate is also in the position to do one harm, then invading privacy in an attempt to counter that threat is justified.

However, that invasion also needs to meet some tests (Schoeman 1984):

- The invasion must be placed in a larger context of facts and history. Since one of the definitions of invasion of privacy is the subject's loss of control over the context of information (Westin 1967), an effort to study character must include enough context to provide meaning.
- The revelation of private facts about political figures should meet the traditional tests of journalistic publicity and evidence. Further, these private facts need to be linked to public, political behaviors before publication or broadcast becomes ethically justifiable.
- The invasion of privacy must further the larger political discourse. Investigation of the character of political figures must meet the most demanding ethical test: the need to know.

Careful reporting on character can pass these tests. However, journalists must also be willing to weigh the harm done to others, particularly those who have not sought the public limelight. While public officials do have the capacity to do harm, that argument is much less compelling when applied to parents, spouses, children, friends and other family members. Journalistic investigation of character may often involve others, but publication or broadcast of what is learned should be considered only if public awareness of such facts furthers the political discourse.

Even reporting that passes these three tests must be filtered through discretion. Merely publishing private information without this tie to a more public role is a form of "tabloid journalism" that casts doubt on journalistic motives and credibility. More seriously, such publication denigrates politicians in such a way that every official becomes a "crook," "liar" or "philanderer" without some larger understanding of why those character traits may or may not be important in doing the public's business.

Reporters covering political character should be aware of some or all of the following building blocks of character:

- The politician's development of a sense of trust.
- A politician's own sense of self-worth and self-esteem.
- The development of a politician's relationship to power and authority.
- Early influences on adult policy outlook.
- How a politician establishes contact with people.
- The flexibility, adaptability and purposefulness of mature adulthood.
- The historical moment.

The media's current emphasis on covering political character provides the best illustration of the need to balance the demands of governing with privacy considerations. No culture has ever expected its leaders to be saints; in fact, some cultures have prized leadership that is decidedly unsaintly. By emphasizing an almost inhuman standard of public behavior, the mass media may be setting a standard of public behavior that may be impossible to meet as well as politically inadvisable.

However, an in-depth and nonjudgmental explanation of character can spur and expand the political debate, particularly if journalists treat character as one political story among many and if they are willing to imbed character in a history and political context Americans share. A deep exploration of character may help Americans think deeply about what we as a political system mean by and need from leadership.

MODERN MEDIATED PROBLEMS: GOVERNING

One of the ironies of democratic politics is that, in order to accomplish something, you first have to get elected. But accomplishing something, not getting elected, is the major work of politics. Many inches of newspaper space are devoted to the process on the local level. Local television news provides much less attention to policy making. Regulatory agencies, the courts, and even Congress are not considered glamour beats by the national press corps, and annual surveys by journalism watchdog groups show a dwindling number of reporters on the regulatory beat.

Yet the national press corps, particularly, has changed how the policy process operates. No one is quite certain when the "media leak" originated, certainly back in the last century and quite likely as early as the founding of the country. Not only has a leak to a reporter become a fact of political life; it appears to alter how policy-makers, and sometimes policy itself, work.

Political scientist Martin Linsky (1986) describes how leaks have become part of the Washington policy-making process. Government officials, both elected and appointed, use the mass media to help make policy in a variety of ways, he says. Sometimes they leak a story to find out how others will react to an idea, a practice known as floating a "trial balloon" in the press. Other times, policy-makers will leak a story because they wish to mount either public or bureaucratic support for or opposition to a set of options.

Sometimes leaks take the form of whistle-blowing when a government employee honestly believes the public good is not being served by working through the system. Watergate's famed and unnamed source, "Deep Throat," apparently was motivated by such a belief when he leaked parts of the government investigation into the break-in to *Washington Post* reporters Bob Woodward and Carl Bernstein. Anti–Vietnam War activist Daniel Ellsberg admits a desire to fuel opposition to national policy was much of his motivation in leaking the Pentagon Papers to the *New York Times.*

Still other times, government officials leak a story to put a particular reporter or publication on notice about who really holds the power in a particular situation. Network news correspondent Bill Moyers was taught that lesson by Lyndon Johnson, who told him that he planned to fire J. Edgar Hoover, a scoop Moyers reported. The very next day Johnson appointed Hoover director of the FBI for life. Moyers was stuck with a story that was accurate but not true. Worse, he had become the subject of Johnson's well-known propensity for power plays. It was a lesson in trust and political power Moyers never forgot.

Linsky's work about the role of the media in the policy-making process raises at least two important points regarding ethical journalistic practice.

First, leaks are becoming a more acceptable way of doing government business, and policy-makers are using them skillfully. In the summer of 1989, when terrorist groups in the Middle East threatened to kill one or more of the Americans they held hostage, then-President George H. W. Bush allowed a staff member to leak a story to a trusted *New York Times* reporter that the United States would retaliate militarily if hostages were killed. Bush's message was sent to the terrorists not through diplomatic back channels but on the paper's front page.

Second, leaks can alter the outcome of the policy process itself. President Bill Clinton's 1993 trial balloon about the potential of freezing the Social Security cost-of-living allowance provoked immediate congressional opposition. But it enlarged the range of politically acceptable options—including taxing a larger percentage of some Social Security benefits—to reduce the nation's deficit.

Of fundamental importance for journalists is the question of whether reporters, editors and their news organizations should become consciously involved in the process of governing, and in what manner? Such willing involvement runs counter to established notions of objectivity but not to the history of the media themselves. Leaks are so common that journalists can no longer plead ignorance either of their existence or of their impact. Instead they must decide if, and how, they are willing to be used—and for what political purposes. These are difficult questions, particularly when big stories, professional prestige and the chance to influence world events hinge on the outcome of ethical decision making.

MODERN MEDIATED PROBLEMS: ARROGANCE WITHOUT AUTHORITY

Although the evolving role of the mass media in a democratic society has been widely analyzed, most ethicists agree that the media's primary function is to provide citizens with information that will allow them to make informed political choices (Hodges 1986; Elliott 1986). As part of performing that job, the media are expected to act as a watchdog on government. This watchdog role arises from the Founders' original skepticism of concentrated political power. The watchdog media enable citizens to learn about and then check inappropriate government activity.

While the Founders built many checks and balances into the original U.S. system, those checks and balances were designed to enable government to continue to function. The Founders tried to guard against any single check fundamentally undermining the American experiment. The watchdog media—examined from this perspective—also have a "guide dog" function. Their goal is to help citizens make their way through the political process, not to immobilize them with a series of false trails or a sense that all political activity is futile.

However, many contemporary media critics argue that a particular style of covering politics, one emphasizing conflict and wrongdoing, has soured both journalists and citizens on American democracy. Political reporter E. J. Dionne in *Why Americans Hate Politics* (1991) argues that definitions of news that emphasize conflict inevitably help to degenerate political debate into a shouting match between diametrically opposed factions that have no reason to compromise. He notes that contemporary debate about both abortion and race has taken on this "us vs. them" quality, one that fails to acknowledge an important series of majority agreements on both issues—namely that abortion is not a particularly good method of birth control and that a sizable majority of Americans accept that human beings are of equal value and that learning to get along with one another is crucial in daily political life.

Dionne adds that politics without government, a concept that seems to have rhetorical support across the political continuum, is an oxymoron. While he does not blame the mass media for creating these sorts of false rhetorical divisions, he does hold those in his own profession accountable for failing to point out what they mean in the context of a democratic form of government. In this, Dionne agrees with Plato, who said that democratic politics, while a "degenerative" form of government, was probably the best available system considering that human beings were its primary components.

Media critic James Fallows goes one step further. He holds a journalism permeated by a cynical and conflict-laden view of politics directly responsible for voter apathy, congressional gridlock and government via opinion polls rather than political leadership (Fallows 1996, 7):

> The harm actually goes much further than that, to threaten the long-term health of our political system. Step by step, mainstream journalism has fallen into the habit

of portraying public life in America as a race to the bottom, in which one group of conniving, insincere politicians ceaselessly tries to outmaneuver another. The great problem for American democracy in the 1990s is that people barely trust elected leaders or the entire legislative system to accomplish anything of value. . . . Deep forces in America's political, social and economic structures account for most of the frustration of today's politics, but the media's attitudes have played a surprisingly important and destructive role.

In fact, media critic Katherine Hall Jamieson (1992) has suggested that, when it comes to politics, journalists should get themselves a new definition of news. Instead of emphasizing events and conflict, Jamieson believes news stories could equally revolve around issues and multiple policy perspectives. This suggestion even has some support in academic research; readers are more interested in coverage that emphasizes policy issues than fights and horse races (Sheehan and Robinson 1984).

Fallows and others insist that journalists have a right to report on government. But implicit in that right is the sense that successful governing is a political outcome for which the media are partially responsible. The cynical assumption that government can never act for the public good, and the arrogant stance that journalists and the media are somehow outside the political system, are almost nihilistic in this view. Many journalists and scholars believe there is real meat behind this critique of "mad dog" journalism. Conscientious ethical practice will allow journalists and media consumers to begin the work of carving out new understandings of our *responsibilities and rights* when the mass media become involved in the American democratic political system.

MODERN MEDIATED PROBLEMS: TERRORISM AND HATE

Terrorism is, at its most fundamental, an act of communication. In fact, scholars suggest that terrorism was not possible before the advent of the mass media. Terrorists and the media have a symbiotic relationship: terrorists need the media to communicate their messages, and the media garner ratings and increased readership when terrorism is in the news, even while deploring the violence. At the same time, the media perform an essential role: acting as a filter on the terrorists' message and as a watchdog on government response.

Terrorism presents journalists with what philosophers call "hard questions." Terrorism is news, but news coverage furthers terrorists' ends and makes more terrorism likely. How to break that cycle has been the subject of much professional anguish throughout the world, beginning in the Middle East (soon after Israel became a state and Palestine did not), continuing with the troubles in Northern Ireland that intensified after 1972 (which provoked the British government to censor the BBC), and culminating in the images of New York's twin towers (and the resulting war that included the military takeover of Iraq).

In the face of some forms of terrorism such as genocide, journalists must take the side of humanity, even if it means abandoning objectivity. CNN correspondent Christiane Amanpour did this when she argued on air with former President Bill Clinton about America's reluctance to involve itself in the racial and civil war that

Cartoon by Walt Handelsman. Copyright© 2003 Tribune Media Services. Reprinted with permission.

developed after the former Yugoslavia disintegrated. Amanpour was not alone in her views, and it should be noted that after extensive debate the United States and NATO did engage in the conflict.

Despite instances where journalists drop their objectivity in favor of advocacy, the more general journalistic understanding is that coverage of terrorism must avoid partisanship and must include context needed to place the act in its historical context. In the long run only this sort of news coverage will make reasoned debate and response possible. However, the reality of more than half a century of war in the Middle East, and the continuing struggles by those who employ terrorist methods to gain power, provides a discouraging reminder that a free media system is an inadequate solution to solve the problems caused by deep-seated hatred and ill-conceived national self-interest.

Terrorism also presents nation-states with hard problems. Nations under attack almost reflexively clamp down on their citizens—particularly those who question or dissent—because leaders believe diplomacy will be ineffective. Democracies pass laws, for example the Patriot Act, that enhance government's powers over its citizens. In the case of the Patriot Act, not only did the law increase the government's powers of search and seizure unchecked by the courts, but it also made possible incarceration of suspected terrorists without bail or public notification. What made the act more devastating, from the journalists' perspective, was the inclusion of a provision that made it impossible for journalists to get information needed to evaluate the effectiveness of the Patriot Act.

In such times, it becomes easier to label those who question particular policies as unpatriotic. When the George W. Bush administration asked news organizations to refrain from broadcasting tapes of Osama bin Laden for fear that hidden messages in the tapes would alert terrorist cells in the United States, all the American news networks complied. The Bush administration had made it clear that failure to honor the request would be considered unpatriotic, and public opinion polls overwhelmingly supported this view. No one was willing to consider that such messages could reach the United States via satellite, since many other news organizations around the world would broadcast the messages. Shortly before the two-year anniversary of the 9/11 event, another bin Laden tape surfaced. This time, the networks broadcast the tape, just as many news organizations around the world did, and the Bush administration remained silent.

Cases about the media and coverage of terrorism can be found throughout this book, and we urge you to revisit them in light of the tension between a government under stress and news media that inevitably will be used by terrorists as news organizations perform their journalistic, institutional role. If truth is the first casualty of war, then independence of thought and action is the first casualty of terrorism.

Journalists perform another role in such historic time—that of moral witness. Ethicist Patrick Plaisance (2002) suggests that when journalists report on such events as terrorism, its causes, its execution and its results, the journalist functions as a "moral witness" because such news stories cannot be understood or reported outside of a moral framework. Plaisance and others assert that to be detached and objective about genocide and hate is to condone it. When journalists write the first draft of history of the early part of this century, they must deal with competing claims about justice, community, truth and power. Such reporting requires excellence in both ethical reflection and professional technique. It has seldom been more difficult—or more important—to do both well.

MEDIATED MODERN PROBLEMS: SOCIAL JUSTICE

Just as there are members of a power elite, there are also those who feel excluded from political society. While some scholars have argued that one interpretation of U.S. history has been the gradual extension of the franchise to ever more diverse publics, that extension of basic rights has been uneven and contentious. All of these minority groups seek access to the political process and, since the mass media have become major institutional forces in that process, they seek access to media as well.

Media ethicists suggest these political and social out-groups provide the mass media with a further set of responsibilities. For instance, they assert that the mass media, and individual journalists, need to become advocates for the politically homeless. Media ethicist Clifford Christians suggests that "justice for the powerless stands at the centerpiece of a socially responsible press. Or, in other terms, the litmus test of whether or not the news profession fulfills its mission over the long term is its advocacy for those outside the socioeconomic establishment" (Christians 1986, 110).

This socially responsible view of the media suggests that journalists have a duty both to promote community and to promote the individuals within it. Those who are in significant ways outside the community—economically, socially or culturally different—need a voice.

By advocacy, Christians does not mean reporting that espouses only one sort of political or social agenda. Rather, he insists,

> Press portrayals feed into public discourse and play a portentous role in the shape our culture and the sociopolitical realm ultimately take. In its loftiest sense, the press ought to amplify public debate and reconstitute the argument so that it becomes an important public forum where significant issues of social justice are fruitfully raised and resolved. (Christians 1986, 123)

Christians' argument can be amplified beyond democracy's racial, ethnic and economic out-groups. In contemporary democratic society, clearly some "things" also are without political voice. The environment, racial equality and events beyond American shores all have difficulty finding a powerful domestic spokesperson. These issues cross traditional political boundaries. Those who will be affected by them also seem to be without a voice.

Communitarian thinking takes social responsibility to the next level. It urges that justice—rather than truth—become the ethical linchpin of journalistic decision making. If justice becomes the fundamental value of American journalism, than the media—functioning at institutional level—have the goal of transforming society, of empowering individual citizens to act in ways that promote political discussion, debate and change (Christians et al. 1995).

What makes journalists uneasy about either the communitarian or social responsibility approaches is that they smack of a kind of benevolent paternalism. If individual human beings carry moral stature, then assigning one institution—in this case the mass media—the role of social and political arbiter diminishes the moral worth of the individual citizen. The mass media become a kind parent and the citizen a sort of wayward child in need of guidance. Such a relationship does not promote political maturity.

While the weight of recent scholarly opinion sides with Christians, such a view is not without risk. If accepted, it means a thoroughgoing change for the mass media in the U.S. political system. That change would bring about other changes, some of them not easy to anticipate. But whether change is what's needed, or merely a return to the strict libertarian view, both call for some sophisticated ethical reasoning. As Thomas Jefferson said, being a citizen of a democracy is not easy—to which journalists might well add, neither is covering one.

Suggested Readings

DIONNE, E. J., JR. 1992. *Why Americans hate politics.* New York: Touchtone.

FALLOWS, JAMES. 1996. *Breaking the news: How the media undermine American democracy.* New York: Pantheon.

FRY, DON, ed. 1983. *The adversary press.* St. Petersburg, FL: The Modern Media Institute.

JAMIESON, K. H. 2000. *Everything you think you know about politics . . . and why you're wrong.* New York: Basic Books.

LINSKY, MARTIN. 1986. *Impact: How the press affects federal policymaking.* New York: W. W. Norton.

MADISON, JAMES S., Alexander Hamilton, and John Jay. *The Federalist papers.*

MERRITT, DAVIS. 1995. *Public journalism and public life.* Hillsdale, NJ: Lawrence Erlbaum Associates.

Cases on the Web

"The David Duke candidacy: Fairness and the Klansman" by Keith Woods
"Whose abuse of power: The *Seattle Times* and Brock Adams" by Lee Wilkins
"Denver's Rocky Flats: The role of the alternative press" by Lee Wilkins
"Terrorist use of the news media: News media use of terrorists" by Jack Lule
"Singapore: Balancing democracy, globalization and the Internet" by Seow Ting Lee

CHAPTER VII CASES

CASE VII-A
The Filmed Execution of Timothy McVeigh
BENJAMIN HU
University of Missouri

Timothy McVeigh was convicted on eight counts of first-degree murder for engineering the April 1995 Oklahoma City bombing, and sentenced to die by lethal injection by a federal court in 1997. The attack on the Alfred P. Murrah Federal Building killed 168 people and injured more than 500 others. Structurally, the blast damaged or destroyed several neighboring buildings in downtown Oklahoma City. McVeigh was arrested an hour later as he sped away on the interstate. Two days later he was formally charged. Even post-9/11, the Oklahoma City bombing remains the single most damaging terrorist attack carried out by an American against a domestic target.

After appeals, McVeigh's sentence was scheduled to be carried out nearly three years later. Prior to his June 11, 2001, execution at the federal prison in Terre Haute, Indiana, McVeigh made an unusual request that his execution be broadcast live. The same request was made by two other parties—lawyers opposed to the death penalty and an online company that intended a private broadcast to raise funds for charity.

Ultimately Attorney General John Ashcroft mandated that the execution would not be broadcast to the general public or to parties other than the bereaved and survivors. The execution would be viewed live by 10 survivors and bereaved (chosen by lottery) at Terre Haute while a special, encrypted broadcast would be carried to Oklahoma for the remainder of authorized viewers there to witness the execution. Also present at the execution were McVeigh's family and friends, and select members of the media. Many anti– and pro–death penalty lobbyists were catered for outside the prison, as were more press members and crew.

The execution itself raised several issues, the first of those focusing on McVeigh. In his request that his execution be broadcast, McVeigh noted: "It has been said that all of Oklahoma was a victim of the bombing," McVeigh wrote to the *Sunday Oklahoman*. "Can all of Oklahoma watch?"

Throughout his incarceration and interviews, and finally his execution, McVeigh was repeatedly described as acting to exercise control over circumstances—for example, eating only vegetarian foods in order to appear emaciated at his execution, and giving a curt nod to each group of witnesses. His request could be viewed as a further means of exerting control over the coverage of his death. Others interpreted it as a further attempt at propaganda for McVeigh's antigovernment political agenda.

Notably, the White House requested that the American Society of Newspaper Editors tone down coverage of the McVeigh case. The request was largely rebuffed by editors, who claimed that President George W. Bush's plea for circumspection, made by a man who presided over 131 executions during his governorship of Texas, seemed contradictory.

A different issue was raised by lawyers representing Joseph Minerd, an accused murderer who, if convicted, could face the same fate. They argued that the tape of the execution would provide material to support a case that lethal injection constitutes cruel and unusual punishment. The film they intended to make would have been used for legal purposes only, and a federal judge had upheld their request. However, Ashcroft denied this request as well, arguing that fears of media sensationalizing and security problems were of overriding concern. Ultimately the U.S. Supreme Court denied the lawyers permission to film.

The final request to broadcast the execution was forwarded by Entertainment Network Inc (ENI), which proposed that the execution be recorded via Web cam and made available to viewers online. To prevent the viewing of the execution by children, ENI proposed a $1.95 credit card charge per viewer, with all proceeds going to charities that directly aided the bereaved. Previously, ENI had a reputation as a "pornography company"—the company had initiated a voyeur camera service whereby college students received free tuition in return for 24-hour online surveillance of their living quarters. Ashcroft denied this request as well.

In this case, the Justice Department overruled the argument that the First Amendment protects the right to broadcast executions. According to federal law, recording devices are forbidden at executions. However, there appears to be some uncertainty on this count, especially as ABC ran audiotapes of executions that took place in Georgia between 1983 and 1998 on its show *Nightline*—a practice that should have been impossible if the Justice Department's ruling could be applied to all state and federal jurisdictions.

Micro Issues

1. Does McVeigh have any privacy in this situation? Can McVeigh himself "give away" his privacy in this instance?
2. Should journalists have downplayed the execution itself, as requested by President Bush? If you answer is "no," are there ever times when it might be appropriate to honor such a request?
3. Using the concepts of ethical news values outlined in Chapter 2, how would you evaluate the newsworthiness of this event?

Midrange Issues

1. Is there an ethical theory that supports the closed-circuit broadcast of the execution to the families and friends of McVeigh and his victims? How would you articulate that argument?
2. If the media has a watchdog role over government, how is reporting about the death penalty to be done if media coverage of executions is curtailed in cases such as this?
3. How would you, using ethical theory, respond to the comments that McVeigh's request was really for propaganda purposes? Does the purpose of McVeigh's request make any difference in an ethical response?
4. Would it have been possible to restrict viewing of the online broadcast of the execution to "paying adults"? Should this matter? Why?

Macro Issues

1. Historically, particularly in Great Britain but more recently in Africa and the Middle East, executions have been quite public—even considered entertainment. Is this a question where culture—as opposed to philosophy—is shaping the decisions that journalists make?

2. Many journalists oppose the death penalty while many others support it. Should how an individual journalist feels about this issue govern whether he is assigned this story?

3. How do conceptualizations of privacy, as articulated in the "no body bag" video policy common at many local television stations, apply—or fail to apply—in this particular case?

CASE VII-B
Victims and the Press
ROBERT LOGAN
National Institute of Medicine, Washington, D.C.

Alice Waters's daughter, Julie, seven, has leukemia. Her illness was diagnosed in its early stages in March 2000. Julie's physicians believe her condition can be successfully treated.

Ms. Waters, 37, lives in a mobile home in an unincorporated area a few miles from Metroplex, a city of 1.5 million. Ms. Waters's street is the only residential section in the area. At the north end of the street—which has 12 mobile homes on each side facing one another—are four large gas stations that catch traffic off the interstate that runs a quarter-mile away to the west. At the south end of the street (about a quarter-mile away) are two large tanks that are a relatively small storage facility for Big Oil Inc. Next to this—starting almost in her backyard—is the boundary of a successful, 700-acre grapefruit orchard, which borders on a municipal landfill. About a quarter-mile away are large well fields that are the principal source of drinking water for Metroplex.

In July 1999, a 6-year-old boy in the household two doors down from Ms. Waters was diagnosed as having leukemia. He was not as lucky as Julie; his diagnosis was late in the progression of his disease, and he died in December 2000. In 2001, an infant girl became the second baby born with birth defects in the neighborhood within seven years. Both families moved before Ms. Waters came to the neighborhood in 1999.

Internal medicine specialists Dr. Earnest and Dr. Sincere met Julie soon after she was admitted to the hospital in October 2000. They were instrumental in getting funding for Julie's care when her mother was unable to pay. They are members of Worried M.D.'s for Social Responsibility, a self-proclaimed liberal, national public-interest group that gets actively involved in national political issues.

The physicians told Ms. Waters that they were suspicious about the causes of Julie's illness. Three cancer and birth-defect incidents on the same street, the physicians said, were not a coincidence.

In November 2001, they began to collect water samples from the wellhead at Ms. Waters's house. They sent the samples to a well-regarded testing lab in another city. Since then, they have tested the water at a professional lab every four months. Every test revealed traces of more than 10 human-made and natural chemicals often associated with oil storage tanks, pesticides, grapefruit orchards, gas-station leaks, lead from automobile emissions, and a large landfill.

However, each chemical occurs consistently at 6 to 15 parts per billion, which is considered safe for drinking water based on standards set by the U.S. Environmental Protection Agency (EPA). At higher levels these chemicals are associated with carcinogenic risks or increases in birth defects, but the levels found at Ms. Waters's wellhead are within safety thresholds set by the EPA. There is no evidence the chemicals are associated directly with the health problems found in Ms. Waters's neighborhood.

At a fund-raising party last night for mayoral candidate Sam Clean, Drs. Earnest and Sincere privately told Clean what they had found. Clean is a well-known public figure, has a reputation as an environmentalist, owns a successful health-food restaurant chain, is media wise, and looks good on television. He is a long shot to become mayor and needs fresh issues to draw attention to his candidacy.

At 11:00 A.M. today, KAOS news radio begins running as the top story in its twenty-minute news rotation "Clean Attacks City Lack of Cleanup." In the story, Clean gives a sound bite attacking city officials for "ignoring cancer-causing agents in water in a neighborhood where children have died, which is next door to the city's water supply." He describes the neighborhood's medical problems and describes (without naming) Julie and Alice Waters. The news report explains that water from the neighborhood has several "toxic agents believed to cause cancer at higher levels" and points out that the city's water wells are within a quarter-mile of oil tanks, gas stations, a grapefruit orchard, a landfill, and septic tanks. County officials are said to be unavailable for comment. The report runs throughout the day at 20-minute intervals.

By 2:30 P.M., calls to the switchboard have jammed the newsroom. The callers who get through are frightened about their drinking water. City Hall's switchboards are jammed. The callers sound upset and ask whether their water is safe to drink.

By 4:00 P.M., reporters from the local ABC affiliate are already knocking on doors in the trailer park and sending live reports from the scene. Neighbors tell them where Alice and Julie Waters live.

At 4:15 P.M., your managing editor gives you the story. You are an ambitious reporter for *Metroplex Today,* the only morning newspaper in Metroplex. Both of you realize this is clearly Page 1 potential, but you have only a few hours before deadline for the next morning's edition. After a few phone calls, you discover that the mayor, the city council, and most city and county officials are all out of town at a retreat and are unavailable for comment. The regional EPA office is not answering the phone.

A trusted spokesperson for Regional Hospital tells you that Drs. Sincere and Earnest are furious at Clean for releasing the story and have no comment. She fills you in with all of the above information.

The same Regional Hospital spokesperson says Ms. Waters does not want to be interviewed. She suddenly realizes that her husband, whom she walked out on several years before, might see the story and return to town.

Sam Clean is more than happy to talk to you.

Micro Issues

1. Is Clean a reliable enough source on whom KAOS radio could base its reports?
2. Should KAOS have broadcast the story?
3. Should you respect Ms. Waters's wishes and leave her and her daughter out of the story?
4. Are Dr. Earnest and Dr. Sincere reliable sources?
5. What do you tell the public about whether the water supply is safe?

Midrange Issues

1. Would you be working on the story if KAOS and ABC had ignored it?
2. Would you be working on the story if there was little public reaction after the KAOS broadcast?

3. If Ms. Waters decides to do an interview on ABC later today, do you then include her in your story?

4. If city and county officials remain unavailable, how do you handle their side of the story? Does that delay publication until you can get more information, or do you go with what is available?

5. Are there unbiased sources you can contact about risk assessment? Who?

Macro Issues

1. How do you handle the discrepancy between the information from the EPA and the skeptical scientists and environmentalists?

2. What is the public's probable reaction to reporting this story? Should your newspaper take any precautions to prevent public panic? If so, what should they be?

3. How risky is the water compared to risks we take for granted, such as traveling by car? Can you think of a relevant comparison for your article comparing the relative risk of the water to a well-known risk?

4. Is it the media's role to speak for a society that is averse to many risks? How might the media accomplish this function?

US MILITARY
IRAQ WAR POW

Edgar Hernandez

**Army Spc.
Joseph Hudson**

**Army Spc.
Shoshawna Johnson**

Pfc. Patrick Miller

Sgt. James Riley

AP Photo/Iraqi TV via APTN

CASE VII-C
Painful Images of War: Too Painful for Whom? When?
BEVERLY HORVIT
Texas Christian University

On March 23, 2003, in the first few days of the second Gulf War in Iraq, U.S. troops traveling in a six-vehicle convoy made a wrong turn and were ambushed by Iraqi forces. Six of the U.S. troops were captured, and nine were killed. That news was confirmed when the Qatar-based satellite network al-Jazeera rebroadcast Iraqi television footage of five captured soldiers—four men and one woman—as well as images of slain soldiers. Pfc. Jessica Lynch was among those captured but not interviewed by Iraqi-state television.

The bodies of four of the dead soldiers were filmed as they lay on the floor of a makeshift morgue. Two of the dead soldiers appeared to have been shot in the head. A fifth body was shown lying on the road behind an ambushed U.S. military truck. The tape also showed five of the captured Americans being interviewed by Iraqi officials, who were off-screen.

U.S. officials, including Defense Secretary Donald Rumsfeld, immediately criticized the Iraqi government for allowing those interviews to be recorded and broadcast. By doing so, Rumsfeld argued, the Iraqis had violated the 1949 Geneva Conventions, which mandate how prisoners of war are to be treated. Article 13 states, in part, that "prisoners of war must at all times be humanely treated" and "must at times be protected, particularly against acts of violence or intimidation and against insults and public curiosity."

The International Committee of the Red Cross concurred.

The Geneva Conventions mandates that prisoners only be asked their name, rank and serial number and that they not be subjected to "degrading and humiliating treatment." The al-Jazeera footage shows the U.S. soldiers—some visibly nervous—being asked additional questions about their hometowns and their reasons for coming to Iraq.

Immediately after al-Jazeera began broadcasting the footage, Rumsfeld told reporters, "Needless to say, television networks that carry such pictures are, I would say, doing something that's unfortunate" (Reid and Doran 2003). Lt. Gen. John Abizaid of the U.S. Central Command went further: "We will hold those [in charge] accountable for their actions" (Reid and Doran 2003).

After the Pentagon said the interview footage violated the Geneva Conventions, al-Jazeera pulled the interviews but temporarily continued to broadcast images of slain soldiers (Hamilton 2003). Similarly, although CBS News briefly showed a clip of the al-Jazeera tape, it stopped after the Pentagon complained and e-mailed U.S. news organizations asking them not to use the tape.

Peter Jennings of ABC News told viewers that pictures of the captured soldiers and probably slain soldiers "have been seen widely throughout the world, including in Iraq. The Bush administration has said very forcefully this violates the Geneva Conventions governing the treatment for prisoners of war, and the president of ABC News has decided not to broadcast the pictures at this time."

In a *Nightline* edition the next night, Dave Marash of ABC News said "one simple rule" at ABC and other networks is not to use such pictures "until we know that families have been informed that their soldier has been captured." And, even when ABC knew the families had been notified, Marash noted there were other limitations on what ABC would show: "Pictures of dead soldiers, in which their wounds are grotesquely obvious, and their faces, perhaps, identifiable. And the real-time depiction of clearly frightened soldiers being asked questions that go well beyond the name, rank and serial number approved by the Geneva Conventions rulebook."

Newspaper editors around the United States also had to grapple with deciding which images, if any, to publish. Some U.S. newspapers chose to publish neither still photographs from the footage nor the soldiers' names. Others opted to run mug shots of the soldiers that had been cropped from the video footage but not still photographs of the slain soldiers. In many cases, the newspapers felt compelled to explain their rationale to their readers.

The *Orlando Sentinel, Atlanta Journal-Constitution,* Portland *Oregonian* and *Nashville Tennessean* are examples of papers whose editors decided not to use any of the still photographs from the al-Jazeera tapes on the first day. Dan Hortsch, public editor of *The Oregonian,* which published mug shots after the soldiers' names were released, told readers that although the Geneva Conventions applied to governments and not the news media, "the media must consider whether their actions further the intent of the captors" (Hortsch 2003).

In its story for March 24, the *Washington Post* told readers it was "not publishing the names of some of the soldiers because they had not been officially released by the Pentagon." The *Post* and *USA Today* did, however, use the name of Army Spc. Joseph Hudson, 23. Hudson was the second soldier to be questioned. When asked why he was in Iraq, Hudson replied: "I follow orders." Similarly, the *Orlando Sentinel* and *Constitution-Journal* ran a mug shot of Hudson.

Other newspapers, including the *Fort Worth Star-Telegram, Hartford Courant, Salt Lake Tribune* and *Sacramento Bee,* ran photos of the five captured soldiers cropped to mug shots. The *Star-Telegram* and *Sacramento Bee* published the mug shots on their front pages. In a Page 1 note to readers, *Star-Telegram* editors said, "We believe it is important for our readers to know their condition after capture, so we have chosen to run photos of their faces." Their actions and explanation did not impress several readers, many of whom sent angry letters to the editor.

A *Star-Telegram* (2003) editorial argued that publishing the photos would hold the Iraqis accountable for the POWs' well-being:

> The photographs . . . make it impossible for Iraqi officials to deny that they have these brave Americans in custody or to explain away possible injuries after their conditions have been documented. . . . Should the unthinkable happen—that they die after appearing in the news—then it will be clear that the soldiers were mistreated as prisoners. . . . Many families of prisoners held during the Vietnam War said that the media reports at least let them know their husbands, fathers, sons and brothers were still alive.

By the time the Pentagon had notified Spc. Shoshana Johnson's family of her capture, her parents already knew: they "had stumbled across it on their own—on a Spanish-language television station they had tuned in so that their granddaughter could watch cartoons" (Kenworthy, Willing and Cauchon 2003).

Complaints of media coverage of POWs cut both ways. One Al-Jazeera employee told the *Los Angeles Times,* "Everyone showed footage of Iraqi prisoners of war just a day ago, and no one said a thing about that" (Pasternak 2003). Likewise, a Red Cross spokesman said, "Images being shown of POWs on both sides are a cause for concern" (Neuffer 2003).

Gina Lubrano, readers' representative for the *San Diego Union-Tribune,* said readers complained when the newspaper published a photograph of a dead Iraqi soldier, a photograph similar to one that appeared on the front page of the *New York Times.* She told readers (Lubrano 2003):

> The reason photographs of prisoners are permissible in the *Union-Tribune* and other newspapers and suspect when supplied by the Iraqis has to do with who is behind the camera and the intent behind the photo. Government-run Iraqi television represents the government holding the prisoners. Photographing them being questioned can be interpreted by some as an attempt by the Iraqi government to ridicule them and hold them up to public curiosity. . . . The photos of the Iraqi prisoners and the dead published in the *Union-Tribune* and other newspapers have been taken by independent photojournalists, not the government, and are an attempt to show the events of war, not *to ridicule them.*

Micro Issues

1. Critique the *Star-Telegram*'s argument that publishing the photos would make the Iraqis more accountable for the welfare of the soldiers.
2. How should American media respond to the threat by the U.S. Central Command officer to hold those in charge "accountable for their actions"?

Midrange Issues

1. Lubrano makes a distinction between the independent U.S. press and the state-owned Iraqi press in justifying her paper's action while condemning a similar action by Al-Jazeera. Is the distinction valid? Justify your answer.
2. Is there a difference between film and still photography of the dead soldiers, and does that difference, if any, justify handling the images differently?

Macro Issues

1. Should the press acquiesce to the government's request to not show photos of the war based on:
   a. notification of families?
   b. taste?
   c. the Geneva Conventions?
   d. national security?
   Justify your answers.

CASE VII-D
Military Censorship of Photographs
PAUL LESTER
California State University—Fullerton

The United States has been engaged in military conflicts both honorable and questionable. Inspired by the need to report each war to an anxious public, journalists have traveled to the front lines to produce stories and pictures both supportive and critical. As the informational and emotional power of visual images has become more understood, military strategists and politicians have instituted various forms of censorship of images in an attempt to protect their troops and to control public opinion.

Termed "Desert Storm" by the military and the "Gulf War" by the media, the clash with Iraq over Kuwait was an example of the often tenuous relationship between government officials and journalists. Hundreds of journalists throughout the world were in Saudi Arabia covering the fight, but only about a hundred made up the official military press pool. With more than 500,000 U.S. troops in the area and fighting erupting on several fronts, newspapers, for example, relied on only 16 journalists to cover every ground unit in the country. Although most reporters accepted the fact that a pool was necessary, many were frustrated by the military's slowness in transporting the pool members to troubled areas. Once there, pool members were accompanied by an ever-present military escort.

U.S. Department of Defense ground rules signed by all journalists prohibited reporting that would in any way endanger the troops. A journalist had to get approval

AP/WIDE WORLD PHOTOS. Used with permission.

before attempting any story. Once the piece was completed, the story and pictures were subject to U.S. and allied military censorship. Although there was no stated prohibition against showing wounded or dead soldiers, some journalists were wondering halfway into the war why they had not "seen one picture of bloodshed [or] anyone who's dead yet." Charges of "news management" and a "credibility gap" between official and pool reporter accounts surfaced. Claiming that press pool restrictions were too harsh, several U.S. publications and a few individual authors asked for a federal court injunction against the Defense Department's pool procedures.

The Gulf War was difficult to cover. It was primarily an air campaign waged in the middle of the night using fast-moving aircraft carrying computer-guided missiles with video cameras in their nose cones to signal the results of their prearranged missions. The Iraqi government was extremely hostile to journalists, only allowing a handful of correspondents to report from its side of the conflict. The isolated nature of the terrain was a further barrier to full-access coverage. It was simply not possible to conveniently drive across the huge desert seeking frontline firefights as in previous wars.

Besides, it was quite dangerous to try such a mission, as Bob Simon and his crew from CBS discovered. Simon and his associates decided to drive to Iraq through the desert on their own because they were frustrated by the military's strict censorship controls over their actions. They were soon captured by Iraqi forces and detained until the end of the conflict. Despite these dangers and restrictions, CNN's coverage of the night bombing of Baghdad was particularly impressive, as was the subsequent damage to buildings in that ancient city reported by Peter Arnett—the only American correspondent able to report with his words and images from Baghdad.

As never before, technology played a significant part in fighting and reporting the war. Arnett and others were able to report from the far-off country because of the use of a portable satellite transmitter. Photographers were able to quickly send their images to their waiting editors because of digital cameras and transmitters. Nevertheless, most still photographers and videographers were frustrated by their lack of access to any real fighting scenes. They were left to cover noncombat scenes involving soldiers drilling. Once the ground war had commenced, a few journalists found themselves riding along with the tank units. But most of the fighting occurred at night, making it extremely difficult to record action scenes. Most of the pictures of the fighting areas in Iraq were of the long lines of Iraqi prisoners captured by military forces.

One highly emotional picture that did get through military censors was taken by *Detroit Free Press* photographer David Turnley. Turnley was riding with the 5th MASH medical unit inside Iraq. A fierce firefight had recently erupted between Saddam Hussein's Republican Guard and the 24th Mechanized Infantry Division.

A helicopter—filled with Turnley, medical personnel and equipment—touched down about a hundred yards from a frantic scene. An American military vehicle had just taken a direct hit. Soldiers on the ground were upset, as they said it had mistakenly been struck by a U.S. tank. The wounded were quickly retrieved from the vehicle and carried to the helicopter. Sgt. Ken Kozakiewicz, suffering from a fractured hand, slumped into the helicopter. The body of the driver of Kozakiewicz's vehicle was placed on the floor of the helicopter inside a zippered bag. A medical staff member, perhaps thoughtlessly, handed the dead driver's identification card to Kozakiewicz. Turnley, sitting across from the injured soldier, recorded the emotional moment with his camera when Kozakiewicz realized that his friend had been killed by the blast. Later at the hospital, Turnley asked the soldiers their names. He also asked if they would mind if the pictures were published. They all told him to get the images published.

The rules of combat enforced by the military required that Turnley give his film to military officials for approval for publication. A day after the incident, Turnley learned that his editors had not yet received his negatives from the Defense Department officials. Military officials insisted that they were holding the film because the images were of a sensitive nature. They also said that they were concerned about whether the dead soldier's family had been informed of his death. Because of Turnley's argument that the family must have been informed by then, the officials released his film.

His photographs were eventually published in Detroit and throughout the world. The picture of Kozakiewicz crying over the loss of his friend was called the "Picture of the War" on the cover of *Parade* magazine. Several months after the war, Turnley spoke to Kozakiewicz's father, who had been in one of the first U.S. military units in Vietnam. Reacting to the censorship of images by military officials, David Kozakiewicz explained that the military was "trying to make us think this is antiseptic. But this is war. Where is the blood and the reality of what is happening over there? Finally we have a picture of what really happens in war." For David Kozakiewicz, showing his son grieving over the death of a fellow fighter gave added meaning to the soldier's death.

Micro Issues

1. Should the photographer have taken the picture? Justify your answer.
2. Should the photographer have asked permission of the injured soldier to take the picture?
3. Does a picture of a grieving soldier belong on Page 1? Under what circumstances, if any?

Midrange Issues

1. Would criticism be lessened if the image were run small and on an inside page?
2. If the soldier is not from your newspaper's local area, why should the picture run?
3. How would you as an editor react to a reader's complaining that the picture demoralizes America's war effort?

Macro Issues

1. What moral philosophies influence an editor who uses the picture and a reader who complains about its use?
2. During a war does the military have the right to censor images produced by a photographer?
3. Does "pool" coverage during a war offer the best solution for informing the public back home?
4. Should an editor wait to publish a picture of a dead person until relatives are informed? Why or why not? Does your answer change if the media is widely reporting the name?
5. Should journalists avoid taking and publishing images that criticize a nation's war effort?

CASE VII-E
Not in Our Name
KARON SPECKMAN
Truman State University

Whether Great Britain should join the United States in war against Iraq was a hot topic among British citizens in the beginning months of 2003.

America's President George Bush was pushing for war, and Great Britain's Prime Minister Tony Blair was advocating joining the United States. The Blair-Bush partnership was strengthened after the 9/11 attack on the World Trade Towers in 2001. Now, Blair was trying to persuade British citizens and his government to join the United States regardless of the outcome of a second United Nations resolution sanctioning the war.

However, many British citizens and even Blair's own Labour Party did not want to join the United States unless the United Nations supported the action. An Independent Television poll of Sept. 25, 2002, had showed that 70 percent of the respondents were against Great Britain going to war alongside the United States without a UN mandate. By Jan. 13, another ITV poll showed that 53 percent would have approved taking part in a U.S.-led war on Iraq as long as such action was approved by a fresh UN Security Council motion. The UN Security Council motion wasn't getting support from other Council members, in spite of intense pressure from both countries' leaders. Yet Blair pressed on with his arguments to join the United States, arguing that Iraq posed a threat to world safety. He addressed the House of Commons and also took his case to the British public on television. Blair also spent an hour Feb. 6 defending his reasons in front of a hostile panel of citizens on BBC's *Newsnight* with Jeremy Paxman.

London's 10 daily national newspapers were vocal about their stance on the war, although the message usually focused on the need for another UN resolution. Six papers were for the war, and three were against the war—the *Guardian,* the *Independent,* and the *Daily Mirror.* The London papers are not owned by particular parties. However, excluding the *Independent,* the papers are considered highly partisan. The *Daily Mirror* took partisanship to a new level with an orchestrated effort against the war that involved reader petitions, slanted coverage with inflammatory photo illustrations and involvement in an antiwar rally.

Because British newspapers are quite different than American dailies, it is helpful to look at some of those differences to understand the *Mirror*'s campaign. London's dailies are considered national because the papers have a national reputation, extensively cover national issues, and are published in the nation's capital. The dailies are divided in two ways: by size (broadsheet or "quality" and tabloid) and also by audience or socio-economic market (elite, mid-market, and popular). With a circulation of 2,100,000 of mostly unskilled working class and underclass readers, the Labour-leaning *Daily Mirror* is one of three tabloids at the "bottom" of the socio-economic categories.

Although London popular tabloids often are dismissed as "trashy," one of the most famous—the *Sun*—has a readership of more than 3.5 million. In fact, most citizens get their news from tabloids that package rehashed news with a heavy focus on entertainment and celebrities. The broadsheets—the *Times, Financial Times,* the

Guardian and the *Independent*—usually restrict blatant partisanship to editorial pages. Not so the tabloids. They are very willing to mix comment with news in headlines, stories, and photo illustrations. Also, competition for readers is keen among all newspapers but especially the tabloids. The *Daily Mirror* was losing readers at this time to the *Sun* and the *Daily Star* and needed to boost its circulation figures.

So with stiff paper competition and a prospective controversial war, the *Daily Mirror* started a petition drive on Jan. 21, 2003, dubbed "Not in Our Name." Its entire front page had a background picture of a soldier and these words:

> Sign this page and send it back to us.
> > You are NOT powerless.
> > You DO have a voice.
> > NO WAR.
> > Mr. Blair, I hereby register
> > my opposition to any war
> > with Iraq not justified by unequivocal UN evidence.
> > Name
> > Address

Thus started a campaign to get reader messages—and e-mail responses—to Blair. The next day's edition also devoted the entire front page to the campaign with the headline "The War is Wrong" and a picture of a Falklands War hero Simon Weston, who was against the Iraqi War. Antiwar coverage consumed six inside pages with several pages of pictures of entertainment celebrities signing the petition.

On Thursday, Jan. 23, the tally of petitions began. The front-page headline read: 15,000 BY FIRST POST, Are you listening NOW Mr. Blair? By Friday, the count was 70,000, and that issue included a giant NO WAR poster. The Friday front page was split into halves—one half devoted to a TV star in a skimpy outfit and the other half devoted to the antiwar campaign.

The number of petitioners continued the second week with 164,500 petitions. The Wednesday Jan. 20 front page had a photo illustration of Blair with bloody hands and the headline: BLOOD ON HIS HANDS. Examples of other front pages that blasted Blair were one with a PRIME MONSTER headline over a picture of Blair, one with a big red VETO stamped on Blair's face, and one with Blair kissing Bush that said Make Love Not War. Inside content matched the subjective tone, much of it in first-person editorials mixed with news coverage so that readers would have difficulty separating opinion from fact.

However, the *Mirror*'s involvement did not stop with the petitions and sensationalized content. The largest antiwar rally in Britain's history was Feb. 15 with estimates varying from 1 to 2 million marchers in London. The *Mirror* staff gave out 30,000 placards to marchers—the original NO WAR poster from the first front page of the campaign. In addition, a giant *Mirror* banner with Not in Our Name was a backdrop at the rally in Hyde Park where speakers addressed the marchers. A similar large banner was unfurled in Bush and Blair's flight patterns near Lajes air base in the Azores—where Bush and Blair held a last-ditch summit over the weekend of March 15–16.

Newspaper petitions are not new to London papers. The *Sun* started a petition drive earlier in January 2003. But its cause was against what it called "asylum madness." Fear of terrorist acts in London sparked much of the fervor over asylum seekers as well as a killing of an unarmed policeman by an asylum seeker. More than 500,000 people responded to the popular and often xenophobic *Sun* petition drive. Other newspaper-led petitions included a 1990 campaign by the *Daily Mail* and the *Daily Star* against the murder charges of a paratrooper for the death of a Belfast teenager.

Newspaper editors often feel the campaigns are successful; however, critics say that unless focus groups also raise the issues, government will not pay attention. A final problem for those who led antiwar campaigns: what happens when the government goes to war? Britain did join the United States on March 18. By then, almost 225,000 readers had signed the petition. Then the *Mirror* had the challenge of convincing readers that although the paper was against the war, it supported the troops. Thus, the March 18 front page said:

> UNlawful
> UNethical
> UNstoppable
> Why we blame Blair but back our forces.

By April 2003, the *Mirror*'s circulation had fallen below 2 million. Editor Piers Morgan said in a *Guardian* article that perhaps the antiwar stance could be blamed for the loss in circulation.

Micro Issues

1. Should newspapers or broadcast media openly support or oppose a war or any other cause with petition drives? If yes, who should decide which causes to openly support?
2. How should a media outlet separate or distinguish its "opinion" or analysis from straight news so readers and viewers know the difference?
3. Do photo illustrations have a place in news?

Midrange Issues

1. Is the "objectivity" or fairness standard of American journalism outdated for modern times and in an era of multiple delivery systems for news?
2. What are the dangers of a similar push by an American media company in a time when so many papers are owned by conglomerates?
3. Is partisanship of a media outlet a problem if people know the media outlet's political leanings?
4. What happens when media outlets find themselves on the unpopular side of a cause? Should the financial implications of such a stance be a factor in whether the unpopular leaning should be revealed.

Macro Issues

1. What is the difference between "reflecting" the view of readers and "setting the agenda"?
2. Are editors abusing or misusing political power with petitions or are they giving voice to the voiceless?

VIII

Media Economics:
The Deadline Meets
the Bottom Line

By the end of this chapter you should be familiar with:

- **how advertisers gain influence in the media economic equation and the ramifications of that additional influence.**
- **the economic realities of the social responsibility theory of the press.**
- **the economic and legislative initiatives that have combined to place control of information in the hands of fewer and larger corporations.**
- **the problems of programming for diversity in a numbers-driven media.**

INTRODUCTION

In the movie *Absence of Malice,* Paul Newman is asked if he has taken his complaint concerning an inaccurate article about him to the newspaper. He replies, "Have you ever tried to talk to a newspaper?" For most Americans, the point is well taken. A faceless, nameless, non–locally owned media is becoming a reality in all but a few communities. Today the media are predominantly corporate owned and publicly traded, with media conglomerates among the largest of the world's corporations. The corporate owners of the average news operation are more insulated from contact with news consumers than virtually any other business owner in America.

The pace and size of the mergers that created these media conglomerates are staggering. In rapid succession the following occurred:

- General Electric bought NBC, Westinghouse bought CBS and later sold it to Viacom, and the Disney Corporation purchased ABC, each deal worth billions.
- Westinghouse/CBS merged with Infinity Broadcasting to create the nation's largest radio chain.
- Time Warner, created by a billion-dollar merger earlier in the 1990s, acquired the Turner Broadcasting System—including such properties as WTBS, TNT, CNN,

and *Headline News*—and then was itself acquired in 2000 by America Online in an ill-fated deal estimated at $115 billion.

- Telephone giant MCI bought an interest in the News Corporation, the parent company of Fox Television, while Microsoft and NBC combined to create MSNBC, a multimedia venture, to name but two.
- NBC joined the ranks of the supersized media companies when it bought the entertainment business of Vivendi Universal, including such holdings as Universal movie and television studios and cable networks USA, Sci-Fi and Trio.
- In many local markets, alliances were formed between the local newspaper and one of the television news outlets, sharing news resources and occasionally Web sites as well.

The CBS sale is illustrative of how intertwined all media have become. In 2000, the FCC gave its approval to the $46 billion merger between Viacom and CBS. Viacom's assets include MTV, VH1, Nickelodeon, Paramount, Blockbuster, Simon and Schuster publishers, and Spelling Entertainment, producers of television programming. At the time of the acquisition of CBS, Viacom also increased its holdings by acquiring television stations, syndicators King World and Eyemark, a radio and outdoor advertising empire, and several cable networks. And even though the merger put Viacom in control of two networks—CBS and UPN—the FCC granted an exception to its rule prohibiting one corporation from owning two television networks.

The twin goals of this rush to consolidation were vertically integrated companies with diverse sources of income. The NBC/Vivendi merger is illustrative of this trend. By acquiring the production facilities of Universal, NBC stands a better chance of owning the shows it puts on its broadcast network. And by acquiring the cable USA network, NBC obtained another outlet for its shows to go into syndication—a textbook model of vertical integration of product from beginning to end. In addition, the new company, named NBC Universal, diversified NBC's income. Its revenues went from 90 percent advertising-based to 50 percent, with the remainder coming from subscriptions, admissions, licensing and other ancillary income.

In June 2003, the Federal Communications Commission, obeying a court order to review all ownership regulations every two years, proposed changes that either eliminated antiquated ownership caps or paved the way to the end of democracy, depending on one's political leanings. The rhetoric was heated in the months leading up to the ruling, with more than 520,000 comments pouring into the commission. The vote for the relaxation of ownership limits was divided 3–2 along party lines, with the Republican majority on the panel casting the deciding votes. Key provisions of the law included:

- Allowing a single company to own multiple television stations in a market.
- Expanding the number of radio stations a company could own in a market.
- Expanding the potential allowable reach of television chains to 45 percent (up from 35 percent) of the total population in the United States.
- Leaving intact a ban on any of the four largest television networks—ABC, NBC, CBS or Fox—from merging their operations.
- Overturning a decades-old rule that prevented newspapers in a monopoly market from owning broadcast properties in the same community.

Groups as disparate as the National Organization for Women and the National Rifle Association criticized the changes. FCC Commissioner Michael Copps, in a dissent, called the changes another step in the "Clear Channelization" of American media, a reference to Clear Channel, a media company that had benefited from earlier relaxation of ownership limits in radio, only to become a lightning rod for consumer complaints about nonlocal ownership of radio stations.

Critics of the decision claim that when the local newspaper is allowed to own two or more television stations and up to eight radio stations in the nation's largest markets, competition in news would no longer exist and the public would lose important viewpoints. Ironically, the commission refused to relax ownership rules in smaller markets, where regulatory relief was presumably most needed to help television stations offset such costly FCC mandates as the move to digital broadcasting.

Others, including newspaper trade associations and large broadcasting groups, heralded the decision as good news for the local news consumer. Chairman Powell sided with these latter groups, saying he was trying to "save free TV" from total ownership by satellite and cable interests. He added that the new rules were "legally enforceable broadcast ownership limits that promote diversity, localism and competition."

Soon after the new ownership rules were announced, they were challenged in court, where they remained when this book went to press. In addition, Congress has called for hearings on the relaxation of ownership limits. As a result, the changes did not create the immediate rush to the bargaining table that happened when radio ownership regulations were relaxed in the 1990s when a third of all stations in the United States changed hands.

Columbia Journalism Review Editor at Large Neil Hickey (2003) summed up the fears of many when he concluded,

> What we risk over the long haul is ownership creep that may eventually see the end of the few remaining rules, and with them, the public's right to the widest possible array of news and opinion—at which point, robust, independent, antagonistic, many-voiced journalism may be only a memory.

One thing both sides agreed on was that media economics was now news, and that the biennial review of ownership limits of broadcast properties would never again be dull, back-page news. How the public interest can best be served through ownership rules will likely be a debate for years to come.

As they get bigger, the media must increasingly satisfy competing publics to survive. The desires of stockholders must be balanced with the mandate to keep the audience happy in programming and content decisions. At the same time, advertisers, who demand large numbers of readers and viewers for their messages, make claims on the media as well. The inherent tension created in trying to satisfy these competing publics creates many of the ethical problems discussed in this chapter.

THE PENNY PRESS REVOLUTION

Financing the American media through advertising is so deeply ingrained in the system that it is hard to imagine any other way. Yet newspapers supported solely by their readers thrived in America for more than a century. As recently as 1920, then-Secretary of Commerce Herbert Hoover argued in vain for a commercial-free broadcast industry to be funded by the sellers of the receivers. While the airways eventually became filled with commercials, Hoover and the Federal Radio Commission (now FCC) won one important battle: the public is the owner of the airwaves and the station is merely the "trustee" of that commodity.

Today each medium has found its own formula to economic security—from "free" network television on one end of the continuum to books, movies and a handful of magazines such as *Ms.* and *Consumer Reports* on the other—that pass on virtually all of the production costs to the consumer. Most media organizations lie somewhere in between.

That formula for contemporary economic security began more than 170 years ago when Benjamin Day, publisher of the *New York Sun,* started a revolution by lowering the price of his newspaper to a penny at a time when his competition was selling newspapers for a nickel. He gambled that he could overcome the printing losses with additional advertising revenue—if circulation increased. When his gamble paid off, virtually every publisher in town followed his lead. Soon after, Frank Munsey lowered the cost of *Munsey's Magazine* from a quarter to a dime and watched as his circulation increased eightfold in two years to a half million readers.

What Day and Munsey did was farsighted. By pricing their products at or below the cost of printing, they cast their economic future with their advertisers. What was not foreseen, however, was the diminished role the consumer would play in the process.

Under the old pricing structure, subscribers were an end in themselves. Each represented a percentage of the profit, no matter how minuscule. Under this system, readers purchased news, entertainment and opinion content. Under the new system, advertisers purchased readers. The individual subscriber became a means to an end. Content is now relegated to the status of "bait" to catch readers and viewers to be sold to advertisers, as Bill Moyers points out in an interview for PBS's *The Promise of Television:*

> Every manager or owner I know in commercial television now simply accepts television as a by-product of the merchandising process. That changes how you regard the people for whom you are producing or creating television. They are there to be seduced, to be sold something that somebody wants to sell. You are simply a transmission belt between someone trying to sell a product and the person who has the money to buy it, and it changes altogether your sense of your mission, your purpose, or your obligations to that viewer.

CASUALTIES FROM THE REVOLUTION

Two problems emerged from the penny press revolution that shifted the profit center from consumers to advertisers. First, in an attempt to attract the largest audience possible, media outlets "homogenized" their content, dealing in topics guaranteed to offend few individuals while hoping to garner large audiences. The result is journalism that takes no risks unless research shows that the audience will follow. In fact, Gannett's *USA Today* was developed from a marketing plan, not as a news concept.

Network news presidents "know," for instance, that the public has an interest in only one foreign story at a time. So while the "pack" went first to the Persian Gulf and then Somalia in the early 1990s, the continuing horrors of Bosnia and the killing fields of El Salvador went unreported or at best underreported. During the buildup and execution of the 2003 war to remove Saddam Hussein, stories of the continuing turmoil in Afghanistan—until 2003 the "hot spot" of foreign affairs—dropped precipitously.

Similarly, events are reported more than processes. Stories written for the masses focus on quick-onset disasters such as Hurricane Andrew but not on the slow-onset disaster of global warming that may be spawning ever larger hurricanes. Every summer, stories of forest fires with their made-for-television visuals are played out with only passing reference to the underlying causes of a drought that may be reaching half a century in length now.

Second, the penny press revolution made it more difficult for diverse voices to find a mainstream forum. The late Randy Shilts of the *San Francisco Chronicle,* the first reporter in the United States assigned to the AIDS beat, claimed that AIDS coverage was stymied in its early stages as it was perceived to be a "gay plague" of interest only to the homosexual community (Shilts 1987). Only when celebrities such as Rock Hudson and "innocents" such as Ryan White contracted the disease did it get widespread mainstream media coverage (Rogers and Chang 1991).

The pursuit of financial interests by publicly traded "Big Media" conglomerates has limited the access to mainstream media for all but mainstream ideas. Scholars (Kessler 1989; Miller 1992) have found a relationship between advertising dollars and editorial content, particularly in the controversial area of tobacco and health. Magazines receiving a great deal of revenue from the tobacco industry were significantly less likely to print articles about the health impact of tobacco. Kessler credits the indirect influence of the tobacco industry on these publications as a factor in the rise of tobacco-related cancers in women during the latter half of the 20th century.

Just what role profit ought to play in the media depends in part on the view one takes of the media's role in society. In the section below, we will examine two important descriptive theories of the press that have dominated American thought and look at the role profit and economics play in each.

LIBERTARIAN AND SOCIAL RESPONSIBILITY THEORIES REVISITED

Mass communication research has several descriptive theories. An underlying assumption of these theories is that any media system "takes on the form and coloration of the social and political structures within which it operates" (Siebert, Peterson, and Schramm 1956, 3). Eventually, theorists predict, a media system will reflect the political and social structure of a society.

Two of the best known descriptive theories of the press are the libertarian and social responsibility theories. Together they describe more than 200 years of thinking on the role of information in a society and how it should be delivered.

The *libertarian theory* of the press grew out of the changes that swept Europe from the Reformation to the Renaissance. In keeping with the basic tenets of the Enlightenment, libertarian theory assumes that people are rational and that truth is discoverable in a secular, empirical way. According to libertarian theory, political authority rests with the individual. Government's role is to ensure the domestic and foreign peace, but the individual is supreme in politics—a belief spelled out in the Preamble to the U.S. Constitution. Because the individual is rational, government should do the individual's bidding. People are viewed as having both the time and the inclination to become literate and involved in public affairs.

With these assumptions, the libertarian theory of the press reflects Milton's concept of the "marketplace of ideas." Anyone could operate a printing press, particularly anyone aligned with a political group. Those who ran the presses of the day, because they were partisan, would provide partisan versions of reality. The rational citizen would select the truth from among the partisan versions available.

Within this theory, the press's most potent antagonist would be government, which libertarians viewed as locked in a perpetual power struggle for political supremacy with the individual. The duty of the press was to support the individual in that fight. The result was a media system that supported a well-informed individual in a quest for well-being and happiness.

The ensuing 500 years have done much to change our view of humanity and of society. Three intellectual changes were instrumental in this shift. First, Freud and modern psychology changed our view of rational humanity. We now believe that people are often illogical, sometimes irrational, and motivated by a variety of needs and drives. People are not uniformly energetic or educated. For this reason, they will not always seek out and sometimes will not understand information to which they have access.

Second, knowledge, indeed reality itself, has been transformed. Societies have begun to realize that what we think of as a "fact" is subject to both perception and change, a philosophical view known as pragmatism. The "fact" that matter cannot become energy was successfully challenged by Einstein. Truth has become ephemeral.

Third, society has become more cosmopolitan. As people moved to cities and as waves of immigrants reached American shores, people discovered they were as different from one another in culture and language as they were alike in their quest for a better life. What was truth for one group was not truth for another. Literacy, at least literacy in English, was a cherished ideal, not a reality. Mass markets of many sorts emerged.

These shifts transformed the press of the 1800s into the mass media of this century. Life today in the United States often seems to comprise a series of self-interested subgroups. A new media system was required. Today, the mass media are no longer the written word, but also television, public relations, advertising, entertainment and every conceivable hybrid, including the Internet. Few people, even in the age of the personal computer, can own a media outlet. Existing outlets are largely corporate owned and eschew partisanship in favor of objectivity. The marketplace of ideas became a monopoly supermarket, and the goods it carried were uniformly "vanilla."

With these changes came a new descriptive theory of the press. The theory was developed in the 1940s by a panel of scholars, the Hutchins Commission, with funding from Henry Luce, the conservative founder of *Time* magazine. No journalist sat on the commission. Despite this, the *social responsibility theory* of the press continues to fascinate both academics and practitioners because it attempts to compensate for changes in modern political, social, and cultural life.

Social responsibility theory acknowledged what was already a reality by the 1940s: the number of media outlets is limited; people are often self-interested and sometimes lazy. Because of these changes, the media have certain responsibilities in the political system. According to the Hutchins Commission, the media have the following five functions in society:

1. To provide a truthful, comprehensive and intelligent account of the day's events in a context that gives them meaning.

2. To serve as a forum for exchange of comment and criticism.

3. To provide a representative picture of constituent groups in society.

4. To present and clarify the goals and values of society.

5. To provide citizens with full access to the day's intelligence.

The goals of social responsibility theory are troubling to journalists. While the theory acknowledges that the world is intellectually and socially a different place from that of the libertarian view, it provides no clear guidelines for journalistic behavior in this new era.

Indeed, some of the guidelines the theory does provide are ambiguous. How should the forums operate? Whose values should be presented and clarified? Others appear to be mutually exclusive. For example, the media's role as mirror and critic may conflict with some interpretations of media objectivity. Other guidelines might simply be impossible to achieve—for example, providing intelligent discourse about the day's events in a nightly newscast of less than 23 minutes.

An even more fundamental problem hobbles social responsibility theory: it gives little attention to modern media economics. This omission occurred in part because the multinational corporations and chain ownership were still on the horizon when the Hutchins Commission codified the theory. Because the theory was developed early in the McCarthy period, there also was an unwillingness to link economic and political power for fear of being labeled Marxist. This central omission means that *the social responsibility theory, like libertarianism, does not deal with the realities of concentrated economic power,* particularly in an era when information has become an increasingly valuable commodity. Today some of the most troubling problems in media ethics stem from journalism's dual responsibilities to citizens and to stockholders, and the social responsibility and libertarian views of the press provide little guidance on these issues.

MEDIA ECONOMICS IN THE MODERN ERA: CUTBACKS AND CONSOLIDATIONS

If the Founders envisioned a marketplace of ideas where all views would be aired and the truth would emerge, by the late 20th century the dream had died. Information in the United States had fallen into the hands of a very few well-financed corporations. In every key media format—radio, television, newspapers, magazines, cable television and motion pictures—more than half of the gross revenues were concentrated in the hands of fewer than five corporations. The result is what media economics researcher Ben Bagdikian has called "a de facto ministry of information within a democracy" (Bagdikian 1990, 5).

The history of newspapers is indicative of the consolidation trend in all media. At the turn of the century, William Randolph Hearst, Joseph Pulitzer and the Scripps family sought to widen their influence and enlarge their bank accounts by building the first newspaper chains. For the first time, profits made by selling information and advertising within a community left that community destined for corporate accounts in distant banks. Gradually, the concept of what a newspaper owed a community changed as well. Newspapers were no longer a public trust, but a public utility akin to a power company. Newspapers were delivering to a community a necessary product—information—without any of the regulations of those companies that deliver electricity and gas, and most often without competition. Consequently, the profits of newspapers are many times higher than most corporations—today averaging between 20 to 30 percent annually. Some niche markets, for example, business publications, are even more lucrative.

James Squires (1993), former editor of the *Chicago Tribune,* claims that the corporate takeover of U.S. newspapers has led to the "death of journalism." Today, corporate chains own nearly 90 percent of the nation's daily newspapers, compared to 20 percent at the end of World War II. Most are monopolies, as the number of cities with competing dailies shrank dramatically in the 20th century. The rise in corporate ownership usually meant immediate changes in the name of corporate profits. Media-acquisitions expert Christopher Shaw tells clients that profits from a newspaper can be tripled in two years through a combination of staff reductions and increases in advertising and subscription rates. "No one will buy a 15 percent margin newspaper without a plan to create a 25 percent to 45 percent margin," Shaw has said (Bagdikian 1987, 7).

In good times and bad, newspapers, largely because of the monopoly status that most enjoy, are among the most profitable of all industries. In the first half of 2003, with the nation mired in recession, newspaper profits, as a whole, rose more than 5 percentage points to 22.3 percent, according to industry analyst John Morton (2003) reporting in *American Journalism Review.* Indeed, for long-term health of the publicly traded corporations owning the newspapers, the bottom line is more important than the headlines. Former Gannett Chairman Allen H. Neuharth told Bagdikian, "Wall

Street didn't give a damn if we put out a good paper in Niagara Falls. They just wanted to know if the profits would be in the 15 to 20 percent range" (Bagdikian 1987, xxi). Apparently, the strategy worked. At one point in its history, Gannett posted increased profits in 87 consecutive quarters, a streak unheard of in most industries.

However, content often suffers in the pursuit of proft. In a move that sent shock waves through the industry, *San Jose Mercury News* publisher Jay Harris resigned his job at the Knight-Ridder paper in the spring of 2001, saying he could not acquiesce to corporate demands for increased profits that would have resulted in newsroom layoffs at a time when the community was hit by the dot.com-led recession in Silicon Valley. Several weeks later, Harris gave an impassioned speech to the American Society of Newspaper Editors in which he said that corporate demands for increased profits were undercutting the journalistic mission.

Broadcasting also has felt the impact of consolidation. With each round of takeovers, the network newsrooms of ABC, NBC and CBS were downsized. At one point, NBC virtually cut its *Nightly News* writing and production staff in half, in part because parent company GE saw nothing wrong with the on-air product during a 17 week writers' strike that caused the newsroom to operate shorthanded (Schoenbrun 1989). Among the casualties of the cutbacks were foreign bureaus—a fact that left the major networks scrambling after the events of September 11, 2001, brought foreign affairs to the forefront once again.

This era of cutbacks and consolidations has been noted by media researcher Robert McChesney (1997), who makes this analogy:

> Imagine if the federal government demanded that newspaper and broadcast journalism staffs be cut in half, that foreign bureaus be closed, and that news be tailored to suit the government's self-interest. There would be an outcry that would make the Alien and Sedition Acts, the Red Scares and Watergate seem like child's play. Yet when corporate America aggressively pursues the exact same policies, scarcely a murmur of dissent can be detected in the political culture.

Not only did the financial environment change, but the legal context for media ownership changed too. The net effect of the Telecommunications Act of 1996 (and the subsequent changes in 2003) was to ensure that media ownership will become increasingly concentrated thanks to more relaxed multiple and cross-ownership rules. In 1996 alone, 2,045 radio stations were sold, for a total of $13 billion. Major radio chains, such as Infinity and Clear Channel Communications, went on cross-country buying sprees for radio stations, driving the prices up as they went. Less than six months after the signing of the Telecommunications Act, both chains owned more than a hundred stations. In some cases, a single chain would own all of the talk radio stations—a major source of news and information—in a single market. In some cases, acquired stations were reformatted with automated programming meaning fewer jobs and higher profits for the new owners.

As the legal landscape was changing, the major media players also discovered the synergy that could be developed through "vertical integration." Under vertical integration, a media empire attempts to own a combination of media properties that take a project from development to distribution. Disney, which in the 1990s added ABC-TV to its ownings, is the industry leader in vertical integration. For instance, the film *Hunchback of Notre Dame* earned a "disappointing" $99 million at the box office but generated more than $500 million in revenues in other Disney ventures (McChesney 1997). Clear Channel, after becoming a leader in owning radio stations, began operating concert venues and packaging tours for major acts.

Becoming a player in the media game today is a far cry from the days of the single editor beginning a partisan newspaper, as envisioned by Milton. When Gannett wanted to launch a national newspaper, the corporation spent more than $800 million before *USA Today* turned a profit. When media mogul Rupert Murdoch wanted to create a fourth television network, he lost nearly $100 million in the first two prime-time seasons of his now healthy Fox network. Even though most newspapers enjoy a lucrative monopoly in their home markets, venture capital to create competing newspapers is nonexistent, with start-up costs for a major daily well above a quarter of a billion dollars. These staggering initial costs have closed the door to all but a few and changed the complexion of the media industry to an exclusive club where only the rich and powerful need apply for membership.

As the mass media have themselves become enormous, economically powerful institutions, they have joined what political scientist C. Wright Mills (1956) nearly half a century ago called the "power elite," a ruling class within a democratic society. Time has proved Mills right. Power is found not only in the halls of government but also on Wall Street. And power is found not only in money or armies; it is also found in information. Media organizations, precisely because they have become multinational corporations engaged in the information business, are deeply involved in this power shift.

This emergence of media as economic and political power brokers leads us to question how a powerful institution such as the mass media, which traditionally has had the political role of checking other powerful institutions, can be checked. Can the watchdog be trusted when it is inexorably entwined with the institutions it is watching? For instance, what media can be trusted to take a critical look at the FCC's consideration of loosening the ownership rules when the media stands to profit from the changes? As media corporations expand exponentially in the pursuit of profit, who will watch the watchdog?

Some researchers (see for instance, *What Liberal Media?* by Eric Alterman) have come to the conclusion that the myth of liberal media bias is wrong. While individual journalists still tilt toward the liberal end of the political spectrum, the powerful corporations they work for are often "tamed" by the stockholding public's demand for profits, sometimes following the temptation to self-censor possible offending content for the sake of ratings. The holders of this view got powerful anecdotal evidence when, during the November "sweeps" period of 2003, CBS pulled the plug on a controversial movie, *The Reagans,* which purportedly showed the ex-president and First Lady in a negative light. Threatened by protests and threats of advertiser boycotts, CBS pulled the show less than two weeks from its air date and pushed the movie over to its sister property, the premium Showtime channel.

In speaking for those who protested the moving of the program, *USA Today* commentator Robert Bianco (2003) said:

> If nothing else, this act of creative sabotage should put to rest the idea that the media are liberal. The networks aren't driven by ideology. They're driven by the fear

of any controversy that would scare off advertisers—which means they bow to the whims of impassioned people on either end of the spectrum.

Government is probably the only institution capable of providing a counter to the massive economic power of the media. Yet government provides a variety of subsidies to the industry. In addition, government functions as a regulator of the broadcast and advertising industries, ensuring profits to both these groups by limiting access to the airwaves and legislating fair play in advertising. So, more often than not, the U.S. government supports big media rather than acting as a counterweight.

ECONOMICS AND NEWS

As media ownership becomes the privilege of the rich, an elite few control an important ingredient of democracy: news. When the few who own the media view it only as a business, the problem gets worse. Dan Rather, CBS's *Evening News* anchor, expressed the concerns of many journalists in a *New York Times* op-ed column he wrote:

> News is a business. It has always been. Journalists understand and accept that. But journalism is something else, too. Something more. It is a light on the horizon. A beacon that helps the citizens of a democracy find their way. News is an essential component of a free society. News is a business, but it is also a public trust. (Rather 1987)

Good journalism is often expensive, and in an era of static subscriptions and sometimes unreliable ad revenues, few newsrooms enjoy budgets as large as in past years. The television networks have closed entire bureaus, and many newspapers have pulled back on overseas correspondents, leaving coverage of foreign news to the wires and CNN.

The effect of these cutbacks is lost news for the consumer. One photojournalist, Brad Clift, told the authors that he went to Somalia months before U.S. troops were dispatched, using his own money because he felt the starvation there was an underreported story. Only an occasional network crew and a handful of newspapers pursued the Somalia story until former President Bush committed U.S. troops to the region in December 1992. Most news organizations, like this photojournalist's employer, declined to cover the emerging story, pleading that they had depleted their international budgets by covering Operation Desert Storm.

In reading the code of ethics of the Society of Professional Journalists, two of the "guiding principles" of journalism speak directly to the ethics of media economics: (1) seek truth and report it as fully as possible; and (2) act independently. Seeking the truth can be personally and financially expensive. These examples, from the "Darts and Laurels" columns of *Columbia Journalism Review* in 2002 and 2003 and other sources, show media outlets still willing to stand up to some of society's most powerful institutions, often at great cost, to help the less powerful and disenfranchised.

The *Boston Globe* and the weekly Boston *Phoenix* spent thousands of hours digging deeply into the troubles of the Catholic Church and its role in covering up the sex scandal caused by priests abusing children in their parishes (Cooper, March/April 2002, 21). Investigative stories revealed that in some of the most egregious cases, priests who failed to change criminal behavior even after stays in psychiatric hospitals were transferred and allowed numerous chances at new parishes. In the end, at least one priest was sent to prison and Boston's Cardinal Law was allowed to resign in disgrace.

The *Chicago Tribune,* along with student journalists from Northwestern University, delved deeply into the records of death row inmates in Illinois, proving several of them innocent in cases that captured the nation's attention (Cooper, March/April 2003, 7). Governor George Ryan commuted the sentences of all 167 prisoners on death row. In his speech, he credited the work of Steve Mills and Ken Armstrong of the *Tribune,* who described the system as "so riddled with faulty evidence, unscrupulous trial tactics and legal incompetence that justice has been forsaken."

In the spring of 2003, *The Wall Street Journal* began a national dialogue about a widely known but rarely discussed fact that the uninsured poor pay far more for medical care than their peers covered by private insurers or Medicare (Cooper, July/August 2003, 6). Using examples dating back more than 20 years, the *Journal* showed that uninsured patients often paid five times or more the cost that Medicare or HMOs reimbursed for identical procedures. They also showed that prestigious not-for-profit hospitals were among the most aggressive of bill collectors from the poor, garnishing wages, placing liens on homes and savings accounts and tacking enormous fees and interest onto unpaid bills. By the end of the summer of 2003, congressional hearings on the matter were proposed and many lawyers were collecting clients for class-action suits against hospitals who had overcharged uninsured patients.

The Atlanta *Business Chronicle* helped to stop a $2.2 billion, 59-mile "Northern Arc" across Atlanta when it revealed several previously undisclosed conflicts of interest between the State Department of Transportation and landowners in the area (Cooper, January/February 2003, 5). The *Atlanta Journal-Constitution* launched its own investigation into the matter and forced the state to put the project on hold until the state assembly could pass more stringent ethics laws.

Along a similar line, *Southern Exposure* magazine ran a 53-page cover package in the summer of 2003 about the high cost of being poor, and of the existence of a thriving "poverty industry" that fleeced low-income people, predominantly minorities looking for money (Cooper, September/October 2003, 6). The article outlined such practices as predatory mortgage lending, high-interest credit cards, bank fees, and outrageous "payday" loans. The most significant finding of the story, however, was that these practices were not merely the domain of the corner pawn store or local loan shark; they were being perpetrated on the poor by local and national banks and well-known lending institutions such as Citigroup and its subsidiaries. The magazine also sought to empower its readers with a package that ended with a section entitled "Fighting Back."

Acting independently, another of the Society of Professional Journalists guidelines, can also be expensive. For some media outlets, independence is as simple as buying tickets to the movies reviewed and sports events covered. However, it can go far beyond that. Both the *Lexington Herald-Leader* and the *Syracuse Post-Standard* faced reader boycotts and threats against individual reporters when they opened investigations of local, successful college basketball programs. Reporters for the *New York Daily News* exposed the numerous allegations of incompetence by a medical doctor who was spending more than $150,000 a year in advertising in the *News.*

Television also provides us with stellar examples of good journalism that was often expensive from a personal and corporate standpoint. KHOU of Houston was credited with setting in motion the massive recall of thousands of faulty Firestone tires on Ford Explorers after thousands of wrecks and injuries and hundreds of fatalities. KTVC in Salt Lake City launched an investigation that showed rampant corruption and bribery in the Olympic bidding process that brought the 2002 games to that city.

Unfortunately, these uplifting stories of personal corporate enterprise are far too rare in an industry that demands more than 20 percent pretax profit from its holdings. This demand for profits generates subsidiary problems as well. Entry-level salaries for journalists in both print and broadcast are among the lowest starting salaries of any jobs requiring a college degree—under $26,000 at the turn of the century.

McKinsey and Company made "excellence" a buzzword in business circles with studies that formed the basis of *In Search of Excellence,* the best-selling business book of the 1980s. In 1985, the firm was hired by the National Association of Broadcasters to study 11 of the nation's great radio stations, such as WGN in Chicago, and report to the group's annual convention about what made an excellent radio station. Their findings were (1) the great radio stations were audience-oriented in their programming, often breaking down the traditional walls that defined formats, and (2) the great radio stations were community-oriented in their promotions, becoming synonymous in their communities with charitable events and community festivities.

The attitude is summed up by WMMS (Cleveland) General Manager Bill Smith (National Association of Broadcasters 1985):

> If you want a car to last forever, you've got to throw some money back into that car and make sure that it's serviced properly on a continual basis. Otherwise, it's going to break down and fall apart. We know that we're constantly rebuilding the station one way or another. We throw the profit to the listening audience . . . to charities, to several nonprofit organizations, to free concerts or anything to affect the listeners of Cleveland as a whole. If we can donate the money to light up Terminal Tower, if that's what it's going to take and nobody else is going to do it, we'll do it . . . and we get and hold our listeners, year-in and year-out, because they identify us as being community-minded.

ECONOMICS AND ENTERTAINMENT: THE DAY THE MUSIC DIED

While digital technology sent shock waves throughout all media industries, the strongest tremors were felt in the music business. There, digital technology arrived at the same time five global companies—Universal Music Group (owned by Vivendi), Warner Music (a division of AOL Time Warner), Sony Music Entertainment, the German firm Bertelsmann Music Group (BMG) and the EMI Group—took control of about 85 percent of the record industry.

The rationale for the conglomeration in the music industry (labeled "dyssynergy" by *New Yorker* writer John Seabrook) was that profits from established labels and artists would be used to promote new talent. However, the corporate approach meant that managers now focused on quarterly profits and selling records rather than making music and promoting art. Corporations wanted mega hits. They were difficult and expensive to make and promote, and impossible to predict.

Chris Blackwell, who began a small record label in the 1970s and sold it to Poly-Gram in 1989, said, "I don't think the music business lends itself very well to being a Wall Street business. You're always working with individuals, with creative people, and the people you are trying to reach, by and large, don't view music as a commodity but as a relationship with a band. It takes time to expand that relationship but most people who work for the corporations have three-year contracts, some five, and most of them are expected to produce. What an artist really needs is a champion, not a numbers guy who in another year is going to leave" (Seabrook 2003, 46).

While corporations were merging, CD technology—made possible by the digital revolution—took over what historians now call the "record" market. By 1986, CD sales had climbed to 100 million copies worldwide. In 1999 CD sales eclipsed those of vinyl records. And, then, the bottom fell out due to an unanticipated consequence of the CD (digital) format: CDs made piracy possible. Digital music, uploaded onto the Internet through MP3 files, made enormous inroads with younger listeners—the generation most comfortable with the computer and its capabilities. In 2002 the industry shipped 33.5 million copies of the year's 10 best-selling albums, barely half the number it had shipped two years before. With Kid Rock and Pink contributing less than anticipated to the bottom line, the corporations tended to play it safe. New music, and new artists, had a much more difficult time.

Most industry experts agreed that the MP3 format was a permanent addition to the ways audiences could access music. The flexibility and specificity of file-sharing programs like Morpheus and Grokster—which enabled person-to-person sharing of music—meant that many more people were sharing music files. Some estimate that as many as 60 million Americans download music in this way. Sir Howard Stringer, the chairman of the Sony Corporation of America, called downloaders "thieves" and compared them to those who shoplift from stores. (For a case study about Napster, the first file-sharing software, go to the Web site for this book.)

The recording industry fired back against file sharing of copyrighted music in the fall of 2003 when the Recording Industry Association of America (RIAA) sued 261 persons (out of an estimated 60 million potential) who had illegally downloaded music. Those selected for the lawsuits had each downloaded more than 1,000 songs, and several of the defendants were minors. Although the liability for those sued was potentially in the millions, a few weeks after the initial suits most of the cases were being resolved for about $2,000, with the added agreement that those who pleaded guilty would take all copyrighted music off their computers and sign a pledge not to engage in file sharing in the future.

A few weeks after the initial suits, the RIAA announced that it would pursue more lawsuits while at the same time offering an amnesty program to those who had downloaded music illegally in the past. The amnesty program required the users to take the same steps required of those sued—deletion of music files and the signing of a cease-and-desist agreement. Indeed, more suits were filed in 2004, with "John Doe" warrants issued while judges forced Internet service providers to turn over the names of offenders.

Some have suggested that the heavy-handed tactics employed show that many in the music industry regard their fan base with suspicion and disapproval. However, some artists were not so quick to condemn, noting that music file sharing/piracy could be considered payback for the way giant corporations had exploited artists. Joni Mitchell, songwriter and artist, called the record industry a "corrupt cesspool." Others have said that if the downloading trend continued unchecked, the recording industry as the world currently knows it will die.

The ethical implications of these two now-entwined trends are obvious. As you read this section, ask yourself when was the last time you bought a music CD as opposed to burning one? Do you agree that person-to-person music sharing constitutes theft? Is Joni Mitchell right, and is file sharing a good way to register such a protest? Is Sir Howard Stringer right that it is equivalent to shoplifting? Would you feel the same way if someone shared *your* works? On an industrywide level, how will new artists, especially those who don't fit the corporate view, emerge and prosper? Can music fans worldwide "afford" to relinquish an art form that for many sustains an emotional connection to some of the most formative times of their lives? Will creative people, who find their energies unusable in the music industry, turn to other mediums? As is often the case in the mass media, the development and adoption of a new medium or delivery technology often has unanticipated consequences on many mediums and formats as well as on content.

BLOCKBUSTER OR BUST: ART IN A COMMERCIAL AGE

It was supposed to be a victory for consumer choice. Satellite and cable systems with more than 100 networks. Unlimited variety on the Internet. Commercial-free radio in your car.

However, recent media mergers have created fewer media corporations with the power to "greenlight" a project—books, films, CDs, television shows—putting pressure on the product that does get produced to return unrealistic profits. Adding to the problem is that all but one of the major worldwide media conglomerates are publicly traded, putting the pressure on managers to produce each quarter so that stock prices remain high. As a result, many studios and record labels now produce only a handful of projects per year, most often featuring well-established stars and recording artists. Money that was once used on new artist development now is re-purposed to hype the latest offering from existing stars.

In the summer of 2002, one major studio announced that it would no longer make medium-budget films—from $40 million to $80 million. Instead, the corporation announced to its shareholders that it would focus instead on occasional "niche" films for $10 million or less and "blockbuster" films with budgets of $100 million or more. According to executives quoted, films in the middle are now considered too risky to make.

With the average price tag for major films soaring, studios run for cover, and most often they find that cover in proven formulas such as sequels. In the summer of 2003, no fewer than six sequels hit the theater, with budgets averaging more than $100 million. Some were sequels of classics, such as the second installment of the *Lord of the Rings* trilogy, while others, such as *Laura Croft, The Cradle of Life,* were sequels of movies panned the first time out. Advertising budgets for these and other sequels were huge, creating large opening weekends that were typically followed by dropoffs in attendance of up to 70 percent as the word of mouth got out that some films were not that good.

The effect of this trend is that midpriced, independent films, with fewer explosions and with no-name actors, have less chance of being made than ever before. And if the independent film has the added "strike" of being controversial, as was the case with the 2004 Mel Gibson film depicting the crucifixion of Christ, distributors blanch. Big-budget films soak up available studio funding and distribution channels—often open on more than 1,000 screens—crowding out the independent films at the bank and the multiplex.

The same phenomenon can be seen in publishing and recording as well. With tiny bookstores in malls and airports ordering only the fastest selling titles, and with "rack jobbers" stocking only the fastest selling CDs in the small square footage given to them by discount retailing chains, publishers and record companies are increasingly hesitant about greenlighting projects that will take time and word of mouth to find their audience.

This "blockbuster or bust" trend will have fallouts similar to the ones mentioned in music above. First, and most immediate, fewer voices with something to say in film, music or printed page will be heard. Second, in years to come, the entertainment industry could experience a shortage of artists, writers and composers in the "pipeline" to replace today's artists.

SOCIAL RESPONSIBILITY IN THE NEW MILLENNIUM

When the social responsibility theory was framed in the 1940s, the primary informational concern was scarcity: people might not get the information they needed for citizenship. Today, however, the primary informational concern is an overabundance of raw data: people might not filter out what they need through all the clutter. Media and their distribution systems changed, but the theory remained silent, especially about the role of profit in the development of systems for gathering and disseminating information. This meant that, until recently, government agencies such as the FCC were still basing policy decisions on the scarcity argument when any consumer with cable or a satellite dish knew otherwise.

The Newspaper Preservation Act of the 1970s, the AT&T antitrust suits of the 1980s, the Telecommunications Act of the 1990s, and other battles finally focused the attention of the U.S. government on the fact that delivery of entertainment and information is indeed big business and is currently in the hands of a very few—something the libertarian framers of the Constitution sought to avoid.

The clash of large, well-financed institutions for control of information is a modern phenomenon. Classical ethical theory, which speaks to individual acts, is of little help in sorting out the duties and responsibilities of corporations larger than most nations that control the currency of the day: information. Political theory, particularly Marxist theory, is of some help in identifying the problem, but communism has been rejected as a potential solution throughout most of the world.

Americans are equally unwilling to accept government as the solution to counter the concentrated economic power of the media, and government has been loathe to break up the large media conglomerates. During the lifetime of the readers of this book, the power and role of "big media," such as AT&T and Time Warner, should emerge as *the* most important issue in media ethics. Can an institution that began as a lone printer with a press "flourish" without a change in vision as a multinational corporation with billions in assets?

History says "no." Adaptability is the key to institutional survival. The Roman Catholic Church lost much of its intellectual and political hold on western Europe when devotion to dogma overruled commitment to parishioners. The Reformation resulted. Likewise, the Mandarin class lost political control in ancient China because it could not change with a country that was moving into the 20th century. Social and political history has not been kind to big entities. Media conglomerates will thrive only to the extent that they can adapt both to serve the diverse communities into which their far-flung empires take them and to react quickly when they fail.

The ones that do it well will survive.

Suggested Readings

AULETTA, KEN. 1991. *Three blind mice: How the TV networks lost their way.* New York: Random House.

BAGDIKIAN, BEN H. 2000. *The media monopoly.* 6th ed. Boston: Beacon Press.

GILBERT CRANBERG, RANDALL BEZANSON, and JOHN SOLOSKI. 2001. *Taking stock.* Ames, IA.: Iowa State University Press.

MILLS, C. WRIGHT. 1956. *The power elite.* New York: Oxford University Press.

ROBERT W. MCCHESNEY. 1991. *Rich media: Poor democracy: Communication politics in dubious times.* Urbana: University of Illinois Press.

Cases on the Web

"Union activism and the broadcast personality" by Stanley Cunningham
"A salesperson's dilemma: Whose interests come first?" by Charles H. Warner
"Turning on the *Light:* The San Antonio newspaper war" by Fred Blevins
"Calvin Klein's kiddie porn ads prick our tolerances" by Valerie Lilley

CHAPTER VIII CASES

CASE VIII-A
Ms. Magazine—No More Ads!
PHILIP PATTERSON
Oklahoma Christian University

Ms. magazine printed its last commercial issue in October 1989 and returned in June 1990 as one of the few mass-circulation magazines in history to eschew advertising and rely entirely on its readers for support.

While vowing to continue in the tradition begun by the group of women activists who founded the magazine in 1972, one thing was now different: the price. Readers would be asked to pay $35 for six issues, a price that has since increased.

The new publisher, David Lang, who bought *Ms.* when it was struggling to make ends meet, at the prompting of the magazine's editors, decided to fund the magazine entirely on readers' subscriptions.

Gloria Steinem, a cofounder of *Ms.,* said the magazine has always walked the line between unvarnished advocacy and the demands of the people who pay the bills. She authored an exposé for the premiere issue entitled "Sex, Lies and Advertising." In it, Steinem revealed the stories of advertisers who didn't want to be placed near articles dealing with abortion, gun control, illness, large-size fashion, anything depressing.

The new editor-in-chief, Robin Morgan, told the *Denver Post,* "Now we can say all the things we never got to say for 18 years. We have to keep reminding ourselves of that" (*Denver Post* 1990).

Andrea Kaplan, spokesperson for Lang Communications, said *Ms.* would need 50,000 to 100,000 subscribers to show a profit, a standard achieved by its third issue. At the time of its suspension in 1989, *Ms.* had 550,000 subscribers but was losing money.

Ms. is not the only magazine to take action against the constraints of advertisers. Some magazines—for example, *Consumer Reports*—refuse advertising altogether. Other publications such as *Modern Maturity, The New Yorker* and *Mother Jones* have implemented strict advertising policies. *Modern Maturity* refuses all ads that depict aging in a negative light, said Robert E. Wood, publishing director of the magazine, claiming in interviews that advertising is as important as editorial in shaping the overall feel of the magazine.

At *The New Yorker* all proposed advertisements are sent to a committee that evaluates each ad's motives and relevance to the magazine's targeted audience. Only if the committee approves the ad will it be published. Similarly, the staff of *Mother Jones* magazine refuses to publish ads that are sexist, racist, or exploitive.

Ms. magazine's decision to eliminate advertising drew attention to the difficulties publishers face regarding ethics and advertising today. It raised questions about the role of the media as an information outlet and questioned the motives of advertisers and publishers alike.

Micro Issues

1. Is *Ms.* infringing on the advertiser's right to freedom of speech?
2. Is *Ms.* courting financial ruin by shunning the advertising that supports it?
3. Is *Ms.* depriving its readers of an informative medium through its elimination of ads?
4. If a magazine edits an article to satisfy an important advertiser, does it have any obligation to inform readers of the decision?

Midrange Issues

1. Are consumers able to distinguish between editorial content and advertisements? Does it matter?
2. How could *Ms.* magazine responsibly satisfy the desires of its advertisers and its readers simultaneously?
3. How would the particular advertiser problems of a liberal feminist magazine such as *Ms.* compare to another periodical such as *Newsweek*?

Macro Issues

1. Is it the media's job to censor advertisements for the public?
2. By running an ad, is a publication endorsing the product being advertised? Should publications be held responsible for the claims of their advertisers?
3. Is a magazine ethically required to be an open forum for all advertisers who have the ability to pay? According to what standards?

CASE VIII-B
Crossing the Line? The *L.A. Times* and the Staples Affair
MEREDITH BRADFORD AND PHILIP PATTERSON
Oklahoma Christian University

The *Los Angeles Times,* in a "special report" on December 20, 1999, called attention to an event its editors perceived as a breach of journalism ethics. The multi-story report was entitled "Crossing the Line." What made this report extraordinary is that it was the *Times* itself that had crossed the line that triggered this journalistic exposé.

A few weeks earlier, the Staples Center, a $400 million sports and entertainment arena in downtown Los Angeles, had opened to great fanfare. Most observers shared the hope that the facility, which would house two basketball franchises and one hockey team, would spark a revitalization of downtown. Staples Inc. had won the naming rights to the arena by paying $116 million.

Tim Lieweke, president of the Staples Center, left with $284 million more to raise, had initiated talks with McDonald's, Anheuser-Busch, United Airlines, Bank of America, and others to become "founding partners." He was eager to have the *Los Angeles Times* as a founding partner because of previous joint successes and because he thought the paper could contribute value beyond cash.

The Staples arena already had a promotional arrangement with the *Los Angeles Times* in exchange for cash payments from the *Times* and free advertising in the paper. "The arrangement is similar to that many big-city papers have with their local professional sports teams," said David Shaw, the *L.A. Times* Pulitzer Prize–winning media critic, in an investigative piece on the controversy (Shaw 1999). "But for the Staples Center, Lieweke wanted more. He wanted the *Times* as a founding partner."

Since the Staples Center could be a major contributor to the revitalization of downtown Los Angeles, *Times* executives were "eager to participate," Shaw said.

The price for founding partners ranged from $2 million to $3 million per year for five years. Jeffrey S. Klein, then senior vice president of the *Times,* who supervised early negotiations on the Staples deal, "didn't think it was worth what they were asking." Negotiations stalled for several months in 1998 until a "Founding Partner Agreement" was accepted on December 17, 1998, between the L.A. Arena Company and the *Los Angeles Times.* Part of the language in the agreement stated the two companies "agree to cooperate in the development and implementation of joint revenue opportunities."

"Although all of the principals in the negotiations say that the precise terms of the Staples deal are confidential," Shaw reported, "information from a variety of sources shows that in effect the *Times* agreed to pay Staples Center about $1.6 million a year for five years—$800,000 of that in cash, $500,000 in profits and an estimated $300,000 in profits from what Lieweke had called 'ideas that would generate revenue for us.' "

This latter part of the deal was clarified in a clause of the final contract that said, in part, that the *Times* and the L.A. Arena Company would agree to cooperate in the development and implementation of joint revenue opportunities such as a special section in the *Los Angeles Times* in connection with the opening of the arena, or a jointly published commemorative yearbook, Shaw said.

These "joint opportunities" were to create $300,000 of net revenue for each party annually. According to the contract, these opportunities would be subject to the mutual agreement of both parties.

On October 10, 1999, the *Times* published a special 168-page issue of its Sunday magazine dedicated to the new Staples Center sports and entertainment arena.

Only after the section was published did most of the paper's journalists learn that the *Times* had split the advertising profits from the magazine with the Staples Center. Feeling that the arrangement constituted a conflict of interest and a violation of the journalistic principle of editorial independence, more than 300 *Times* reporters and editors signed a petition demanding that publisher Kathryn Downing apologize and undertake a thorough review of all other financial relationships that may compromise the *Times'* editorial heritage.

The petition, in part, stated "As journalists at the *L.A. Times,* we are appalled by the paper entering into hidden financial partnerships with the subjects we are writing about. The editorial credibility of the *Times* has been fundamentally undermined."

Less than two years before the episode, Downing had been named publisher by Mark Willes, the new chief executive of Times Mirror Corporation, parent company of the *Los Angeles Times,* despite having no newsroom background. Her previous experience had been as a legal publicist. Willes had moved from General Mills to Times Mirror in 1995. Willes had made no secret of his desire to " 'blow up the wall' between business and editorial" (Rieder 1999). He was also on record as telling *American Journalism Review* in 1997 that "[the] notion that you have to be in journalism 30 years to understand what's important, I find rather quaint" (Rieder 1999).

Downing did apologize, calling it a "major, major mistake." After taking questions at a two-hour staff meeting on October 28, she admitted that she and her staff "failed to understand the ethics involved" (Booth 1999). Downing meanwhile canceled all future revenue-sharing deals with Staples, promised to review all contracts with advertisers, and ordered up awareness training for the ad side.

For his part, Willes seemed to reverse his earlier stance when he said, "This is exactly the consequence of having people in the publisher's job who don't have experience in newspapers" (Rieder 1999).

On the business side of the paper the arrangement was widely known and discussed openly for most of 1999. Downing says she deliberately withheld the information from Michael Parks, the paper's editor, but did not direct her subordinates on the business side not to talk about it to him or to anyone else in editorial, according to several reports.

Shaw reports that Willes argued that the absence of such discussion only shows the need for "more communications, not less. . . . The profit-sharing deal happened not because The Wall came down," Willes says, "but because people didn't talk to one another when they should have."

In an interesting argument, Downing claimed if the editorial side of the paper did not know about the profit-sharing deal with the Staples Center before printing, then the Sunday magazine devoted to the Staples Center would be unbiased. The uninformed editorial staff would have no reason to be biased.

Many critics from inside and outside the newspaper agree with Shaw that "readers have no reason to trust anything the *Times* wrote about Staples Center, or any of its tenants or attractions, anywhere in the paper, now or in the future, if the *Times* and Staples Center were business partners." He adds that readers will wonder whether other improper arrangements, formal or informal, might also exist or be created in the future with other entities, agencies and individuals covered by the *Times*.

Whether connected to the Staples affair or not, massive changes were in store for Willes, Downing, Parks and the *Times*. The newspaper was bought by the Tribune Company, publisher of the *Chicago Tribune,* in March 2000. All three employees were gone within a year.

Micro Issues

1. Critique Willes's early and late statements about journalistic experience in newspaper management positions.
2. Is the actual loss of credibility as disastrous as the reporters felt, or does the public really have the same sensibilities as those in the profession?
3. How does entering into the contract with the Staples Center differ from the sports department accepting press passes for the events held in the arena?

Midrange Issues

1. If one acknowledges that "the wall" is good and necessary, how does that affect media engaged in advocacy journalism?
2. Shaw entitled his article "Journalism Is a Very Different Business." In what ways do you think journalism differs from other businesses?

Macro Issues

1. In the new information age, where so many competing views can be found on most issues, is "the wall" still relevant?
2. When a newspaper is a publicly traded company, do the loyalties of the paper shift from the public to the shareholders? If not, how can you justify a move that might be counterproductive to profits?

CASE VIII-C
"Bonding" Announcements in the News
JOANN BYRD
Seattle Post-Intelligencer

The "Wedding Book" in the Sunday "Northwest Life" section of *The Herald* in Everett, Washington, includes weddings, engagements, and 25th and 50th wedding anniversaries. Each event submitted is reported with a one-column picture and about 2 inches of copy. People who want a more detailed announcement or their own language can buy a reduced-rate display ad, for which they write the copy.

In the fall of 1990, a lesbian couple filled out the form used to collect information and submitted it for the "Wedding Book" page. The women wanted to announce they had made a lifetime commitment to each other in a bonding ceremony attended by family and friends in a local park.

The *Herald* serves an area combining the suburbs of Seattle and surrounding rural communities. Many in the core communities had made it clear over the years that they expected the paper to reflect and reinforce conservative family values. The county had grown 36 percent in the previous decade and showed an increasing diversity of races, cultures and lifestyles. Other institutions, including the state's biggest bank, had adopted policies recognizing unmarried relationships, and the city of Seattle had recently been involved in a visible campaign to have domestic partners of city employees declared eligible for medical insurance.

The decision to accept the announcement was made almost instantly. Simultaneously, Stan Strick, the paper's then-managing editor, suggested expanding the page to include, as the in-paper announcement put it, "significant personal milestones in people's lives, everything from adoptions to retirements."

Readers were notified of the change Sunday morning, November 25, 1990, in a story alongside the jumps of section-front pieces about gay couples who had exchanged vows and ministers discussing church positions on gay commitment ceremonies. The paper, with its page renamed "Celebrations," would be "one of the first in the nation to accept bonding ceremonies other than weddings," said the announcement.

The decision was condemned from pulpits in the county that morning, and people in the community began to protest. The women's announcement ran on the revamped page December 2, under a standing head, "Bondings," that matched the labels for "Weddings," "Engagements," "Anniversaries," and "Birthdays."

The community reaction became intense. Hundreds of angry subscribers canceled their subscriptions (as did some people who didn't have subscriptions). Letters and phone calls flooded the newsroom; a local businessman organized a protest group and visited the *Herald* advertisers, urging, although unsuccessfully, a boycott of the paper. Delegations from the conservative Christian community came to the paper to demand that the policy be rescinded.

Seattle television covered the debate, and national media interviewed Strick. The storm continued for months. Letters to the editor and organized letter-writing and telephoning campaigns followed national news stories. As other newspapers across the country were approached to publish gay bonding ceremonies, editors phoned for details of the *Herald*'s experience.

Most of the complaints centered on Biblical interpretations condemning homosexuality. Those callers and letter writers felt the *Herald* was endorsing sin, and giving to homosexual relationships the sanction that should be reserved for heterosexual marriages, engagements, and wedding anniversaries.

The *Herald's* position was that sexual orientation was not a morally relevant basis for refusing to accept the announcements, that a page of reader-generated "significant personal milestones" simply had to give people equal access.

The policy has not been changed, but no other gay couple in the county submitted an announcement in the years following. One advertiser quit advertising for several weeks. Many of those who canceled subscriptions have not returned.

Micro Issues

1. Should the paper have accepted the announcement?
2. What options could you imagine? (Should the paper, for instance, have treated it as a news story rather than institutionalizing gay commitments on its announcement page?)
3. Some critics thought the *Herald* was bragging about being "one of the first" to accept gay bonding announcements. Would it have been better to skip the advance notice and simply publish the bonding ceremony and the new publication procedures for the page?
4. Some defenders likened the paper's decision to publishing mixed-race marriages before such notions were thought "socially acceptable." Is that a legitimate parallel? Are there others?

Midrange Issues

1. Gay commitments are not recognized by most state laws. Should the paper publish any arrangements that do not have legal status?
2. This case arose on a page where "news" is defined by people who want to make the announcements, not by reporters working a beat. Does that raise different ethical questions in the newsroom?
3. How far should the newspaper go in giving people equal access to its pages? Is anything anybody wants to announce okay?

Macro Issues

1. Offending people and their most deeply held beliefs is not morally justified unless there is an overriding moral obligation. How much should the paper weigh the probability of offending a large portion of its audience by doing what it considers morally correct in this case?
2. Chances are that there would have been less dispute if the change had occurred at a paper in a big city. Are the values at stake here different from community to community, and should all newspapers' decisions recognize that?
3. How much should a secular entity like a newspaper reflect religious beliefs?
4. The women involved in this case were harassed by conservative groups for months afterward. Does a newspaper have an obligation to censor news that may harm those submitting it? If so, what are the criteria?

CASE VIII-D
Punishing the Messenger: The Tobacco Industry and the Press
STEVE WEINBERG, Former Associate Editor, *Columbia Journalism Review*
University of Missouri—Columbia

When ABC News, under the cloud of a $10 billion libel suit, apologized to Philip Morris in August 1995 for an award-winning investigation entitled "Smoke Screen," most journalists were stunned. The network's action damaged the credibility of a top-notch news organization, perhaps undermined investigative reporting as a journalistic genre, and encouraged lingering questions about the impact of the bottom line on corporate decision making regarding news stories.

The two-part investigative piece reported by Pulitzer Prize winner Walt Bogdanich stated that tobacco companies, including Philip Morris and others, added nicotine to cigarette tobacco with the purpose of keeping smokers hooked on the drug. The story itself had been exhaustively researched for more than a year, and all of the sources but one—"Deep Cough"—had agreed to go on the record with their comments. In the process of researching the story, Bogdanich learned that during the manufacturing process, nicotine is actually removed from tobacco at one point only to be added back into the tobacco later.

Less than a week before the show aired on the news magazine *Day One,* the U.S. Food and Drug Administration (FDA) issued a letter stating that it believed there was mounting evidence that nicotine is "a powerfully addictive agent" and that "cigarette vendors control the levels of nicotine that satisfy this addiction" (Weinberg 1995, 27).

Spokespersons for the tobacco industry were quoted in the segments, and Philip Morris, just days before the show was to air, sent ABC News a two-paragraph statement that said, in part, "Nothing done in the processing of tobacco or manufacture of cigarettes by Philip Morris increases the nicotine in the tobacco blend above what is naturally found in the tobacco." The investigative report never made the allegation that nicotine levels were increased beyond those that occur naturally; rather it suggested the tobacco companies had the ability to remove some of the drug from cigarettes and had chosen not to do so.

Controversy erupted after the first part of the story aired on February 28, 1994. A second segment, which aired one week later, focused on the list the tobacco companies had supplied to the federal government of 700 cigarette ingredients. Thirteen of those ingredients are banned in food. Philip Morris was not mentioned at all in the second segment.

Journalists applauded the work. The coverage won a George Polk award and a DuPont/Columbia University award. Congressional hearings into the tobacco industry were called as a result of the story. One day before those hearings were to begin, Philip Morris sued for libel, asking for $5 billion in compensatory damages and $5 billion in punitive damages, despite the fact that Virginia law capped punitive damage awards at $350,000. The story about the libel suit ran nationally, often without the notation about the award restriction. In addition, the tobacco giant gave every indication that it would pursue the suit vigorously, spending more than $1 million per month for more than a year on the litigation.

At ABC, newspeople saw what they perceived as an immediate chilling effect. The day Philip Morris filed the lawsuit, two independent producers were notified by a producer at ABC's program *Turning Point* that their documentary on the tobacco industry's advertising tactics and production transfers to overseas sites was being shelved, despite the outlay of about $500,000.

Legally, the going was equally difficult. Although the network gave every indication that it intended to fight and win the libel suit, discovery tactics by Philip Morris bedeviled the process. Documents that normally would have been public were marked as trade secrets, thus sealing them and making them impossible to report on. Worse yet, from the journalists' point of view, Philip Morris attempted to unearth Deep Cough's identity by subpoenaing records of reporters' phone bills, credit card purchases and travel in an attempt to retrace the journalist's footsteps to Deep Cough's door. A judge initially approved of the subpoenas in the discovery process but later reversed himself after the network contested the decision.

As in many expensive lawsuits, talk about a settlement surfaced from time to time, starting in the summer of 1994, just three months into pretrial discovery—and just as rumors began that Disney might make ABC part of its entertainment empire. Insiders weren't surprised. But it wasn't until almost a year later, on June 30, 1995, that *The Wall Street Journal* reported that settlement talks had begun anew. By that time, and despite assurances from ABC's trial lawyers, other lawyers and some ABC managers had decided that portions of the investigative report would not withstand trial scrutiny.

It turned out that the trial lawyers had been kept away from the settlement negotiations. In-house lawyers, who were joined in the final days by renowned First Amendment lawyer Floyd Abrams, worked with Philip Morris's litigators on the language of an apology to the two tobacco companies. (Abrams had been involved in the case briefly, before the settlement talks began.) The network's statement ultimately ran in more than 700 publications under the headline "Apology Accepted." Philip Morris dropped the suit.

The apology was clearly a victory for Philip Morris, but was it a sellout for ABC? If "Smoke Screen" contained one or more factual errors, it might be possible to consider the extremely limited language of the apology and the absence of any monetary awards (ABC did agree to pay the other side's legal fees, at least $15 million), a victory of sorts for the network. ABC's assertion in the apology letter that it stands behind the show's intended principal focus and the signing of the reporter and producer to new long-term contracts with substantial raises—even though both refused to sign the settlement agreement—are a vindication of sorts for the show.

ABC was purchased by Disney after the suit was settled.

Micro Issues

1. Should Deep Cough have been allowed to remain off the record?
2. What standards of evidence should journalists doing investigative work demand from their sources and documents?
3. How should other news organizations that covered the libel suit have reported it?

Midrange Issues

1. Should journalists work out agreements about legal liability with their editors in advance of broadcast or publication?
2. Should the journalists have been willing to wait on the story and work with government regulators on the issue?
3. What professional values are served by stories such as "Smoke Screen?"
4. Does reporting on undesirable products or issues—toxic waste or tobacco, for example—demand a different professional standard than reporting on city government?

Macro Issues

1. What is the responsibility of "corporate ownership" to encourage and protect investigative reporting?
2. Do journalists, who increasingly work for large corporations, have a responsibility to the public to find mechanisms to counter the demands of the bottom line?
3. Do journalists have a watchdog role when it comes to covering corporations and economically powerful interests?
4. Compare "Smoke Screen" to Upton Sinclair's classic *The Jungle*. Would such a treatment of the tobacco industry be possible today?

IX

Picture This: The Ethics of Photo and Video Journalism

By the end of this chapter, you should be familiar with:

- **the legal and ethical issues involved in photojournalism in the area of privacy.**
- **the technology available for altering photos and of the ethical and epistemological issues those possibilities raise.**
- **the legal and ethics problems of "eyewash."**

INTRODUCTION

Decades of technological developments have dramatically shortened the time between the occurrence of a news event and the dissemination of photos or video of it to the public. Digital photos can be posted to the Web almost instantaneously. Video is routinely beamed live into television homes across America. Once, the most instantaneous of ethical decisions in the mass media was the one made by the photographer at the scene of a news story: "Shoot or don't shoot?" Today the question has added layers that must be answered: "Post or don't post?" Or: "Go live or not?"

Decisions that once could be made in the relative calm of the newsroom following a dramatic tragedy now must be made in the field or at the computer screen immediately in an increasingly competitive media environment. And making the right decision can be the difference in being applauded for beating the competition and bringing a compelling visual to readers or being criticized by thousands of readers or viewers for lack of taste or sensitivity.

How a photographer or editor prepares for such moments, and what decisions he or she makes when a questionable situation arises, is sometimes thought to be the only issue in photo and video ethics. However, a number of ethical issues surround the visual part of the business, many of them evolving rapidly with new technology. In this chapter we will discuss the following:

1. Balancing the right to privacy and newsworthiness.
2. Staging video and news photographs.
3. Changing images electronically.
4. Selective editing to support a point of view.
5. Using unrelated "eyewash" photography in news.

What do these issues have in common? Perhaps it is that they all seem to center on the twin themes of fairness and accuracy. However, once the problems are identified, the answers are not that simple. What is fair? What is accurate?

While each photographer and photo editor will have to answer these questions individually, perhaps some minimum standard can be established: No image used in the news, whether video or still photograph, is ethical unless it treats the subjects or topics fairly and attempts to present an accurate and unambiguous picture of reality.

We will examine the inherent problems of visual communication, then look at specific ethical issues.

PROBLEMS IN THE PROCESS

Age-old axioms assure us that "The camera never lies" and that "Seeing is believing." Yet no photograph or videotape can be completely accurate, since the mechanics of photography demand that the lens and film make choices the eye is not required to make. These differences between the eye and the camera influence perception, as Arthur Berger points out in *Seeing Is Believing.* Because of the many variables in photography—camera angles, use of light, texture and focus—Berger says a picture is always an *interpretation* of reality, not reality itself. He adds that a dozen photographers taking pictures of the same scene would produce different views of the reality of it. For instance, one photographer, Nat Fein, won the Pulitzer Prize for photography while taking a picture of an event dozens of photographers were shooting—the retirement of Babe Ruth. By moving to the rear of his subject, Fein captured a different angle and told a different and more dramatic story with his photo.

Not only does the camera differ from the eye in its ability to manipulate angle, light and focus; cameras also capture an isolated reality by presenting us with a slice of life, free from context. In *About Looking,* John Berger (1980, 14) says:

> What the camera does, and what the eye can never do, is to fix the appearance of that event. The camera saves a set of appearances from the otherwise inevitable supersession of further appearances. It holds them unchanging. And before the invention of the camera nothing could do this, except in the mind's eye, the faculty of memory.

Although the camera and the eye are vastly different in their functions and their abilities, most media consumers believe the photographs they see because most people assume their eyes don't deceive them. In this unguarded assumption lies the possibility for manipulation and deception.

Compounding the reality problem is the importance of visuals to both the electronic and print media. No major story is complete without a photo or footage. In this rush to shoot compelling visuals to accompany a story, photojournalists must juggle deadline and competitive pressures with other, less tangible qualities, such as privacy.

TO SHOOT OR NOT TO SHOOT?

Each day, before photos or video are chosen by the appropriate editor, another important decision is made in the field by photographers. Arriving on the scene of newsworthy events, she must make several decisions. The most basic of these is whether or not to shoot the photo of a subject who is in no position to deny the photographer access to the event. Often these vulnerable subjects are wounded, in shock, in grief. In that newsworthy moment, the subject of the photograph loses a measure of control over his or her circles of intimacy. That control passes to the photographer, who must make a decision.

Goffman (1959) claims people possess several "territories" they have a right to control. Included in Goffman's list are two territories that are problematic to the visual journalist: the right to a personal space free from intrusion (i.e., by a camera lens) and the right to preserve one's "information," such as a state of joy, or grief, from public view.

By its very nature, photojournalism is an intrusive and a revealing process—two violations of Goffman's sense of self. In many cases, it appears that someone else's misfortune is good fortune for the photojournalist. One study (Junas 1980) found that more than half of the winning images in top photography contests were pictures of violence and tragedy.

Inevitably, every photojournalist happens on an assignment that will intrude on a subject's privacy. Garry Bryant (1987), a staff photographer with the *Deseret News* of Salt Lake City, offers this checklist he goes through "in hundredths of a second" when he reaches the scene of events such as the ones just described:

1. Should this moment be made public?
2. Will being photographed send the subjects into further trauma?
3. Am I at the least obtrusive distance possible?
4. Am I acting with compassion and sensitivity?

To this list, however, Bryant adds the following disclaimer (1987, 34): "What society needs to understand is that photographers act and shoot instinctively. We are not journalists gathering facts. We are merely photographers snapping pictures. A general rule for most photojournalists is 'Shoot. You can always edit later.' "

Editors argue that decisions cannot be made concerning photos that do not exist. Not every picture of grief needs to be ruled out just because the subject is vulnerable. For instance, newspaper readers and television viewers need to know that drinking and driving can kill and leave behind grieving parents and friends. Where to draw the line is a decision best made in the newsroom rather than at the scene. The photographer who attempts to perform a type of ethical triage at the scene of a tragedy might find his career in jeopardy if the assignment fails to capture the pathos of the event when all other photographers succeeded. In addition, the photographer who fails to capture some of the event, for whatever reason, fails to capture some of the truth for the audience.

However, the window of time for deciding later is closing. Today's microwave technology means that the media can be "Live at Five" on the scene of a tragedy, broadcasting footage even before the immediate family is alerted. Scenes that might once have been edited as the story was compiled now go straight on the air. An important stage in the ethical decision-making process is bypassed when such stories are aired live.

How can the victims of these tragedies come to life as vulnerable humans with feelings to a professional who sees the world most of the time through a lens? That question was asked at a conference held on the campus of Texas Christian University entitled "Crime Victims and the News Media." The conference brought together victims of violent crime and the journalists who covered their stories. One participant, Jeff Greenfield, who was ABC's media critic at the time, noted, "Once a journalist hears their simple, eloquent stories of what happened to them, he will never approach the story of a human tragedy in quite the same way."

Essentially, the photographer who is deciding whether and how to photograph a tragedy is wrestling with the dilemma of treating every subject as an end and not merely a means to an end. We can agree that powerful images of accident victims may cause some drivers to proceed more safely, but if that message often comes at the expense of an accident victim's privacy, is it a message that needs to be told? Bovée (1991), in an essay entitled "The Ends Can Justify the Means—But Rarely," offers this set of questions to help the photographer find the answer.

1. Are the means truly morally evil or merely distasteful, unpopular, etc.?

2. Is the end a *real* good or something that merely *appears* to be good?

3. Is it probable that the means will achieve the end?

4. Is the same good possible using other means? Is the bad means being used as a shortcut to a good end when other methods would do?

5. Is the good end clearly greater than any evil means used to attain it?

6. Will the means used to achieve the end withstand the test of publicity?

While application of this test might help the photographer make some decisions, the choices will always be tough. The line between newsworthiness and intrusiveness, between good pictures and bad taste, is often blurry. Donald Gormley, formerly the general manager of the *Spokane Spokesman-Review,* offers some insight into the difference between photos that are universally offensive and photos that are simply tough to view:

> Compassion is not the same as good taste. If a reader knows the person pictured in a very dramatic photograph, he may find it offensive. That's a sin against compassion. If he is offended whether he knows the person or not, the sin is probably one against good taste. (1984, 58)

STAGING PHOTOGRAPHS

Every photographer has had this feeling: you are about to capture that perfect moment on film, except _____. You can fill in the blank with any number of problems. For the photographer at a birthday party, the issue is inconsequential. You simply remove the offending child, relight the candles or arrange the scene and try again. To the photojournalist attempting to convey the truth of a story, however, the issue is much more complex: to tamper with the subject is to rearrange reality.

The issue is not a new one. As early as 1876, an enterprising photographer staged a picture of his own death allegedly to dodge his creditors (Lester 1992). More than a hundred years later, the ethics of the issue of staging remain unresolved, even in major news organizations.

For instance, during the 1992 November sweeps period, NBC's magazine show *Dateline* aired an 18-minute segment on a faulty design of General Motors pickup trucks that concluded with video of a truck exploding into flame immediately after a side-impact collision. More than 300 people had died in such collisions since GM had introduced the trucks. The story included gripping still photographs of charred bodies pulled from accident scenes, court documents from the many suits filed against GM over the truck's design and videotaped testimony from independent auto safety experts and a former GM engineer, all saying that the corporation had known about the design flaw yet had chosen to do nothing.

However, NBC did not inform viewers that, in order to ensure fire in the closing video, "sparking devices" had been mounted on the test cars by the independent testing agency the network had hired as part of its investigation. Even with the addition of the sparking devices, only one of two test vehicles had exploded on cue and the fire had gone out almost immediately.

About two months after the story aired, a jury returned a $105 million damage judgment against the automaker in a wrongful death suit that centered on the truck's design flaws. The NBC story had not been introduced in the court case. A week after the jury returned the verdict, General Motors filed a libel suit against the network, charging—among other things—that the network had staged the concluding video. In an unprecedented move, anchors Jane Pauley and Stone Phillips read a 3-minute retraction of the original *Dateline* story, admitting that the network had aired the concluding video even though it was staged. The NBC–General Motors confrontation proved to be the end for network news president Michael Gartner. He resigned less than a month later.

Calvin and Hobbes

by Bill Watterson

The NBC incident raises several questions. Is there a place for reenactment in the news? If so, when? How should such photos and video be labeled? The issues are not trivial, nor are they resolved. In a poll conducted by the National Press Photographers Association, the number-one ethical problem reported by photojournalists was setup shots.

"Your work sounds interesting." Francesca said. She felt a need to keep neutral conversation going.

"It is. I like it a lot. I like the road, and I like making pictures."

She noticed he'd said "making" pictures. "You make pictures, not take them?"

"Yes. At least that's how I think of it. That's the difference between Sunday snapshooters and someone who does it for a living. When I'm finished with that bridge we saw today, it won't look quite like you expect. I'll have made it into something of my own, by lens choice, or camera angle, or general composition or all of those.

"I don't just take things as given; I try to make them into something that reflects my personal consciousness, my spirit. I try to find the poetry in the image."

The Bridges of Madison County
Robert James Waller

The questions surrounding fakery and staging speak to the purpose of news photography. Two possible purposes exist: the "mirror" and the "window" photograph (Szarkowski 1978).

The mirror photograph attempts to subjectively re-create the world in whatever image suits the photographer. Anything can be manipulated: light, proportion, setting, even subject. On the other hand, window photographs should be as objective a picture of reality as the medium will allow, untouched by the bias of the lens or the photographer.

Each type of photography has a function. A large percentage of the government-commissioned Dust Bowl–era photographs that have seared our memories of the Depression would fit into the mirror category. Photographers searched for settings, posed people and shifted props to achieve the maximum effect.

On the other hand, the photos that show us the horrors of war and famine, and arouse public opinion, are windows, where the photographer captures the moment with no attempts to alter it. *The problem comes in the substitution of one for the other.* When a photograph mirrors a photographer's bias, yet is passed off as a window on reality, the viewer has been deceived.

ELECTRONIC MANIPULATION

Another major ethical issue in visual reporting is manipulation. Again, the history of photo manipulation is long. It has included such crude drawing-board techniques as cropping with scissors and paste, darkroom techniques such as "burning" and "dodging," and, more recently, airbrushing. Today, technology allows increasingly sophisticated changes to be made to an image after it has been captured. Any person familiar with PhotoShop or any of many other software packages is keenly aware of how photos can be manipulated.

Technology has, in fact, made the word "photography"—literally "light writing"—obsolete, as a lighted reality no longer must exist in order for a "photograph" to be created. Photos and video are now what Reaves (1987) calls a "controlled liquid," capable of being manipulated into a seamless, yet totally un-realistic image. What this technology will ultimately lead to, Reaves claims, is an epistemological shift away from photography as irrefutable evidence of a story to photography as changeable story illustration. Eventually, she argues, as the pub-lic realizes that photographs can be—and frequently are—electronically altered, photos could lose their "moral authority." Tomlinson (1987) adds that technology could render photos nonadmissible as legal evidence once they lose the assump-tion of validity.

With an overwhelming amount of technology available for enhancing pho-tos, editors must consider the ethical ramifications of their use. Once expensive technologies such as "morphing" one image into another, creating images di-rectly from pixels with no real image required or the digital insertion of existing images into new contexts are now common software applications on home com-puters. As a more sophisticated audience approaches the video or photography in the media, viewers will bring with them a skepticism not present in previous gen-erations of consumers.

Most editors and photographers agree that manipulation or staging of news photos is generally more culpable than manipulation or staging of feature pho-tos. During the 2003 war in Iraq, a photojournalist for the *Los Angeles Times* was fired for combining two similar photographs into one more aesthetically pleas-ing one (see case IX-C). While the resulting photo was so similar to the "real" ones that the difference escaped the eye of the photo editor, a line had been crossed, and the photographer was dismissed. The reasoning for this differing standard for news as opposed to feature photography or advertising photogra-phy is a presupposition that *while art may be manipulated, information may not* (Martin 1991). Such a flexible standard would be allowed under a categorical imperative as a permissible act, provided that:

- the photographer's intent is to merely make the photo more aesthetically pleasing and not to deceive; *and*
- the intended audience recognizes the difference; or
- the difference does not make audience members think or act in a manner in which they might not otherwise have thought or acted.

The problem for audiences is compounded by the fact that both advertising and entertainment and even non-news sections of the newspaper make frequent use of these techniques. Confusion over what is appropriate in one context and not another is bound to occur, but we suggest that the same issue of visual truth telling can and should be applied to advertising as well.

SELECTIVE EDITING

Another ethical question centers on the video editing process: whether editing itself renders a story untrue or unfair. While this complaint is not new to television, the charges leveled against video editing are more vociferous, since editing for time considerations is a much more noticeable constraint than editing for space. Scenes aired out of sequence, answers dubbed behind questions that were not originally asked, and a preponderance of one view dominating the final cut at the expense of another view are some of the most frequently cited instances of "selective editing."

Actually, the term "selective editing" is redundant. *All* editing is selective. The issue is who does the selecting, and what predispositions they bring to the process. Some observers have noted that a dual standard has emerged between words and photos. A strange ethical dichotomy has long existed in the business of creating and processing print news and the photos that accompany it. The writer is allowed to reorder facts and rearrange details into an inverted-pyramid story on the rationale that the reader wants the most important facts taken out of sequence, and even out of context, and placed first in the story for more efficient reading. The result is praised as good writing and is taught in every journalism program.

However, should a photographer attempt to do the same thing with a camera—rearrange reality to make a more interesting photo or videotape—the result is called "staged." Our unwillingness to allow visual journalists the same conventions as print journalists says something fundamental about the role of visuals in the news. Media tradition says that while the truth in a print story about an explosion can contain only the highlights, the truth of a photo about the same explosion should be kept in context.

Such an analogy to print is important. When a writer edits, it makes for a more readable story, and the act is applauded. When a photographer or video editor does the same thing, he or she is open to accusations of distortion. That is because we evaluate news photos according to print standards: linear and logical. Yet video and photographs are neither. They have a quality Marshall McLuhan called "allatonceness" that we are not quite comfortable with as a technology. Just what the photographer can do with the visual truth the camera uncovers is still a topic of debate.

Some photographers argue that to take away the possibilities that computer technology allows is to put them at a disadvantage in trying to tell a story visually. Should a photographer attempt to rearrange reality to make a more interesting photo or piece of film, the photograph is denigrated as "staged." And if a computer is used to correct focus or remove distractions, the photograph is derided as being "manipulated." In either case, the photographer could face sanctions.

However, as long as readers hold the view that "Seeing is believing," that view—whether based in reality or not—becomes a promise between the media and their audience that photographers and videographers should be hesitant to break. While many photojournalists argue that "Seeing is believing" should have never been a cultural truism (see Lester 1992), others argue that we must work within our readers' or viewers' predispositions about the truth of what they see. Steve Larson, (quoted in Reaves 1991, 181) director of photography for *U.S. News & World Report,* summarized this viewer-based rationale:

> The photo is a record of a moment in time. We're on shaky ground when we start changing that. We must maintain this pact. Catching a moment in time has history. When you look at a Matthew Brady photo there is that sense "this really happened." I believe strongly that's where photography draws its power.

EYEWASH

Another ethical issue in photojournalism is the controversial use of stock photos or file footage to illustrate news stories. Such "eyewash" is used regardless of the context of the original photograph and sometimes without the consent of the subject (Tomlinson 1987).

For instance, an article on compulsive gamblers might show a woman enjoying herself on a sunny afternoon at the races. While her action is taking place in public view, she might or might not be a victim of the syndrome addressed in the article, although the casual reader might infer that she is, indeed, a compulsive gambler. In this context, the photo is serving the purpose of eyewash, decoration for a story that bears no genuine relationship to it.

Eyewash has had a brief history in the courts. A Washington, D.C., television station used a tight shot on a pedestrian facing the camera, chosen at random, to illustrate the "twenty million Americans who have herpes." The court ruled that the combination of the film and the commentary was sufficient to support an inference that the plaintiff was a victim of herpes, which she contended was not true.

However, not all plaintiffs are successful. One young couple photographed in a public embrace in the Los Angeles Farmer's Market later saw their private moment published in *Harper's* illustrating an article entitled "Love Makes the World Go 'Round." The California Supreme Court noted that the couple had "waived their right of privacy" by their voluntary actions and said that publication of the photograph merely extended and increased the public who could view the plaintiffs in their romantic pose.

With the rulings of the courts ambiguous on the matter of eyewash, the media have created divergent policies to cover the issue. Some newspapers and television stations, for instance, will use no picture not directly related to the story. Others limit the use of file or stock footage to that which is clearly labeled. Others limit the shooting of eyewash only by insisting that it occur in public view.

The issue is exacerbated by the voracious appetite that both television and the print media have for visuals. Virtually all surveys have shown that the presence of a photo adds to the number of readers for a newspaper story, while television news consultants insist that viewers will watch "talking heads" for only a few seconds before diverting their attention elsewhere. The answer to the question "Have you got art?" often means the difference in running or killing a story. At other times, good visuals can get a story in the coveted first slot on the nightly news or the front page of the newspaper.

Given the importance of visuals to a story, it is not surprising that ethical lines blur. Coleman (1987) tells the story of his young son's falling off a horse and breaking his arm. A photographer friend took a picture of the boy "dirty, tear-stained, in great pain, slumped in a wheelchair with his arm in a makeshift sling" on his way to the operating room. About a year later, a textbook publisher ran across the photo and wanted it as an illustration for a book on child abuse. Coleman denied the request but added that the photo could have run with little or no repercussion if he had not been easily available for the publisher to ask. Had that happened, the public would have been deceived by a photograph of a boy who had been a victim of nothing more than a childhood accident.

CONCLUSION

Visual ethics is emotionally charged and constantly changing with new technology. *What this means is that the consumer of news photography is being presented with a product that is sometimes too raw to be palatable and sometimes too polished to be believable.*

The problem lies in the nature of the photojournalist's job. On a day-to-day basis, photography can be a mundane and poor-paying job. When an opportunity for a gripping photo does arise, like word that police are searching for a drowning victim, the desire to break out of the daily grind can lead to one of the two extremes stated above: a photo too raw or a photo too polished.

Photojournalists should operate under this version of Kant's categorical imperative: *Don't deceive an audience that expects your pictures to be an accurate representation of a particular quality of reality.* Fortunately, only a small percentage of photos offend, and only a small percentage of photos are staged or electronically manipulated. However, photographers are dealing with a trust that readers and viewers have placed in them. If that trust is betrayed, it will be slow to return.

Suggested Readings

BERGER, ARTHUR ASA. 1989. *Seeing is believing.* Mountain View, CA: Mayfield Publishing Co.
BERGER, JOHN. 1980. *About looking.* New York: Pantheon Books.
Journal of Mass Media Ethics. 1987, Spring–Summer. Special issue on photojournalism.
LESTER, PAUL. 1991. *Photojournalism: An ethical approach.* Hillsdale, NJ: Lawrence Erlbaum Associates.
———. 2003. *Images that injure.* 2nd edition. Westport, CT: Greenwoood Press.

Cases on the Web

"Film at 10: Handling graphic video in the news" by Sonya Forte Duhé
"Raid, reunion or neutral coverage? The Elian Gonzalez story" by Paul Lester and Deni Elliott
"Looking at race and sex: When do photographs go too far?" by Beverly Horvitt
"Faking Photos: Is it ever justified?" by James Van Meter

CHAPTER IX CASES

CASE IX-A
Daniel Pearl and the *Boston Phoenix:* Too Much of a Bad Thing?
TIMOTY RAGONES
University of Missouri

On January 23, 2002, *Wall Street Journal* reporter Daniel Pearl was on his way to interview an Islamic fundamentalist leader in Pakistan when he was abducted. A month later, on February 21, FBI officials received a video entitled "The Slaughter of the Spy Journalist, the Jew Daniel Pearl" confirming that Pearl's abductors had killed him. The 3-minute video included footage of Pearl confessing his Jewish roots and reading a statement denouncing U.S. foreign policy in the Middle East and Afghanistan. Pearl is then decapitated. Later, an unidentified man holds Pearl's head aloft. That image remained on screen as the National Movement for the Restoration of Pakistan Sovereignty listed demands, among them return of Pakistani prisoners to Pakistan, the delivery of U.S.-made F-16s that Pakistan paid for but which were never shipped, and an immediate end to U.S. presence in Pakistan.

U.S. news media had access to the video in the weeks after it surfaced. On Tuesday, May 14, an edited portion of the tape appeared on the *CBS Evening News.* The 4.5-minute story, which was about use of the Internet to spread propaganda, showed about 30 seconds of the Pearl tape, not including the decapitation. In prefacing the story, anchor Dan Rather said, "We're about to show you edited portions of it so that you can see and judge for yourself the kind of propaganda terrorists are using in their war against the United States." Executive producer Jim Murphy noted, "[Dan and I] very, very carefully crafted this story to report what people have to know. We used very little of the video at all."

The network aired the story despite fielding calls from Secretary of State Colin Powell's office, the Justice Department, *The Wall Street Journal* and several members of Pearl's family. After the broadcast, Pearl's family accused the network of playing into the hands of terrorists by airing material that was bound to become propaganda and that spread a message of hate. Barbara Comstock, Justice Department spokeswoman, said the network had opened the door for others to use even more graphic parts of the tape.

Her fears came true on May 31, when the *Boston Phoenix*, an alternative paper that had garnered a Pulitzer Prize for criticism in 1994, posted a link to the unedited tape on its Web site. The paper had a circulation of 118,000 in the Boston area. When the link appeared, traffic on the Web site jumped to 40,000 hits. In an online note below the link, *Phoenix* publisher Stephen Mindich wrote:

> This is the single most gruesome, horrible despicable and horrifying thing I've ever seen. If there is anything that should galvanize every non-Jew hater in the world— of whatever faith, or of no faith—against the perpetrators and supporters of those who committed this unspeakable murder, it should be viewing this video.

The *Phoenix* link connected to Prohosters.com, a Virginia-based Web-hosting company. Mindich said he decided to publish the link after learning that the FBI had pressured Prohosters to remove the video from one of its client sites. Prohosters said the FBI had threatened the client with legal action, and objected to the government pressure on First Amendment grounds.

The *Phoenix* took another step into the controversy one week later when it published still photographs of Pearl talking to the camera and Pearl's decapitated head in the hard copy version of the paper. Warnings about the nature of the photographs, which had been available on the Web, were not included in the newsprint paper. An editorial defending the decision to run the photos noted, "The silence on this issue—the U.S. government's attempt to censor politically sensitive, yet legal content from our leading pundits and opinion makers has been deafening." The editorial compared footage of Pearl's murder to widely disseminated images of the Nazi concentration camps, the 1986 *Challenger* space shuttle explosion, and the 9/11 World Trade Center footage.

"Beyond its repugnance, though, it has value in reminding us, as did the September 11 footage, what anti-American terrorists are capable of. It's hard to find language strong enough to decry the impulse to keep this information from the public."

Micro Issues

1. Should CBS have aired even a portion of the tape? Justify your answer.
2. What portion of the tape, if any, should the *Phoenix* have placed on its Web site? Justify your answer.
3. Is there a morally relevant distinction between the tape of Pearl and the 9/11 World Trade Center footage?
4. In considering all the stakeholders in the decision to print the photos, how can the *Phoenix* justify its decision to the wife of Daniel Pearl? Should she be considered in the equation when making the choice whether to run the photos, or does that send the process towards "quandary ethics?"

Midrange Issues

1. Was publication of the video and the stills necessary for the *Phoenix* to accomplish one of its stated goals: educating the American public about terrorism?
2. Is posting on the Web somehow ethically distinct from publication in a tangible newspaper?
3. Does the alternative press, papers like the *Phoenix* and New York's *Village Voice,* play a professionally distinctive role in the American media mix? Do they operate under any different ethical mandates than the mainstream press? Justify your answer.
4. In the 1980s, a Pennsylvania elected official, moments from surrendering to authorities to begin a prison sentence, called a news conference where he was expected to resign his post. Instead, he surprised everyone in the room when he pulled out a gun, put it in his mouth and pulled the trigger. Video and still images were available of the suicide, and some media outlets chose to run them. In what way, if any, does that suicide differ from the Pearl case?

Macro Issues

1. Could words have adequately described what happened to Daniel Pearl? What does your answer say about the role of images in your definition of truth? Of privacy?
2. Is it ever appropriate for the government to pressure news media not to publish? Under what circumstances?
3. What is the relationship between news and propaganda? Is it appropriate for journalists to be concerned about the use others will make of their stories, particularly when that story focuses on hate?
4. How is the government's attempt to censor the tape relevant in the decision to post the tape on the Web or publish the stills?

CASE IX-B
Problem Photos and Public Outcry
JON ROOSENRAAD
University of Florida

Campus police at the University of Florida were called on a Saturday to a dorm to investigate "a large amount of blood on the floor of a women's bathroom," according to police reports. They determined that the blood "appeared to have been from a pregnancy miscarriage" and began searching the dorm area. Some time later a police investigator searching through a trash dumpster behind the dorm found bloody towels, plastic gloves, and a large plastic bag containing more towels and the body of a 6- to 7-pound female infant.

Police discovered no pulse. Rigor mortis had set in. After removing the body from the bag, the police briefly placed the body on a towel on the ground next to the dumpster. The photographer for the student paper, the *Independent Florida Alligator,* arrived at this time and photographed the body and dumpster.

Later on Saturday, the 18-year-old mother was found in her dorm bed and taken to the university's hospital. The hospital exam revealed "placenta parts and the um-

Photo courtesy of the Independent Florida Alligator. *Used with permission.*

bilical cord in her" and she was released later in good health. A local obstetrician contacted about the case said that judging by the size of the infant, it was likely a miscarriage and not an abortion. The infant was determined to be about seven months developed.

The story began on the front page of the Monday issue, across the bottom of the page, under the headline "UF police investigate baby's death at dorm." It jumped inside to Page 3 and was accompanied by the photo.

It was a dramatic photo, contrasting two well-dressed detectives and one uniformed policeman with the naked body and contrasting the fragile human form with the harsh metal dumpster filled with pizza and liquor boxes. The photo was played 7 by 5 inches.

The story was well written and the photo dramatic but likely offensive to many—potentially so offensive that the newspaper's staff debated most of Sunday about how to use it. The editor decided to run it, but in an unusual move she wrote an editor's column explaining why that appeared on the opinion page of the same issue. It showed a scene one might visualize in a ghetto but not on a college campus. It showed that supposedly sexually educated and sophisticated college students still need help. The editor wrote:

> Even with these legitimate reasons we did not run the picture on the front page. This is partially in response to our concern that we do not appear to be exploiting this picture to attract readers. . . . We also examined the photographer's negatives to see if there were any less graphic prints. . . . Is the message perceived by the reader worth the shock he or she experiences? After pondering what we feel is a very profound photo, we decided there is. This was a desperate act in an area of society where it is not expected. The picture shows it.

The local daily covered the story Monday in a police brief. No photo ran.

It was determined that the body was from a miscarriage. The woman involved left school. The campus paper got several letters critiquing its coverage of the story. Many chose to criticize the editors for running the photo, while some praised the staff for pointing out the problem and for listing places on campus where sex and pregnancy counseling was available. Some letters did both.

An example of some of the outrage over the running of the photo by the *Alligator* came from a female student who called the coverage "the most unnecessary, tactless piece of journalism I've ever encountered." Another letter from a male student called the photo "in poor taste and extremely insensitive." The writer added, "There are times when good, sound judgment must override 'hot' copy."

Perhaps the most pointed comment came from a female writer who added 24 other names to her letter. The letter stated:

> The incident *could* have been used to remind people that they need to take responsibility for their own sexuality. The story *could* have been used as a painful reminder that there are many un-educated, naïve people out there who need help. But, unfortunately, the *Alligator* chose to sensationalize the story with a picture, completely nullifying any lesson whatsoever that might have been learned.

Micro Issues

1. Should the photographer have taken the picture? Justify your answer.
2. Is this a legitimate story, and if so, does it belong on Page 1?
3. If this was the only photo available, did the paper then have to run it?
4. Various letters to the editor called the photo "unnecessary," "tactless," and "insensitive." What would you say to those charges if you were on the staff?

Midrange Issues

1. Does running the photo inside lessen any criticism of poor taste? Did its placement mitigate any ethical criticism?
2. If the staff was so unsure, was the editor correct in writing a same-day rationale for its publication?
3. Critique the reasoning stated by the editor in running the photo. What moral philosophy, if any, would lead one to agree with the action?

Macro Issues

1. Should a paper play a story and photo like this to crusade about a problem?
2. Is the perceived social value of such a picture worth more than the shock and criticism?
3. Was the writer correct in her assessment that the shock of the photo negated any good that might have been done by the story?
4. Should a campus newspaper have a different standard—of taste, play, news value—than a "regular" daily?

CASE IX-C
Manipulating Photos: Is It Ever Justified?
LEE WILKINS
University of Missouri

Authors Note: *By the decision of the* Los Angeles Times, *the photos in question in this case are not available. However, various Web sites have covered this controversy and some include the photos.*

The visual images of the 2003 war in Iraq were extraordinarily controversial. Photo editors, particularly at large media outlets, had to make decisions about hundreds of photographs every day. Sunday, March 30, was no exception. That night, *Los Angeles Times* director of photography Colin Crawford had edited about 500 photos of the war when he saw a picture from staff photographer Brian Walski. The photo depicts a group of Iraqi citizens sitting on the ground as an American soldier, armed with a rifle, stands in the foreground.

The *Times* ran the photo on Page 1, and so did sister publications the *Hartford Courant* and the *Chicago Tribune.* Thom McGuire, the *Courant's* assistant managing editor of photography and graphics, said, "It was a great image."

But a *Courant* employee, who was looking through the images for a friend, thought he noticed a problem—what appeared to be a duplication of the Iraqi citizens in the background of the picture. He brought the problem to the attention of a copyeditor, who alerted McGuire. "After about a 600 percent magnification in Photoshop, I called Colin to ask for an investigation," McGuire said.

In Los Angeles, Crawford was disbelieving. He thought the apparent duplication of the background crowd was probably due to some sort of technical, satellite-related glitch. "He sent us 13 very good images Sunday," Crawford recalled. "We had to get information and give him the benefit of the doubt."

As it turned out, Walski had used his computer to combine elements of two photographs, taken moments apart, in order to improve the composition. Once that admission was made, Crawford fired him. All the publications that ran the composite photo ran corrections.

In his apology, Walski told other *Times* employees, "I deeply regret that I have tarnished the reputation of the *Los Angeles Times,* a newspaper with the highest standards of journalism . . . and especially the very talented and extremely dedicated photographers and picture editors and friends. . . . I have always maintained the highest ethical standards through my career and cannot truly explain my complete breakdown in judgment at this time."

Another *Times* staff photographer, Don Barletti, told the Poynter Institute's online discussion group that he recalled seeing Walski after he returned. Walski told him, "Now no one will touch me. I went from the front line of the greatest newspaper in the world, and now I have nothing. No cameras, no car, nothing."

Barletti also said he understood how the alteration might have happened. Walski had been in the desert for days under harsh conditions with little sleep and food and under enormous pressure.

"He got into a zone," Barletti said. "He was on a head roll, making fantastic images, and it got out of hand. He told me that he did not plan to send the image and was just messing around. He sent it anyway . . . didn't know what he was doing, but he did it. With all that he was facing, how did he have the presence of mind? It just got out of hand."

When asked about the issue, *New York Times* photographer Vincent LaForet agreed that the breach was serious. "There is not ever a good time for such manipulation, but this is the worst time. What really differentiates us from other photographers and media is our credibility. We have a history of getting it right, accurately. . . . Our credibility is all that we have."

Micro Issues

1. How should the newspapers that ran the original photo have corrected the error?
2. Should Walski have been fired? Why?
3. Many journalists who examined the photo did not notice the problem until it was pointed out to them. Is the minor nature of the alteration relevant in the ethical discussion? Why or why not?

Midrange Issues

1. Suzanne Lainson, also commenting on the issue on the Poynter Web site, said, "Why is the culture of the photojournalist supposed to be different than that for the print, audio, or video editor . . . rather than condone editing photos, perhaps we should not condone editing print, audio and video data." Evaluate this comment.
2. What should be the role of editors—in an ethical sense—in the newsroom?
3. Should employees blow the whistle on colleagues when they think there has been an ethical breach? If not, why not? If so, how should they do it?
4. How does the electronic manipulation of the persons in the background differ from the photographer simply asking the people to move to a certain location before the photo is taken? Are they equally culpable from an ethical sense?

Macro Issues

1. "People do not expect 'truth' or 'reality' from their media—today's media audience is much more aware of the doctored nature of everything they read, see and hear than we like to think. I'm sure this *LA Times* story did not come as a surprise to most people," wrote Mark Deuze. Analyze this statement. How might media organizations assure viewers and readers of the veracity of the information they publish?
2. Eric Meyer, who commented about the issue on the Poynter Web site said, "A photo is like a direct quote. You chose what to quote or what to photograph. But, when you run a direct quote or a photograph, you don't alter it to 'make it better.'" Evaluate this statement.

CASE IX-D
"Above the Fold": Balancing Newsworthy Photos with Community Standards
JIM GODBOLD, MANAGING EDITOR
JANELLE HARTMAN, REPORTER
Eugene Register-Guard, *Eugene, Oregon*

Author's Note: *On November 10, 1993, a nightmare unfolded in Springfield, Oregon, a quiet town adjoining the university community of Eugene, as Alan McGuire held his 2-year-old daughter, Shelby, hostage in their house. By the end of the standoff both were dead and the media had captured some horrific photos.*

Seven children had died as a result of child abuse in Lane County, Oregon, in the 20 months prior to that day and the media had just witnessed the eighth. Jim Godbold was the assistant managing editor of the Eugene Register-Guard *at the time. The remarks below are from an interview with him months after the event.*

Godbold: The call came over the police scanner shortly after noon. We responded to a hostage situation, a man holding someone at knife point in a Springfield neighborhood. We knew it was probably 20 minutes from the *Register-Guard* in the best of possible circumstances so we really scrambled. Photographer Andy Nelson and police reporter Janelle Hartman went as fast as they could to the area.

We got there when the police were trying to set up a perimeter to get people away from the area. It was real pandemonium right when Andy arrived. The situation didn't unfold for more than a few minutes before there was a burst of flame inside the house that caught the attention of the police officers, and they immediately made the decision that they were going to have to go inside.

A group of officers ran at the door, and then all of a sudden Alan McGuire, the man who was in the house, came hurtling through the front window on fire. I am not even sure if police officers knew how many people were in the house at the time. His wife had escaped from the home. She had been held at knifepoint and bound, and she had somehow gotten out and she let police know that their two-year-old daughter, Shelby McGuire, was in the house.

Shelby was a hostage and being held at knifepoint. Police saw her and tried to set up a telephone line so they could negotiate with McGuire, but the events unfolded rapidly, and after Alan McGuire jumped through the front window police broke down the door. Two officers hauled McGuire's flaming body to the ground and tried to douse the flames with a garden hose. Inside the house one of the officers saw Shelby McGuire sitting upright on the couch. She had a plastic grocery produce bag over her head, and it apparently had been duct-taped in some fashion, maybe around the neck.

They immediately tore the bag away. A detective picked Shelby up and sprinted out of the house with her. It was at that moment that Andy Nelson snapped his picture of one of the officers with Shelby's body in his arms, running out, two other officers standing on the side of the doorstep, another officer with a hose near Alan McGuire, and Alan lying on the ground. The flame's now out, but the charred and still smoking body was present in the viewfinder as Andy snapped the picture.

At that moment the officer with Shelby McGuire, the 2-year-old, began mouth-to-mouth resuscitation on the front lawn. Andy subsequently took a photograph of

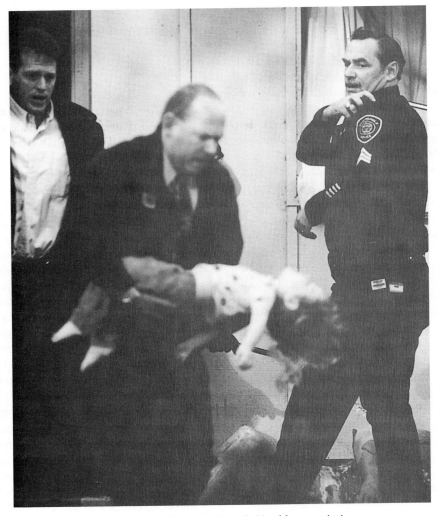

Photo courtesy of the Eugene Register-Guard. *Used by permission.*

that. Then they rushed both Alan and Shelby McGuire to the hospital. We did not know Shelby's condition. The police didn't respond about whether she was able to be resuscitated.

We have a standing policy at the newspaper that as a general rule we don't run photographs of dead bodies of children. That immediately triggered the kind of re-view that we would go through to determine where this particular incident was go-ing to stand up on our policy, whether or not anyone was going to argue for publication or against publication.

We began to talk about the policy and the potential community reaction that we might face. The discussion was pretty brief. The photo was so compelling and the situation that it sprang from so horrifying that we began looking at the photograph and saying,

"Well, I don't know, but, look at what the photo has captured."

"People are going to be upset."

"This is potentially a photograph of a dead 2-year-old child."

"Look at the concern and the expression on the police officers' faces. This is an example of what they deal with day in and day out. They are up against this kind of domestic violence hostage situation and people don't realize that."

So, the debate was intense, and yet pretty short. We prepared a selection of pictures, and we brought those to the then-managing editor Patrick Yak and made the case that this is going to be a tough photograph for us to run. This is going to be one that we are going to have to be prepared to defend. But we believe it's that kind of exception to the rule that we look for.

The public response to the publication of the Shelby McGuire photograph was unprecedented in my 22 years in journalism and unprecedented at this newspaper. I have not come across a case, having been shown a number of them subsequently, that is of the magnitude per capita of reader response to a single photographic image. We received on the order of 450 telephone calls that began the moment people got the newspaper, which started at 6:00 A.M. First they came into our circulation department. The circulation department switchboard became overloaded and gave them the main newsroom switchboard, which didn't open until 7:30. At 7:30 when they threw the switch, all 20 of our incoming phone lines lit up, and the calls began to roll over into a holding pattern that had never been utilized by our switchboard before.

I was called at home by Al Gimmell, the corporate controller, who said, "We are inundated with telephone calls. We need some help." So I immediately came in to try to handle telephone calls and I tried to find the time in between phone calls to call other editors in but the calls were coming so rapidly that every time I hung up it rang again. When I picked up my voice mail messages, I had 31 unanswered messages, and that was probably 7:45 in the morning.

The range of responses weren't monolithic, except in their anger. But the anger came from different places. For some people the anger came from a belief that we had simply stooped to a tremendously sensational graphic crime picture

Photo courtesy of the Eugene Register-Guard. *Used by permission.*

trying to sell newspapers. For others the anger came from the terrible sense of violation that the surviving mother and brother of Shelby McGuire would have to wake up to the morning after their ordeal and see this on the front page of the hometown newspaper.

Another component argued that this was wholly inappropriate for the kind of newspaper the *Register-Guard* has been and continues to be. That 5-year-olds and 6-year-olds were sharing the newspaper at the breakfast table and parents were finding themselves in a position of having to explain this horrifying incident and having the question "How is the little girl?" asked again. And there was also a range of response from people who were themselves victims of domestic violence or spouses of victims or had family members who were involved in it. For them it was a combination of anger and pain.

I spoke with literally dozens of people through tears. It was an emotional response that was overwhelming and people were extremely upset by the picture. Most asked the question "Why? I need to understand why the newspaper published this picture."

We were really, I think, at a loss initially to respond to that question. I think a lot of that had to do with being in a very real sense out of touch with a substantial number of readers. The kind of reaction that we had was not anticipated by anyone in the news department.

If we were presented with a similar situation and a similar photograph today, we would absolutely not do it the way that we did it in the Shelby McGuire case. Thousands of our readers have defined for us a boundary in this community and for this newspaper that I don't think until we began to see it materialize we had any sense of exactly where it was.

Micro Issues

1. Look at the photos that accompany this text. The photo of the officer carrying out Shelby McGuire ran in full color above the fold, two-thirds of the page wide and 6 inches tall. Does a photo of that size oversensationalize the story?

2. The photo of Sergeant Swenson's attempts to resuscitate Shelby ran below the fold in a small two-column photo. Why do you think the decision was made to run this photo smaller and lower?

Midrange Issues

1. Does the fact that Shelby died influence your decision on whether to run the photos? If so, in what way?

2. Does the fact that at least one television station and the local Springfield newspaper were there with photographers influence your decision to run the photos? If so, in what way?

3. Does the fact that seven other children had died in Lane County in less than 2 years affect your decision to run the photos? If so, in what way?

4. The biweekly *Springfield News* chose to run a front-page photo of Alan McGuire falling out of the front window of his home, his badly burned flesh still in flames. However, they covered the front page with a wrapper that read "Caution to Readers" and explained the content of the stories and photos underneath the wrapper. Critique that approach to handling the story.

5. A local television station showed a few seconds of the scene described above after warning viewers of the violent nature of the video that followed. The station got fewer than 20 complaints. How do you explain the vast difference in the reaction to the broadcast and print photos?

Macro Issues

1. What are the privacy rights of:
   a. Shelby McGuire?
   b. Shelby McGuire's mother and 4-year-old brother?
   c. Sergeant Swenson?
2. Critique the argument that these photos should be shown because they illustrate the type of tragedy that law enforcement officers are often called upon to handle.
3. Critique the argument that these photos should be shown because they illustrate the horror of domestic violence.
4. Critique the statement that "If we were presented with a similar situation and a similar photograph today, we would absolutely not do it the way that we did it in the Shelby McGuire case." In your opinion is that based on sensitivity to reader concern or caving in to reader pressure?

CASE IX-E
Horror in Soweto
SUE O'BRIEN, FORMER EDITORIAL PAGE EDITOR
The Denver Post

On September 15, 1990, freelance photographer Gregory Marinovich documented the killing, by a mob of African National Congress supporters, of a man they believed to be a Zulu spy.

Marinovich and Associated Press reporter Tom Cohen spotted the man being led from a Soweto, South Africa, train-station platform by a group armed with machetes and crude spears. Marinovich and Cohen continued to witness and report as the man was stoned, bludgeoned, stabbed, doused with gasoline, and set afire.

It was one of 800 deaths in two months of factional fighting among blacks as rival organizations vied for influence in the declining days of apartheid.

The graphic photos stirred intense debate among editors. In one, the victim, conscious but stoic, lies on his back as a grinning attacker poises to plunge a knife into his forehead. In the final photo of the series, the victim crouches, engulfed in fire.

As the series was transmitted, several member editors called up to question what the photographer was doing at the scene—could he in any way have stopped the attack? In response, an advisory went out on the photo wire, saying Marinovich had

AP/WIDE WORLD PHOTOS. Used with permission.

tried to intervene and then, when told to stop taking pictures, had told mob leaders he would stop shooting only when they "stopped hurting that man."

Decisions on what to do with the photos varied across the country, according to a survey. If any pattern emerged, it was that newspapers in competitive markets such as Denver, Minneapolis–St. Paul and New York were more likely to go with the harsh graphics.

The burning photo was the most widely used, the stabbing the least. Several editors said they specifically rejected the stabbing as too extreme. "It showed violence and animalistic hatred," said Roman Lyskowski, graphics editor for the *Miami Herald.* Another editor, who agreed that the stabbing was much more disturbing than the burning, said he recalled immolation pictures from the Vietnam era. "That's not as unusual an image as that knife sticking right out of the skull."

When the Soweto series cleared at the *Miami Herald,* the burning photo was sent to Executive Editor Janet Chusmir's home for her approval. At her direction, the immolation picture ran on the front page, but below the fold and in black and white. The detail revealed in color reproduction, Chusmir and her editors agreed, was too graphic.

At the *Los Angeles Times* and *Dallas Morning News,* however, the burning photo ran above the front-page fold—and in color.

The *St. Paul Pioneer Press* chose the stabbing for front-page color. "I look at the moment that the photo freezes on film," said News Editor Joe Sevick. "Rarely do you see a photo where a knife is about to go into somebody." The photo ran in color on the *Pioneer Press* front page, accompanied by the story Cohen had written on the attack and a longer story on the South African government's attempt, announced that day, to crack down on black-on-black violence.

In Denver, at the *Rocky Mountain News,* Managing Editor Mike Madigan wanted to run a comprehensive package on the Soweto story. The tabloid's only open page was deep in the paper, but a Page 3 box referred readers to the story with a warning the photos were "horrific and disturbing." Inside, stories on the attack and government crackdown and an editor's note on Marinovich's intervention accompanied three photos: the victim being led away from the train station, the stabbing, and the burning.

Most papers that ran the more challenging photos involved top management in the decision. Frequently, top editors were contacted by telephone, or came in from home, to give the photos a final go-ahead.

In most newsrooms, the burning or stabbing photos made it to the news desk for approval or rejection. But there, they sometimes were killed abruptly. "The editors at that point said no," one picture editor reported. "They would not take the heat."

Several editors deferred to the so-called breakfast test. "The question is 'Which of those photos would help tell the story without ruining everyone's breakfast?' " asked Rod Deckert, managing editor of the *Albuquerque Journal.* One editor said his paper is especially likely to de-emphasize disturbing material in the Sunday paper, which children often read with their parents.

But many editors who rejected the more brutal pictures said the "breakfast test" is irrelevant. "If you're putting out a paper in New York and don't have something that's going to cause some discomfort over breakfast, then you're probably not putting out the full paper you should," said Jeff Jarvis, Sunday editor at the *New York Daily News.* "I don't think the breakfast test works for the nineties."

AP/WIDE WORLD PHOTOS. Used with permission.

Others cited distance tests. Some newspapers, in deference to victims' families, are less likely to use death photos from within their own circulation areas. Another editor, however, said his paper is *less* likely to run violent photos unless they are local and have a "more immediate impact on our readership."

Newspapers also differed widely on how they packaged the Soweto story. Some accompanied a photo series with the Cohen and crackdown stories, and a note on Marinovich's intervention. Some ran a single photo, often the burning, with only a cutline and a brief reference to the train-station incident in the "crackdown" story. Two respected big-city dailies, which omitted any reference to the Soweto attack in their accompanying stories, ran cursory cutlines such as "Violence continues: A boy runs away as an ANC supporter clubs a Zulu foe who was beaten, stabbed and set ablaze."

Although 41 papers used at least one of the Marinovich photos, only four—the *Charlotte Observer, Akron Beacon-Journal, Rocky Mountain News* (Denver) and *USA Today*—told the story of Marinovich's attempt to halt the attack.

Among collateral considerations at many news desks was the coverage of South African troubles that had gone before. At least one editor said the Soweto photos, which followed several other beating and killing photographs from South Africa that had been used earlier in the week, were "just too, too much."

With only three exceptions, editors said race did not figure in their considerations. One white editor said the fact that both attackers and victim were black deprived the series of clarity: "You don't have a sense of one side against another. You don't have a sense of right or wrong." Two editors who identified themselves as African-American, however, argued for aggressive use of the photos. Both work in communities with significant black populations. "I think black readers should be more informed about this," one said. "Across the board, black Americans don't realize what's going on with the black-on-black violence."

Front-page placement and the use of color frequently triggered reader objections, but the adequacy of cutline information and accompanying copy also appear significant. The *Albany Times Union* was flooded by phone protests and subscription cancellations. Two other papers perceiving significant reader unrest—the *Dallas Morning News* and *Los Angeles Times*—ran the burning photo in color on their front pages. But each of the three papers also ran the front-page photos with only cutline accompaniment, referring readers inside to the stories that placed the images in context.

In retrospect, *Rocky Mountain News'* Madigan said he was very pleased with the final Soweto package and readers' reaction to it.

> It wasn't so much the idea that, "Yeah, we ran these really horrific pictures and, boy, it knocked people's socks off." I don't think that was the point. I think it was more the way we handled it. Just one word or the other can make a terrific difference in whether the public starts screaming "sensationalize, sensationalize," or takes it as a thoughtful, important piece of work, which is what we were after.

Micro Issues

1. In all but the most important stories, would you support a ban on dead-body photos in your newspaper or newscast?
2. Some editors believe it is their ethical duty to avoid violating readers' sense of taste or compassion. Others argue that it is their duty to force society to face unpleasant truths, even if it means risking reader anger and rejection. Whose side would you support?
3. Many readers suspect that sensational photos are chosen to sell newspapers, or capture rating points, by appealing to morbid tastes. Do you believe they're right?

Midrange Issues

1. Editors sometimes justify running graphic photos by saying they can provide a "warning bell," alerting people to preventable dangers in society. What values might the Soweto photographs offer readers?
2. Is the desire to avoid offending readers an ethical consideration or a marketing consideration?
3. Is it appropriate to base editorial decisions on what readers are likely to be doing at home: to edit newspapers differently, for instance, if they are likely to be read at the breakfast table, or present newscasts differently if they are to air during the dinner hour rather than later in the evening?
4. As an editor, would you be more likely to run a photograph of someone being murdered if the event happened in your own community, or if it happened thousands of miles away and none of your readers would be likely to know the victim or his family?
5. Do you see any distinction in:
   a. whether a violent photo is run in color or black and white; or
   b. whether it is run on the front page or on an inside page?

Macro Issues

1. Is aesthetic, dramatic or photographic value ever reason enough to run a picture, regardless of how intrusive it may be or how it may violate readers' sensitivities?
2. Is it your responsibility as an editor to find out if a photographer could have saved a life by intervening in a situation rather than taking pictures of it? Is that information you need to share with your readers?
3. Is it your responsibility as an editor to find out if the presence of the camera at the scene in any way helped incite or distort an event? Is that information you need to share with your readers?
4. When dramatic photographs are printed, how important is it for readers or viewers to be told all the background of the story or situation?

X

Ethics in Cyberspace: New Questions and New Roles

By the end of this chapter, you should be able to:

- spot "old" ethical issues in their Internet incarnations.
- understand the role of copyright law in ethical decision making about Internet content.
- develop professional strategies for using the Internet as a reporting tool.
- delineate important policy issues the Internet raises for journalists.

Academic philosophers sometimes debate whether any really new ethical issues emerge over time, or whether old issues merely resurface. Students of applied ethics (and by reading this book you are one) have a tentative answer to that question. The core ethical issue may remain the same, but its real-world manifestation, and the morally relevant facts, often call for original thinking.

In no field of media ethics is this truer than when thinking, talking and working with the Internet. The technology itself has transformed the culture of the developed world so dramatically that ethical issues that might have bothered only a very few editors or advertising copywriters in previous generations now wind up on everyone's desktop workstation.

COOKIES . . . AND THE RIGHT TO READ UNMOLESTED

Take cookies, that electronic "marker" particular Web sites attach to your computer when you access them. Those advertising on the Web want to know who is looking at their site and whether they will purchase the advertised product. In rough parallel, cookies might be thought of as a sophisticated version of eye tracking—a research technique used by marketers literally to trace how the human eye moves across the page. The results of eye-tracking studies, for example, have taught us that the upper righthand corner of the newspaper page is where the human eye most often focuses and that a single dominant picture can encourage the eye to move around the page in the way the designer intended. Advertisers also use eye-tracking research to determine what part of a particular design catches and holds consumer attention. Media researchers have used eye tracking for decades, and no one has claimed that it presented an ethical problem. Cookies, the electronic equivalent, should be treated the same way, right?

Not exactly.

Because the cookie is a marker that's attached to your computer hard drive (and in the earliest days of "cookies" you did not know when you had received one), it's capable of providing its originator with a great deal of information about you. What kind of computer do you own? What sorts of Web sites do you visit? For how long? What do you purchase? Did you use a credit card? The cookie gives marketers this kind of information without asking your permission and sometimes, for the Web neophyte, without your knowledge.

In short, a cookie on your computer hard drive can mean that you lose control of a great deal of information about you. Furthermore, the marketers can use the information they gain about you to find better, more effective, ways to sell you things. Law enforcement, or even the spouse you are divorcing, can subpoena such information. Marketers can, and do, sell the same information to other marketers. And, the United States, unlike the European Union, does not make such action illegal.

If phrases in the preceding paragraph sound familiar, they should. Recall that part of the definition of privacy (see Chapter VI) is the ability to control information about you and how that information is interpreted and used. What seemed like a great idea to marketers—to track consumer Web use through the novel approach of a cookie—raises important privacy questions. Those questions seem more urgent because of the nature and amount of information one can collect and connect by accessing the multiple consumer databases of which we are all a part. The privacy issue raised by cookies, in fact, is so significant that some suggest consumers should have a legal right to access the World Wide Web without fear of their every movement being tracked, analyzed and potentially resold. You have the right to read anonymously (Cohen 2000); information about you is your private property. Your computer constitutes your private space in much the same way your home does. Those who enter your home must do so, except in very rare circumstances, only with your permission.

It is our contention that the Internet, using cookies as a good example, doesn't raise unique ethical questions so much as it asks us to rethink our standard answers to similar questions. The impact of speed—and the trade-off between speed and accuracy in what used to be referred to as the drive for the "scoop"—is another question that the Internet has brought to the foreground. And, because the Internet is a system, it also asks us to broadly consider the systemwide implications of ethically informed choices. Speed, accuracy and privacy are not new ethical issues to journalism and mass communication; the Internet simply asks that we examine them in light of new facts, some of which may be morally relevant.

OWNERSHIP OF INFORMATION: LEGAL HINTS BUT NOT HELP

In October 1995, the *New York Times* found itself under siege from a distinguished group of authors, all of whom contributed occasionally to the paper. More than 300 writers and scholars—among them Norman Mailer, Alice Walker, Garry Trudeau, Kurt Vonnegut, Barbara Raskin, Roger Rosenblatt, Ben Bagdikian and Carolyn Bird—signed a petition protesting the *Times'* newly implemented policy requiring writers to surrender syndication, electronic and other secondary rights to their work after articles were published in hard copy in the *Times*.

In an internal memorandum, the *Times* had announced it would require its free-lancers to sign "work-made-for-hire" contracts. It read: "The position on this is un-ambiguous: if someone does not sign an agreement, he or she will no longer be published in the newspaper." The writers responded that the memorandum was a historic break with publishing tradition where freelancers had been allowed to re-tain copyright to their own work.

What was really at issue, of course, was money. The freelancers wanted to be paid for the original publication of their efforts and for all subsequent publication of their work—regardless of medium. The *Times,* which was struggling to develop an Internet presence and to make money from that effort, was attempting to cut both costs and subsequent legal problems by demanding copyright ownership of its or-ganizational contribution to the Information Superhighway. Since the *Times,* like all other news organizations, had been unable to turn the Internet into a profit center, it sought to reduce some expenses by curtailing its payments to freelancers. The writ-ers, in turn, wanted the Internet to be governed by the same professional norms that had governed the print media—in other words, the writer retains the copyright and each user must pay for the privilege of reproduction.

Ultimately the protest turned into legal action—and the courts ruled in favor of the writers. But, the suit itself still raised a fundamental issue: in an Internet world, who owns—and who can profit from—a work product, be it words, a design, a pho-tograph, a melody or a film.

While the recording industry, and to a lesser extent other media outlets, regard piracy as theft, consumers and some journalists are not so sure. United States copy-right law, as it has evolved over the past 200 years, can be boiled down to two suc-cinct concepts. The first is that the courts have repeatedly ruled "You can't copyright an idea." As Justice Louis Brandeis observed in *International News Service v. As-sociated Press,* "The general rule of law is that the noblest of human productions—knowledge, truths ascertained, conceptions and ideas—become voluntary communication to others, free as the air to common use."

What can be copyrighted, however, is the particular execution of an idea. Mozart could not copyright the order of the keys on the harpsichord, but he could copyright the particular order of notes played on that instrument—the execution of an idea—in *The Magic Flute.*

The second basic concept of copyright law is that an idea that is sufficiently novel and concrete enough does warrant protection. This "novel and concrete" ap-proach to ideas is rooted in the 17- and 18-century notion that ideas are like private property and, like private property, are worthy of protection. An entire line of cases involving television and radio formats has developed essentially through regarding particular formats and plot lines as concrete expressions of ideas that can be copyrighted. One legal scholar has noted that the essential feature of this branch of copyright law is "the right to determine what shall be done with an idea."

The courts currently protect ideas that are bound through contracts—what is called "expressed contract theory." This means that copyright is related not so much to ownership as to sales. In fact, some scholars assert that copyright doesn't protect ownership so much as it protects the right to copy (Halbert 1999). A contract may be expressed through money changing hands or a promise to disclose the idea to a third party (for instance, a publisher's promise to publish a novel). Even if an idea is obtained fraudulently, the courts have been willing to protect its originator. The courts also protect ideas under what is called "implied contracts." A freelancer submitting an article to a magazine in the hopes that it will be published is functioning under an implied contract that the publisher will consider the article but not steal it.

Finally, the courts have developed a doctrine designed to impede unjust enrichment. Under this view, ideas should be protected because, failing to do so would allow one person or organization to enrich themselves while failing to compensate the original developer of the idea. For instance, in 1990 humorist Art Buchwald was awarded $900,000 when the courts found that his idea for the movie *Coming to America* had been developed into a successful film without any compensation to him.

However, Internet-based technologies have allowed those who create information to bypass industry delivery systems and deliver their products directly to the consumer (Halbert 1999). Popular author Stephen King in 1999 bypassed his own publisher and agreed to market a new novel on the Web, providing those who accessed the book chapters would directly pay King $1 for every chapter they downloaded. King curtailed his experiment after about 6 months, but not before he had sent a message to the publishing world that the Internet—at least for popular and well-known artists—could replace some of the marketing support the publishing industry normally provides. King's book, however, remains incomplete.

THE LAW LAGS BEHIND

Legal theories and case rulings have not kept pace with the technology. The courts would normally consider a photograph a concrete expression of an idea. But what happens when the photograph has been cut into pixels, the individual pixels' colors changed, the shape of the pixels reorganized—say, from a camel to an elephant—and then the resulting image, which now looks a great deal like an elephant and lacks a negative to indicate that it was once a camel, is downloaded onto a Web site that belongs to your news organization? Is linking to another site some form of copyright infringement? Is it like using "freelance" work in a publication? Could links constitute unjust enrichment? Or are they more like the harpsichord keys—a good idea that cannot be copyrighted although it can be used in many different ways?

Is the execution of the idea that the photograph represents the property of the photographer who shot the original image, the property of the multimedia author

Copyright © Ed Stein. Reprinted with permission of Rocky Mountain News.

who took the photograph of the camel and changed it to an elephant, or the property of the news organization that ultimately distributed it in the form of electrons on a Web site? How about the designer or the content creator of the page you are linking to? Is there an express or implied contract in any of these actions? Does the creator of the elephant image owe royalties or acknowledgement to the creator of the camel? Adding to the complexity is another question: Do these issues persist after death? For example, who gets paid for, and who holds the copyright to, an image of television star Lucille Ball who, years after her death, is electronically reproduced and inserted into a 1996 television ad for Service Merchandise? Furthermore, what if the creator of the ad could prove that the image of Ms. Ball was created out of a group of uncopyrighted pixels? Who then would own the Ball image? On such complex issues, the courts have been silent.

Right now, it is unclear how the use and development of the Internet will influence these trends. Common ownership muddies the professional waters even further. Thinking about copyright has always included an element of "this came first," but that issue was defined in terms of weeks or years rather than nanoseconds.

Historically, when one medium—for example, radio—has surpassed another—say, newspapers—in an important dimension such as timeliness, both mediums have evolved to take advantage of their unique strengths. Thus, as broadcasting developed, that medium tended to emphasize immediacy while print emphasized depth. With the emergence of broadcasting as a dominant medium, journalists began to rethink the ethics of "the scoop" and to insist that accurate news reporting was more important in both a professional and ethical sense than mere speed. This same debate—the balance between accuracy and speed—is now taking place among news organizations with a substantial Internet presence.

This Internet-focused debate has also added renewed energy to questions regarding corrections of inaccurate, but speedy, reports. Corrections of news stories, in either the traditional print or broadcast media, have some permanence. On the Internet, it is possible to simply blow away the page—or even the site—that contains an error, leaving no permanent record of either the mistake or attempts to rectify it. But with so many pages out there, and so many links, errors may persist in ways that were unimaginable 20 years ago. Journalists working in many venues, as well as media ethicists, have long agreed that errors merit permanent correction. Should the same professional standard be applied to Internet coverage? If it should, how then might it be achieved so that readers who access the page months, or even years, later know that an error was made and have access to the correct information?

The ability to digitize information also challenges our intuitive assumptions about a variety of things—everything from the "reality" that a picture represents to the external symbol systems that words and images together create. Digitization enables media designers to confound the external referent as never before. Students at the turn of the century will recognize that John Wayne's image has been digitized and electronically inserted into a Coors ad. But students in 2050 may not recognize the original John Wayne, may not know that he was a film star and may not be aware that he has been dead for decades. They will have "lost" the external referent to the image. One consequence of that loss is that the Coors commercial may not be as meaningful, or seem as clever. There are more sinister possibilities, such as the twisting and destruction of meaning that Orwell raised in *1984.*

In addition to what may be copyrighted, the Internet emphasizes questions of when. We now work in a 24-hour news cycle. Stories must be updated almost constantly. The 1990s phrase "All news all the time" has been narrowed in focus to "All terrorism all the time," "All stock market all the time," or "All presidential scandal all the time" by cable and the Internet. Many professionals insist that the 24-hour news cycle has resulted in the trivialization of news and a sensationalistic approach to news. Rumor can pass for information on the Web, further confounding traditional efforts at fact checking and decreasing the time for thoughtful decision making.

Some have suggested that the Web can make news journalists lazy; finding information on the Web in many news organizations has nudged out interviewing as the primary method of information collection. This means journalists have to learn to discriminate between "quality" Web sites and those that, while creative, do not adhere to the facts. The ethical issue—a professional drive for accuracy and, when possible, truth—remains the same. But the Internet requires that journalists not only be able to discern when a source is "lying" (what some professionals refer to as the "sniff" test) but also need to recognize when a Web site is inaccurate, perhaps deliberately so.

Ethical thinking combined with sound professional practice can provide some paths out of this virtual swamp. The first, and probably the most basic, maxim arises from the habits of sound professional performance. Cite the source of your information—or your electronic bytes. After all, journalists are required to note the originators of their information when reporting on documents or interviews. Multimedia designers should be subject to the same standard, just as music arrangers (as opposed to composers) or screenwriters currently are. Just as important, that source needs to be credible—even accurate. Newspapers and broadcast outlets eschew publishing rumors; Internet news—if it is to succeed as a genuine information medium—needs to consider the same standard. Just as in the days of the film *The Front Page,* scoops for the sake of scoops are ethically suspect.

If noting the originators of your information creates problems, as it did for the *New York Times,* then be willing to accept those problems as the price of using the information. Many publications require that journalists avoid sourcing their stories exclusively from the Internet; some demand confirmation of an Internet source with additional verification from nonvirtual documents and in-person interviews.

In an ethical sense, such professional standards allow news organizations and those who work for them to achieve two results. In the Judeo-Christian tradition, you have avoided information theft, an ethically culpable act, and fulfilled the ethical duty of beneficence, sharing credit with the originator of your information, whether that is a particular author or the source of a quote in a feature story. You've also done your best to uphold the professional standards of accuracy and truth. In this world of bits and bytes, application of a maxim of "Cite the source of your bytes" will prejudice you to the development of original and creative work, including multiple sources. And, using your own stuff, and not someone else's, improves performance.

The second maxim that emerges from a discussion of deception is this: information that has the capacity to deceive the rational audience member as to its origin, original referent, or source must be regarded as suspect. While journalistic discussion of deception has generally focused on practices used to obtain stories, we believe the concept also applies to the relationship between the journalist and his audience. The issue is whether using digitized information is intended to mislead the audience. Thus, an October 1996 cover of *Life* magazine that combined more than 400 previous covers into an image of Marilyn Monroe does not intend to deceive the audience because the editors clearly explained what they did. But lifting an image from one Web site, downloading sentences from another, and combining them for your own news story without citing your original sources is an attempt to deceive both your editors and your audience.

While both plagiarism and forgery are clearly deceptive practices (Bok 1983, 218), the Web, with its nearly infinite possibilities as a source of information, has highlighted the need for journalists to take care. Even in a new era of pixels and bytes, journalists must maintain old-fashioned credibility with our audiences about the sources of our information and the means and methods of gathering that information.

SOURCES: NEW TECHNOLOGY BUT CONTINUING ISSUES

New technology often raises old ethical issues with additional permutations, and the subtleties of sourcing on the Internet don't all focus on accuracy and speed. Journalists accept that readers and viewers may better understand and evaluate news if those stories identify information sources. Identification often goes beyond a mere name and address: journalists may provide background so audience members understand why a person or document is cited. The professional standard is that sources should be named and that journalists must have compelling reasons for withholding a source's identity. Implicit in this standard is that sources are aware that they are talking to a journalist—or that a specific document has been requested for a journalistic purpose. The Internet can confound these implicit assumptions.

First, granting anonymity requires a mutual agreement between reporter and source, not a unilateral understanding imposed on one party by the other. Anonymous sources are expected to be the exception rather than the journalistic rule. Professional mores dictate that, should a reporter decide to grant anonymity, she does not have to divulge the source's identity to editors, other supervisors or, in rare instances, the courts.

Like many contemporary professional practices, sourcing is not firmly rooted in journalistic history. In the era of the partisan press, story sources were most often the printers who controlled the presses. Further, printers were paid for their efforts by political partisans. Historians suggest that reader understanding of sources in the Revolutionary era parallels contemporary understanding of a signed editorial.

Even the traditional practice of interviewing, now considered commonplace, was controversial at its inception. The critics claimed that interviewing would destroy reporting. Critics argued that if journalists adapted this reporting technique, they would slip into a moral morass, fall prey to aggressive exploitation and manipulation and would no longer serve the public. One *New York World* correspondent referred to the practice as a "modern American inquisition." In 1869, the *London Daily News* castigated those journalists who were practicing this new form of reporting, saying they brought the profession of journalism "into contempt." Editors and publishers feared then that reporters' use of the interview would lessen the control of the editor over the reporter.

Reporters' power grew with the use of the interview because they could select which persons to question and determine which comments to include. As the journalistic practice of the interview developed concurrently with the rise of the professional ideal of objectivity, identifying news sources became accepted professional practice (Schudson 1995; 1978).

The role sourcing plays with readers and viewers has also been questioned in mass communication research. One of the most widely accepted findings in the field is that audience members tend to disassociate the source from the message, what is known as the "sleeper" effect (Lowery and DeFleur 1988). Studies confirm that most people tend to retain the fact of what is said while forgetting the context in which they "heard" it. Practitioners, from Nazi master propagandist Joseph Goebbels through contemporary political consultants, have intuitively understood this human tendency to disassociate the source from the message. But readers and viewers are morally autonomous actors. Identifying news sources allows audiences to evaluate reports in terms of both content and a source's motives for divulging information.

The motives for providing and withholding information are sometimes central to political coverage, and political reporters have added an element of elasticity to the practice of anonymous sourcing.

The phrase "not for attribution" means journalists may quote what is said but agree to veil the source. Thus, the attribution "a high-level White House source" may mean anyone from the president himself to cabinet officers to other, well-connected administrative appointees. The phrase "on background" means journalists should consider the information given as an aid in placing facts in context. Background information also may be used as part of a sourcing trail: journalists in possession of background information may use their knowledge to try to get other sources to provide them with the same information on the record.

Journalists continue to debate allowing sources to go "off the record" or "on deep background." A strict interpretation of these synonymous phrases means that the journalist who accepts such information may not quote the specific source and, in addition, may not use his knowledge to pry the same information from other sources. This stringent interpretation has meant that editors have instructed reporters literally to leave the room when a source asks for such anonymity. Journalists have spent time in jail rather than reveal a source's identity. Less stringent interpretations suggest that journalists who accept information off the record may not name or in any way reveal the identity of the source but may use the information itself to leverage similar or related information from other sources.

Until quite recently such agreements were arrived at through face-to-face conversation and negotiation. However, the advent of the Internet and the ability of journalists to lurk at many places on the Information Superhighway have stripped many interviews of their context and nonverbal cues that have traditionally signaled whether information is on or off the record. Such agreements most often focused on the willingness of the source to be identified, but the Internet can alter this view. Journalists surfing for story sources or leads must be careful to identify themselves professionally on the Internet when they begin "conversing" with another Internet user.

Some publications, for example *The Wall Street Journal,* maintain an informal policy that requires reporters to identify themselves as reporters when they begin their Internet conversations so there is less confusion about the role the journalist plays. The reasoning behind such requirements is that people, in this instance people who are "telepresent" through the Internet, need to know that they are dealing with a journalist working in a professional capacity when they respond to questions about either story ideas or Internet content.

Such professional identification—the Internet version of identifying yourself at the beginning of a telephone conversation—also raises additional professional issues. For example, it is possible for competitors, who also may be surfing the Net, to learn about the direction of a story or even of its specific content during the reporting process. This increases the chance that other news organizations will learn about stories or angles they have missed sometime before actual publication. While this sort of competitive consideration has always influenced journalism, the Internet makes it easier and faster to learn what other news organizations are doing. However, most professionals agree that identifying yourself as a journalist is just as important when working on the Net as it is in face-to-face situations. Since journalists are well aware of the pitfalls of being deceived by a source, "wired" reporters should be more than sensitive to these problems when they become the party to the conversation with the power to deceive.

Whether in person or through fiber optics, journalists who cover police, the courts and other areas of public life often develop informal agreements with frequent sources about when and how information may be attributed. Such relationships are necessary but risky. Many journalists have had to decide whether they will "burn a source," that is, to reveal the identity of a source who has been allowed to remain veiled in earlier stories for a particularly important story. Burning a source means terminating a relationship that worked well for both parties. It is considered a form of promise breaking.

Keeping the trust between reporter and source intact is one reason that larger news organizations will often send an investigative reporter to cover a particularly sensitive story that arises on another reporter's beat. Sending an investigative reporter allows the beat reporter's sourcing agreements to remain undisturbed, ensuring a continuing flow of routine information while the investigation continues.

There are significant ethical justifications for using anonymous sources. They are:

- Preventing either physical or emotional harm to a source.
- Protecting the privacy of a source, particularly children and crime victims.
- Encouraging coverage of institutions, such as the U.S. Supreme Court or the military, which might otherwise remain closed to journalistic and hence public scrutiny.

It is this final justification that is used most frequently by journalists. Reporters maintain that only when sources are allowed to remain anonymous will they provide newsworthy information that would otherwise place their careers or their physical safety at risk. While using the Internet as a reporting tool does not alter these justifications, it foregrounds the need for disclosure when working with sources in ways that nonvirtual journalists seldom encounter. The thinking may be the same, but the situation that prompts such reflection may look very different at first glance.

POLICY OPTIONS: THE ROLE OF THE PROFESSION

Unlike some media technologies such as the printing press, the Information Superhighway was initially developed by the government for political reasons. The original Internet was a computer network designed first to support the military and then, in the 1960s, reorganized to allow scientists working primarily at universities and government laboratories worldwide to communicate quickly and easily among each other. This system remained confined to the intellectual and military elite until the early 1980s, when the Internet, as we now know it, began to take shape.

This unusual history—a mass medium that was "invented" to support government policy—has made the Internet a difficult fit for both academic study and journalistic necessity. Unlike the printing press, which began as a private invention and remained private property, the Internet has historically owed a great deal to the government in both conceptual and financial terms. Because journalists never were part of the early history of Internet development, the notion of using the Internet as a profit-oriented mass medium is a very recent invention. Grafting a concept of mass communication onto a system designed for government-supported communication is fraught with the potential to raise some difficult questions.

The contemporary conceptualization of the Internet has government supporting a system that will wire and link all schools, libraries and hospitals. This proposal, which has been partially funded but will cost billions, is rooted in both practical politics and ethical theory.

The political aspects are fairly straightforward: by linking schools, hospitals and libraries, the government is supporting an infrastructure that will promote education and learning and thus strengthen the economy through providing a better educated workforce. A better educated workforce is also generally considered a more efficient one, thus making U.S. workers more competitive worldwide as well as driving down production costs domestically. A better educated populace, of course, also has military implications: it enables the military to draw from a more qualified pool of recruits who are being asked to operate increasingly more complicated weapons. Thus, the reasoning goes, the federal government fulfills its constitutional responsibility to protect Americans from international as well as domestic threats by supporting a system that will promote the country's growth and development in many obvious and subtle ways.

Linking hospitals, of course, is also viewed as one way to simultaneously improve the quality of health care for many Americans while holding down medical costs. Again, the reasoning is that private, for-profit medicine would not be as likely to connect all hospitals; through government support the projected benefit can be distributed throughout American society.

This conceptualization of the Internet is also founded in ethical theory. As you may remember from the discussion of utilitarianism in Chapter I, the notion of the greatest good for the greatest number has profoundly democratic implications. Wiring schools and libraries should, in theory, provide access to the Internet for every American. Indeed, some libraries in California have experimented with "Internet addresses" for the homeless. Universal access to the Internet through education also would follow Rawls's theory—it would allow the maximization of freedom (access) while protecting weaker parties (people of color, the poor) who might not have access to many other goods in U.S. society but can use the Internet as a way to better their individual and potentially collective lots in life.

Of course, journalists and journalism have not been included in this conceptualization. Yet many journalists have argued that access is only part of the picture—it does people little good to access information if they can't make sense of it. Some scholars have suggested that, as the Internet develops, journalism itself will change from a profession that primarily gathers facts—something anyone can now do on the Internet—to a profession that places those facts within a context and makes them meaningful. If the development of the Internet does indeed encourage professional development along these lines, then ethical thinking would demand that access to news coverage be distributed as widely as possible among the population and that it remain economically affordable.

That stance, of course, puts journalists at odds with all those segments of U.S. society that view the Internet as another potential profit center, including the multinational corporations for which increasing numbers of journalists now work. Insisting that affordable news become part of the policymaking that is currently swirling around the Information Superhighway would challenge the long-standing U.S. tradition of regarding journalism and government as irreconcilable adversaries. Yet ethical (and in some ways political) thinking would seem to suggest that making news coverage accessible to every American via the Internet has significant potential benefits for the individual and society at large. It also would make journalists and the government partners, a true philosophical shift in the conceptualization of a "free" press.

Finally, such a partnership would demand that journalists themselves take an active part in developing and implementing legislation that will affect their working lives. Such a change in attitude also would require a philosophical shift, one that places journalistic responsibility to political society on an even plane with worker responsibility to profitable media industries.

THE FRAGMENTATION OF POLITICAL CULTURE

In the 1980s, Nicholas Negroponte, the head of MIT's Media Lab and an Internet guru of some note, created a unique publication he called the *Daily Me*. Negroponte programmed his MIT computer to develop a daily newspaper based on his information needs and desires as well as past information preferences. The *Daily Me*, for example, carried a great deal of news about computers and universities and relatively less news about sports, U.S. politics, and the environment. Negroponte, acknowledging that he had a good chance of missing stories that he either should know about or would be interested in that would fall outside his desired categories, programmed his computer to select 10 percent of the *Daily Me*'s content literally at random.

Today, all of us now have the capacity to develop a *Daily Me* from the vast collection of information now on the World Wide Web. Of course, reader and viewer selectivity is nothing new. How many people do you know who always read the sports page and never anything else? If most contemporary newspaper readership surveys are correct, about 35 percent of regular newspaper readers fit this profile. Or take the reverse problem. What if something new—say the emergence of a potentially deadly virus—is noted by doctors but given little media attention? How will you know to tell your *Daily Me* that, instead of looking at the *New York Times*, the better sources are the alternative press in the gay community in San Francisco and New York? This was exactly the case from 1981 through 1986, when many major publications, including the *New York Times*, refused to carry front-page stories about the AIDS virus at the same time the gay press was covering the epidemic.

If every member of a society has access to personalized news, the implications for democracy are enormous, as Cass Sunstein (2001) points out in Republic.com. He writes that democracy demands two imperatives. First, people must be exposed to materials that they would not have chosen in advance and come across views that they would not have previously selected or even agree with. Second, many, or at least most, citizens should have a range of common experiences. In the absence of shared experiences, society will have a much harder time addressing social problems, Sunstein contends.

Philosopher Jürgen Habermas is another advocate of this approach, arguing that one of the preconditions of a deliberative democracy is a large number of public forums where people meet by chance and begin a dialogue—none of which is possible in a society where everyone subscribes only to the *Daily Me*. Sunstein concludes that "The imagined world of the 'Daily Me' is the farthest thing from a utopian dream, and it would create serious problems from a democratic point of view."

Journalists acknowledge that newspapers and magazines produced in such a customized fashion as the *Daily Me* will give the reader more editorial control, but worry not only for their financial future but also about the impact of such enhanced selectivity on the larger political culture. The Internet, by placing responsibility squarely on the shoulders (or at least in the computers) of users, has the potential to fragment U.S. culture even more deeply than is the current case. For instance, political conservatives could read only certain points of view; many others would choose to read nothing about politics altogether. At some point, Americans may lose the shared political vocabulary and experience that is the foundation for representative, democratic government.

It is even more unclear what journalists themselves can do to alter this potential trend. News organizations are experimenting with interactive stories and individual editions tailored to particular groups of subscribers. Cable channels, newspaper sections, and magazine titles continue to search for select "niche" audiences, a fact that was true before the Internet but absolutely necessary for survival today. No one yet knows what will work, what readers and viewers will accept, and what the impact of these changes will be on the larger political culture. What is clear is that journalists need to develop a better sense of how their work helps people make sense of their political, economic and social lives. The Internet has pointed out as never before the need for journalists to connect themselves to readers and viewers or face the consequences of being considered irrelevant and annoying. If there was ever a goad to improved professional performance, the Internet may be providing it.

Suggested Readings

GODWIN, MIKE. 1998. *Defending free speech in the digital age.* New York: Times Books.
HALBERT, DEBORA J. 1999. *Intellectual property in the information age.* Westport, CT: Quorum Books.
NEGROPONTE, NICHOLAS. 1995. *Being digital.* New York: Alfred A. Knopf.

Cases on the Web

"The witch and the woods mystery: Fact or fiction?" by Karon Reinboth Speckman
"The Napster debate: When does sharing become thievery?" by Laura Riethmiller
"Digital sound sampling: Sampling the options" by Don Tomlinson
"Cry Wolf: *Time* magazine and the cyberporn story" by Karon Reinboth Speckman
"Filmmaking: Looking through the lens for truth" by Kathy Brittain McKee
"The Madonna and the web site: Good taste in newspaper online forums" by Philip Patterson

CHAPTER X CASES

CASE X-A
Ethics on the Internet: Abiding by the Rules of the Road on the Information Superhighway
BRUCE LEWENSTEIN
Cornell University

ComNet is a commercial online service with a wide range of options available to its subscribers. These include databases, e-mail capabilities and forums for discussion of many topics. Some of these forums are available to all subscribers, while others require a separate sign-up system and are available only to registered users. In the case of JourForum, a discussion group for journalists, only working journalists may post or read messages to the group. Working journalists are defined as those employed by newspapers, magazines or other legitimate publications; those whose names appear on the masthead of a regularly published magazine; those who belong to one of several professional organizations (such as the Society of Professional Journalists or the American Society of Newspaper Editors); or those who prove their legitimacy by presenting clips of their published work. ComNet is available both through direct modem connection and through the World Wide Web.

Subscribers to ComNet agree to abide by the service's "Rules of Behavior," which include prohibitions against objectionable or lewd language, illegal activity and "abuse of the service." Journalists signing up for JourForum are reminded of these rules and requested to use only their true names, as well as limiting their discussion to issues directly related to journalism. No specific statements are made about whether JourForum (or other parts of ComNet) are on or off the record. Mark Morceau is the "moderator" of JourForum—as well as its creator—and, through contractual arrangements with ComNet, the person responsible for ensuring that uses of JourForum abide by ComNet's rules.

In a new message to the JourForum, Miriam Zablonsky identifies herself as the editor of a newsletter about "alternative" (nontraditional) medical treatments. She presents many details about a new drug treatment for AIDS, including information about the research leading to the treatment. She wonders why the media has failed to cover the story, she says.

In a response, Harry Lee, a reporter for an online magazine about medicine, suggests that the media usually cover medical stories only after they appear in medical publications such as *The New England Journal of Medicine*.

Zablonsky goes ballistic. In a long, biting, bitter message, she complains about a major medical journal that, she says, refuses to publish information about the new treatment. She calls the editor of the journal, Katherine Kelly, "a fat, sexist, lying slob." Kelly is a well-known commentator on the excesses of tabloid journalism (especially its coverage of medical topics); her columns are often accompanied by her photo, showing a slim, stylish, beautiful woman of 42.

A flood of messages appears, condemning Zablonsky's comments. To each one, Zablonsky responds with long, rambling diatribes about conspiracies of "them" (unspecified) to control the world, about the deep distrust that a journalist should have toward all major institutions, and about her own unwillingness to change or even compromise her positions, no matter what information is presented to her.

At this point (less than a day after the original message from Zablonsky), Mark Morceau posts a message reminding Zablonsky of ComNet and JourForum's rules about objectionable language and abuse of the service (including posting long messages on topics that aren't germane to journalism). In addition, he asks her to apologize to Kelly and to avoid libelous statements in the future.

Zablonsky refuses, citing (among other arguments in another long, rambling message) her rights to free speech and freedom of the press.

Morceau tells Zablonsky that JourForum is not a publication, so it is not subject to rules of free press. It is, he says, more akin to a private club, which can enforce rules on its members. He points to the requirement that contributors belong to professional journalism organizations as one of the ways that JourForum maintains its limited membership. (Zablonsky once worked for a daily paper, and she maintains her membership in SPJ.)

If JourForum is a private club, responds Zablonsky, what she said isn't libelous, because the club isn't a public place or publication. (All of these messages, as with all JourForum messages, are publicly posted so any subscriber to JourForum can view them.)

The next day, Katherine Kelly joins the online discussion. She threatens to sue Zablonsky, claiming that she has been libeled in a public forum. The international community of journalists with access to JourForum is so large that it cannot be considered a "private" club, she argues. Any one of those subscribers can read this forum, she reminds Zablonsky, making it equivalent to a trade paper or magazine. It is as public as any traditional publication, Kelly argues. Moreover, she says, in a landmark decision in June 1996, a federal appeals court described online forums as one of the most important contributions to free exchange of ideas since the development of the printing press. Clearly, Kelly says, the canons of a free press—including the responsibility of avoiding libel—apply to online forums.

Cynthia Smith has been following the online discussion. She finds the issues of potential censorship, free press and free speech fascinating. She writes an article about the fracas for her own newspaper's weekly "News from Cyberspace" page. That page appears on Thursdays in the business section of the paper; it is also available in the newspaper's online edition. In her story, Smith includes quotes from Morceau, Zablonsky, Kelly and other members of the forum; the quotes are taken not from interviews but from the messages those people had posted online.

When Smith's story appears, she is accused (in another round of postings in JourForum) of violating the expectation many journalists had that their words in the online forum were "off the record" and would not be quoted.

Micro Issues

1. Can Zablonsky be sued for libel? Should she be sued for libel?
2. Should Smith have asked for permission to quote?
3. Does Morceau have the right to control what material appears in JourForum?

Midrange Issues

1. Does it matter if Smith's article appeared only in the traditional paper format, only in an on-line supplement to the newspaper, or in a separate online magazine that does not have ties to a traditional-format publication?
2. Is there a moral difference between Zablonsky's potentially libelous statements and Smith's potential violation of the standards of on- and off-the-record?

Macro Issues

1. Is JourForum a public or private place? What difference would it make if any ComNet subscriber could read messages in JourForum, though only registered members could post messages there? (Compare JourForum to the floor of a convention, where members of the press are often identified with badges so that speakers know they are talking to a reporter.)
2. Under what circumstances does a reporter need to identify himself or herself? At what point do "private" conversations become open to reporting by others?
3. Are online publications subject to different rules than are traditional publications? If so, how do you distinguish between the rules that apply to publications that appear only online and those that appear in both online and offline versions? Does it matter if the online and offline versions are different or edited differently?

CASE X-B
What Were You Linking?
PAUL VOAKES
University of Colorado

One of the oldest controversies in southern politics helped to create one of the newest controversies in media ethics.

In May 2000, the South Carolina legislature voted to remove the Confederate flag from the Capitol dome in Columbia and to have it placed behind the nearby Confederate Soldiers Monument, but the issue had far broader appeal than just to South Carolinians. Activists on both sides in Alabama, Arkansas, Florida, Georgia and Mississippi were carefully monitoring the debate, expecting it would influence debates in their states over various displays of Confederate symbols. The National Association for the Advancement of Colored People (NAACP) was organizing a national boycott of South Carolina even after the compromise that put the "Rebel" flag behind the monument. The NAACP action included boycotting the products of several manufacturers that had recently built facilities in South Carolina. The national media were paying close attention to the story.

A few months earlier, the Associated Press had begun routinely adding URLs (Uniform Resource Locators, or Internet addresses) to its stories, which would link readers to related sources of information on the World Wide Web. This practice had by now become fairly common on the Web sites of many national news organizations, but the AP's handling of its links on this particular story illustrated the ethical pitfalls that can await online journalists.

For several weeks, at the bottom of every story involving the Confederate flag controversy in South Carolina, the AP listed the Web addresses of three prominent stakeholders in the story: the NAACP, the South Carolina Heritage Coalition, and the Sons of Confederate Veterans. Surfers to the Heritage Coalition's site found the group's position on the flag issue, and more: calls for "the confederate curriculum to be taught in all South Carolina public schools"; for "recognition of South Carolinians as Confederate/Southern Americans for National Origin status" on government forms; for state holidays commemorating the birthdays of Confederate leaders Robert E. Lee and Jefferson Davis; and for "civil rights protection for Confederate/Southern Americans in the workplace." By providing the link to this organization, the AP had given it unprecedented access to the U.S. public.

When a news organization offers a hypertext link to another site, is it responsible in any way for the content of that site?

This wasn't the first time the question had surfaced. In 1997 the *New York Times* published a story about efforts to establish the innocence of convicted killer Charles Manson, complete with links to "Access Manson" and other sites that suggest Manson's innocence.

In the early days of online journalism—way back in the mid-1990s—few editors thought to provide links to external Web sites as part of a news or feature story. Once editors became more enchanted by the ways in which a Web site "added value" to the printed version, links became frequently embedded in stories. By the end of the decade, however, a modest backlash had occurred as editors realized that

(1) readers using the links were leaving the news site and quite often not returning and (2) readers may be associating the tone and views of the linked site with the provider of the original site.

In many cases, the linked Web sites simply add more detailed information or opinions to what was presented in the original story. This is often "unmediated" material that can pass directly from a source or advocate to the reader, without passing through the filters of journalists. Many Web observers and editors celebrate this capability, especially when the link goes to a site produced by a widely known, reliable organization. "I don't see that as a danger to democracy or the public interest," Jonathan Wolman of the Associated Press told the *American Journalism Review.*

But what if the journalist links readers to sites that publish more propaganda than fact, or that advocate racism, violence or pornography?

News organizations have taken different approaches to the "linking" debate. Some don't link at all, except to other pages within the same site. CNN.com tries to make sure its external links are balanced to represent the major positions of a controversy. The *New York Times* says it will link to no sites that "celebrate violence," present sexual content or advocate bigotry or racism. Other online newspapers, such as the *Chicago Tribune,* warn readers generally that by clicking on the hypertext, readers will be leaving the *Tribune*'s site. Other sites warn readers that not only are they leaving the site but external sites "are not endorsed" by the original site. Other sites warn readers that the information in external sites has not been checked for accuracy by the staff of the original site. Still others offer more specific warnings, such as the *Los Angeles Times'* warning to readers that if they linked to the site of the rock band Rage Against the Machine, they would encounter "adult language."

The AP has instructed its editors to use their "best news judgment" to determine which external sites to include.

As with most ethical controversies raised by fast-changing online technologies, there is no consensus at this time. Most online news providers do agree, however, on this much: linked sites do reflect, at least to some extent, on the journalistic decisions being made by the link provider.

Micro Issues

1. Does each reporter have a responsibility at least to "check out" every Web site his or her story links to, if only to make sure the linked site still exists?
2. Should each reporter be able to vouch for the accuracy and reliability of each linked site?
3. A significant percentage of readers who follow a link will not make it back to the newspaper's site. Is this reality a relevant factor in deciding how often to link or to whom you should link?

Midrange Issues

1. Should news organizations provide any disclaimers about links before taking readers to the linked sites? If yes, what should those disclaimers say?

2. Should mainstream news organizations link only to Web sites of established, "respectable" organizations, in order not to be associated with fringe or extremist positions? Does linking imply endorsement?
3. Who makes the call on what is respectable? Is this decision-making process a form of censorship or is it gatekeeping, or something else entirely?
4. In what way, if any, does checking the accuracy of a cited Web resource differ from checking out the veracity of an individual quoted in the story. Should the same rules apply?

Macro Issues

1. What is the media's responsibility to society in terms of expanding the "marketplace of ideas" via the Web?
2. Will the free exchange of ideas and democratic debate be enhanced, or is widespread, unchecked linking more likely to distort and discourage honest debate?

CASE X-C
ELLEgirlBuddy: Girl Meets Bot
MARIA CARTER
University of Missouri

At the beginning of 2002, teen fashion magazine *ELLEgirl* was looking for a way to increase its readership. The magazine is targeted at teenage girls interested in fashion and beauty. Seeking to establish a larger readership and differentiate itself from other teen magazines, *ELLEgirl* decided to use instant messaging, one of the most popular methods of communication among teenagers, to interest girls in subscribing. *ELLEgirl* teamed up with software developer ActiveBuddy to create an instant message bot to chat with potential *ELLEgirl* readers. The ELLEgirlBuddy chat bot is a software program that works with AOL Instant Messenger and Microsoft Messenger to provide information from *ELLEgirl* magazine while realistically chatting like a teen.

To engage potential subscribers, ELLEgirlBuddy not only uses teenage lingo and chat acronyms but also is given a history and personality. According to an article in the *Los Angeles Times* (Frey 2000), ELLEgirlBuddy represents herself as not just a bot but an actual person. She describes herself as a 16-year-old girl, who is 5'6" tall with straight red hair, green eyes and freckles. She lives in San Francisco with her parents and older brother. Her interests include listening to music, chatting online with friends, and polishing her nails. Her favorite band is No Doubt. Her favorite book is *Catcher in the Rye,* and her favorite television show is *Buffy the Vampire Slayer.* When she grows up, she would like to own a bookstore café, design handbags or work as a foreign correspondent. These and many other details give ELLEgirlBuddy a personality that appeals to teenage girls.

One month after the launch of ELLEgirlBuddy, traffic at ELLEgirl.com increased 83 percent, and *ELLEgirl* magazine subscriptions rose 50 percent. One in ten people who saw an advertisement on ELLEgirlBuddy visited the advertiser's Web site (ActiveBuddy 2002).

While subscription rates and Web site usage certainly indicate the effectiveness of ELLEgirlBuddy as an advertising tool, the bot does seem to be connecting to its target audience on a personal level. In an e-mail to ActiveBuddy (2002), one ELLEgirlBuddy wrote about the company's various bots: "My favorite so far is ELLEgirlBuddy she is so cool and gives really great tips and quizzes about fashion." Another user wrote, "ELLEgirlBuddy is awesome as well! I love her beauty and fashion tips!"

Anecdotal evidence also suggests that some people use ELLEgirlBuddy and other bots as confidants. They provide the bots with information about their feelings and events in their lives, and in some instances they develop feelings toward the bot. SmarterChild, ActiveBuddy's prototype bot, readily acknowledged that it was not human, although it was also programmed to respond "I love you too!"

ELLEgirlBuddy also collects information provided by the user for future use. For example, if the user says she is looking forward to seeing the next Harry Potter movie, the bot may begin its next conversation with the user by referring her to an article about the film in *ELLEgirl.*

Micro Issues

1. Does creating bots constitute some form of deception?
2. While most teens "catch on" to the fact that the bot is a computer program, should the bots' creators consider the fact that more naive users may not be as quick to catch on?
3. Does the fact that ELLEgirlBuddy was created as an entertaining and informative advertisement pass the TARES test outlined in the advertising chapter?
4. Does collecting information from users raise some privacy questions?

Midrange Issues

1. Anecdotal evidence suggests that users tell ELLEgirlBuddy about breakups with boyfriends, family problems and the rigors of school. Since ELLEgirlBuddy can't gossip and is programmed not to be judgmental, might this be a positive use of the Internet?
2. Would if be appropriate to have ELLEgirlBuddy make its advertising function more prominent? How might that be accomplished?
3. How might the creators of ELLEgirlBuddy respond to questions of authenticity that are raised in discussions of persuasion ethics?

Macro Issues

1. In the late 1930s after the "War of the Worlds" radio program resulted in a national furor, the FCC required that broadcast stations regularly identify themselves so audiences would have external cues to help them distinguish entertainment from news. Would it be appropriate for the Federal Trade Commission to adopt a similar policy regarding bots? In what ways are the two different, if at all?
2. At what point should those who provide media content, regardless of the form of transmission, have to consider the impact of that content on naive or psychologically at-risk users as opposed to the much larger, general audience? Are these standards the same for information and entertainment?

CASE X-D
The Case of Banjo Jones and His Blog
CHRIS HEISEL
University of Missouri

Bad pancakes at a Denny's restaurant set in motion the first reported case of a journalist being fired for running a "blog," the popular name for a Web log, an Internet-based diary that is often equal parts news and subjective observation.

Steve Olafson joined the staff of the *Houston Chronicle* in May 1995 after the *Houston Post* closed. He had been with the *Post* for more than 14 years, and before that, he had been at the *San Antonio Light* and the *Wichita Falls Times & Record News* in north Texas. While at the *Chronicle,* he covered Brazoria County—the large, rural area on the Gulf Coast with many small towns—from his home (a requirement of his job with the *Chronicle*).

Sometime in the spring of 2001, Olafson said he doesn't remember exactly, he had gone to a local Denny's and had some bad pancakes. Before that, he had read about the growing phenomenon of blogs—shorthand for Web logs—which are personal sites that contain a variety of items, including original reporting, links to other blogs, interesting articles on the Internet, and diary-type entries. Many well-known journalists have blogs. Both readers and editors consider some to be required reading. Olafson started up *Brazosport News* (named for one of the more populous regions of the county), and wrote it under the pseudonym "Banjo Jones."

"The first entry was just sort of a throwaway one that said something about how the pancakes at Denny's were cold, toxic waste floating down the San Bernard river and 'stay tuned,'" Olafson said via an Internet interview.

He said the motivation to create the blog was "chiefly self-amusement" and a long-running desire to be a columnist. He added he decided to write the blog under a pen name because he "knew the powers that be at the *Houston Chronicle* probably wouldn't like their reporter's opinion on the Web. I figured, well, nobody will know it's me, so no harm, no foul."

The blog started off focusing on the personal, but eventually items about events in and near Brazoria County appeared. The *Houston Press* reported that some items dealt with local politicians Olafson covered as a *Chronicle* reporter.

Some of the more controversial content included this article from August 8. Buster Brown was, in the May 30, 2001, edition of Jones' Web site, "the state senator with the Hair Club For Men Wig." When a local city council had problems complying with the Open Meetings Act, the headline was, "Angleton Council: Shining Beacon of Open Govt. or Taliban-like Nest of Lawbreakers?" (Connelly 2002)

The Register analysis also suggested the blog mocked two local papers, one entitled *The Facts* and the second Olafson's employer in an entry written after the *Chronicle* ran the story about the "Women of Enron" appearing in *Playboy* magazine on the front page.

Yvonne Mintz, a reporter at *The Facts* who eventually wrote the story that exposed Olafson, told the Poynter.org "E-media Tidbits Weblog" that Olafson's site "gained a strong following, and was entertaining and often insightful."

For his part, Olafson maintained he never published any information he gathered as a *Chronicle* reporter, nor did he use any "off the record" or "background" information.

After the controversy over the blog had ended, *The Register,* a British online magazine that covers technology topics, analyzed the archives of the *Brazosport News,* which are no longer available today. That analysis found that about 20 percent of the blog coverage was related to Brazoria County politics.

The events surrounding the disclosure of Banjo Jones's identity are still contentious.

The Facts published a story on July 26 naming Olafson as the writer. Earlier in the week, Olafson's *Chronicle* editors were contacted by a *Facts* reporter who told them about Olafson's alter ego. Olafson says that his *Chronicle* editor Jeff Cohen called him and said, "I'm running a mainstream American newspaper. There's no place here for gonzo journalism. . . . Take the f——ing site down!"

However, *The Facts* story reported that Cohen would not comment on whether Olafson's blog violated the paper's ethics code. That same news story also noted that Hearst Newspapers, the *Chronicle*'s parent corporation, adopted a statement of professional principles that said employees should avoid active involvement in community issues or organizations "to the extent that their participation might cause the paper's objectivity to come into question" (Mintz 2002).

Olafson took down his Web site and was fired by the *Chronicle.* He maintained there was "no concern" in the community about the blog.

Kelly Hawes, managing editor of *The Facts,* said he published the story because he believed a journalist was using the blog to "take anonymous potshots. . . . If he had been a reporter taking shots at his competitor, I might have called his boss, but I still don't think I'd have published a story. We ran this story for one reason. Steve Olafson had a public trust as a journalist, and he violated that trust."

Micro Issues

1. What would you consider to be appropriate content for a blog written by a local reporter? Sports? Entertainment?
2. Was the *Chronicle*'s action appropriate?
3. How is a blog by a local reporter like or unlike an editorial? Should it enjoy the full First Amendment protection of more traditional journalistic endeavors?
4. Does the fact that this blog was written under a pen name make any difference?
5. Would it be appropriate for another reporter to use information from the blog as part of research for a news story? A column?

Midrange Issues

1. Many well-known journalists publish blogs. Do columnists have greater latitude than reporters in this area?
2. Does the fact that this blog was published on the Internet make an ethical difference? Why?
3. In a competitive industry, is this sort of "outing" appropriate? What ethical theory supports your view?

Macro Issues

1. Do blogs, columns, and other sorts of opinion-influenced writing compromise journalistic objectivity? Does that matter?
2. Some commentators have suggested that Web ethics are distinct from the ethics of print journalism. Evaluate this statement.
3. Was the newspaper's code of ethics appropriately used in this case?

XI

The Ethical Dimensions of Art and Entertainment

By the end of this chapter you should be able to:

- understand the link between aesthetics and excellent professional
    performance.
- explain Tolstoy's rationale for art and apply it to issues such as
    stereotyping.
- understand the debate over the role of truth in popular art.

During the 20th century, the predominant use of the media shifted from the distribution of information to entertainment and the popularization of culture. In this chapter we will examine the ethical issues that arise from the field of aesthetics. We will apply these principles, plus some findings from social science, to the art and entertainment components of media industries, focusing on the responsibilities of the public as well as the creators of mediated messages.

AN ANCIENT MISUNDERSTANDING

Plato did not like poets. The ancient Greek's reasoning was straightforward. Poets, the people who dream, were the potential undoing of the philosopher king. They were rebels of the first order, insurrectionists on the hoof. He banned them from the Republic.

But Plato's skepticism about the role of art is alive in contemporary culture. Few weeks elapse without a news story about an artist or entertainment program that has offended. You are probably familiar with at least some of the following:

- Attempts to ban books such as *Catcher in the Rye* or *Lady Chatterley's Lover* from public and/or school libraries for being too sexually explicit.
- The controversy over government funding of art that some claim is obscene.

- Calls by conservatives and liberals to boycott television networks and their advertisers over allegedly objectionable content.
- The furor over rappers such as Eminem whose homophobic, misogynistic and sometimes clever lyrics offend many while earning nominations for the industry's top awards.
- The public outcry and political posturing that followed Janet Jackson's breast-baring episode at the Super Bowl in January 2004.

Such a response to works of art and entertainment, whether it is by public officials or individuals, is essentially Platonic. Like Plato, those who would restrict the arts do so because they mistrust the power of the artist to link emotion and logic in a way that stimulates a new vision of society, culture or individuals.

Calvin and Hobbes

by Bill Watterson

OF TOLSTOY AND TELEVISION

Tolstoy was the sort of artist Plato would have feared. In his famous essay, "What Is Art?" Tolstoy argued that good art had one dominant characteristic: it communicated the feelings of the artist to the masses in the way in which the artist intended.

> To evoke in oneself a feeling one has once experienced and having evoked it in oneself then by means of movements, lines, colors, sounds or forms expressed in words, so to transmit that feeling that others experience the same feeling—that is the activity of art. . . . Art is a human activity consisting in this, that one may consciously by means of certain external signs, hand on to others feelings he has lived through, and that others are infected by these feelings and also experience them.

Tolstoy's application of his own standard—one that sounds remarkably like artistic social responsibility—was so demanding that he rejected the works of both Shakespeare and Beethoven as being incapable of being understood by the masses. While you may not agree with all of Tolstoy's specific applications, we believe his philosophical rationale has much to recommend it.

Tolstoy's rationale is particularly pertinent to photographers and videographers who, through their visual images, seek to arouse emotion as well as inform. Haunting pictures of starvation from Bosnia and Ethiopia have provided a spur for international concerns. Award-winning dramas such as *Angels in America,* the AIDS quilt, movies such as *Philadelphia* in which Tom Hanks won an Academy Award for his portrayal of an AIDS victim and obituaries of famous artists who have succumbed to the disease have all aroused both our intellects and our emotions regarding AIDS. They invite action. Television and film documentaries have made viewers more aware of the plight of the mentally ill and homeless, raised important public policy questions, and occasionally made us laugh, through a unity of purpose and craft.

Such work reminds readers and viewers of the moral impetus of art by putting us in touch with characters and situations more complex than our own lives. By thinking about these fictional characters, we enlarge our moral imaginations. Both artists and journalists can provide such a stimulus, although it will not be reflected in every song, story or film.

Unfortunately, Tolstoy's assertion that great art is defined by how it is understood by an audience also includes a genuine dilemma. There are those who, given even Tolstoy's life experiences, could not articulate the deep truths about human nature Tolstoy wrote about in *War and Peace.* Worse yet, we might not be able to sell those insights to a sometimes lukewarm public, or to produce them on demand for an hour a week, 36 weeks a year. The result might be popular art that loses its critical edge and takes shortcuts to commonplace insight. In fact, some mass communication scholars have argued that the unstated goal of popular art is to reinforce the status quo; popular culture, they say, blunts the individual's critical-thinking abilities.

Storytellers have a history as popular artists, and the mass media have become the primary cultural storytellers of the era. In *Propaganda,* Jacques Ellul (1965) argues that in a modern society storytelling is an inevitable and even desirable tool to stabilize the culture. To Ellul, this "propaganda of integration" is not the deliberate lie commonly associated with propaganda but the dissemination of widely

Philosophers, sociologists and artists have debated the meaning of art for the past 150 years. Prior to the Industrial Revolution, art was something only the well educated paid for, produced and understood. Mozart had to capture the ear of the Emperor of Austria to get a subsidy to write opera. Such "high" or "elite art" provided society with a new way to look at itself. Picasso's drawings of people with three eyes or rearranged body parts literally provided Western culture with a new way of seeing. Michelangelo's paintings and sculpture did the same thing in the Renaissance.

But patronage had disadvantages. The patron could restrict both subject matter and form, a reality depicted in the film *Amadeus* where the Emperor informed Mozart that his work, "The Marriage of Figaro" had "too many notes." Gradually artists discovered that if they could find a way to get more than one person to "pay" for the creation of art, artistic control returned to the artist. The concept of "popular art" was born.

Scholars disagree about many of the qualities of elite and popular art; some even assert that popular art cannot truly be considered art. While both kinds of art are difficult to define, the following list outlines the major differences between popular and elite art and culture:

1. Popular art is consciously adjusted to the median taste by the artist; elite art reflects the individual artist's vision.
2. Popular art is neither abstruse, complicated, nor profound; elite art has these characteristics.
3. Popular art conforms to majority experience; elite art explores the new.
4. Popular art conforms to less clearly defined standards of excellence, and its standards are linked to commercial success; elite art is much less commercially oriented, and its standards of excellence are consistent and integrated.
5. Popular artists know that the audience expects entertainment and instruction; elite artists seek an aesthetic experience.
6. The popular artist cannot afford to offend a significant part of the public; the elite artist functions as a critic of society, and his or her work challenges and sometimes offends the status quo.
7. Popular art often arises from folk art; elite art more often emerges from a culture's dominant intellectual tradition.

held mores to the culture at large. This is precisely where the entertainment media get their power—not in the overt programming messages but in the underlying assumptions that (if unchallenged) will become widely held societal values.

Many observers complain that the media reinforce the status quo by constantly depicting certain social groups in an unflattering and unrepresentative way, presenting a distorted picture of reality to the reader or viewer. For example, when was the last time you saw an Arab on television as anything other than a terrorist or religious fanatic? Or a beautiful blonde woman who also happened to be an engineer? Depictions and omissions such as the ones above reinforce cultural stereotypes and offend the groups involved. They also leave the media in the position of constantly having to explain why the media world is so different from the real world.

At least some such distortion is the natural outcome of compression. Just as substances such as rubber change form when compressed, so do media messages. Given only 30 seconds to register a message in a commercial, an advertising copywriter will resort to showing us the stereotype of a librarian, a mechanic, or a pharmacist. Using stereotypes as a form of mental shorthand is a natural way media work and was noted as early as 1922 by Walter Lippmann in his classic work *Public Opinion.* Lippmann said that for economy of time and maintenance of the status quo, we hold to stereotypes by "defining first and seeing second." Soon, we expect reality to imitate art.

Mass communicators know the power of stereotypes and deeply held notions and use them. According to advertising guru Tony Schwartz (1973), advertising messages are often constructed backward. The communicator actually starts with what the receiver knows—or believes he knows—and then constructs a message that fits within that reality. Schwartz calls it hitting a "responsive chord."

It works the same in entertainment.

If you need a pimp to further the plot and time is tight, dress an African-American male appropriately and let the audience fill in the details. If you need a terrorist, anyone of Arab descent will usually do. The audience gets the idea of a pimp or a terrorist, but another idea has been planted as well—the racist notion that most pimps are minorities or that all Arabs are terrorists. While these images suit the artist's purposes, they are problematic.

Some scholars have made a more universal argument. Meyrowitz (1985) argues that television has become a "secret-revelation machine," bringing behaviors once confined to the "backstage" to the screen. The result is a loss of faith in institutions such as government, religion and parenthood, with a resulting loss of stability. This loss of stability, Postman (1986) claims, can happen in one of two ways. In the Orwellian concept (found in *1984*) culture becomes a prison; in the Huxleyan concept (found in *Brave New World*) culture becomes a burlesque. Postman believes we are in more danger of the latter. Television is a threat to society precisely because most of its messages are so common yet people take them so seriously. Fore (1987) argues that every culture reveals itself through its underlying assumptions—the decisions it makes about what to value, how to solve problems, who is powerful and what is taboo. In earlier cultures, these values were transmitted around the campfire; in our society, they are transmitted via television to a viewer who is separate from feedback and outside points of reference. These conditions, Fore argues, make the viewer subject to "a tunnel vision that encourages unquestioning acceptance of the world view he or she sees on the screen" (Fore 1987, 4).

The unquestioning acceptance of an unchanging reality is the antithesis of the effect Tolstoy intended art to produce. In Tolstoy's vision, art introduces the reader or viewer to the novel with such power and depth that what is novel can become known and what is known can become understood.

TRUTH IN ART AND ENTERTAINMENT

No question in the field of aesthetics is more thoroughly debated with less resolution than the role of truth in art. Most philosophers seem to agree that artists are not restricted to telling the literal truth. Often artistic vision can reveal a previously undiscerned truth, a new way of looking at the world or understanding human nature that rings deeply true.

But just how much truth should the audience expect from entertainment? And how entertaining should the audience expect truth to be? There are several opinions. At one point on the continuum is the argument that there is no truth requirement at all in art. At another point on the continuum is the belief that one person's truth should be established as the accepted truth for all. This imposition of a specific moral, as opposed to ethical, "truth" is common to all cultures and political systems. In *The Republic* Plato had Socrates argue against allowing children to hear "casual tales . . . devised by casual persons." Its result, when applied to the mass media, is usually some form of licensing or censorship. In U.S. society, that battle historically has raged over library books.

Classics such as *Huckleberry Finn, Of Mice and Men, The Grapes of Wrath,* and *The Merchant of Venice* are but some of the long-revered and award-winning works that now face censorship by various school systems. The American Library Association reports that incidents of book banning rise each year and now reach more than one thousand instances annually, with little or no impedance from the courts. In 1982, the U.S. Supreme Court allowed a lower court ruling to stand that forced the Island Trees, New York, school district to reexamine a list of books considered objectionable (most of them by minority writers or about minority experiences) and to justify the censor's motives, but since that time the high court has not heard another book-banning case.

While books are important because they form the most permanent part of our cultural and intellectual web, television has been the medium that has been the most frequent contemporary target of censorship and protest. The protests began early in the medium's history. The 1951 airing of the show *Amos 'n' Andy* was condemned by the National Association for the Advancement of Colored People for depicting "Negroes in a stereotyped and derogatory manner." In 1964 the United Church of Christ set a legal precedent when it successfully challenged the license renewal of WLBT in Jackson, Mississippi, on the grounds that the owners had blatantly discriminated against African-Americans.

In the 60s, 70s and 80s a variety of special-interest groups used more subtle methods to influence entertainment programming. Some, such as the Hispanic advocacy group Nosotros, worked closely with network bureaucracies, previewing potentially problematic episodes of entertainment programs, often altering program content before it reached the airwaves. Other advocacy groups employed strategic campaigns with advertisers and affiliates to influence the airing of certain episodes of popular shows or to make certain that some characters certain segments of society might find objectionable remained scripted in prime time.

The networks opted for a policy of balance, believing that co-option was superior to confrontation and that muting criticism in advance would have a positive impact on the networks' image and the bottom line. Yet, *New York Times* television critic Jack Gould framed the problem of artistic accountability in the early days of the ascendancy of advocacy groups: Such agreements hold "latent dangers for the well-being of television as a whole. An outside group not professionally engaged in theatre production has succeeded in imposing its will with respect to naming of fictional characters, altering the importance of a leading characterization and in other particulars changing the story line" (Montgomery 1989, 21). For the artist, network attempts to "balance" competing advocacy-group interests had come close to recreating the patronage system, albeit a far more sophisticated one.

The struggle over censorship, which some label as disagreement over taste, becomes even more acute when governmental sponsorship is at stake. Some argue that because tax dollars are extracted from all, the programs they fund should be acceptable to all. Federal support for programs such as the National Endowment for the Arts (NEA) has been repeatedly questioned in Congress for the last decade, the latest in a series of congressional initiatives. Conservatives objected to funding artists such as photographer Robert Mapplethorpe, whose blend of homoerotic photos and traditional Judeo-Christian symbols offended many. Eventually, the criticism was a factor in the resignation of one of the NEA's directors, Robert Frohnmayer.

The government also censors in other ways. On multiple occasions Infinity Broadcasting has been fined several hundred thousand dollars for disc jockey Howard Stern's on-air profanity and offensive racial slurs. Stern protested that the FCC's action amounted to an enforcement of political correctness, and his supporters point to Stern's show being dropped by Clear Channel in the spring of 2004 as proof that he was being censored. But those who supported the FCC's action noted that Stern most often castigated disadvantaged people and groups. In early 2004, the FCC began another series of fines for indecency, and Congress was asked to raise the fine for a single count of indecency from $27,500 to $275,000. Because of the potential liability for crippling fines, producers of live programming such as the Grammy awards and the Oscars were forced to put a delay on the broadcast to bleep out indecent language or nudity. As this book is going to press, Stern has been forced off the air by a number of stations, in partial response to the Janet Jackson episode in 2004.

COP TV: ENTERTAINMENT, INFOTAINMENT OR NEWS?

In his ingenious and award-winning satirical film, *Network,* the late writer-director Paddy Chayefsky envisioned a time when the lines would be blurred between entertainment and news, rendering them indistinguishable. By the late 1980s, television was proving him right. However, Chayefsky was wrong in one detail. News did begin to take on the look of entertainment as he predicted it would; however, he did not predict that entertainment would also begin to look increasingly like news. Consider these television shows: *America's Most Wanted,* reenactments of crimes with photos or line drawings of the suspects, in which the audience is encouraged to help by calling in tips for police; *Unsolved Mysteries,* with its focus on the criminal and the paranormal; *Inside Edition,* a voyeuristic look at stories dubbed "too hot to handle" for traditional network news; and others of the same breed, including *A Current Affair, Hard Copy, COPS* and *Rescue 911.*

In what genre do these shows belong? When *America's Most Wanted* follows a bounty hunter on an illegal trip into Mexico to bring home a nationally known fugitive, as it did in the summer of 2003, is the resulting program news or entertainment? When it turns out that the trip to Mexico was illegal under that country's laws, was the media culpable for the act in any way? Which set of standards of truth should the producer of that show (and others like it) operate under—the artistic license of entertainment or the more rigorous truth standard of news?

Currently, dozens of such pseudo-news shows are in production simultaneously. From arrests to court trials to public confrontations, very little escapes our fascination. Dubbed "infotainment" by critics, these shows are hot with television programming executives and audiences alike. Such programming provides relief from re-runs of situation comedies and the sameness of game shows and draws large ratings. When produced by syndicators, the shows are prepackaged with ads embedded in them, making them attractive to station owners.

Much attention was focused on the syndicated talk-show genre in the late 1990s when one guest on the *Jenny Jones Show* later murdered another guest when it was revealed on the air that the victim (a male) had a crush on the perpetrator (also a male). The revelation came as a total surprise to the show guest, who admitted to committing the murder. As a condition of being on the show, he had been told that he would be meeting a secret admirer, and was even told that person could be male or female, but he was unprepared for the embarrassment he allegedly felt when it turned out to be a same-sex crush. The family of the victim sued the show for its part in the murder. After a highly publicized trial, the television show won in court, but public opinion was clearly divided on the show's culpability.

Voyeurism can take many forms. A teenaged girl became a national celebrity when she put her life on the Web for all to view from a camera mounted on a computer in her bedroom that she called "Jennicam." A man in Dallas changed his legal name to "dotcomguy" and let the nation watch as he moved into a vacant house in 2000 with only a computer and lived an online life for 365 days before emerging in early 2001. Ironically, in his exit interviews, he refused to reveal his real name, claiming that he wanted to retain his privacy.

The blending of facts and entertainment is not restricted to the small screen. Films such as *The Alamo, Nixon, Hoffa,* and *Thirteen Days* reflect a particular artistic vision based on fact. *Hoffa* director Danny DeVito sought to make an entertaining film of the major facts of the controversial missing labor leader's life, but took symbolic liberties with many events and people. DeVito told the *Today* show audience in early 1993 that what he sought was entertainment—"not sitting down and reading a book."

Though these films and reality-based television shows differ in format and content, they are alike in invoking the license allowed entertainment programming while retaining the authority of fact—a risky combination. By blending information and entertainment into an internally coherent package, the possibility for abuse of an unsuspecting audience exists. To understand how this can happen, we must look to the mass-communication theory of "uses and gratifications." Phrased simply, the theory says audience members will use the media to gratify certain wants and needs. People bring something to the message, and what they bring affects what they take away.

For example, seeking news and information is a common use of the media, with an expected gratification of getting information necessary for citizenship. Entertainment is another common media use, with its own expected gratification. Infotainment, in keeping the look of news yet airing the content of lowbrow entertainment, may be produced to entertain but often has had the unintended "use" of informing. The problem arises when the information such entertainment programming provides about important institutions in U.S. culture, such as the court system or medical practice, or important political figures such as Malcolm X, is fundamentally flawed.

This confounding of unexpected and unintended uses and gratifications is important. *New York Times* columnist A. M. Rosenthal (1989) compared airing these tabloid television shows to buying news programming "off the shelf." The stations airing these programs should add the disclaimer, "We did not put this stuff in the bottle, whatever it is," Rosenthal added.

With a look of authority (an anchor's desk, a courtroom, a police precinct) and the hype of their importance (e.g., "200 lives saved so far!"), these cop-based reality shows appear to be useful for acquiring information, thus gratifying the human need to know. However, by invoking their license as entertainment, such shows are free to bypass accuracy, fairness, balance and other standards normally associated with news and to focus on more sensational elements to gather larger ratings.

REALITY TELEVISION: OXYMORON, PROFIT CENTER, AND USING THE AUDIENCE

They eat cow's lips, let their families pick their mates, and routinely lie about their financial and physical assets. It's all part of the reality television craze that made strong inroads into prime-time entertainment programming in the new millennium. Most media critics suggest the craze began with the wildly successful *Survivor* series, which ran first as a summer replacement show and garnered ratings that impressed network executives. Since television entertainment is nothing if not imitative and reactive, *Survivor* quickly spawned other reality shows, among them *Amazing Race, Danger Island, Road Rules* (which actually preceded *Survivor* on MTV), *The Osbornes, The Real World, Fear Factor* and *American Idol*, again borrowed from the British *Pop Idol*.

Why the rush to reality programming? Ratings and money. During the 1980s and 1990s, traditional network programming lost audience share to cable television and the Internet. At their height, the original three American networks, ABC, CBS and NBC, could count on attracting approximately 90 percent of American homes with televisions on any given evening; the rest tuned in a few fledgling independents playing mostly reruns. Today, the audience for what is now five broadcast networks with affiliate stations has plunged to about half of all households, with the number slipping every season. Compounding the problem, those who continued to watch the traditional networks were an older demographic not popular with advertisers.

Reality television was the first programming genre to pull viewers away from cable and computers and back to the networks. Not only did reality shows draw viewers, but the audience they drew centered on 18- to 49-year-olds, including young men. The result was a ratings bonanza in the preferred demographic, a very potent inducement to produce more reality programming.

Reality programming was not only popular with viewers, but cheap to produce. There was little need to pay writers, since scripts as such weren't generally part of the shows, and the actors who populated them worked for scale or less. Unlike shows such as *Friends, ER* and others where the popularity of the show caused cast members' salaries to skyrocket, salaries never became an issue for producers of reality programming. Compared to most entertainment shows, including evening news magazines, reality programming costs less to produce and provided bigger, and more demographically desirable, audiences.

Reality shows even added to American slang. Getting "voted off the island" became a catch phrase for everyone from politicians to news journalists. "You're fired" entered the American vernacular after the popular show *The Apprentice* starring Donald Trump. However, making money is not considered morally culpable. Neither is popularity. So, if there is an ethical angle to reality shows, what might it be?

History provides a partial answer. The new century version of reality was really a second pass at the genre. The first attempt at reality television took place in the 1950s with quiz shows such as *21* and *The $64,000 Question.* These shows were enormously popular and, as it turned out, could be rigged. Popular contestants were given the answers to general-knowledge questions beforehand; what the audience saw was a scripted contest with the winner predetermined. Winners came back from week to week to continue the game, and some gained a national following. Not surprisingly, the predetermined winner was the one the various shows' creators believed would sustain the ratings or increase them. The quiz show scandals, as they are referred to in media history, were followed by congressional hearings and even some legislation (for more information on this phenomenon, see the Web site for this text).

The new reality shows suffered from some of the same problems. When it was discovered that those who advanced on one or more popular reality shows had actually been determined in advance, it became national news. Soon after, audiences learned that participants in the various reality shows were not always novices to the medium but were often recruited from ranks of fledgling actors. Furthermore, the notion of spontaneity, crucial to getting the audience to believe the premise of the reality show, was false. The producers of shows such as *Survivor, Joe Millionaire* and the like most often shot hundreds of hours of video only to edit it into a few hours, confounding the entire concept of viewers "seeing" events as they occurred.

Some reality shows were based on legally questionable premises, such as the series that proposed to capture men hiring prostitutes—the reality of "johns"—or cop shows that allowed media to capture arrests inside homes only to be successfully sued for invasion of privacy later. Others were based on ethically questionable premises, such as the lies told to the female cast of *Joe Millionaire.* In the final installment, the truth was revealed and Joe Millionaire didn't get the girl, a conclusion with multiple interpretations depending on one's point of view.

While some shows, such as *America's Most Wanted,* claimed a purpose more noble than ratings, others seemed notable for their complete lack of a moral compass. *Temptation Island* put couples and relationships in physical and emotional jeopardy for the entertainment of the audience, who became much more like voyeurs than traditional viewers as they watched to see which relationships would end. And then there was the train wreck of former stripper Anna Nicole Smith, whose real-life 16-year-old son refused to appear on her show (modeled after *The Osbornes,* perhaps television's most dysfunctional family of all time) because he was so ashamed of his mother.

But, still, America watched.

Reality television raises an important ethical question: what constitutes reality? As you'll remember from Chapter I, definitions of truth and the relationship between truth and reality have changed throughout the millennia. Reality television is a lot like the computer-generated matrix in the film *The Matrix.* Reality shows used participants for other purposes, and along the way, a lot of people in the matrix world of reality TV were entertained.

The Matrix illustrates how difficult truth and authenticity are to come by. Reality isn't always what we see, and that insight is important, not only because it has philosophical roots but also because it encourages critical thinking.

The early part of this century has been a scary time, and watching Joe Millionaire bungle his relationships is lot easier than taking the chance of going out on a first date. However, that scary first date has the chance of turning into something wonderful or awful—neither outcome one that Joe Millionaire had to face. Truth in relationships matters because it's how people form connections. Reality television was people, inside a box, having a planned and edited experience. That planning wasn't about truth. It wasn't even particularly personal. Just like in the matrix world, it was a code.

The promise of television is found in the Greek roots of its name—"to see from afar." Falling short of the promise of the medium is an ethical issue, one that surfaces again and again as each entertainment craze hits the small screen.

As the reality television craze gathered momentum, a scripted program, *The West Wing,* about a fictional president in a fictional White House, gained critical and popular approval while dealing with political questions closely resembling those of the real world. During this time, *The West Wing* was the only television programming (news included) to raise the issue of what constitutes a "just war" simultaneously with America's war against Iraq. *The West Wing* took on social justice, lying to Congress, racism, professional ethics and the trade-offs and the compromises that real public policy requires. During this same time, some opinion polls showed that many Americans would rather have had the fictional President Bartlett sitting in the White House.

In the process of entertaining us, *The West Wing* also helped us understand ourselves. It let us "see from afar" some of the difficulties of governing in a democracy, and in doing so fulfilled the promise of art in general and television as an artistic medium. Philosophers would suggest that reality television at the height of its popularity threatened to drive out the opportunity for such higher quality programming. In fact, the final episode of *Joe Millionaire* trounced *The West Wing* in the ratings, even though the latter show had garnered multiple Emmy awards for its scripts and its cast.

The shortsighted view of using cheaply produced reality programming to garner huge ratings will have consequences for years to come. In the financial world of network television, quality shows such as *ER* and *The West Wing* are quite expensive to produce and often take time to find an audience sufficient to sustain these shows. What the producers hope for is a chance to air enough episodes—typically 60 or more—to make it to the lucrative syndication market, where they live on for years and produce a sizable return on the initial investment.

By eating up entire chunks of the network schedule, reality television pushed many quality shows into an early retirement and kept many more out of production. The result will be fewer quality programs in syndication for years to come and, worse than that, fewer producers of quality shows able to get their product an initial airing in the reality-laden schedules of the major networks. The light-viewing months of the summer were once a time when networks took some chances on genre-defining shows to see if they could find an audience. Now that season is given over to reality television that turns immediate profits with no regard for the future.

AESTHETICS IS AN ATTITUDE

Artists see the world differently. While most people perceive only what is needful for a particular purpose, the artist works with what some philosophers call an "enriched perceptual experience." This aesthetic attitude is one that values close and complete concentration of all the senses. An aesthetic attitude is a frankly sensual one, and one that summons both emotion and logic to a particular end.

For example, the theatre audience knows that Eugene O'Neill's plays are "merely" drama. But they also provide us with an intense examination of the role of family in human society—an experience that is both real and personal to every audience member. Such intense examination is what gives the plays their power to move.

We believe that the makers of mediated messages, whether they are the executive producers of a television sitcom or the designers of a newspaper page, share this aesthetic impetus. These mass communicators are much like architects. An architect can design a perfectly serviceable building, one that withstands the elements and may be used for particular purposes. But great buildings—St. Paul's Cathedral in London or Jefferson's home at Monticello—do more. They are tributes to the human intellect's capacity to harmoniously harness form and function.

In fact, philosophers have argued that what separates the commonplace from the excellent is the addition of an aesthetic quality to what would otherwise be a routine, serviceable work. These qualities of excellence have been described as:

- An appreciation of the function realized in the product.
- An appreciation of the resulting quality or form.
- An appreciation of the technique or skill in the performance.

These three characteristics of aesthetic excellence characterize excellence in mass communication as well.

Take the newspaper weather page. Before *USA Today* literally recalibrated the standard, weather pages were generally restricted to the upper right hand quadrant of the second page of a newspaper section. They were printed in black and white, in columns of tiny type. Newspaper editors believed that most people weren't interested in the weather—unless it was weird—and designed their pages accordingly.

USA Today editors, on the other hand, understood that their readers agreed with the observations of political columnist Molly Ivans: when people aren't talking about football, they talk about the weather. The editors devoted more space to it and printed it in color. They added more information in a more legible style and form. In short, they gave newspaper weather information an aesthetic quality. While much about *USA Today* has been criticized, its excellent weather page has been copied.

Although mass-communication professionals are infrequently accused of being artists, we believe they intuitively accept an aesthetic standard as a component of professional excellence. As philosopher G. E. Moore (1903, quote at p. 83) noted in *Principia Ethica:*

Let us imagine one world exceedingly beautiful. Image it as beautiful as you can; put into it whatever on this earth you most admire: mountains, rivers, the sea, suns and sunsets, stars and moon. Imagine these all combined in the most exquisite proportion so that no one thing jars against another, but each contributes to increase the beauty of the whole. And then imagine the ugliest world you can possibly conceive. Imagine it just one heap of filth, containing everything that is most disgusting to you for whatever reason, and the whole, as far as may be, without one redeeming factor. . . . Supposing (all) that quite apart from the contemplation of human beings; still it is irrational to hold that it is better that the ugly world exist than the one which is beautiful.

Substitute film, compact disc, poem, news story, photograph or advertising copy for Moore's word "world" and we believe that you will continue to intuitively agree with the statement. While we may disagree on what specifically constitutes beauty in form and content, the aesthetic standard of excellence still applies.

Philosopher John Dewey noted, "Aesthetic experience is a manifestation, a record and celebration of the life of a civilization, a means of promoting its development, and is also the ultimate judgment upon the quality of a civilization." Perhaps the most important positive effect is the media's ability to pull people away from the routine of everyday life and provide an outlet for escape. In an interview on the PBS series *The Promise of Television,* commentator Bill Moyers (1988) said:

The root word of television is vision from afar, and that's its chief value. It has brought me in my stationary moments visions of ideas and dreams and imaginations and geography that I would never personally experience. So, it has put me in touch with the larger world. Television can be a force for dignifying life, not debasing it.

Though Moyers's comments were made specifically about television, the same argument can be made for a good book, a favorite magazine, music or a film. And whether the media are a force for dignifying humanity or debasing it is largely in the hands of those who own it and work in it.

Suggested Readings

CALVERT, CLAY. 2000. *Voyeur nation: Media, privacy and peering in modern culture.* Boulder, CO: Westview Press.

LIBERTY, ROBERT M., JOYCE N. SPARKING, and EMILY S. DAVIDSON. 1982. *The early window: Effects of television on children and youth.* New York: Paragon Press.

MEDVED, MICHAEL. 1992. *Hollywood vs. America.* New York: HarperCollins Publishers.

MONTGOMERY, KATHRYN C. 1989. *Target: Prime time. Advocacy groups and the struggle over entertainment television.* New York: Oxford University Press.

POSTMAN, NEIL. 1986. *Amusing ourselves to death: Public discourse in the age of television.* New York: Penguin Books.

Cases on the Web

"How to remember Malcolm X" by Dennis Lancaster
"Beavis and Butthead: The case for standards in entertainment" by Philip Patterson
"Joe Klein and the authorship of *Primary Colors*" by Lee Wilkins
" 'Bamboozled:' Truth (or prophesy) in satire" by Lee Wilkins

CHAPTER XI CASES

CASE XI-A
Truth in Filmmaking: Removing the Ugliness from *A Beautiful Mind*
PHILIP PATTERSON
Oklahoma Christian University

In 1950, at the age of 22, mathematician John Forbes Nash Jr. revolutionized game theory. Since the 1920s, game theorists had attempted to explain how "players," whether friends in a poker game, nations in a strategic alliance or animals in the evolutionary cycle, make choices to contribute to an optimal result. Nash improved game theory to predict the behavior of multiple rational players in games when they hold complete knowledge of the other players' preferences and abilities.

Nash's theory of the "equilibrium point" in game theory has been described as the economics equivalent of Newton's theory of gravitation or Darwin's theory of natural selection—not only revolutionary but also so simple and necessary as to be inevitable in its discovery (Nasar 1998, 98). Today, its uses range from economics to biology to international diplomacy. It was most recently used in creating the bidding format for the successful $7 billion auction of the electronic spectrum by the U.S. government in 1994 to cooperating and competing communications conglomerates after the ill-conceived auctions of two other nations had failed.

More than 40 years later, Nash's contribution would be recognized by the Royal Swedish Academy of Sciences with the 1994 Nobel Prize in Economics. But the most interesting part of this story is the fact that Nash, hailed by a cover story in *Forbes* magazine in 1958 as one of the most brilliant mathematicians in the nation, had spent most of the ensuing years in the deep clutches of schizophrenia. Furthermore, against all odds and after decades of cruel and unenlightened medical treatment, he had experienced a spontaneous, if tenuous, recovery. A Hollywood movie was inevitable.

The film, *A Beautiful Mind,* starred Russell Crowe as Nash and Jennifer Connelly (who won an Oscar) as his wife, Alicia. It was directed by Ron Howard. The film heralded the life of the brash young genius from Bluefield, West Virginia, who changed economic theory forever after taking a single undergraduate class in economics from Princeton. After following Nash from his college years to his appointment to the mathematics faculty at MIT, the movie depicts his quick downward spiral into schizophrenia in a series of scenes where he interacts with an imaginary government agent. The agent instructs him to look for codes and sequences embedded by America's enemies in ordinary newspapers and magazines.

Nash's colleagues report a similar story. According to his biographer, his first case of erratic behavior seems to have come when he laid a *New York Times* on the table and told his colleagues that the story in the upper lefthand corner had a coded message in it from alien beings that only he could decipher. Within months, he had been taken out of the classroom, been forcibly hospitalized in a mental institution and had angrily denounced his professorship at MIT.

A Beautiful Mind chronicles his descent into mental illness, his tortured marriage, his problems at MIT and his eventual partial recovery from schizophrenia. It ends with the 66-year-old Nash accepting his Nobel Prize in Stockholm.

Left out of the script, however, are several of the most troubling details of Nash's life that were included in detail in *A Beautiful Mind,* the book by Sylvia Nasar (1998) that was the basis of the movie. While the film was vivid in its depiction of Nash as a schizophrenic, a malady suffered by approximately 1 percent of the population, it was silent about his arrest on a complaint of indecent exposure and his fathering of a child out of wedlock.

In August 1954, Nash was working during the summer for RAND, a government contractor, when he was apprehended in a police "sting" operation aimed at stopping homosexual activities in public bathrooms near the Santa Monica beaches. Caught in the grip of Cold War fears that homosexuals (as his employers now assumed Nash to be) were more susceptible to blackmail by America's enemies, RAND had no choice but to let Nash go. Nash never expressed embarrassment to his employers, explaining to them that his 2 A.M. walk in Palisades Park had been part of an "experiment." He further produced a photo of a woman and boy, saying that she was the woman he was to marry and the boy was their son.

That much was true.

As a young professor at MIT, Nash had met a nurse named Eleanor Stier while in the hospital for a procedure to remove varicose veins. At 29, Stier was five years older than Nash and considerably less educated. Her accent and grammar revealed her hardscrabble upbringing in Jamaica Plain, a lower-class, blue-collar portion of Boston. In her book, Nasar compares their differences to those of Professor Higgins and Eliza Dolittle of *My Fair Lady.* Stier became pregnant in November 1953. Nash claimed to be pleased with the prospect of being a father. But by the time the baby arrived in June 1954—three months before Nash's arrest when he showed the baby's picture—he had made it clear that he was not interested in marrying someone not his intellectual equal.

Nor did Nash allow his name to be put on the baby's birth certificate. Ironically, years later Nash would suggest to his grown son at age 44 that he should change his name to Nash. John David Stier refused.

Although Nash visited the baby frequently, he never helped financially, and eventually Eleanor was forced to put John David in foster care. Even then, the affair between Nash and Eleanor continued, with surreal visits to whatever foster home or orphanage John David was in on Sundays.

During this period in their relationship, Nash had an affair with an MIT undergraduate, Alicia Esther Larde, who eventually became his wife. Eleanor and Alicia's chance meeting at Nash's apartment signaled the end of his relationship with the mother of his illegitimate son. Nash chose the beautiful, young and intelligent Alicia over Eleanor, a move his biographer called "a part of Nash's genius to choose a woman who would prove so essential to his survival" (Nasar, p. 199), a sort of game theory move with real-life consequences.

The frankness of the script of *A Beautiful Mind* about the mental illness of John Forbes Nash Jr. is matched by the paucity of information about the arrest, the illegitimate son and the complicated relationships that could have made the subject even more complex to the discriminating viewer.

Micro Issues

1. Media must discriminate in presenting facts. The process is called editing. What do you think was the motive of the filmmaker in "editing" the facts of Nash's arrest and fatherhood from the film?
2. In what way would scenes recounting the arrest of Nash and his fathering of John Stier have changed the movie *A Beautiful Mind*?
3. The 44 pages of source notes for Nasar's book contain no mention of an interview with Nash, although Eleanor, Alicia, John David and many of Nash's colleagues cooperated. Should the movie have been based on a biography in which Nash did not cooperate?

Midrange Issues

1. As a public figure, what privacy rights, if any, does Nash enjoy? How do his rights differ from ordinary individuals, if at all? Does your answer change if Nash is dead when the film is made?
2. Nash enjoyed the spotlight in his chosen field of mathematics and even cultivated his academic celebrity. However, he did not choose to be mentally ill. Does this fact influence the way he should be covered by the media?
3. The film omits any account of Nash's violence toward members of his family or his continuing problems with an adult son (by Alicia) who also suffers from schizophrenia. Do these omissions fall into the category of acceptable editing or do they constitute an attempt by the filmmaker to sanitize the story of anything that would detract from a "feel-good" ending?
4. The type of remission Nash experienced is sometimes called "spontaneous remission" and it is rare. Does its inclusion in the movie create a false impression of the disease as something one "gets over"? Does it create false hope for the families of current victims of schizophrenia?

Macro Issues

1. When a film is based on a "true story," what obligation does the filmmaker have to present a complete portrait?
2. *A Beautiful Mind* is not only the story of a man; it is the story of a disease that might affect more than 2 million people in the United States. About a quarter will die prematurely, most from suicide. Of the rest, most will never experience remission. What obligation does the filmmaker have to society to accurately depict the facts of the disease?
3. In refusing to deal with Nash's arrest, has the filmmaker made any value judgment that homosexuality is somehow a culpable situation while mental illness is not? Justify your answer.

CASE XI-B
Playing Hardball: The Pete Rose–Jim Gray Controversy
BEN SCOTT
The University of Colorado–Boulder

Author's Note: In January 2004, in his second autobiography and subsequent book tour, Pete Rose admitted betting on baseball. In an interview with Barry Horn (2004) of the Dallas Morning News, *Gray recalled the incident below, which resulted in intense scrutiny of his actions by his media peers and death threats against him that were investigated by the FBI.*

"*To this day, I can't tell you why people line up to support Pete," he told Horn. Even though Rose admitted betting on baseball, he and Gray continue to disagree over the events outlined below and whether Rose knew the betting questions were coming in the live interview. Rose has acknowledged that his answers to the questions were lies.*

Shortly before game two of the 1999 World Series, the All-Century baseball team was introduced to a sellout crowd in Atlanta and a nationwide television audience. Pete Rose received the longest ovation. But unlike his fellow honorees, most of whom were in the Baseball Hall of Fame, Pete Rose was not—he'd been banished from Major League Baseball for life for gambling on baseball while he was the manager of the Cincinnati Reds.

Known as "Charlie Hustle" during his lengthy major league career, Rose collected more base hits than any player in history. In the decade since his banishment by Bart Giamatti, the former Ivy League university president turned commissioner of baseball, fans on both sides have debated his banishment. Rose has always adamantly denied that he bet on baseball. The appearance at the World Series game was Rose's first appearance at a baseball game in more than 10 years.

After the on-field ceremony, Jim Gray, an Emmy Award–winning reporter for NBC, caught up with Rose and asked him for an interview before the live television audience. But instead of lauding Rose and welcoming him back to the game, Gray immediately grilled the legend about his refusal to admit any guilt regarding the gambling allegations.

Gray had earned acclaim for confronting Mike Tyson about his actions immediately after a 1997 fight in which Tyson bit off a chunk of his opponent's ear. He has a reputation for standing up to star athletes and asking the tough questions.

"Are you willing to show contrition, admit that you bet on baseball and make some sort of apology?" Gray asked Rose.

"Not at all," Rose replied. "I'm not going to admit something that didn't happen."

Gray, who had interviewed Rose more than 50 times in the past, didn't let the subject drop. He continued to badger Rose, stating that the evidence against him was overwhelming and added, "Some people say you are your own worst enemy."

Finally, Rose said, "Jim, I'm surprised you're bombarding me like this on such a festive occasion."

NBC switchboards across the country were immediately deluged with calls complaining about Gray's interview, including 2 hours nonstop in Cincinnati, where Rose had played and coached. The majority of the callers felt that Rose had paid the price for his past troubles and should have been allowed to enjoy his moment of recognition as one of the game's greatest.

New York Yankee outfielder Darryl Strawberry, a player in the World Series game and a man who was no stranger to bad press and bad choices, said, "It was a night of celebration for Pete Rose. Every player who has ever played cares about Pete Rose. It was embarrassing."

Yankee manager Joe Tore agreed. "For some reason, we've lost sight of the word 'respect.' We deal too much in shock value."

Yankee players decided to boycott Gray for the remainder of the Series. When Yankee outfielder Chad Curtis hit a game-winning home run in the next game, he made his feelings about Gray evident in a live postgame interview. "Because of what happened with Pete, we decided not to say anything," Curtis told a live audience, leaving Gray to shout questions after him as he walked away. "It's not a personal thing between me and Jim Gray," Curtis said later. "It's a thing the team decided."

NBC was forced to move another reporter into Gray's slot for the remainder of the Series. Despite the animosity of the fans and players, NBC still supported Gray and his interview. Dick Ebersol, chairman of NBC Sports, called Gray "the best sports reporter of his generation."

Despite the public sentiment, Gray refused to apologize. "I stand by it and think it was a proper line of questioning," he said. He added that reporters had asked Rose the same questions at a press conference before the ceremony.

In a later interview with *Sports Illustrated,* Gray said he believed the forum for the questions was appropriate. "It was not overdone. Rose has put himself in a position to be pressed like that. Pete knew what was coming. I was trying to give him a window of opportunity to take his case to the public."

The *Boston Globe*'s Bob Ryan criticized Gray, saying, "After two questions he should have realized it was going nowhere, that Rose would cling to the fiction that he did not bet on baseball as manager of the Cincinnati Reds" (Ryan 1999). Bob Raissman (1999) of the *New York Daily News* wrote, "It was just another case of a guy on TV, who is supposed to supplement the moment, trying to make himself bigger than the game."

More than 50 sports editorials were written nationwide on the controversy, and the reaction to Gray's conduct was evenly split among his print peers.

Micro Issues

1. Given the manner and context of the Rose interview, was Jim Gray out of line?
2. Does Rose's celebrity status have an impact on how much latitude a reporter like Gray has in the questioning?
3. Given what Gray knew would be Rose's response, was the interview necessary?
4. Should Gray have apologized? Justify your answer.

Midrange Issues

1. Was NBC correct in standing behind its reporter. If not, why? If so, then how can the network justify moving Gray out of the Yankees' dugout after the player boycott?

2. Did Gray do his employer a disservice by making himself less useful during the several games left in the Series?
3. Critique the quote by Ryan. At what point should a journalist quit trying to get an answer from a reluctant interviewee? How is the standard different for public figures, if at all? For elected officials?

Macro Issues

1. Sports reporters need athletes, and athletes, to maximize their earnings potential, need coverage. Given this symbiotic relationship, is objectivity possible? Desirable?
2. Is the public's reaction a factor in determining whether a journalistic action was ethical? Are the reactions of one's professional peers, as represented by Ryan and Raissman, a factor in determining if a journalistic action was ethical? Justify your response, and if you answer no, supply a list of stakeholders whose reactions should be considered when judging a professional action.

CASE XI-C
Hate Radio: The Outer Limits of Tasteful Broadcasting
BRIAN SIMMONS
Cascade College

Trevor Van Lansing has what some would call the greatest job in the world. He is employed by KRFP-AM, an all-talk-format radio station in a large city in the West. His program airs weekdays from 3:00 P.M. to 7:00 P.M., and he is currently rated number one in his afternoon drive-time slot. Van Lansing is, quite simply, the most popular radio personality in the market. He is also the most controversial.

Each afternoon Van Lansing introduces a general topic for discussion and then fields calls from listeners about the topic. However, Lansing's topics (and the calls from his listeners) revolve around a recurring theme: the world as viewed by a Caucasian, Anglo-Saxon Protestant who also happens to be vocal, uncompromising and close-minded.

A sampling of his recent programs typifies his show. On Monday, Van Lansing discusses a woman in a small Indiana town who quits her job in a convenience store to go on welfare because there is more money to be made on the federal dole than in the private sector. Says Van Lansing, "All these irresponsible whores are the same. They get knocked up by some construction worker, then expect the taxpayers to pay for them to sit around the house all day and watch Oprah Winfrey."

Callers flood the airwaves with equally combative remarks in support of and opposition to Van Lansing's comments. On Tuesday, the topic of racial discrimination (always a Van Lansing favorite) comes up. According to Van Lansing, "Those Africans expect us Americans to make up for two hundred years of past mistakes. Forget it. It can't be done. If they are so keen on America, let them compete against Caucasians on an equal basis without the 'civil rights crutch.'"

When one African-American caller challenges Van Lansing's thinking, the host responds, "Why don't you tell your buddies to work for what they get like us Caucasians? All you do anyway is steal from the guys you don't like and then take their women."

Wednesday finds Van Lansing lashing out against education: "The problem with today's schools is that our kinds are exposed to weird thinking. I mean, we tell our kids that homosexuality is okay, that we evolved from a chimp, and that the Ruskies are our friends. It all started when we elected women to school boards and started letting fags into the classroom. It's disgusting."

Thursday features an exchange between Van Lansing and an abortion-rights activist. At one point they are both shouting at the same time, and the airwaves are peppered with obscenities and personal attacks. By comparison, Friday is calm, as only a few irate Jews, women, and Mormons bother to call in.

Critics have called Van Lansing's program offensive, tasteless, rude, racist, obscene and insensitive. Supporters refer to the program as enlightening, refreshing, educational and provocative. The only thing everyone can agree on is that the show is a bona fide moneymaker. Van Lansing's general manager notes that the station's ratings jumped radically when he was hired, and that advertising revenues have tripled.

In fact, Van Lansing's popularity has spawned promotional appearances, T-shirts, bumper stickers and other paraphernalia, all designed to hawk the station. "Sure, Trevor is controversial, but in this business that's good," says KRFP's general manager.

"Van Lansing is so good that he will make more money this year than the president of the United States. Besides, it's just a gimmick."

Does Van Lansing see a problem with the content and style of his program? "Look," he says, "radio is a business. You have to give the audience what they want. All I do is give them what they want. If they wanted a kinder, gentler attitude, I would give it to them." He continues, "Don't get mad at me. Thank God we live in a country where guys like me can express an opinion. The people who listen to me like to hear it straight sometimes, and that's what the First Amendment is about, right?"

Finally, Van Lansing points out that if people are really offended by him, they can always turn the dial. "I don't force these people to listen," he pleads. "If they don't like it, let them go somewhere else."

Others disagree. The National Coalition for the Understanding of Alternative Lifestyles, a gay- and lesbian-rights group, calls Van Lansing's show "reprehensible." "Trevor Van Lansing is hiding behind the First Amendment. What he says on the air isn't speech; it's hate, pure and simple," says the group's director. "His program goes well beyond what our founders intended."

Adds a representative of the National Organization for Women, "Van Lansing is perpetuating several dangerous stereotypes that are destructive, sick and offensive. Entertainment must have some boundaries."

Micro Issues

1. Would you be offended by Van Lansing's program? If so, why?
2. Would Van Lansing's program be less offensive if the station aired another talk show immediately after his that featured a host holding opposite views?
3. How are the lyrics of rapper Eminem like or unlike Van Lansing's rants? Is an artist subject to different restrictions?

Midrange Issues

1. Who should accept responsibility for monitoring this type of program? Van Lansing? The radio station, KRFP? The FCC? The courts? The audience?
2. What, if any, are the differences between Van Lansing's *legal* right to do what he does and the *ethical* implications of what he does?
3. Legal scholar Mari Matsuda (1989) has called for a narrow legal restriction of racist speech. She notes, "The places where the law does not go to redress harm have tended to be the places where women, children, people of color, and poor people live" (Matsuda 1989, 11). She argues that a content-based restriction of racist speech is more protective of civil liberties than other tests that have been traditionally applied. Could such an argument be applied to entertainment programming?

4. In the current American media landscape, talk radio is supposedly the stronghold of the right while the majority of major daily newspapers are supposedly controlled by the left. Does the evidence validate this widely-held assumption? Is democracy well-served by this arrangement of entire media systems leaning to one side of the political spectrum?

Macro Issues

1. Are entertainers relieved of ethical responsibilities if they are "just giving the audience what they want"? Do Van Lansing's high ratings validate his behavior, since many people are obviously in agreement with him?

2. How does Van Lansing's narrow view of the world differ from a television situation comedy that stereotypes blondes as dumb, blue-collar workers as bigoted, etc.?

3. Van Lansing says that it's great that a guy like him can have a radio show. Is tolerance one of the measures of a democracy? If so, are there limits to tolerance, and who draws those lines?

4. Supreme Court Justice William O. Douglas has said, "If we are to have freedom of mind in America, we must produce a generation of men and women who will make tolerance for all ideas a symbol of virtue." How should democratic societies cope with unpopular points of view, particularly as expressed through the mass media?

CASE XI-D
How Much Coverage is Appropriate? The Case of the Highly Paid Athlete
MATT KEENEY
University of Missouri

Randy Moss, one of the highest paid players in the National Football League, has received a great deal of media attention both on and off the field. Moss has had a number of run-ins with authorities, dating back to high school days, and with league officials after he turned professional. In high school, he was arrested and sentenced to 30 days in jail for assaulting a classmate. Florida State University kicked him off the football team for smoking marijuana. In 1999, the NFL fined Moss $35,000 for verbal abuse and squirting an official with a water bottle. A year later, the league fined Moss $55,000 for taunting and other violations.

All this was well known when, on September 24, 2002, Moss was arrested and charged with careless driving and failure to obey a traffic officer.

In an Associated Press account that was widely reprinted, the Minneapolis police department said Moss was cruising around the city in his Lexus when he attempted to make an illegal turn. A traffic officer stepped in front of his car to prevent him from making the turn, and Moss failed to stop. He used his car to push the officer about half a block down the street, eventually tapping the accelerator to make her fall off the car and onto the pavement. Police officers arrested Moss, and he spent the night in jail.

The media reported the incident immediately. Moss, who was in jail, could not be reached for comment. Reporters did attempt to contact the Minnesota Vikings' representative; team representatives also refused to comment. One witness to the incident, quoted on ESPN's Web site, put a positive spin on Moss's actions. "If he had been a madman, he would have just run over her and kept going" (ESPN.com, 9-24-02). However, Moss's version of events had not been told.

Journalists attempted to get a comment from Moss the next day when he was released from jail. A gang of reporters rushed him with cameras, lights and microphones as he opened the door, covering his head with a jacket in an attempt to hide his face. The reporters followed Moss as he attempted to walk away from the police station; no one obtained a significant comment. Moss did not apologize, nor did he admit fault.

Moss's unwillingness to speak to journalists was not out of character. He was well known for his somewhat less than "can-do" attitude. He had been caught bickering with his teammates on the sidelines during games. He had previously told reporters that he did not try on every play of the game. "When I want to play, I'll play," he said.

Footage shot at the jail popped up on many sports programs that evening. At this time, the police said Moss was being formally charged with careless driving and failure to obey a traffic officer, both misdemeanors, far less serious charges than those given in initial news accounts.

After avoiding reporters, Moss agreed to an exclusive interview with ESPN that was aired on the network's SportsCenter show and repurposed as a news article on the network's Web site. In that interview, Moss said the officer confused him with her orders, and he didn't know what to do. "I'm trying to be there, trying to change, trying to change for the best," Moss said.

ESPN did not retract an earlier, incorrect account of alleged impending felony charges against Moss. The interview also noted that police had found a small amount of marijuana in Moss's car. The receiver denied the substance belonged to him. On October 1, 2002, Moss was charged with misdemeanor possession of a controlled substance.

A few months later, on December 12, 2002, Moss appeared in court and pleaded guilty to the two traffic charges. The marijuana charge was dropped as part of a plea agreement. The court ordered Moss to complete 40 hours of community service.

There were far fewer news stories about the disposition of the case than reports of the original arrest. ESPN did report the disposition as a news story and on its Web site.

Micro Issues

1. What makes Moss's story newsworthy?
2. Should his previous "bad acts" have been reported as part of the incident? Why or why not?
3. Was the mob of journalists at the jail an appropriate way to try to get Moss's version of events?

Midrange Issues

1. Do athletes deserve a different level of media attention than other categories of people? Justify your answer.
2. Should ESPN have issued a retraction when it became apparent that its initial report about the severity of the charges was wrong?
3. In these days of the 24/7 news cycle, is it professionally possible to wait for charges to be filed before airing anything about them? What role does competition play in your answer?

Macro Issues

1. Sports pages are among the most widely read of any newspaper section, and among the most watched television programming. How does the popularity of this topic influence news coverage? Is such influence ethically justifiable?
2. Compare this case with the case of Naomi Campbell in this chapter. What are the morally relevant differences?
3. Former NBA All-Star Charles Barkley made headlines when he claimed that parents, not athletes, were supposed to be role models, and that he felt no responsibility as an athlete to be a role model. Is the media culpable in making heroes of athletes who may later prove to be less than model citizens?

CASE XI-E
Schindler's List: **The Role of Memory**
LEE WILKINS
University of Missouri

In 1982 director Steven Spielberg purchased the rights to Australian novelist Thomas Keneally's retelling of the story of the "Schindler Jews," a group of about 1,100 Krakow, Poland, residents who survived the Holocaust because Czech businessman Oskar Schindler was willing to cajole, bribe and bully the Nazis for their lives. Today, Schindler, a Roman Catholic by birth, is known in Israel as a "righteous person"; he is the only Nazi buried in Jerusalem's Mount Zion cemetery.

By 1992 when Spielberg began work on the film, both he and the world had changed. Bosnia was in the midst of "ethnic cleansing," as were nations in Africa and in the Far East, such as Nepal. Some polls indicated that more than half of the U.S. teenagers living in that decade had never heard of the Holocaust; about 23 percent of the U.S. public at the time maintained the gassing of 6 million Jews plus 5 million other "undesirables" in Germany and its occupied territories never happened.

"I think the main reason I wanted to make this film was as an act of remembrance," Spielberg told the film editor of the *Atlanta Journal-Constitution.* "An act of remembrance for the public record. Maybe it won't be seen by gallons of people who see my other movies, but it might be the kind of movie shown one day in high schools. I also wanted to leave this story for my children. I wanted to leave them a legacy of their Jewish culture."

What Americans, as well as Spielberg's children, will see is a 3-hour-and-15-minute examination of the conscience of Oskar Schindler, who entered World War II on the side of the Nazis, intending to make a profit. He hires Jews to work in his enamelware factory because they work for less than slave wages. Initially, he befriends the Nazis and the SS to help expedite his purchase and takeover of the plant. Later, after the Nazis have first ghettoized and then attempted to exterminate the Jewish population of Krakow, Schindler uses his personal charm, his connections and most of his war-amassed wealth to have "his" Jewish workers first labeled as essential to the German war machine and later moved from Germany and into Czechoslovakia for safekeeping. None of the bombs manufactured at Schindler's plant ever exploded.

Spielberg shot the film in black and white on location in Poland. Much of the movie has a documentary feel; cinematography is at eye level. It was often Spielberg himself who focused the handheld camera. Hitler appears only once—in a photograph on someone's desk. And, by centering on Schindler, Spielberg captured the conscience of an uneasy hero.

As Keneally's book indicates, Oskar Schindler was a complex man. He managed to maintain outward friendships with many Nazis whom he despised. He was a sensualist who enjoyed good food, expensive possessions and carnal knowledge of women who were not his wife. Spielberg's film, which was rated

"R," depicted all of this, including scenes of lovemaking that involved full, frontal nudity and more distant shots of concentration camp existence in which Jewish inmates were required to run naked in front of their guards to determine who remained well enough to work and who was sick enough to be murdered.

Perhaps the most disturbing element of the film was Spielberg's portrait of the violence embedded in Hitler's "final solution" and of the banality of evil (Hannah Arendt's phrase used to describe convicted war criminal Adolph Eichmann) that individual human beings can come to represent. That sundered humanity is symbolized by Amon Goeth (played by Ralph Fiennes), the amoral and, some have suggested, sociopathic commandant of the labor camp from which many of the people who worked for Schindler survived. Whether it is the Nazis hunting the Jews who remain in hiding in the Krakow ghetto or Goeth's randomized murder of the men and women who lived in his camp as before-breakfast sport, the violence in the film is devastating not just for its brutality but also for its casualness.

When Spielberg's mother told him making "*Schindler's List* would be good for the Jews," Spielberg responded that "it would be good for all of us."

Critics, who had a difficult time accepting that the same man who directed *Jurassic Park* could also produce *Schindler's List* in the same year, praised the film for its aesthetic qualities and for its retelling of the story of the Holocaust in such a powerful fashion. The film also brought Spielberg multiple Oscars, an award that had eluded him despite his enormous popular success. After the film's release, President Bill Clinton said that every American should see it.

Writing in the *Washington Post,* Rita Kempley saw more than a superficial resemblance between Schindler and Spielberg. "And Schindler, played with élan by [Liam] Neeson, is really a lot like Spielberg himself," she wrote, "a man who manages to use his commercial clout to achieve a moral end."

Micro Issues

1. Should a film like *Schindler's List* receive the same R rating as films such as *Road Trip?*
2. What is the appropriate role of a film critic for films such as *Schindler's List?* Should different standards be used to evaluate this film than some other Spielberg successes, such as *E.T.* or *Jaws?*
3. Would you allow a child under 17 to see this film?

Mid-range Issues

1. Should news accounts focus on events such as the ethnic cleansing in Bosnia with the goal of changing public opinion?
2. Are docudramas that focus on social issues such as spouse abuse or child molestation the appropriate mechanism to engage the public in debate or discussion about such serious questions?
3. Some people have argued that certain historical events, such as the Holocaust or the recent genocide in Rwanda, should never be the subject of entertainment programming because entertainment can never capture the true horror of what has happened. How would you evaluate such an assertion?

Macro Issues

1. Compare the moral development of Oskar Schindler with that of the main characters in a film such as *Gandhi.*

2. John Dewey wrote about "funded memory," by which he meant how a culture remembers and reconstructs its own history. What is the role of entertainment programming in funded memory? What should be the role of news programming in such cultural constructions?

3. Tolstoy argues that good art communicates the feelings of the artist to the masses in such a way that others may experience the same feeling as the artist. How does this film accomplish that purpose?

CASE XI-F
Naomi Campbell: Do Celebrities Have Privacy?
LEE WILKINS
University of Missouri

Supermodel Naomi Campbell is an international celebrity. Campbell was discovered in London's Covent Garden when she was only 15 and soon became one of the best paid and most often photographed supermodels, earning more the $1 million a year. Her worldwide celebrity was helped, in part, because of her physical image; a native of the United Kingdom, Campbell is black. She was often the focus of media coverage in both Britain and the United States and, in the years after her discovery, developed a reputation for being a prima donna—irritable and manipulative. She was dropped by her agency in 1993, although she was later reinstated, and she was once arrested for assaulting her personal assistant. These stories about Campbell were news.

Campbell often sought the media spotlight. And, like many models, among them Britain's Kate Moss, Campbell was rumored to use drugs—specifically cocaine, which depresses the appetite and hence helps with weight control. Campbell publicly denied any drug addiction on multiple occasions, including in 1997 when she had been rushed to a hospital in Gran Canaria following an alleged drug overdose. After that incident, she told Britain's *The Daily Telegraph,* "I didn't take drugs."

Then, in February 2001, London's *Daily Mirror,* one of Britain's most widely read tabloids, published a photograph of Campbell leaving a Narcotics Anonymous meeting in King's Road, Chelsea, a wealthy London neighborhood. The article that appeared with the photograph included details of the meeting she attended.

Campbell sued in British courts—not for libel but for invasion of privacy. The suit was the first brought under laws governing the European Union, which includes in its charter protection of individual privacy under the Human Rights Convention. Britain is a member of the EU. Campbell's attorneys reasoned that the EU statutes, which are more specific about privacy than legal precedent in either Britain or the United States, gave them the best chance of winning the suit.

Speaking later, Campbell said the *Mirror* photograph and articles made her feel as if she had been raped. She characterized the article as "very damaging."

However, things got more complicated when the case actually went to Britain's High Court. During that proceeding, Campbell maintained that she was not a drug addict and denied that she had been receiving therapy for some years. She did admit that she was "notorious for tantrums."

In its ruling in March 2002, the High Court awarded Campbell 3,500 pounds (about $6,000) in damages and ordered that the newspaper pay additional court costs equal to about $110,000 (70,000 pounds). The judge in the case noted that even celebrities were entitled to some privacy. "Although many aspects of the private lives of celebrities and public figures will inevitably enter the public domain, in my judgment it does not follow that even with self-publicists every aspect and detail of their private lives are legitimate quarry for the journalist." The judge noted that Campbell's attendance at the Narcotics Anonymous meeting and the details of her therapy clearly related to her physical and mental health and therefore met the standard of "sensitive personal data."

However, the judge also noted that the public clearly had an interest in knowing that Campbell had been misleading them by her denials of drug addiction. "Clearly *The Mirror* was fully entitled to put the record straight and publish that her denials of drug addiction were deliberately misleading. She might have been thought of and, indeed, she herself seems to be a self-appointed role model to young black women." The judge also noted, "I am satisfied she lied when making denials about her drug addiction."

News organizations in Britain generally treated the ruling as a victory, noting that the small damage award served as much as a rebuke to Campbell than as a punishment to the often invasive tabloids. Campbell, too, seemed to regret many aspects of the suit. She said the case had left her unable to sleep. "I didn't expect it to be the way it's blown up like this. . . . Recovery is something that takes time. You feel that you're getting better in the right direction. I wasn't hiding. But first of all an addict had to admit to themselves that they have a problem before they can admit it to anybody else. That is the first step."

Piers Morgan, editor of the *Mirror,* characterized the judgment as "derisory. . . . This is a case that should never have been brought. It is quite clear that the judge thought we had every right to say she was a drug addict. We have every right to tell the public that she was having treatment. The only thing we couldn't do—and this was what the whole case came down to—was say she was going to Narcotics Anonymous."

Micro Issues

1. If Campbell had admitted her drug addiction when first asked, would it have been ethical to publish the story?
2. Was it appropriate for other media outlets—the mainstream press in both Britain and the United States—to publish the *Mirror* photo and story details once the *Mirror* had published them?
3. Are the details of Campbell's drug treatment ethically distinct from the fact that she is in treatment? Justify your answers in terms of ethical theory.

Midrange Issues

1. How should Campbell's character influence media coverage of her, particularly her private life?
2. Are celebrities morally distinct from other categories of people when it comes to privacy issues? Would you make the same or a different argument for public officials?
3. Is there something more invasive about a photograph of Campbell leaving the meeting than a story that recounted the event? Was a photograph necessary for a journalistic purpose?
4. Should there be different standards for the tabloid press than for more mainstream media? If there are different standards, how do you account for them?

Macro Issues

1. In a commentary that ran after the court decision was announced, British journalist Kim Fletcher noted: "There is more at stake here than the right to write about what famous people do in their own time. The fear is that lawyers will extend the notion of what can be regarded as confidential—conversations between business colleagues, tax discussions—to prevent newspapers gaining and publishing information that may be of greater significance and more in the public interest than a model's drug addiction." Analyze and evaluate this statement based on ethical theory.

2. How do you believe this case would have been resolved in the United States, had Campbell chosen to sue there? Is your analysis based in legal precedent? On ethical theory? Which is more appropriate in privacy cases?

XII

Becoming a Moral Adult

By the end of this chapter you should:

- **know the stages of moral development as described by Piaget and Kohlberg.**
- **understand the ethics of care.**
- **understand the stages of adult moral development.**

INTRODUCTION

Graduation is not the end of the educational process; it is merely a milestone marking the beginning of a new era of learning. If delivered properly, college studies not only equip you for entry into the workforce (or for the adult student perhaps a promotion in the workplace) but also equip you to be a lifelong learner.

The same is true about moral development. There is no "moral graduation," marking you as an upright person capable of making right choices in all of life's personal and professional dilemmas. It is a lifelong process of steps, some of which you have taken, while others lie ahead. Where you are now is a function of both age and experience, but no matter what your circumstances, the person you are now is not the person you will be 10 years from now. In a decade, you will have added insight. Growth may, and probably will, change your decisions. This process is not only inevitable but also desirable.

This chapter is designed to provide you with an overview of some psychological theories of moral development. It attempts to allow you to plot your own development not only in terms of where you are but also in terms of where you would like to be.

BASIC ASSUMPTIONS ABOUT MORAL DEVELOPMENT: THE RIGHTS-BASED TRADITION

People can learn to develop morality just as they can learn to think critically (Clouse 1985). Scholars base this assertion on the following premises.

First, *moral development occurs within the individual.* Real moral development cannot be produced by outside factors, nor can it be produced merely by engaging in moral acts. People develop morally when they are aware of their reasons for acting a certain way.

Second, *moral development parallels intellectual development.* Although the two may proceed at a slightly different pace, there can be little moral development until a person has attained a certain intellectual capacity. For this reason, we exempt children and people of limited mental ability from some laws and societal expectations. While one can be intelligent without being moral, the converse is not as likely.

Third, *moral development occurs in a series of universal, unvarying and hierarchical stages.* Each level builds on the lower levels, and there is no skipping of intermediate stages. Just as a baby crawls before walking and babbles before speaking, a person must pass through the earlier stages of moral development before advancing to the later stages.

Fourth, *moral development comes through conflict.* As moral development theorist Lawrence Kohlberg notes (1973, 13), "A fundamental reason why an individual moves

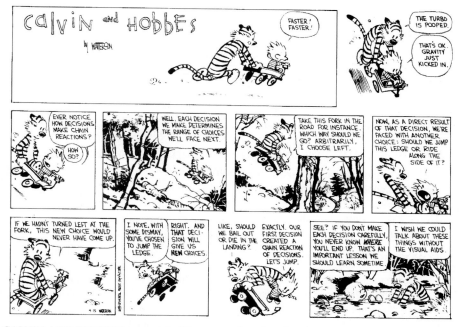

CALVIN AND HOBBES copyright Watterson. Reprinted with permission of Universal Press Syndicate. All rights reserved.

from one stage to the next is because the latter stages solve problems and inconsistencies unsolvable at the present developmental stage." Just as a baby soon learns strategies other than crying to get its needs met, the developing moral being learns more complex behaviors when older, more elementary strategies no longer work.

The two developmental psychologists who are the most cited experts in the field did their work decades and continents apart yet came to remarkably similar conclusions. Jean Piaget conducted his research in Switzerland in the 1930s by watching little boys play marbles, and in the 1960s Lawrence Kohlberg studied Harvard students. Together they have produced many of the most provocative insights in the rights-based tradition. They are often called "stage theorists" for their work in identifying and describing the stages of moral development.

THE WORK OF PIAGET

Swiss psychologist Jean Piaget turned his attention to children's moral development in the 1930s. He watched as boys between the ages of 3 and 12 played marbles, and he later tested his assumptions about their playground behavior in interviews. The box below presents the basics of Piaget's theory.

The children under ages 5 to 7 didn't really play a game of marbles at all. They made up their own rules, varied them by playmate and game, and delighted in exploring the marbles as tactile objects. Their view of the game-playing universe was centered exclusively on what each individual child wanted.

Piaget's Stages of Moral Development

EARLY DEVELOPMENT (before age 2)

- Interest in marbles is purely motor, e.g., put the marbles in your mouth.

FIRST STAGE—egocentrism (years 3–7)

- Children engage in "parallel play"; there is no coherent set of rules accepted by all.
- The moral reasoning is "I do it because it feels right."

SECOND STAGE—heteronomy (years 7–8)

- Children recognize only individual responsibility; obedience is enforced through punishment.
- Each player tries to win.
- Rules are regarded as inviolate, unbreakable, handed down from

outside authority figures, usually older children.
- The children do not understand the reason behind the rules.

THIRD STAGE—autonomy (begins about age 11)

- Children internalize the rules; they understand the reasons behind them.
- They develop an ideal of justice and are able to distinguish between individual and collective responsibility.
- They ensure fair play among children.
- Children can change the rules in responses to a larger set of obligations.
- Authority is internal.
- Children understand universal ethical principles that transcend specific times and situations.

Piaget found that younger boys (ages 7 and 8) played marbles as if the rules had been taught to them by their parents or other authority figures and as if violations of those rules would result in punishment. The boys believed the rules were timeless and that "goodness" came from respecting the rules. Boys in this stage of moral development believed "Right is to obey the will of the adult. Wrong is to have a will of one's own" (Piaget 1965, 193).

Children progressed to the next stage of moral development when the boys began to develop notions of autonomy. As they became more autonomous, they began to understand the reasoning behind the rules, and that the reasons (i.e., fair play and reciprocity) were the foundation of the rules themselves. Children in this stage of moral development understood that the rules did not originate from some outside authority figure but rather received their power from the group consensus.

These children had internalized the rules and the reasons behind them. Understanding the rules allowed the boys to rationally justify violating them. For example, children in this stage of moral development allowed much younger children to place their thumbs inside the marble circles, a clear violation of the rules. But the younger boys' hands were smaller and weaker, and by allowing them a positional advantage, the older ones had—in contemporary language—leveled the playing field. They had ensured fairness when following the rules literally would have made it impossible.

Although Piaget worked with children, it is possible to see that adults often demonstrate these stages of moral development.

Take the videographer whose primary motivation is to obtain a great shot, regardless of the views of those he works with or his story subjects. This journalist operates within an egocentric moral framework that places the primary emphasis on what "I" think, "my" judgment, and what's good for "me."

Beginning journalists, the ones who find themselves concerned with the literal following of codes of ethics, may often be concerned with the heteronomy stage of development. This journalist knows the rules and follows them. She would never accept a freebie or consider running the name of a rape victim. It's against organizational policy, and heteronomous individuals are motivated largely by outside influences.

Just as the boys at the third stage of moral development were more willing to alter the rules to ensure a fair game for all, journalists at the final stage of moral development are more willing to violate professional norms if it results in better journalism. The journalist at this stage of moral development has so internalized and universalized the rules of ethical professional behavior that he or she can violate some of them for sound ethical reasons.

Proceeding with a story that is unpopular, expensive or out of the norm could be considered an example of journalism at the highest level of Piaget's schema. For instance, the Pulitzer Prize–winning series by the *Des Moines Register* regarding the rape, recovery and trial ordeal of a rape victim who volunteered to have her story told is an example of journalism that breaks the mold and goes far beyond the norm of stories of its type. Also indicative of this level of journalism is the painstakingly detailed series of articles written by two enterprising *Detroit Free Press* reporters who read volumes of the federal tax code and found it to be loaded with one-of-a-kind tax loopholes for individuals and businesses with political connections.

However, people seldom remain exclusively in a single stage of moral development. New situations often mean that people, including journalists and their sources, regress temporarily to a previous stage of moral development until enough learning can take place so that the new situation is well understood. But, such regression would not include behaviors that would be considered morally culpable under most circumstances, for example, lying or killing, despite the new context.

THE WORK OF KOHLBERG

Harvard psychologist Lawrence Kohlberg mapped six stages of moral development in his college-student subjects. The accompanying box outlines Kohlberg's stages of moral development, divided into three levels.

Kohlberg developed a lengthy set of interview questions to allow him to establish which stage of moral development individual students had achieved. He asserted that only a handful of people—for example, Socrates, Gandhi, Martin Luther King or Mother Teresa—ever achieved the sixth stage of moral development. Most adults, he believed, spend the greater portion of their lives in the two conventional stages. They are motivated by society's expectations.

Doing right, fulfilling one's duties and abiding by the social contract are the pillars upon which the stages of Kohlberg's work rest. Under Kohlberg's arrangement, justice—and therefore morality—is a function of perception; as you develop, more activities fall under the realm of duty than before. For instance, reciprocity is not even a goal for students in the earliest stage, yet it is an essential characteristic of people in upper stages of moral development. Conversely, acting to avoid punishment is laudable for those in the first stages yet might not be as praiseworthy for someone who is operating on universal ethical principles. The further up Kohlberg's stages students progressed, the more they asserted that moral principles are subject to interpretation by individuals and subject to contextual factors.

Kohlberg's stages are descriptive and not predictive. They do not anticipate how any one individual will develop, but suggest how most will develop. In addition, there is a difference in moral reasoning and moral behavior. They are correlated but not totally overlapping phenomena. Kohlberg focused not on the goodness of moral decisions but on the adequacy of the cognitive structures underlying them.

Kohlberg's formulation has much to recommend it to journalists, concerned as they are with concepts such as free speech, the professional duty to tell the truth and their obligations to the public and the public trust. However, Kohlberg's work was not without its problems. At least two aspects of his research troubled other moral development theorists.

Many scholars have argued that any generalizable theory of moral development should allow people who are not saints or religious leaders to attain the highest stages of moral development. While it has been argued that only saints can be expected to act in a saintly manner most of the time, history is replete with examples of ordinary people taking extraordinary personal or professional risk for some larger ethical principles. Many scholars felt that Kohlberg's conception—unlike Piaget's—was too restrictive.

The Six Moral Stages of Kohlberg

Level 1: Pre-conventional
Stage 1: Heteronomous morality is the display of simple obedience.
Stage 2: Individualism is the emergence of self-interest. Rules are followed only when they are deemed to be in one's self-interest and others are allowed the same freedom. Reciprocity and fairness begin to emerge, but only in a pragmatic way.

Level II: Conventional
Stage 3: Interpersonal conformity is living up to what others expect, given one's role, e.g., "brother," "daughter," "neighbor," etc. "Being good" is important, and treating others as you would have them treat you becomes the norm.
Stage 4: Social systems is the recognition that one must fulfill the duties to which one has agreed. Doing one's duty, respect for authority, and maintaining the social order are all goals in this level. Laws are to be upheld unilaterally except in extreme cases

where they conflict with other fixed social duties.

Level III: Post-conventional
Stage 5: Social contract and individual rights is becoming aware that one is obligated by whatever laws are agreed to by due process. The social contract demands that we uphold the laws even if they are contrary to our best interests because they exist to provide the greatest good for the greatest number. However, some values such as life and liberty stand above any majority opinion.
Stage 6: Universal ethical principles self-selected by each individual guide this person. These principles are to be followed even if laws violate those principles. The principles that guide this individual include the equality of human rights and respect for the dignity of humans as individual beings regardless of race, age, socioeconomic status, or even contribution to society.

Still more troubling was how those students who were tested on Kohlberg's scale performed. In study after study, men consistently scored higher than women on stages of moral development. This gender bias in Kohlberg's work—coupled with other findings from developmental psychology—prompted discussion about a different concept of moral development, founded on notions of community rather than in the rights-based tradition. It is called the ethics of care.

PARALLEL ASSUMPTIONS ABOUT MORAL DEVELOPMENT: THE ETHICS OF CARE

The psychologists who developed the ethics of care disagree with at least two of the fundamental assumptions underlying Piaget and Kohlberg.

First, while moral development occurs within the individual and parallels intellectual development, moral development does not always occur in a series of universal, unvarying and hierarchical stages. Second, moral growth emerges through understanding the concept of community, not merely through conflict.

The rights-based scholars believe that moral development emerges from a proper understanding of the concept "I." Proponents of the ethics of care say that moral development arises from understanding the concept of "we."

Carol Gilligan's (1982) work provides the clearest explanation of the ethics of care. Gilligan studied women who were deciding whether to have abortions. As she listened to them, she learned that they based their ethical choices on relationships. The first thing these women considered was how to maintain a connection. Gilligan argued that the moral adult is the person who sees a connection between the "I" and the "other." The women spoke in a "different voice" about their ethical decision making.

For example, Gilligan presented the women with Kohlberg's classic ethical dilemma: the case of the desperate man and the greedy pharmacist. In this scenario, a man with a terminally ill spouse doesn't have enough money to purchase an expensive and lifesaving drug. When he explains the situation to the pharmacist, the pharmacist refuses to give him the medication.

Under Kohlberg's system, it would be ethically allowable for a man at the highest stages of moral development to develop a rationale for stealing the drug, an act of civil disobedience for a greater good. However, women made this particular choice less often. Instead, they reasoned that the most ethical thing to do was to build a relationship with the pharmacist, to form a community in which the pharmacist viewed him/herself as an active part. In that situation, the women reasoned, the pharmacist ultimately would give the man the drug in order to maintain the connection.

Gilligan proposed that the women's rationale was no more or less ethically sophisticated than that expected under Kohlberg's outline. However, it was different, for it weighed different ethical values. Whether those values emerged as the result of how women are socialized in Western culture (an assertion that has often been made about Gilligan's work) or whether they merely reflected a different kind of thinking still remains the focus of heated academic debate. For our purposes, the origin of the distinction—and whether it is truly gender-linked—is not as important as the content of the thought itself.

Gilligan's notion of moral development is not neatly tied into stages and does not borrow as heavily from the tradition of logic and rights-based inquiry. Her closest theoretical counterpart is probably communitarianism with its emphasis on connection to community and its mandate for social justice.

If one were to carve stages from Gilligan's work, they would resemble:

- First—an ethic of care where the moral responsibility is for care of others before self.
- Second—an acknowledgment of the ethic of rights, including the rights of self to be considered in ethical decision making.
- Third—a movement from concerns about goodness (women are taught to believe that care for others is "good" while men are taught that "taking care of oneself" is good) to concerns about truth. It is at this stage of moral development where commitment to a universal ethical principle begins, with truth at the core of that universal principle.

A complete sense of moral development, Gilligan observed, requires the ability "to [use] two different moral languages, the language of rights that protects separations and the language of responsibilities that sustains connection" (Gilligan 1982, 210).

Contemporary journalists have struggled with the issues of connection. Since much of our profession is based on an understanding of rights as outlined in various legal documents, ethical reasoning for journalists almost always assumes a rights-based approach. This historically well-founded bias, however, has led journalists into some of their more systematic and profound errors in decisions about privacy, attitudes of arrogance toward sources and readers, and an unwillingness to be genuinely accountable to anyone.

News organizations can work to sustain community. If journalism as a profession is to mature ethically, it must see itself as the vehicle to help people become the citizens they can be and to help reconnect and sustain communities that have become increasingly fragmented, often by the very media that should have brought us together.

In 1992, the streets of Los Angeles erupted into deadly riots when a jury acquitted two L.A. police officers in an assault trial, despite videotape evidence that the officers had beat the detainee, Rodney King, into submission. In an essay entitled "Whose Values," written in the wake of the Los Angeles riots following the Rodney King verdict, *Newsweek* author Joe Klein wrote:

> Television brought the nation together in the '50s; there were evenings when all of America seemed glued to the same show—Milton Berle, "I Love Lucy" and yes, "Ozzie and Harriet." But cable television has quite the opposite effect, dividing the audience into demographic slivers. . . . Indeed, if you are a member of any identifiable subgroup—black, Korean, fundamentalist, sports fan, political junkie—it's now possible to be massaged by your very own television and radio stations and to read your own magazines without having to venture out into the American mainstream. The choices are exhilarating, but also alienating. The basic principle is centrifugal: market segmentation targets those qualities that distinguish people from each other rather than emphasizing the things we have in common. It is the developed world's equivalent of the retribalization taking place in Eastern Europe, Africa and Asia. (Klein 1992, 21–22)

If there was one common denominator from the vast variety of projects that claimed to fall under the "civic journalism" umbrella in the late 1990s, it was the fact that almost all of them had as a goal to bring people back together and foster a sense of community using the media as a primary tool in the process. To that end, the movement was a laudable one.

DEVELOPING AS AN ETHICAL PROFESSIONAL

Moral development theory helps to explain the decisions of everyday people. However, for the past three decades, scholars have attempted to apply the understandings of moral development to professionals—among them journalists.

James Rest, a psychology professor at the University of Minnesota, took Kohlberg's schema of moral development and used it to create a paper-and-pencil test to measure moral development among various professions. In the ensuing 30 years, the test, called the Defining Issues Test, has been administered to more than 20,000 professionals, among them doctors, nurses, dentists, accountants, philosophers and theologians, members of the U.S. Coast Guard, surgeons, veterinarians, graduate students, junior high students, prison inmates and others. Those taking the test read four to six scenarios (including the Heinz dilemma used by Kohlberg and described earlier in this chapter). They are then asked to make a decision about what the protagonist should do, and then to rate the factors that influenced that decision. Because the test is based in Kohlberg's understanding of moral development, those who take the test who rely on universal principles and who consider issues of justice score well. In general, most people who take the DIT score in the range of what Kohlberg would have called conventional moral reasoning—stages three and four on the Kohlberg scale.

Recently, scholars (Wilkins and Coleman, in press) have asked journalists to take the DIT and have compared journalists' scores to those of other professionals. Perhaps to the surprise of the general public, journalists do well on the DIT, scoring below only three other professions: philosophers/theologians, medical students and practicing physicians. This finding is significant because the single biggest predictor of a good score on the DIT is education, and journalists as a group have less formal education than the three professions with scores "above" those of journalists as well as several professions, for example orthopedic surgeons, that score lower on the test.

The scenarios on the DIT are not directed at any particular profession but rather try to determine how people think about "average" moral questions. When journalists are presented with scenarios that deal directly with journalism, for example, problems involving the use of hidden cameras or whether to run troubling photographs of children, they score even better. In these tests, journalists often score in the fourth and fifth stage of Kohlberg's moral development schema, indicating not only that professionals are capable of thinking well about these issues but also that when their domain (journalism) is the issue, they are very good ethical thinkers indeed. In studying journalists, scholars have also learned that having a visual image, such as a photograph, of some of the stakeholders in an ethical dilemma elevates ethical reasoning.

Scholars have studied journalists' ethical decision making in other ways. Investigative reporters make moral judgments about the subjects of their stories, even though when they talk about their work they are reluctant to leave the terrain of professional objectivity (Ettema and Glasser, 1998). Journalists who have been sued for invasion of privacy don't often think about the ethical issues their reporting creates, an indirect indication that solid ethical thinking may sometimes keep journalists out of court—an indirect measure of professional performance (Voakes 1998).

Finally, journalists do agree on what constitutes "good work" in their profession—an emphasis on truth telling, taking a role as government watchdog, investigative reporting and treating the subjects of their stories with dignity. However, journalists believe that the single biggest threat to continuing professional excellence is the increasing pressure to make a profit that characterizes so many media and corporations. Professionally, journalists are out of joint with a mission that includes both public service and profit making (Gardner et al. 2001). How that tension is resolved will either help to create a professional environment that encourages ethical behavior and sparks better performance or help create an environment where money matters more than content.

WHERE DO YOU GO FROM HERE?

Perry (1970) postulates that one of the major accomplishments of college students is to progress from a simple, dualistic (right vs. wrong) view of life to a more complex, mature and relativistic view. Perry states that students must not only acknowledge that diversity and uncertainty exist in a world of relativism but also make a commitment to their choices (i.e., career, values, beliefs, etc.) out of the multiplicity of "right" choices available. And ethical choices abound in mass media careers. For instance, even the daily routine of setting the news agenda is an ethical issue, since those decisions are often made by Caucasian males for others who are unlike them in significant ways. Even word choice is an ethical issue. Why do we see stories about "working mothers," yet none about "working fathers"? Why are criminal suspects more often referred to by ethnicity when black than when they are white?

Unlike physical development, moral development is not subject to the quirks of heredity. Each individual is free to develop as keen a sense of equity as any other individual, yet few reach their full potential. About your attempts to "grow" ethically, Kohlberg (1970) has offered one observation: we tend to understand messages one stage higher than our own moral judgment stage. Through "aspirational listening"— that is, picking an ethical role model on a higher level and observing that person— you can progress to a higher stage of moral development. This observation is not a new one. In fact, it dates to Aristotle, who suggested that virtues could be learned by observing those who possess them.

This book uses the case study method so that you may see ethical decisions that were made at higher and lower levels of moral reasoning and aspire to the former. Often in case studies, it is the reasoning behind the answer rather than the answer itself that is the best determiner of moral growth (Clouse 1985). *An important part of moral development is the recognition that motive, not consequence, is the critical factor in deciding whether an act is ethical.*

Elliott (1991) illustrates the difference in the following scenario. Imagine a situation where you are able to interview and choose your next-door neighbor. When you ask Jones how she feels about murder, she replies she doesn't kill because if she got caught she would go to jail. When you interview Smith, he says he doesn't kill people because he believes in the sanctity of life. It takes little reflection to decide which neighbor you would prefer. Elliott concludes:

"Ethics involves the judging of actions as right or wrong, but motivations count as well. Some reasons for actions seem better or worse than others" (1991, 19).

Suggested Readings

BELENKY, MARY F., et al. 1988. *Women's ways of knowing: The development of self, voice and mind.* New York: Basic Books.

COLES, ROBERT. 1986. *The moral life of children.* New York: Atlantic Monthly Press.

ETTEMA, JAMES, and THEODORE CLASSER. 1998. *Custodians of conscience: Investigative journalists and public virtue.* New York: Columbia University Press.

GARDNER, H., CSIKSZENTHMIHALYI, MIHALY, and DAMON, WILLIAM. 2001. *Good work: When excellence and ethics meet.* New York: Basic Books.

GILLIGAN, CAROL. 1982. *In a different voice: Psychological theory and women's development.* Cambridge, MA: Harvard University Press.

LEVINSON, DANIEL J. 1978. *Seasons of a man's life.* New York: Alfred A. Knopf, Inc.

WILKINS, LEE, and COLEMAN, RENITA. at press. *The moral media.* Mahwah, NJ: Lawrence Erlbaum and Associates.

Bibliography

ActiveBuddy (2002). Case D Study: ELLEgirlBuddy. Retrieved November 21, 2002. http://www.activebuddy.com/welcome/

Agence France Presse (2003, March 26). "The war as seen on US TV: More sand sweat than blood and tears." Accessed on LexisNexis Academic.

Alderman, E. and Kennedy, C. (1995). *The right to privacy.* New York: Alfred A. Knopf, Inc.

Allossery, P. (2000, January 21). Benetton sparks controversy again: Series of magazine ads attack death penalty. *Financial Post,* p. C3.

Arendt, H. (1970). *The human condition.* Chicago: University of Chicago Press.

Aristotle. *The Nicomachean ethics.*

Auletta, K. (1991). *Three blind mice: How the TV networks lost their way.* New York: Random House.

Axelrod, R. (1984). *The evolution of cooperation.* New York: Basic Books.

Bagdikian, B. H. (1990). *The media monopoly.* (3d ed.). Boston: Beacon Press.

———. (2000). *The media monopoly.* (6th ed.). Boston: Beacon Press.

Baker, S. and Martinson, D. (2001). The TARES test: Five principles of ethical persuasion. *Journal of Mass Media Ethics* Vol. 16, No. 2 & 3, pp. 148–175.

Beasley, M. H. and Harlow, R. R. (1988). *The new majority: A look at what the preponderance of women in journalism education means to the schools and to the professions.* Lanham, MD: University Press of America.

Becker, L., et al. (2000). Undergrad enrollments level off; graduate enrollment declines. *Journalism and Mass Communication Educator, 55: 3,* pp. 68–80.

Belenky, M., et al. (1988). *Women's ways of knowing: The development of self, voice and mind.* New York: Basic Books.

Bennett, L. (1988). *News: The politics of illusion.* Longman: New York.

Bentley, R. (1986, August 4). Lessons sought from tragic events. *Bakersfield Californian,* p. 15.

Berger, A. (1989). *Seeing is believing.* Mountain View, CA: Mayfield Publishing Co.

Berger, J. (1980). *About looking.* New York: Pantheon Books.

Bianco, R. (2003, Nov. 5). "Cowardly CBS unfair to viewers, not Reagans." *USA Today,* p. D-1.

Black, J., Steele, B. & Barney, R. (1993). *Doing ethics in journalism.* Greencastle, IN: The Sigma Delta Chi Foundation and The Society of Professional Journalists.

Bok, S. (1978). *Lying: Moral choice in public and private life.* New York: Random House.

———. (1983). *Secrets: On the ethics of concealment and revelation.* New York: Vintage.

Boorstin, D. (1962). *The image.* New York: Antheneum.

Booth, C. (1999, November 15). Worst of Times. *Time,* pp. 79–80.

Bovée, W. (1991). The end can justify the means—but rarely. *Journal of Mass Media Ethics,* 6, pp. 135–145.

Braun, S. (1994, November 2). Tuning out the hype and gore. *Los Angeles Times,* p. 1.

Brooks, D. E. (1992). In their own words: Advertisers and the origins of the African-American consumer market. (A paper submitted to the Association for Education in Journalism and Mass Communications), Montreal, Canada, August 5–8.

Bryant, G. (1987, Spring-Summer). Ten-fifty P.I.: Emotion and the photographer's role. *Journal of Mass Media Ethics,* pp. 32–39.

Buckner, J. (2000, Jan. 30). Horrific photo forces us to face a painful past. *Charlotte Observer,* p. 3C.

Calvert, C. (2000). *Voyeur Nation: Media, privacy and peering in modern culture.* Boulder, CO: Westview Press.

Carey, J. W. (1989, Autumn). Review of Charles J. Sykes' "Profscam." *Journalism Educator,* p. 48.

Christians, C. (1986). Reporting and the oppressed. In D. Elliott (ed.),*Responsible journalism* (pp. 109–130) Newbury Park, CA: Sage Publications, Inc.

Christians, C. G., Ferré, J. P. & Fackler, M. (1995). *Good news: Social ethics and the press.* New York: Longman.

Christians, C., Rotzoll, K. & Fackler, M. (1987). *Media ethics: Cases and moral reasoning.* (2d ed.). New York: Longman.

Clark, C. (1997, Summer). In favor of civic journalism. *Harvard International Journal of Press/Politics,* vol. 2, no. 3, pp. 118–125.

Clouse, B. (1985). *Moral development.* Grand Rapids, MI: Baker Book House.

Cohen, A. (2000, Oct. 2). A crisis of content. *Time,* pp. 68–73.

Coleman, A. D. (1987, Spring/Summer). Private lives, public places: Street photography ethics. *Journal of Mass Media Ethics,* pp. 60–66.

Coleman, P. A. (2000). "Fighting a fair war or tilting at windmills?" An unpublished master's thesis. University of Missouri. Columbia, Missouri.

Coles, R. (1986). *The moral life of children.* New York: Atlantic Monthly Press.

Commission on Civil Disorders. (1989). The role of the mass media in reporting of news about minorities. In T. Goldstein (ed.), *Killing the messenger:100 years of media criticism.* New York: Columbia University.

Committee on the Judiciary—Tash Statement. (May 21, 2000). Available: http://www.house. gov/judiciary/10148.htm.

Cooper, Gloria (March/April 2002). "Darts and laurels." *Columbia Journalism Review,* p. 21.

———. (January/February 2003). Darts and laurels. *Columbia Journalism Review,* p. 5

———. (March/April 2003). Darts and laurels. *Columbia Journalism Review,* p. 7.

———. (July/August 2003). Darts and laurels. *Columbia Journalism Review,* p. 6.

———. (September/October 2003). Darts and laurels. *Columbia Journalism Review,* p. 6.

Cranberg, G., Bezanson, R. & Soloski, J. (2001). *Taking stock.* Ames, IA.: Iowa State University Press.

Crouse, T. (1974). *The boys on the bus: Riding with the campaign press corps.* New York: Ballantine.

Cunningham, B. (2003, July/August). Re-thinking objectivity. *Columbia Journalism Review,* pp. 24-32.

Cutlip, S. (1994). *The unseen power: Public relations—A history.* Hillsdale, NJ: Lawrence Erlbaum Assoc.

Daniel, C. (1989). National security and the Bay of Pigs invasion. In T. Goldstein (ed.), *Killing the messenger:100 years of media criticism.* New York: Columbia University.

Daniels, J. (1965). *They will be heard: America's crusading newspaper editors.* New York: McGraw-Hill.

Dates, J. L. (1990). Advertising. In J. L. Dates and W. Barlow (eds.), *Split image: African Americans in the mass media.* Washington, DC: Howard University Press.

Davies, J. C. (1963). *Human nature in politics.* New York: John Wiley & Sons.

Day, L. A. (1991). *Ethics in media communications: Cases and controversies.* Belmont, CA: Wadsworth, Inc.

Deaver, F. (1990). On defining truth. *Journal of Mass Media Ethics, 5* (3), pp. 168–177.

Deford, F. (1992, April 20). Arthur Ashe's secret. *Newsweek,* pp. 31–32.

Dionne, E. J. (1991). *Why Americans hate politics.* New York: Simon & Schuster.

———. (1996). *They only look dead.* New York: Simon & Schuster.

Doyle, M. (2003, March 26, 2003). Photos of POWs raise legal questions. *Star Tribune* (Minneapolis), p. 10A.

Eisenberg, E. M. (1984, September). Ambiguity as strategy in organizational communication. *Communication Monographs, 51,* pp. 227–242.

Elliott, D. (1986). Foundations for news media responsibility. In D. Elliott (ed.), *Responsible journalism.* (pp. 32–34). Newbury Park, CA: Sage Publications, Inc.

———. (1991, Autumn). Moral development and the teaching of ethics. *Journalism Educator,* pp. 19–24.

Ellul, J. (1965). *Propaganda* (Trans. by K. Kellen and J. Lerner). New York: Alfred A. Knopf.

Emery, E. and Emery, M. (1978). *The press and America: An interpretative history of the mass media.* (4th ed.) Englewood Cliffs, NJ: Prentice-Hall.

Encabo, N. (1995). Ethics of journalism and democracy. *European Journal of Communication, 10* (4), pp. 513–526.

Epstein, E. J. (1974). *News from nowhere.* New York: Random House.

Ettema, J. and Glasser, T. (1998). *Custodians of conscience: Investigative journalists and public virtue.* New York: Columbia University Press.

Etzioni, A. (1993). *The spirit of community.* New York: Crown Publishers, Inc.

Fallows, J. (1996). *Breaking the news: How the media undermine American democracy.* New York: Pantheon.

Farrow, B. (2000, April 06). Connected: Taking the movies to market. *Daily Telegraph,* London, p. 8.

Festinger, L. (1957). *A theory of cognitive dissonance.* Stanford, CA: Stanford University Press.

Fink, C. (1988). *Media ethics: In the newsroom and beyond.* New York: McGraw-Hill.

Fischer, C. T. (1980). Privacy and human development. In W. C. Bier (ed.), *Privacy: A vanishing value?* (pp. 37–46). New York: Fordham University Press.

Fitzgerald, M. (1995, November 11). Decrying public journalism. *Editor and Publisher,* p. 20.

Fletcher, G. P. (1993). *Loyalty: An essay on the morality of relationships.* New York: Oxford University Press.

Fore, W. F. (1987). *Television and religion.* New York: Augsburg Publishing House.

Fort Worth Star-Telegram unsigned column. (2003, March 26). "Painful images." *Fort Worth Star-Telegram,* Metro, p. 14.

Frey, C. (2002, July 18). *Web friend or faux.* Los Angeles Times, p. C-1.

Fry, D. (ed.). (1983). *The adversary press: A modern media institute ethics seminar.* St. Petersburg, FL: The Poynter Institute.

Fuss, P. (1965). *The moral philosophy of Josiah Royce.* Cambridge, MA: Harvard University Press.

Gans, H. (1979). *Deciding what's news: A study of CBS Evening News, NBC Nightly News, Newsweek and Time.* New York: Vintage.

Gardner, H., Csikszenthmihalyi, M. & Damon, W. (2001). *Good work: When excellence and ethics meet.* New York: Basic Books.

Gerbner, G. (1987, Summer-Fall). Television: Modern mythmaker. *Media and Values,* pp. 8–9.

Gert, B. (1988). *Morality, a new justification of the moral rules.* New York: Oxford University Press.

Gilligan, C. (1977). In a different voice: Women's conceptions of self and morality. *Harvard Educational Review, 47,* pp. 492–505.

Gilligan, C. (1982). *In a different voice: Psychological theory and women's development.* Cambridge, MA: Harvard University Press.

Godwin, M. (1995). The shoddy article. *JournoPorn on HotWired (Online).*

Godwin, M. 1998. *Defending free speech in the digital age.* New York: Times Books.

Goffman, E. (1959). *The presentation of self in everyday life.* New York: Anchor.

Goldstein, P. (2000, January 1). The year of unconventional wisdom. *Los Angeles Times,* p. 1F.

Goldstein, T. (ed), (1989). *Killing the messenger: 100 years of media criticism.* New York: Columbia University Press.

Gormley, D. W. (1984). Compassion is a tough word. *Drawing the Line,* pp. 58–59. Washington, DC: American Society of Newspaper Editors.

Graham, B. and Weisman, J. (2003, March, 24). "Display of 5 POWs draws firm rebuke." *Washington Post,* p. A1.

Grcic, J. M. (1986). The right to privacy: Behavior as property. *Journal of Values Inquiry, 20,* pp. 137–144.

Gross, L., Katz, J. S. & Ruby, J. (eds.). (1988). *Image ethics: The moral rights of subjects in photographs, film and television.* New York: Oxford University Press.

Grunig, J. E. and Hunt, T. (1984). *Managing public relations.* Fort Worth: Holt, Rinehart and Winston.

Gurevitch, M., Levy, M. & Roeh, I. (1991). The global newsroom: Convergences and diversities in the globalization of television news. In P. Dalhgren and C. Sparks (eds.), *Communication and citizenship.* London. Routledge.

Haiman, F. (1958). Democratic ethics and the hidden persuaders. *Quarterly Journal of Speech, 44,* pp. 385–392.

Halbert, D. J. (1999). *Intellectual property in the information age.* Westport, CT: Quorum Books.

Hamilton, A. (2003, March 25). 5 GIs held in Iraq, shown on Arab TV. *The Dallas Morning News,* p. 1A.

Hanson, K. (1986). The demands of loyalty. *Idealistic Studies, 16,* pp. 195–204.

Hart, A. (2003, July/August). Delusions of accuracy. *Columbia Journalism Review,* p. 20.

Henry, W. H., III. (1994). *In defense of elitism.* New York: Anchor Books.

Hess, S. (1981). *The Washington reporters.* Washington, DC: The Brookings Institution.

Hickey, N. (2003, July/August). FCC: Ready, set, consolidate. *Columbia Journalism Review,* p. 5.

Hixson, R. F. (1987). *Privacy in a public society.* New York: Oxford University Press.

Hobbes, T. (1958). *The Leviathan* (Reprints from 1651). New York: Bobbs-Merrill.

Hodges, L. W. (1983). The journalist and privacy. *Social Responsibility: Journalism, Law, Medicine, 9,* pp. 5–19.

———. (1986). Defining press responsibility: A functional approach. In D. Elliott (ed.), *Responsible journalism.* (pp. 13–31). Newbury Park, CA: Sage Publications, Inc.

Horn, B. (2004, January 10). Any more questions? *Dallas Morning News,* p. C-2.

Hortsch, D. (2003, March 30). Photos of dead and POWs raise thorny questions. *The Oregonian,* C1.

House, D. (2003, March 30). Worth a thousand words. *Fort Worth Star-Telegram Weekly Review,* p. 3.

Hoyt, M. (1990, March-April). When the walls come tumbling down. *Columbia Journalism Review,* pp. 35–40.

James, C. (2000, Dec. 3). In a gay world, without the usual guides. *New York Times,* Section 2, p. 27.

Jamieson, K. H. (2000). *Everything you think you know about politics . . . and why you're wrong.* New York: Basic Books.

———. (1992). *Dirty politics.* New York: Oxford University Press.

Jamieson, K. H. and Campbell, K. K. (1992). *The interplay of influence: News, advertising, politics and the mass media.* (3d ed.). Belmont, CA: Wadsworth, Inc.

Joy, D. M. (1983). *Moral development foundations.* Nashville: Abingdon Press.

Junas, L. (1980, February 23). Tragedy and violence photos dominate in news prizes. *Editor and Publisher,* p. 17.

Kaid, L. L. (1992). Ethical dimensions of political advertising. In R. E. Denton (ed.), *Ethical dimensions of political communication,* (pp. 145–169). New York: Praeger.

Kant, I. (1785). *Groundwork on the metaphysics of morals.*

Keleny, G. (2003, March 25). The Iraq conflict: Prisoners of war, photographs used for propaganda, and the Geneva Convention. *The Independent* (London), p. 9.

Keleny, G. (2003b, March 25). The MoD wants face of Iraqi POWs to be obscured. *The Independent* (London), p. 9.

Kenworthy, T., Willing, R. & Cauchon, D. (2003, March 28). TV coverage takes toll on families of POWs. *USA Today,* p. 9A.

Kessler, L. (1989). Women's magazines' coverage of smoking-related health coverage. *Journalism Quarterly, 66,* pp. 316–22, 445.

Klein, J. (1992, June 8). Whose values? *Newsweek,* pp. 19–22.

Koehn, D. 1998. *Rethinking feminist ethics.* New York: Routledge.

Koff, S. (2003, March 25). "Did the U.S. violate Geneva Convention?" *Plain Dealer* (Cleveland), p. A9.

Kohlberg, L. (1968, September). The child as a moral philosopher. *Psychology Today,* pp. 25–30.

———. (1973). The contribution of developmental psychology to education. *Educational Psychologist, 10,* pp. 2–14.

Landsman, S. (1984). *The adversary system: A description and defense.* Washington, DC: American Enterprise Institute.

Lebacqz, K. (1985). *Professional ethics: Power and paradox.* Nashville: Abingdon Press.

Leiss, W., Kline, S. & Jhally, S. (1986). *Social communication in advertising: Person, products and images of well being.* New York: Methuen Publications.

Leland, J. (1999, August 16). The Blair Witch Cult. *Newsweek.* p. 44.

Lester, P. M. (1992). *Photojournalism: An ethical approach.* Hillsdale, NJ: Lawrence Erlbaum and Associates.

———. (1996). *Images that injure.* Westport, CT: Greenwood Press.

Levinson, D. (1978). *Seasons of a man's life.* New York: Alfred A. Knopf, Inc.

Liberty, Robert M., Joyce N. Sparking & Emily S. Davidson. 1982. *The early window: Effects of television on children and youth.* New York: Paragon Press.

Linsky, M. (1986). *Impact: How the press affects federal policymaking.* New York: W. W. Norton.

Lippmann, W. (1922). *Public opinion.* New York: Free Press.

———. (1982). *The essential Lippmann.* Cambridge, MA: Harvard University Press.

Lippmann, W. and Merz, C. (1989). A test of the news. In T. Goldstein (ed.), *Killing the messenger: 100 years of media criticism.* New York: Columbia University.

Long, E. V. (1995, July 3). To our readers. *Time,* p. 4.

Lowery, S. & DeFleur, M. (1988). *Milestones in mass communication research* (2d ed.). New York: Longman.

Lubrano, G. (2003, March 31). "Images of POWs—and questions." *San Diego Union-Tribune,* p. B1.

Madison, J., Hamilton, A. & Jay, J. *The Federalist papers.*(pp. 17–28). Urbana-Champaign: University of Illinois Dept. of Advertising.

Martin, E. (1991). On photographic manipulation. *Journal of Mass Media Ethics, 6,* pp. 156–163.

Matsuda, M. (1989). Public response to racist speech: Considering the victim's story. *Michigan Law Review, 87,* pp. 2321–2381.

Matthews, A.W. and Steinberg, B. (2003, Nov. 19). FTC examines health claims in KFC's ads. *Wall Street Journal,* p. B1, 2.

McCarty, J. F. (1996, February 23). Son's new evidence in Sheppard case is put before the judge. *The Cleveland Plain Dealer,* p. 1A.

McChesney, R. (1991). *Rich media: Poor democracy: Communication politics in dubious times.* Urbana: University of Illinois Press.

———. (1997). *Corporate media and the threat to democracy.* New York: Seven Stories Press.

Medved, Michael. (1992). *Hollywood vs. America.* New York: HarperCollins Publishers.

Merrill, J. C. (1974). *The imperative of freedom: A philosophy of journalistic autonomy.* New York: Hastings House.

Merritt, Davis. (1995). *Public journalism and public life.* Hillsdale, NJ: Lawrence Erlbaum Associates.

Meyrowitz, J. (1985). *No sense of place: The impact of electronic media on social behavior.* New York: Oxford University Press.

Mill, J. S. (1859). *On liberty.*

———. (1861). *Utilitarianism.*

Miller, E. D. (1994). *The Charlotte Project: Helping citizens take back democracy. The Poynter Papers: No. 4.* St. Petersburg, FL: The Poynter Institute.

Miller, K. (1992, December). Smoking up a storm: Public relations and advertising in the construction of the cigarette problem, 1953–1954. *Journalism Monographs, 136.*

Mills, C. W. (1956). *The power elite.* New York: Oxford University Press.

Mills, K. (1989, Winter). When women talk to women. *Media and Values, 12.*

Mitchell, W. J. T. (1995). *Picture theory.* Chicago: University of Chicago Press.

Molotch, H. and Lester, M. (1974). News as purposive behavior: On the strategic use of routine events, accidents and scandals. *American Sociological Review, 39,* pp. 101–112.

Montgomery, K. C. (1989). *Target: Prime time. Advocacy groups and the struggle over entertainment television.* New York: Oxford University Press.

Mooney, C. (2000, November 6). "The Virtual Campaign". *The American Prospect,* Vol. II, No. 23, pp. 36–39.

Moore, G. F. (1903). *Principia ethica.*

Morton, J. (2003, June/July). Less of a loss. *American Journalism Review,* p. 68.

Moyers, B. (1988). Quoted in '*The promise of television,*' episode 10. Produced by PBS.

Murrdow, A, (2000 January). Ad Men Walking—Benneton is facing its biggest advertising backlash yet, with a new campaign about Death Row. *The Irish Times,* p. 61.

Nasar, Sylvia (1998). *A Beautiful Mind.* New York: Simon & Schuster.

National Association of Broadcasters. (1985). *Radio: In search of excellence.* Washington, DC: NAB.

Negroponte, Nicholas. (1995). *Being digital.* New York: Alfred A. Knopf.

Nelkin, D. (1987). *Selling science: How the press covers science and technology.* New York: W. H. Freeman.

Neuffer, E. (2003, March 24). Airing of POW footage blasted. *The Boston Globe,* p. A19.

Neville, R. C. (1980). Various meanings of privacy: A philosophical analysis. In W. C. Bier (ed.), *Privacy: A vanishing value?* (pp. 26–36). New York: Fordham University Press.

Newsom, D. (1993). *This is PR.* Belmont, CA: Wadsworth.

Newsom, D., Turk, J. V. & Kruckeberg, D. (1996). *This is PR: The realities of public relations.* Belmont, CA: Wadsworth.

Nimmo, D. and Combs, J. (1985). *Nightly horrors: Crisis coverage in television network news.* Knoxville, TN: University of Tennessee Press.

Nuttall-Smith, C. and Davies, F. (2003, March 25). "Name, rank and serial number." *The Gazette* (Montreal, Quebec), p. A-4.

O'Toole, J. (1985). *The trouble with advertising.* New York: Times Books.

Oldenquist, A. (1982). Loyalties. *Journal of Philosophy, 79,* pp. 73–93.

Olsen, Jack. (1985). *Give a boy a gun.* New York: Delacorte.

Oran, D. (1975). *Law dictionary for non-lawyers.* St. Paul, MN: West Publishing Co.

Orwell, G. (1949). *1984.* San Diego: Harcourt, Brace, Jovanovich.

Palmer, E. L. and Door, A. eds. (1980). *Children and the faces of television: Teaching, violence, selling.* New York: Academic Press.

Pasternak, J. (2003, March 24). Treatment of POWs is said to violate treaty. *Los Angeles Times,* p. 4.

Patterson, T. E. (1980). *The mass media election.* New York: Praeger.

Patterson, T. E. and McClure, R. D. (1972). *The unseeing eye.* New York: G. P. Putnam's Sons.

Peters, John D. (2000). *Speaking in the air: A history of the idea of communication.* Chicago: University of Chicago Press.

Perry, W. O. (1968). *Intellectual development in the college years: A scheme.* New York: Holt, Rinehart and Winston.

Piaget, J. (1965). *The moral judgment of the child.* Translated by Marjorie Gabain. New York: Free Press.

Plaisance, Patrick L. (2002). The journalist as moral witness: Michael Ignatieff's pluralistic philosophy for a global media culture. *Journalism: Theory, Practice & Criticism, 3* (2), pp. 205–222.

Plato. *The republic.*

Pojman, L. (1998). *Ethical theory: Classical and contemporary readings.* Belmont, CA: Wadsworth Publishing Co.

Postman, N. (1986). *Amusing ourselves to death: Public discourse in the age of television.* New York: Penguin Books.

Powell, T. F. (1967). *Josiah Royce.* New York: Washington Square Press, Inc.

Price, M. (2000, Dec. 10). Showtime's "Queer as Folk" gives voice to a love that dared not speak its name on TV. *Charlotte Observer,* p. F1.

Raissman, B. (1999, October 27). In baseball vs. Rose, Gray is not a player. *New York Daily News,* p. B1.

Rather, D. (1987, March 10). From Murrow to mediocrity? *New York Times,* Sec. I, p. 27.

Rawls, J. (1971). *A theory of justice.* Cambridge, MA: Harvard University Press.

Reaves, S. (1987, Spring-Summer). Digital retouching: Is there a place for it in newspaper photography? *Journal of Mass Media Ethics,* pp. 40–48.

———. (1991). Personal correspondence to the author quoted in digital alteration of photographs in consumer magazines. *Journal of Mass Media Ethics, 6,* pp. 175–181.

Reid, T. and Doran, J. (2003, March 24). "Mistreating prisoners is a war crime, says Bush." *The Times* (London), p. 2.

Rieder, R. (1999, November/December). A costly rookie mistake. *American Journalism Review,* p. 6.

Robertson, N. (1992). *The girls in the balcony.* New York: Random House.

Robinson, M. and Sheehan, G. (1984). *Over the wire and on TV.* New York: Basic Books.

Rogers, E. M. and Chang, S. B. (1991). Media coverage of technology issues: Ethiopian drought of 1984, AIDS, Challenger and Chernobyl. In L. Wilkins and P. Patterson eds., *Risky business: Communicating issues of science, risk and public policy,* pp. 75–96. Westport, CT: Greenwood Press.

Rosen, J. (1995). What should we be doing? *The IRE Journal, 18,* pp. 6–8.

Rosen, J. (2000). *The unwanted gaze: The destruction of privacy in America.* New York: Random House.

Rosenthal, A. M. (1989, October 10). Trash TV's latest news show continues credibility erosion. Syndicated column by *New York Times* News Service.

Ross, W. D. (1930). *The right and the good.* Oxford, England: Clarendon Press.

Royce, J. (1908). *The philosophy of loyalty.* New York: The Macmillan Co.

Russell, B. (ed.). (1967). *History of Western philosophy.* New York: Touchstone Books.

Ryan, B. (1999, October 27). Rose's case doesn't deserve your sympathy. *Boston Globe,* pp. C1.

Sabato, L. J. (1992). *Feeding frenzy: How attack journalism has transformed American politics.* New York: Free Press.

Safer, M. (1992, January 30). Keynote address at the annual Alfred I. DuPont—Columbia University Awards ceremony.

Sandel, M. J. (1982). *Liberalism and the limits of justice.* Cambridge, MA: Harvard University Press.

Sanders, M. and Rock, M. (1988). *Waiting for prime time: The women of television news.* Urbana: University of Illinois Press.

Schaffer, J. and Miller, E. D. (1995). *Civic journalism: Six case studies.* St. Petersburg, FL: The Poynter Institute.

Schoeman, F. D., (ed.). (1984). *Philosophical dimensions of privacy: An anthology.* Cambridge, MA: Harvard University Press.

Schoenbrun, D. (1989). *On and off the air: An informal history of CBS news.* New York: E. P. Dutton.

Schudson, M. (1978). *Discovering the news.* New York: Basic Books.

———. (1984). *Advertising: The uneasy persuasion.* New York: Basic Books.

———. (1995). *The power of news.* Cambridge, MA: Harvard University Press.

Schwartz, T. (1973). *The responsive chord.* Garden City, NY: Anchor Press.

Seabrook, J. (2003, July 7). "The money note." *New Yorker,* p. 46.

Shaw, D. (1999, December 20). Journalism is a very different business—Here's why. *Los Angeles Times,* p. V3.

Shilts, R. (1987). *And the band played on.* New York: St. Martin's Press.

Siebert, F. S., Peterson, T. & Schramm, W. (1956). *Four theories of the press.* Urbana: University of Illinois Press.

Silver, R. (1989, Winter). The many faces of media women. *Media and Values*, pp. 2–5.

Smith, C. (1992). *Media and apocalypse.* Westport, CT: Greenwood Press.

Smith, D. (2000, Dec. 19). Flap over gay kiss photo proves instructive. *Charlotte Observer,* p. 17A.

Smith, R. (2000, Jan. 13). Critic's notebook: An ugly legacy lives on, its glare unsoftened by age. *New York Times,* p. E1.

Squires, J. (1997). *Read all about it! The corporate takeover of America's newspapers.* New York: Basic Books.

Stamper, C. (1999. July 15). Blair Witch, a scary home brew. *Wired News.*

Stein, M. L. (1986, June 21). Covering a disaster story. *Editor & Publisher,* p. 17.

Stone, I. F. (1988). *The trial of Socrates.* Boston: Little, Brown and Co.

Sunstein, C (2001). *Republic.com.* New Haven: Princeton University Press.

Szarkowski, J. (1978). *Mirrors and windows.* New York: Museum of Modern Art.

Thomas, B. (1990, January 19). Finding truth in the age of 'infotainment.' *Editorial Research Reports.* Washington, DC: Congressional Quarterly, Inc.

Tomlinson, D. (1987). One technological step forward and two legal steps back: Digitalization and television news pictures as evidence in libel. *Loyola Entertainment Law Journal, 9,* pp. 237–257.

Toronto Star unsigned column (March 23, 2003). A note to readers about photos. *Toronto Star.* p. A2.

Vonnegut, K. (1952). *Player piano.* New York: Dell Publishing Co.

Watkins, J. J. (1990). *The mass media and the law.* Englewood Cliffs, NJ: Prentice-Hall.

Weaver, D. H. and Wilhoit, G. C. (1986). *The American journalist: A portrait of U.S. newspeople and their work.* Bloomington: University of Indiana Press.

Weinberg. S. (1995, Nov/Dec.). ABC, Philip Morris and the infamous apology. *Columbia Journalism Review,* pp. 29–37.

Werner, M. R. and Starr, J. (1959). *Teapot Dome.* New York: Viking.

Westin, A. F. (1967). *Privacy and freedom.* New York: Atheneum.

Wicker, C. (1990, March 7). Awhile back, everyone was doing it—but not anymore. *Dallas Morning News,* pp. 1–2C.

Wilkins, L. (1987). *Shared vulnerability: The mass media and American perception of the Bhopal disaster.* Westport, CT: Greenwood Press.

Wilkins, L. and Coleman, R. (at press). *The moral media.* Mahwah, NJ: Lawrence Erlbaum and Associates.

Williams, B.A. and Carpini, M.X.D. (2002, April 10). Heeeeeeeeeeere's democracy! *Chronicle of Higher Education,* p. B14.

Wilson, E. (1940). *To the Finland station.* New York: Doubleday & Co.

Woods, G. (1996). *Advertising and marketing to the new majority.* Belmont, CA: Wadsworth.

Index